FROM THE FIRST HISTORY OF MUSIC IN GERMAN

Philosophies of Music History

A Study of General Histories of Music
1600-1960

by Warren Dwight Allen,

Ph.D., Mus. Doc.

Professor Emeritus, Stanford University
Professor of Musicology, Florida State University, 1950-55

Dover Publications, Inc., New York

Published in Canada by General Publishing Company, Ltd., 30 Lesmill Road, Don Mills, Toronto, Ontario.
Published in the United Kingdom by Constable and Company, Ltd., 10 Orange Street, London WC 2.

This Dover edition, first published in 1962, is an unabridged and corrected republication of the work originally published by the American Book Company in 1939. A new Preface by the author has been specially written for this Dover edition.

International Standard Book Number: 0-486-20282-8
Library of Congress Catalog Card Number: 63-1070

Manufactured in the United States of America
Dover Publications, Inc.
180 Varick Street
New York, N. Y. 10014

PREFACE TO DOVER EDITION

THIS SURVEY of general histories of music and of the assumptions involved in such works was first published in 1939. It had been written a few years earlier as my dissertation "in partial fulfillment of the requirements" for the degree of Doctor of Philosophy at Columbia University. The work was and is again dedicated to my friend and former editor, Dr. Edwin J. Stringham, who contributed a preface to the first edition. We were both gratified that the 1939 edition was well received among readers here and abroad. Now I am grateful to the readers who have urged Dover Publications, Inc. to bring out this new edition, and for them I append a brief discussion of some of the more important music histories published since 1939.

MUSIC HISTORIES SINCE 1939

It is only fair to say that the great strides made by American musicology in the last twenty years are due largely to the influential energy and erudition of one man. Paul Henry Lang, historian, critic, journalist, and editor, finished his magnum opus, so that my entry [314] in the bibliography should now read:

314. Láng, Paul H., *Music in Western Civilization.* 1107 pp. W. W. Norton & Co., New York, 1941.

However, his influence on musical scholarship has gone far beyond that wielded by his book alone. As editor of the *Musical Quarterly* (*MQ*) he has steered a lofty but humanistic course, correcting now and then the sterility of academic thinking so prevalent among our younger, ultra-*seri*-ous pedants. It is as editor of the Norton shelf of "Books That Live in Music" that Lang has turned the light on fellow scholars who have written some special studies that comprise a series unique in the history of music histories.

Gustave Reese was the first of these men with his *Music in the Middle Ages* (1940), even antedating Lang's own book; Reese's *Music in the Renaissance* appeared fourteen years later, and is a monumental work marred only by the fact that the author considers the Renaissance as a period in time and includes his comments on the music of the Lutheran Reformation in the same volume! The two movements were poles apart; Will Durant was so right in devoting a separate volume to each.

Lang then rescued the Swiss-American scholar Manfred F. Bukofzer from what might have been tragic oblivion. In a short time Bukofzer became the leader in American musicology with his *Studies in Medieval and Renaissance Music* (1950) and his *Music in the Baroque Era* (1947). His untimely death in 1955 will always be mourned as a great loss to American research.

Curt Sachs, dean of the group, came late to the Norton fold with *The Rise of Music in the Ancient World* (1943). Until his death in 1959 he was an apostle of evolutionary anthropology as shown in his *World History of the Dance* (1937), published by Seven Arts. Sachs' inquiring mind led him to *The Commonwealth of Art* (1946), his most interesting book. His textbook, *Our Musical Heritage*, was brought out by Prentice-Hall in 1948 and was about the last textbook on the subject written by request. Since the end of World War II publishers had been vying with each other for "music histories" which might be "adopted" by schools giving survey courses for college students financed by the GI bill. When this lucrative source of quantity orders dried up there was no longer such demand for the "general histories of music" that had satisfied superficial readers.

My book was inspired by the need for more thoughtful, critical approaches to the subject. Such studies began to appear in the 1940's with the specialized histories reviewed above, and I am happy to report that the scholars responsible for the most important of them (Professors Lang, Reese, and Bukofzer) were among those who gave me the greatest encouragement. I could never have completed this work without them and the critical help of my editor, Edwin John Stringham.

Even in the 1930's, in the University of California at Berkeley, I had begun to assemble material for my Master's thesis under Professor Frederick J. Teggart (A.B., Stanford), who had founded his own department of Social Institutions, having been unable to work with other historians. This fledgling thesis, "A Critique of Music Histories," lies buried in the University of California Library at Berkeley. It was the seed from which this book has grown.

Oliver Strunk's *Source Readings in Music History* (1950) also belongs in this list of notable works. Some collections, led by *Masterpieces of Music Before 1750* (1951) by Parrish and Ohl, were inspired by Arnold Schering's great *Geschichte der Musik in Beispielen*, reprinted by Breitkopf & Härtel in 1955. *Die Musik in Geschichte und Gegenwart; allgemeine Enzyklopädie der Musik*, edited by Friedrich Blume and published in Kassel by Bärenreiter, is the most extensive and ambitious work on the subject published in modern times. The first volume was published in 1949 and it is still appearing in installments. Eight volumes are now available, covering the subject from A to Mejtus. The fifth edition of *Grove's Dictionary of Music and Musicians*, which was published by Macmillan in 1954 in nine volumes under the editorship of Eric Blom, is, unfortunately, carelessly put together. The material on American music is inexcusably inaccurate.

Today, the only general history that can be called a scholarly work is Donald J. Grout's *A History of Western Music* (Norton, 1960). My review of this book appeared in the *Journal of Research in Music Education*, Vol. VIII, No. 2, Fall 1960, pp. 124-6; I reprint it here because it summarizes my own philosophy:*

"This is a greatly needed text based largely upon secondary but scholarly sources published since 1900. Heretofore the historian has felt obligated to cite primary sources that are out of the reach of modern teachers and students. Intended to supplement Lang's pioneer work, *Music in Western Civilization*, Grout's book is luxuriously supplied with over three hundred illustrations and musical examples and is the first recent history of music based upon 'style-criticism.' This limits the author to published, printed music, and he makes the confession that he deals only with "art-music." This made it necessary to ignore those processes of music history, such as the improvisation of folk-music and popular music, without which our musical art could never have been developed. For example, Ruth

---

*Reprinted by permission of the Music Educators National Conference, publisher of the *Journal of Research in Music Education*.

Hannas has shown how important the popular *L'homme Armé* tune was in the history of the papacy, but the 'style-critic' is only interested in its use as a *cantus firmus* in the compositions of Dufay, Okeghem, and Josquin. The tune itself, like Topsy, 'just grew.'

"The title lays an obligation on the author to define 'Western' as contrasted with 'Eastern' Music, but he fails to do this. He repeats conscientiously old theories concerning Greek modes and Byzantine *echoi,* none of which had anything to do with the beginnings of Western Music. The fact is, Western Music had its beginnings in monkish revolts *against* Byzantine dogmatism. As Egon Wellesz has shown, chants in the Eastern Church had to employ approved formulas which made them as nearly alike as ikons in painting. Free improvisatory deviation was impossible. In the Western Church, the early popes may have wanted to exert that sort of control, but were quite powerless to do so. When John XXII issued his famous edict about 1324, the jolly, disobedient monks went right ahead with their ecclesiastical 'jam sessions.'

"A. Pirro has shown how rich, though chaotic, was the music of the 14th century. Instruments were invented, improved or discarded, and used in the church in spite of ecclesiastical disfavor. All attempts to keep plainchant in the pure austerity of the 'Gregorian' tradition were in vain (a glance at the *Liber Usualis* shows how the style of Roman chant became lyric and romantic around and after the 10th century). Guillaume de Machaut, great and most versatile master of the 14th century, said that music was the *gay* science, but Grout seldom smiles. Choirboys and their teachers mastered difficulties undreamed of today; the written page was a mere skeleton for which musical flesh and blood had to be supplied while improvising counterpoint. If in future years, an historian of twentieth century music should try to reconstruct a "hit-song" from music sold over the counter, what would he learn? Dr. Grout says that jazz has its own 'mystique,' by which he must mean that we 'squares' fail to 'dig it.'

"For Grout, the improvisatory style is florid, cadenza-like, free meandering; that was certainly not the case in the 14th century or the Baroque period any more than it is today in jazz improvised by well-trained musicians who bring in all sorts of fresh glances at the 'classics' while continuing over the 'solid eight-beat.'

"One disappointing, although tacit, assumption is that the history of music can be divorced from that of contemporary events. Just after 1453 Dufay composed a *Lamentation* over the fall of Constantinople, but where are the musical lamentations of today over the fall of great Western empires and the rise of tyrannies worse than that of Byzantium? The history of the West and that of Western music cannot be studied in air-conditioned isolation, disturbed only by the dissonances of 'rock and roll' on the one hand and of artistic dode*ca*cophony on the other. (The added syllable is my own.)

"This book probably will be adopted as a definite text far and wide and may deserve the success it surely will have. But teachers should beware; no text can tell the whole story and this large book is woefully incomplete as a landmark of American scholarship. One would never know that the author is an American. Perhaps that is a good thing, but I hope it is not chauvinistic to point out that this country, after all, has made some unique contributions to Western music, from the pioneer 'fuguing tunes' of Billings and the vigorous legacy of 'Sacred Harp' harmony to the artistic gems of our stage music from Sousa to Broadway musical shows that are so lustily applauded by cosmopolitan critics. 'American music' is not even mentioned in the index and the two scant pages under 'The United States' include mention of Villa-Lobos and Carlos Chavez."

The task before us is more difficult than ever; not only are Western music and civilization threatened, but all life on this planet is involved. In this atomic age all of us need to push aside our parochial barriers. Getting down on our knees, we need to pray that we may have a Future, after all, a future in which music and the arts may still flourish, and in which Man may have another chance.

W.D.A.

June, 1962
Seattle, Washington

EDITOR'S PREFACE

IN THE search for knowledge, one comes inevitably to the basic question, What, after all, is truth? Pursuing this direction of thought further, one discovers that there is nothing absolute, immutable, forever fixed and true, and unalterable in truth save what man, in his agreement with his fellow men, sets forth as such.

All students will agree, I believe, that man is conditioned in his thoughts, as well as in his actions, by his fellow man, by his immediate spatial and temporal environment, by influences less contiguous, by world-wide conditions, and by accumulations of the past. So much so that a one-time truth may now be considered as untrue, and vice versa. In fact, the immediate emotional and physical state of an individual may influence his conception of truth, and that conception may, at times, become generally agreed upon—for good or ill. One may continue with this sort of reasoning even to include the so-called "exact sciences."

At any rate, one cannot ignore the part the individual himself plays in the verdict of what he considers "the truth," so that in every pronouncement of "fact" one should enquire into the "how" and the "why" of the process of arriving at the "fact," and the state of being of the very individual or individuals through whom the pronouncement is issued.

General historiographers have long been cognizant of these determinants of truth and have, at least in some of their more recent works, made due allowances for the human factors involved. Certain political propaganda the world over has made deliberate use of the plausibility of error inherent in historical thinking, with the result that not a few "time-honored facts" are being invested with new and strange significances — an expedient as old as man himself. The science of history is becoming more and more a scientific pursuit of comparisons. Man is in earnest search for the truth of truth in order to revaluate his knowledge and find a firmer basis of reasoning. There may be exasperating cross currents and diverting tacks here and there, but the trend for free questioning and re-examination of long-accepted "truths" in history is very real and irresistible.

No doubt it is a signal victory for the student to be able and permitted to question and to revaluate time-honored data; but the reader must still bear in mind that the vista of the past will be viewed through the glasses of our own time and that the "new" truths will be colored, in turn, by the spirit of our present age. This state of affairs is as interesting as it is valuable to contemporary as well as future scholarship. The "handwriting on the wall" has character as well as substance, and we should be aware of both elements.

This volume in an outstanding example of contemporary scholastic trends applied to a specific field. I do not hesitate to state that, in several salient aspects, this work is one of the most significant documents of its kind that has yet appeared in the English language.

Historiological methods have been very rarely applied to the specialized field of music histories. Music historians have apparently been quite content to continue in old worn-out grooves of a past century or more. The methods underlying music history writing have lagged far behind other specialized fields (*vide* painting, sculpture, and architecture), largely because the scholars in that field have not seriously questioned either the established methods of philosophy applied to that field or to the generally accepted basic data and their implications. Musicology, in America at least, is a very recent science and it has hardly had sufficient time to know itself, to establish a character of its own, or to achieve unchallenged authority in its own sphere of thought. Thus the science of music-history writing has had little opportunity to make itself felt and respected in the world of serious scholarship. But such conditions are slowly changing and it is very likely that Professor Allen's work will play an important part in the future of music-history writing and have a marked effect upon the formulation and establishment of foundational philosophy and methodology of the science of musicology in America. It is with confidence that I anticipate a widespread salutary effect of the author's ideas upon the teaching of music history in our schools and colleges.

In this volume, the author examines and analyzes the histories of music from the first recorded document up to the latest as this book goes to press. He has inquired into such basic and controversial topics as origins, analogy, periodization, continuities, the great-man theory, theories of "progress," "growth," "development," "revolution," "evolution" (words that have long been inexact though of unquestioned currency, but which must henceforth have a new connotation), and the influences of other sciences and philosophies upon the methodology of music-history writing. He parades before the reader excerpts in large numbers and in very unusual amounts, especially translated quotations of ancient and foreign tongues and discussions of works not generally available. This feature alone is of inestimable value to the reader. The text is copiously documented with pertinent references and contains a bibliography that will be of great service to scholars in the field and to writers of music histories.

Professor Allen applies highly skilled logic and reasoning to the examination of music histories of the past; he shows how they were products of their own time and how they reflected current influences just as surely and justifiably as did the artistic creations of their respective years. The author goes on to indicate a present-day interpretation of the "truths" and "facts" set forth in historical treatises of the past in the light of their own time and in comparison with other ages, including our own. In this sort of treatment, the music histories of the past take on new significances, new horizons, and, if you will, new limitations.

For many years past, the teaching of music appreciation has been presented very largely from the historical, or chronological, approach. The underlying supposition has been that music grows, develops, or evolves as time goes on, from simple and crude beginnings to the complex works of today, and that the proper manner to learn to appreciate music is to experience it as it was recorded in the annals of Time. Professor Allen shows the fallacy of this contention and I believe that if his ideas are applied to the study of the appreciation of music, the subject will take on significant meaning and be of vital interest to the average student of our own day to a degree impossible of achieving through the pursuit of a strict chronological sequence.

The proper way to study the music of the past, or the present also for that matter, is to study it in relation to the time and the circumstances that produced it, for art is a reflection as well as an expression of its own time and culture, against the background of all that has preceded the actual moment of creation. The moment of creation is charged with the sum total of esthetic feelings and experiences of man expressed through the sensitive articulation of an individual. The more we can learn about all the concomitants, the closer we shall be to the artistic truth of a work of art. This is the way to appreciation.

Students of general history, philosophy, esthetics, social studies, and other courses in the humanities have in this volume a highly concentrated survey of the entire field of literature pertaining to the history of the art of music.

EDWIN J. STRINGHAM, MUS. D.
General Music Editor

INTRODUCTION

I. THE SCOPE OF THE INQUIRY

THE original purpose of this study was to write a history of an interesting body of literature known as "general histories of music." To this end, the needs of students and teachers of the subject were to be kept primarily in mind. But as this is the first time that such a survey has been attempted, it has seemed wise to broaden the scope of the inquiry to include a study of the philosophies of music history that have tried to picture the subject as a whole. This literature bears important relationships to general trends in thought and culture, in the environment of each author and in his musical and intellectual heritage. Furthermore, concepts have been borrowed from other disciplines to make "general histories" of music possible. The processes of music history have been explained in terms of theology, mathematics, biology, mechanics, and psychology. Therefore an attempt has been made to point out the historical sources of these concepts and analogies and the fallacies involved.

Finally, this study has come to be concerned with the separation that exists between the "scientific" and the "popular" approach to the history of music. It is suggested (in Chapter 13) that both types of inquiry can co-operate to explain (without analogies) how our musical arts, preferences, and prejudices have come to be what they are.

II. THE DIFFICULTIES INVOLVED

Any inquiry of this sort faces certain difficulties which are peculiar to the literature and the teaching of music. In the first place, older literature about music is rare and inaccessible in this country. This is true to an extent that is inconceivable to teachers of other arts, or to teachers in the social studies. In all these fields, the classics of the literature are still available in anthologies, translations, and reprints. Only two histories of music written before 1890 are available in second editions. The larger and most scholarly foreign treatises have not been translated, and most current findings in recent research are only available to those who read foreign languages. The *Musical Quarterly* is our only journal devoted entirely to musicology, and the foreign journals have few readers in this country. The three most recent histories published in this country have begun to provide up-to-date information, but all authors or compilers of music-history texts will admit honestly that their works are replicas, in form and method, of some European pattern. The original patterns are only to be found in our largest libraries; they constitute an unknown body of materials for most students and teachers. Because of this, copious use is made of direct quotation. In dealing with Vasari's *Lives,* first published in 1550, a history of art histories would need only comment and reference. But very few know John Brown's *Dissertation on the Rise, Union and Power of Music* [20],[1] published in 1763 and translated into two other languages. Thus Part I may serve as source book and bibliography as well as commentary and as a stimulus, it is hoped, to other efforts in this direction.

In the second place, examination of the bibliography raises the puzzling question, What constitutes a " General History of Music "? Some works bearing that title are merely histories of ancient music, like Martini's *Storia della musica* [19] and Rowbotham's influential three volumes [113], which go as far as the troubadours. Unfinished " general histories " by such leaders as Fétis [81] and Ambros [67], in the mid-nineteenth century, include only the late Renaissance. But all these men had general concepts of organization; and the philosophies of these men are important for this study. Richard Wagner, on the other hand, wrote no history of music, but his *Oper und Drama* [61] embraces a philosophy of music history which has been taken very seriously by many. The length of the work is no criterion: Calvisius [1], in 1600, reviewed history from Creation to his own day in sixty-five small pages, but the incomplete works mentioned above are on a very large scale. The solution has been to include all general contributions in their historical setting, and to study their persistent assumptions.

Then there arises the puzzling question as to whether an expert historian would say that we have any general histories of music at all. The problems of " historical method " have not been debated in this field. The literature on method is enormous in general history; history's relationship to social science is a subject of serious

[1] The reader is asked to note that numbers in brackets after an author's name or after a quotation refer to the bibliography of general histories of music at the end of the book.

concern to the professional historian. But very few of the latter
have concerned themselves with histories of music; these have
usually been written by amateurs in historical writing. In the seventeenth century, the pioneer work was done by three Lutheran musicians (see Chapter 1) who were interested in students and patrons
of music. But their contemporaries, priests who were interested in
ethical, naturalistic, and mathematical theory, have been more influential than those who were interested in the social scene. In the
eighteenth century, journalists, men of letters, philologists, lawyers,
and esthetes began to take up the subject, and since 1900 anthropologists, conservatory professors, psychologists, physicians, clergymen, theosophists, mathematicians, and musical critics have tried
it. Here again it has been necessary to introduce these works as they
are, not for what they lack.

The final and perhaps the greatest difficulty is the lack of agreement regarding the place in our curricula for the study of music
history. On looking back over the materials reviewed, it appears
that many of the first "histories" were written for theory students
to confirm rules and precepts of composition. Then, after the rules
became thoroughly fixed, as so-called laws of Nature, the subject
of history was no longer considered necessary for students of theory
and composition. In the late eighteenth century *history* became
primarily *biography,* for the edification of the dilettante and the
inspiration of the budding virtuoso. At the present time, conservatories of music place very little stress on history for either "theoretical" or "applied" music students. *Appreciation* is the substitute
for history in many of our public-school curricula. History is only
brought in, as shown in Chapters 11 and 12, to help "elevate taste,"
to show that our great music developed from earlier, less advanced,
and less important forms. Finally, there are the questions: What
is "good" music? What is "classical" music? What is "modern"
music? These questions are all closely related to one another, as in
the mind of the good woman who thought all composers were dead.
Most historians have feared to get down to their Present except for
some critical evaluations or mere mention of a few selected composers. The notion that music must be seen in perspective in order
to evaluate it is pitted against the radical theories of those enthusiasts who think they can break with the Past.

Summarizing these difficulties, we find that the literature on the
history of music is, for the most part, inaccessible to most students

and teachers; and when we test music histories by the criteria applicable to other histories, we get into grave difficulties. So although the term "history" appears in the title that does not imply that this discussion is devoted to the study of historical method in general. There have been endless arguments, whether history is an art or a science (the same arguments still go on with reference to music) and the experts themselves are far from agreement. It is possible for a scholar to have command of consummate knowledge, to be quite sure that everything everybody else is doing is entirely wrong, and yet to be unable or unwilling to show how to do it. Unless that man can leave his ivory tower of knowledge, to help the eager student and teacher in the classroom, his achievements are without influence and his critical labors in vain.

A similar situation is easily possible in the study of music. Today the scholars in musical research are not what popular opinion represents them to be and what they were in years past, namely, mere "slaves of the lamp," interested only in musty documents. They are in possession of knowledge which shows that many of our elementary approaches to music and its history are narrow and antiquated. But if the scholar shows only contempt for the popularizer who is doing his best in the light of his knowledge, the two can never get together to raise the standards of music education and music research. The aim of this study is to help all teachers of music and its history to see more clearly the historical background of present-day confusion in the subject. For one thing, the scholar can co-operate with the popularizer and become one himself, if he would have the popularizer become more scholarly. He might contribute to non-technical lectures and texts which will demonstrate the importance of music in history and social life.

"Such lectures are important; they have a bearing on the development of the art of music in the liberal arts college by arousing general interest in the study of music. Furthermore, such lectures are distinctly helpful to students of history, literature, and the arts. Several German and French universities have recently started lectures for the entire student body. The result has been astonishing. As a consequence, the work of the departments of music has been reorganized so as to offer special laboratory work for students in musicology and lectures for the general public." [2]

[2] Paul H. Láng, "The Place of Musicology in the College Curriculum," M.T.N.A. *Proceedings*, 1934, p. 148. This same scholar is preparing a new text, on *Music in the History of Western Civilization*. [314].

These considerations indicate a vast gulf between the scholar and the popularizer which does not exist in other fields. It is due, as already pointed out, to the inaccessibility of scholarly materials. Those who have access to the latter are doing rigorous scientific work in a new and special discipline known as *musicology*.[8] But while the musicologist is concerning himself with specific techniques in limited areas of inquiry, he has not yet formulated a general *method,* a philosophy with reference to the whole field. One of the leaders, Guido Adler, will be quoted for his treatise on "Method in Music History," but this turns out to be merely a discussion of *techniques* for style-criticism and identification. It is significant that Adler himself, although editor of a great *Handbuch,* has written no general history, but it will be shown (in Chapter 11, under "Periodization") that when he tried to outline a *method* for the whole, he fell back into the evolutionary pattern devised during the nineteenth century.

III. THE OBJECTIVES OF THIS STUDY

This volume is devoted, therefore, not to historical but to musicological method, in grateful appreciation for the research by others who have made it possible. It could never have been done without the technical assembly of accurate, verified data provided by such men as Grove, Riemann, Einstein, Moser, Adler, Combarieu, and others in the Old World, and also Pratt, Sonneck, Kinkeldey, Engel, and others who have done pioneer work in this country. We are all indebted to men like Parry, Lavignac, MacDowell, and Mason, who have done so much to popularize the study of music in public education in three countries. In recent years Marion Bauer has brought twentieth-century music into the historical picture, and others in this country, notably Ferguson, Finney, Leichtentritt, and Einstein, have rendered signal service by bringing general histories up to date. The reader is begged to remember that this inquiry is in pursuit not of men but of assumptions, in the tracking

---

[8] This science is so new, in fact, that the word *musicology* is not yet found in all standard dictionaries. On that account there may be those who object to the use of the word, forgetting that dictionaries do not list words until they acquire meaning through use. For the first statement "On Behalf of Musicology," by Waldo Selden Pratt, see the *Musical Quarterly,* Vol. I, No. 1, 1915, p. 1. For later elucidation of the term in the light of recent achievement, see L. Harap, "On the Nature of Musicology," *ibid.,* Vol. 23, No. 18, pp. 18–25. *Musicologie* is well known and established in France.

down of persistent notions that have tended, apparently, to perpetuate old methods and to prevent formulation of new ones. The critical conclusions reached in this volume may provoke argument,
but that is to be hoped for as a healthy sign of interest.

This volume is not addressed to any one type of reader. It is
hoped that its audience may include the student, teacher, and popularizer who have never known older literature and sources of their
notions, as well as the research scholars who have known the literature and have never taken the time to study it in just this way.
The student of philosophy and of the history of ideas may be interested in the problems of a new *Geisteswissenschaft* that is making worthy efforts to rank with the others. Many lay readers are
showing the keenest curiosity concerning music and its history,
judging from the flood of explanatory books and articles addressed
to them.

A. An Exposé of Word-magic and Confusion

All of these potential readers have seen numerous references to
the "origins of music," and to its growth, development, rise, decline, separation, corruption, progress, decadence, unity, and evolution. These are merely popular words which have been used to
explain the history of music. These words have not explained anything. They are words which have a history which is closely bound
up with the history of our ideas. Few of these readers realize the
extent to which these words have aroused controversy and confusion. Take, for example, the search for the ultimate *origins of music*.
In contemporary European histories, the arguments over origins
are as heated, confused, and inconclusive as those over the origins
of the World War. Consequently, after the historical survey in Part
I of this book, the quest for origins forms the subject for Chapter
9. Some of these words also give rise to arguments over *value*.
Somehow value judgments have been confused with historical time-
sequences. Naturally, there can be no quarrel over a time-sequence
if dates are scientifically verified. People may set up their own standards of value to suit their interests, needs, and tastes, but the confusion appears when the arguments begin over "priority," "inferiority," or "superiority," or over the influences of antecedents upon
consequents. The source of hierarchical scales of fixed value, and
of the notion of the development of "form" through these stages
in time is located in the organism analogies of medieval theology

(Chapters 7 and 10). Sources of the belief in triad and triunity theories, also in the "growth" and "decay" of musical "forms" are found in the pseudo-mysticism and evolutionary theologies of nineteenth-century popular science (Chapters 6 and 12). These are the more complex uses of sequential patterns. The simplest and oldest combination is in the great-man theory (Chapter 6). A genealogical time sequence appears with each "inventor" or "genius" towering above his fellows in a scale of value, each adding his contribution, until there is a "culmination" in the art of one supreme composer. The difficulty here is, of course, in the choice of great men. (Chapter 6, 1.) But the greatest confusion results when many of these analogies are jumbled together in one volume, in order to make the study of history an "attractive" instead of a "dry" discipline. (See Chapter 12.)

Historians of music have been forced to use sequential concepts because they were the only tools made available by influential contemporary thought. Turgot's plea, in 1750, to start with "Nature as it *is*," and Goethe's warning concerning the dangerous nature of too much concern with origins have gone unheeded.

B. A Summary of New Possibilities

After all this, the reader might well ask, What other ways are possible? Four answers to that question have been given: *first,* the recognition of the value of the new knowledge now available and of its meaning for a richer musical life here and now; *second,* analysis of the social factors overlooked in evolutionary theory; *third,* presentation of the pros and cons of the nationalistic point of view. (It will be pointed out, from time to time, that the histories of national musical life and the music of one's own area have tended to become neglected in a democratic country like our own and overstressed under dictatorships.) *Fourth,* the suggestion for a new concept of the persistent continuity of music which goes on with relatively little change. Against such backgrounds musical changes can be better understood.

Style-criticism is a new emphasis which is quite different from the "form and analysis" courses in most curricula. Styles change in response to social conditions, but forms frequently remain unchanged, notably so when authority sees to it that they should be fixed or when popular taste rebels at the unfamiliar. It is urged, therefore, that style-criticism may also help us to recover the spirit

of the Lutheran pioneers (Chapter 1), who studied music in terms
of *use and function,* not merely as an art of design. Music is the
latter, of course, among many other things, but studies of pure
design seldom indicate what the music is designed *for.*

C. Recognition of the Dependence of Music upon Social Conditions

With a "clearer view," the subject of music history should be
one of the most fascinating and enlightening of the humanities.
What is necessary?

"To define the essential characteristics of an epoch, historical research, after ransacking all the documents, is still confronted with the
major part of the work. The spirit of an epoch is not reflected in the
arts only. It covers every field of human endeavor, from theology to
military science, and it is a great mistake to think the family of arts
alone can convey this spirit to us. . . . It is a futile undertaking to
separate music from the conglomeration of arts and letters and try to
view it, as we do in our schools today, as a self-sufficient and independent branch of human inventiveness. A sister science — history of fine
arts — realized the awkwardness of such a procedure, and during the
last quarter of a century developed methods of research and teaching
far in advance of those used by music teachers in American colleges." [4]

Why should the teaching of art be in advance of the teaching
of music, as this careful scholar asserts? Two answers are suggested.
In the first place, Chapter 2 will show that the history of art was
started before that of music, in an age when controversy was rife
in the latter over theory and practice; that there is much less separation and division in the graphic and plastic arts than in music,
which has to deal with the physical elements of sound and the
human elements of vocal tone and rhythm. In the second place,
the analogies of organismic "growth, development, and progress"
have not been nearly so important in art history. Youngsters begin
to draw and model by first observing and imitating line, contour,
and form in the things and people about them. They also pick up
the songs and systematic rudiments of the music of their own environment just as they learn the language. Progressive teachers in
both music and art start "from the known to the unknown" in
order to begin with the student as he is, in his own setting; but
the evolution doctrine is deeply ingrained in some romantic sys-

[4] Paul H. Láng, "The Place of Musicology in the College Curriculum," M.T.N.A.
Proceedings, 1934, p. 147.

tems of education. It is often suggested that the student go back to "primitive" conditions, like a little savage, in order to "progress" through the various "stages of evolution" that history has postulated. Then, in higher grades, "appreciation courses" have been apt to begin, not with observation and critical analysis of the music heard about us every day, but with simple folk melodies "out of which musical classics have evolved." Composers have been studied not so much in relation to the epochs in which they lived but as "forerunners" or "successors." (Chapter 12.)

It is obviously true that beginners should not be given complex tasks which are beyond their capabilities. However, it is equally true that untrained young people of today are familiar with musical idioms, chords, and melodic skips which would have been and are complex, difficult, and advanced for an older generation.

At least one French pedagogue (see Chapter 8, p. 157), uses the evolutionary view of history as a method of teaching composition. Without going back to primitivism in savagery, he does nevertheless suggest that the student begin by copying models of early Christian music and old monody in general. Polyphonic art is to be mastered by beginning with the study of organum and descant, coming on down through the "evolution" of counterpoint to the Renaissance, acquiring harmonic technique by emulating older forms before attempting to evolve a "modern" idiom.

The writer knows of no comparable attempt in art teaching which has children begin by painting animals on the walls of caves, and "progress" in their studies through "the early stages of art" up to the present, or art schools which have students attempt to imitate the masterpieces of medieval art as preparation for art work in the modern world.

There is another field in which the artist has had the advantage of the musician, and that is in the field of public recognition and objective criticism. During the last half of the nineteenth century there developed the first successful revolt against the absolutism of the French Academy, but success came to the painters and authors long before it came to the musicians. Claude Monet's *Impression* was hung in the *Salon des Réfusés* in 1863, under the direct encouragement of Emperor Napoleon III; the Pre-Raphaelites, organized in 1848, had at least been tolerated by a large portion of the British public; and the American Whistler had enjoyed no small measure of success. But in 1889 César Franck's symphony, first performed in the last year of his life, was contemptuously dismissed by Gounod, favorite of the Academy, the conservative public, and the critics.

" The composer of Faust, escorted by a procession of worshippers, male and female, decreed pontifically that this symphony was *l'affirmation de l'impuissance poussée jusqu'au dogme* . . . While one professor said: ' Name one symphony by Haydn or Beethoven where you will find an English horn! Call it what you please, but not a symphony!' " [5]

Today this symphony is one of a few so fixed in popular favor that a contemporary Franck has the same old difficulty. In the nineties, Debussy was startling his colleagues with new concepts of melodic line and sonority,[6] inspired by the vital art of Russia and the exotic music of a Javanese orchestra at the Paris Exposition (1900). But the music of Moussorgsky, Franck, and Debussy was not generally accepted until long after modern tendencies in painting and literature had become commonplace.

In England " it required some moral courage in Parry in 1893 (ten years after Wagner's death) to accord to Wagner's music-dramas the place he gives them as ' the high-water mark of music of the present.' " [7]

This may help to explain the fact that late nineteenth-century studies of the history of art and literature go much more deeply into the study of social factors than do the histories of music. As early as 1863 Hippolyte Taine published his *Histoire de la littérature anglaise,* reviving old theories of the influence of climate and geography upon art but attempting to explain art as the product of

[5] V. d'Indy, *César Franck,* 4th ed., Paris, 1908, p. 30.

[6] For a conservative historian's bewilderment over Debussy, see Combarieu's comment, quoted on p. 288 of this book. This is one phase of criticism which is condemned in this volume. The popular notion of music criticism has obsessed many historians since the eighteenth century. The latter, thinking it necessary to pass judgment according to a sequential pattern of value, too often succeed in merely reflecting the esthetic prejudices of their day. For the defense of this point of view, see Élie Faure, *History of Art,* Vol. I, N. Y., 1921, tr. by Walter Pach, p. xl. That may be journalism but it is not objective history.

Style-criticism is not concerned, however, with value judgments that give grade-ratings to works of art. Modern research decides, for instance, that *Tenebrae factae sunt,* heretofore credited to Palestrina, was written by a pupil, Ingegneri. Modern methods of comparison, with scientific study of style, time, place, and personality, made this decision possible, not a vote of judges sitting about to discuss " merit."

[7] Parry, *Evolution of the Art of Music,* 1935 edition, final chapter by H. C. Colles, p. 463.

social environment. His influence was manifest in Parry's contemporary, Alfred C. Haddon, who said, in 1895:

"in order to understand the designs of a district, the physical conditions, climate, flora, fauna, and anthropology, all have to be taken into account; thus furnishing another example of the fact that it is impossible to study any one subject comprehensively without touching many other branches of knowledge." [8]

Ernst Grosse,[9] in 1893, showed how the sociological problems of art and literature have been studied since the days of Abbé Dubos,

"who started the inquiry into the causes of the different artistic talents of different peoples and different ages, in 1719, in his *Réflexions critiques sur la poésie et la peinture.*"

As for Herder, his

"General thoughts on the influence of national climate and character upon poetry" were forgotten by Germans who "let the airy construction of philosophy rise into the clouds."

H. M. Posnett, in 1886, declared that "the comparative method . . . is in one sense as old as thought itself, in another the peculiar glory of our nineteenth century." *Simple comparisons* permit very penetrating observations concerning the relationships of literature to the social group in and for which it is written. For example:

"If we are determined to lay down the dogma that Shakespeare, or Dante, or any other poet wrote above space and time, above the social and physical conditions under which he lived, we really exclude historical propriety by a creed of literary inspiration which has been frequently asserted, if not believed in, with theological assurance." [10]

It will be shown in these pages that the "theological assurance" of nineteenth-century Romanticism allowed the "general history of music" to be influenced by a "creed of literary inspiration" in the mystic belief that a "scientific," "comparative" method was thus possible. This belief was admirably stated in these words:

"The philosophy of history deals not exclusively but to a great extent with laws of progress, with laws of evolution; and until the idea of progress was firmly and *clearly* apprehended, little could be done in it.

[8] *Evolution in Art, as Illustrated by the Life-Histories of Designs,* London, 1895, p. 7.
[9] *The Beginnings of Art,* English ed., N. Y. and London, 1914, pp. 12 ff.
[10] *Comparative Literature,* N. Y., 1902 ed., pp. 29, 73.

" And only slowly, only by innumerable short stages, only owing to the consecutive and concurrent action of countless causes, has humanity fully awakened to the consciousness of its unity, and the possibility been admitted of surveying the whole of the past and present of society, from a certain *single lofty point of view.*" [11]

" The single lofty point of view " was, in the first place, what the music scholars of the seventeenth century certainly did *not* have (except for the theologians); in the second place it was the only method the nineteenth-century scholar *did* have with which to make a " general history of music." Whether such " clear apprehension " of progress has made the picture clearer is very doubtful. This volume is devoted to the proposal that we abandon the " single lofty point of view " of music as a mystic entity, in order to find a pluralistic method by which we may deal in a scientific way with different arts of music in different areas, with different peoples made up of different individuals.

[11] Robert Flint, *History of the Philosophy of History,* N. Y., 1894, pp. 87, 88, 104.

ACKNOWLEDGMENTS

I AM deeply grateful to the following scholars who have read all or part of this work in manuscript: Professor Edwin J. Stringham for invaluable suggestions which have led me to carry the inquiry into the field of music appreciation; Professor Paul H. Láng for suggestions in relation to graduate research in musicology; Professors George S. Counts, John Hermann Randall, Jr., John L. Childs, Irwin Edman, and Merle Curti for criticisms in the fields of sociology, philosophy, and history; and Dr. Otto Kinkeldey, Librarian and Professor of Musicology at Cornell University.

I am grateful also for all the courtesies shown by the music staff at the New York Public Library, where Dr. Carleton Sprague Smith has shown great interest and given access to sources of very valuable information. The same courtesies and help were available on my visits to the Library of Congress, where Dr. Harold Spivacke performed similar services, as did his predecessor, Dr. Oliver Strunk. The Slavic Division was very helpful in locating and summarizing the Russian histories of music.

This enterprise was started several years ago at the University of California. To Professor Margaret Hodgen of the Department of Social Institutions I am indebted for some constructive suggestions concerning the problems of analogy, borrowed concepts in social science, and possible ways of facing them.

In quoting from foreign texts, I have used authorized translations when they were available. In other cases I have made my own.

For permissions for the use of copyrighted material from books and magazines, grateful acknowledgment is made to the following publishers and authors:

Félix Alcan, Paris: H. Collet, *Le mysticisme musical espagnol;* L. Bourguès and A. Dénéraz, *La musique et la vie intérieure;* Vincent d'Indy, *César Franck.*

George Allen & Unwin, Ltd., London: Otto Jespersen, *Language, Its Nature, Development, and Origin.*

American Journal of Psychiatry, New York: Frederick H. Allen, " Some Therapeutical Principles."

D. Appleton-Century Company, New York: A. Lavignac, *Musical Education*, translated by Esther Singleton; H. M. Posnett, *Comparative Literature*.

Breitkopf & Härtel, Leipzig: Hugo Riemann, *Handbuch der Musikgeschichte*.

Cambridge University Press, London: Otto Gierke, *Political Theories of the Middle Ages*, translated by F. W. Maitland.

Honoré Champion, Paris: H. Gillot, *La querelle des anciens et des modernes en France*.

J. & W. Chester, London: A. Casella, *The Evolution of Music throughout the History of the Perfect Cadence*.

Librairie Armand Colin, Paris: J. Combarieu, *Histoire de la musique*.

P. F. Collier & Son Corp., New York: Montaigne, "Essay on the Education of Children," translated by John Florio, *The Harvard Classics*, Vol. 32.

Columbia University Press, New York: F. J. E. Woodbridge, *The Purpose of History*; Karl Nef, *An Outline of the History of Music*, translated by Carl Pfatteicher.

J. M. Dent & Sons, Ltd., London: Margaret H. Glyn, *Theory of Musical Evolution*.

Oliver Ditson Company, Philadelphia: D. G. Mason, *From Song to Symphony*; M. Meyer, *Musician's Arithmetic*.

M. M. Durand & Cie, Paris: Vincent d'Indy, *Cours de composition musicale*.

Encyclopaedia Britannica, New York, 14th ed.: article "Dictionary."

Raffaello Giusti, Leghorn: A. Bonaventura, *Manuele di storia della musica*.

H. W. Gray Co., New York: T. W. Surette and D. G. Mason, *The Appreciation of Music*.

Librairie Hachette, Paris: F. Clément, *Histoire de la musique*.

S. Hirzel Verlag, Leipzig: Karl Bücher, *Arbeit und Rhythmus*.

Henry Holt and Company, New York: A. Lavignac, *Music and Musicians*, translated by William Marchant; Preserved Smith, *A History of Modern Culture*; Karl Bücher, *Industrial Evolution*, translated by S. M. Wickett.

Kegan Paul, Trench, Trubner & Co., London: J. Combarieu, *Music, Its Laws and Evolution*, translated by F. Legge; Cecil Gray, *The History of Music*; C. H. H. Parry, *The Art of Music*; Richard Wagner, *Prose Works*, translated by W. A. Ellis.

Alfred A. Knopf, Inc., New York: Winthrop Parkhurst, *The Anatomy of Music*; Alfred Einstein, *A Short History of Music*; Wanda Landowska, *Music of the Past*.

H. Laurens, Paris: M. Emmanuel, *Histoire de la langue musicale*.

Larousse, Paris: Alice Gabeaud, *L'histoire de la musique*.

Longmans, Green & Co., New York: R. Wallaschek, *Primitive Music*.

The Macmillan Company, New York: William Wallace, *The Threshold of Music;* Roscoe Pound, *Interpretation of Legal History;* Plato, *Timaeus,* edited by R. D. Archer-Hind; Baldwin's *Dictionary of Philosophy and Psychology;* Stanford and Forsyth, *History of Music;* D. G. Mason, *Beethoven and His Forerunners;* J. B. Bury, *The Idea of Progress.*

The Modern Language Association of America, New York: E. Claasen, "A Theory of the Development of Language," *Modern Language Review,* Vol. 12.

W. W. Norton & Company, New York: Carlos Chavez, *Toward a New Music;* Joseph Yasser, *A Theory of Evolving Tonality.*

Oberlin Press, Oberlin, Ohio: Paul Láng, "The Place of Musicology in the College Curriculum," M.T.N.A. *Proceedings,* 1934; O. G. Sonneck, "The History of Music in America," M.T.N.A. *Proceedings,* 1916.

Open Court Publishing Company, La Salle, Ill.: L. Lévy-Bruhl, *A History of Modern Philosophy in France.*

Oxford University Press, London and New York: George Dyson, *The Progress of Music;* R. Vaughan-Williams, *National Music; The Works of Aristotle,* edited by W. D. Ross; Jowett, *Aristotle's Politics;* Arnold Toynbee, *A Study of History;* Cecil Gray, *A Survey of Contemporary Music; The Oxford History of Music.*

Auguste Picard, Paris: J. Combarieu, *La musique et la magie.*

Theodore Presser Company, Philadelphia: Percy Goetschius, *The Structure of Music.*

The Psychoanalytic Quarterly, New York: Siegfried Bernfeld, "Psychoanalytic Psychology of the Young Child," Vol. IV.

G. P. Putnam's Sons, New York: Satis Coleman, *Creative Music for Children;* Marion Bauer, *Twentieth Century Music;* John Dewey, *Art as Experience.*

Quelle & Meyer, Leipzig: Curt Sachs, *Vergleichende Musikwissenschaft in ihren Grundzügen.*

Rider & Company, London (The David McKay Company, Philadelphia): Cyril Scott, *Music, Its Secret Influence throughout the Ages,* formerly entitled *The Influence of Music on History and Morals.*

G. Schirmer, Inc., New York: W. A. Ambros, *The Boundaries of Music and Poetry,* translated by J. H. Cornell, copyrighted 1893; Ferruccio Busoni, *A New Esthetic of Music,* translated by Dr. Th. Baker, copyrighted 1911, 1935; Edward J. Dent, "The Relation of Music to Human Progress," *Musical Quarterly,* July, 1928; R. D. Chennevière, "The Rise of the Musical Proletariat," *Musical Quarterly,* October, 1920.

The Arthur P. Schmidt Co., Boston: Edward MacDowell, *Critical and Historical Essays.*

Charles Scribner's Sons, New York: J. F. Rowbotham, *A History of Music;* McKeon, *Selections from the Medieval Philosophers; Selections from Schopenhauer;* W. S. Rockstro, *A General History of Music;* Robert Flint, *History of the Philosophy of History.*

Smithsonian Institution, Washington, D. C., and the *Zeitschrift für Ethnologie,* Berlin: Willy Pastor, "Music of Primitive Peoples," *Smithsonian Report.*

G. E. Stechert & Co., New York: Ludwig Gumplowicz, *Outline of Sociology,* translated by F. W. Moore.

University of Chicago Press, Chicago: Albion W. Small, *Origins of Sociology.*

The Vanguard Press, New York: Charles D. Isaacson, *The Simple Story of Music.*

Joseph Williams, Ltd., London: Herbert Antcliffe, *Living Music.*

WHEN it has been necessary to visit the New York Public Library or the Library of Congress in order to consult rare works, that fact is indicated with the initials NY or LC in the bibliographical notes. In addition to library files, a bibliography of musical bibliographies by Michel Brenet (Mlle. Bobillier) in *L'année Musicale*, Paris, 1911, provided an excellent starting point for bibliographical research. The following studies on the literature of music in general have been helpful:

J. N. Forkel, *Allgemeine Literatur der Musik*, Leipzig, 1792, 540 pp. NY.

Carl F. Becker, *Systematisch-chronologische Darstellung der musikalischen Literatur von der frühesten bis die neueste Zeit.* 1836, 605 pp. NY.

James E. Matthews, *The Literature of Music*, London, 1896.

Julia Gregory (Library of Congress Music Division), *Catalogue of Early Books on Music* (before 1800), Washington, 1913.

Adolf Aber, *Handbuch der Musikliteratur*, Leipzig, 1922, 695 pp. NY.

Eric Blom, *General Index to Modern Music Literature in English*, London, 1927, 159 pp.

Ludwig Schiedermair, *Einführung in das Studium der Musikwissenschaft*, Bonn, 1930, 107 pp.

Bibliographies of music history also appear under the title "History of Music" in Grove's *Dictionary of Music and Musicians*, 1928 edition [99], and the *Musiklexicons* of Hugo Riemann [107] and H. J. Moser [287]. Current and past issues of the Peters *Jahrbuch der Musikwissenschaft* (Leipzig), the *Acta Musicologica* (Copenhagen), the *Musical Quarterly* (New York), *Music and Letters* (London), and *La Revue Musicale* (Paris) provide book lists that are constant and growing sources of information.

LEOPOLDVS GVILIELMVS
ARCHIDVX AVSTRIÆ
BELGII et BVRGVNDIÆ
GVBERNATOR

FROM THE DEDICATION OF PART II, VOLUME I, OF PRAETORIUS' "SYNTAGMA
MUSICUM," 1615

CONTENTS

PART I. HISTORY OF MUSIC HISTORIES

Evolution as a Basic Explanation — Music History and Nationalism — The Marxian
Interpretation — Music Histories in Other Countries

PART II. PHILOSOPHIES OF MUSIC HISTORY

Continuity and Analogy — Continuity in Human Experience — Change against
Continuity

The Fascination of the Inexplicable — Origins in " Laws of Nature " — Origins
in " Laws of Human Nature " — Origins in Musical Structure

The Comparative Method — The Analogy of Development — The Idea of Progress

History without Gaps — The Problem of Periodization — The Analogy of Growth
— The Wagnerian Influence — The Confusion of Analogies

Their Influence on Music Education — A Few Quotations — Critical Summary

Comparison, Continuity, and Change — Musicology and Comparison — The
Processes of Modification — Competition in Modification — Different Systems in Different Areas — Conclusion

PART I

HISTORY OF MUSIC HISTORIES

FRONTISPIECE TO KIRCHER'S "MUSURGIA," VOLUME II

CHAPTER I

MUSICAL RESEARCH IN THE BAROQUE ERA

UNTIL very recently the arts of the seventeenth century were dismissed with contempt. Today new methods of style-criticism are restoring the music and other arts of the Baroque era to their rightful place of honor in our cultural heritage.[1] Gone are the days when the term Baroque meant meaningless ornament; it is no longer used as a synonym for that which is *närrisch* or *lächerlich*[2] and "in bad taste."[3]

The nineteenth century was greatly indebted to the seventeenth—more so than Wagnerians and Victorians ever realized. Baroque ideals were revived in the arts under new names, and the speculations of Baroque scholars came to be basic assumptions in social science.

Modern research now shows that between the beginnings of modern chronology,[4] around 1600, and the formulation of modern Ideas of Progress, around 1690,[5] some very interesting work was done by pioneer musicologists. Studied for content alone, one can find much that shows their dependence upon the legendary, the miraculous, and the eccentric. Carl Engel in his *Musical Myths and Facts* [91] put them into his chapter on "Curiosities," and Matthew emphasized that phase of Baroque texts in his *Literature of Music* (London, 1896). The general verdict seems to agree with the state-

[1] For a further discussion of this subject see Allen, "Baroque Histories of Music," *Musical Quarterly*, April, 1939. Acknowledgment is made herewith of permission to use certain statements from that article in this chapter.

[2] See Schilling, *Encykl. der ges. mus. Wissenschaften*, 1835, Vol. I, "Barock." For modern treatments, definitions, and criticisms see "Baroque Architecture," *Encyc. Brit.*, 14th ed.; for evidence of this as a reversal of judgment, see "Baroque," in the 11th ed., as late as 1910.

[3] According to J. W. Mollett, *An Illus. Dictionary of Words used in Art and Archaeology*, Boston, 1883.

[4] Joseph Justus Scaliger's *De Emendatione Temporum* appeared in 1583, 2nd ed. in 1594.

[5] See pp. 245–247.

3

ment of Flint that serious history worthy of the name did not appear
until the Idea of Progress came to be the governing principle of
successive advance from antecedent to consequent. But it is maintained here, and at the end of this volume, that the modern student
of music history can learn much from the breadth of view of some
seventeenth-century writers, and that there is a laudable method to
be observed, even in some works that seem to be hodgepodges of
unorganized material.

Some earlier works lack " chronological order," the *sine qua non*
of modern historiography. Evidently this accounts for the fact that
most bibliographies find no *History of Music* until 1690. But it can
be established definitely that at least one important history appeared
in 1600 and another in 1615.

The year 1600 is a traditional milestone in the history of Western
music. As will be shown later, the quarrels over the respective merits
of ancient and modern music were then at their height. It will also
be pointed out that " modern music," then, and for the next two
hundred years, referred to music of the Christian era as distinct from
music of the ancient Greeks and Romans.[6] But in the nineteenth
century, with the periodization of Ancient, Medieval, and Modern,
the latter term comes to mean music since 1600, the year which saw
" the birth of modern opera." At any rate, it was in that year that
Jacopo Peri's *Euridice* was written for the marriage ceremonies of
Henri IV of France and Maria de' Medici, in Florence, and pré-
sented as the first public performance in the *nuovo stile*. This was
the name given to a style fostered by some Florentine experimenters
who had been endeavoring to apply the principles of Greek declamation to dramatic Italian verse. *Euridice* is usually regarded as
" the first opera " by modern historians.[7] " The first oratorio," [8] or

---

[6] Guido d'Arezzo (early 11th cent.) is the figure chosen by early historians to
mark the beginnings of " modern " music. Because of his activities as a teacher he was
credited with having fixed the scales or *genera* of modern music. As late as 1703,
Brossard, in his *Dictionnaire de musique,* translated by Grassineau (*A Musical Dictionary,* London, 1740) says: " About the 11th century, one Guido Arentine began to
revive this art; 'tis from him we derive what is called the modern music; but his
manner is widely different from that of the Grecians. He brought into one system
two of the ancient *genera,* viz., the diatonic and chromatic; but these not without
some alteration, and omitted the enharmonic, by reason of the minuteness of its
intervals." (Preface, p. ix). Not until the twentieth century has " modern " come to
refer to contemporary music.

[7] E.g., Donald Ferguson [300], p. 179; Theodore M. Finney [301], p. 216;
Karl Nef [210], p. 147.

[8] Ferguson [300], p. 182; Finney [301], p. 225; Nef [210], p. 148.

sacred opera, is, according to general agreement, the *Rappresenta-zione del Anima e del Corpo,* by Emilio del Cavalieri, performed in Rome that same year.

One cannot assert positively that these were really the *first* opera and the *first* oratorio. The word *opera* is not used to describe music-drama until around 1650, and any attempts to locate the first music-drama might bring forth champions of an Italian madrigal-comedy, or a French *ballet de cour* of the late sixteenth century, or a medieval mystery play, or even a masterpiece of Greek or Oriental drama. Similarly, there are no books definitely entitled *Histories of Music* until 1690–1715 (see Section III of this chapter); but on the other hand, literature concerning music, with historical references to older music, music theory, and musicians was by no means a novelty in 1600. Numerous Greek and medieval texts on music and much early Renaissance literature had been devoted to the subject. But in certain respects the work of two Lutheran scholars marks a new departure — in the same sense in which *Euridice* and the *Rappresenta-zione* were the " first." That is to say, the composers and authors of these works, as far as the writer is able to ascertain, were the first publicly to attempt, in these particular fields, to connect ancient tradition, usage, and practice with contemporary needs, usages, and practices.

After discussing the works of Calvisius and Praetorius, the two Lutherans, a brief survey will be made of the researches by Catholic scholars in the Romance countries, and finally of the work of the " nationalists," that is to say, those historians who first abandoned Latin as the language of music history, to write histories of music in German, Italian, French, and English.

I. THE LUTHERAN PIONEERS

In 1600, Seth Kallwitz, Cantor of the Thomasschule and Musik-director of the Stadtkirche in Leipzig, having Latinized his name as Sethus Calvisius, published one of several important works on musical theory. The first of these had been printed in the year of his double appointment (1594), a *Compendium musicae practicae pro incipientibus,* which reached a third edition in 1612, under the title *Musicae artis praecepta nova et facillima.* His original and compilatory work in hymnology is also known to all students of the Lutheran chorale and its history. There is evidence, therefore, for his active interest in music education and in the general Lutheran tendency to *simplify* and *popularize* the music of the church.

But the work published in 1600 is a distinct novelty in the field of theoretical treatises, because the book contained an Historical Supplement, entitled *De origine et progressu musices* [1].

Calvisius was one of a long line of distinguished cantors at the Thomasschule. This double post, as schoolmaster and director, was the same position to which Johann Sebastian Bach was appointed in 1723.[9] But Calvisius was also a mathematician, and it will be pointed out later that his studies in chronology must have prompted him to give this special attention to history. Furthermore, he was a teacher; the titles above indicate that he was interested in giving the boys in the Thomasschule precepts for both theory and practice which would be new and elementary (*nova et facillima*) for beginners (*pro incipientibus*).

Now a great change was taking place in musical styles when Calvisius went to the Thomaskirche. Palestrina and Orlandus Lassus had passed away in the year of his appointment (1594). Their death marked, not the "end of a polyphonic period," as most textbooks explain (for "many-voiced," contrapuntal music did not cease entirely), but a swing in popular fancy toward simpler musical communications in which one principal melody predominated. At the same time there was no small amount of confusion and argument, as the next chapter will show, because of the new emphasis on keyboard instruments. So with the training of young students in singing, organ playing, orchestral routine, and composing (all part of the cantor's job, in addition to teaching Latin, and his own directing and composing), Calvisius evidently felt the necessity of an appeal to history, to show, in a brief review, what the successive steps had been in developing the art which he believed was just about perfect in his own day. So to show his students the value of modern "precepts" and conventions, he wrote this sketch *Of the Origin and Progress of Music.*[10]

[9] See Charles Sanford Terry, *Bach, a Biography*, London, 1928, pp. 162–163.

[10] Calvisius wastes no time in getting at his history; deeming traditional eulogies of the art unnecessary and taking origins for granted, he begins as follows:

"Verum cum brevitatis rationem in primis habendam duxerim, et Musica per se satis laudata sit, omissa omnes alia commendatione, priusquam ad ipsa praecepta transeamus, unicam tantum caput, quod ad Historiam Musices praecipue facere videtur, tractabo.

Quibus videlicet initiis Musica coeperit, quae incrementa sumserit, et quomodo ad eam perfectionem, qua hodie floret pervenerit, de qua re si breviter quae dá

Before Calvisius, many a book had been written on the origins of music.[11] Judging from the evidence offered in the histories to be reviewed in Chapter 3, there was general agreement in all of these early works concerning the divine origins of the art. Calvisius accepts this explanation for *initio musices,* but finds much to admire in the music of his contemporaries and immediate predecessors. In this respect he was unique. Theorists interested in the origins of music had not connected their theories with contemporary practice, unless to condemn the latter. On the other hand, composers with new ideas, and their defenders, were not apt to bother with ancient theory. (See Chapter 2 of this book.)

But this divine-origin theory is not sufficient. Calvisius also quotes Lucretius on the origins of music in *Nature.* Lucretius will be found again in Chapter 3 of this book, quoted by a nineteenth-century English writer. But no conflict exists until eighteenth-century notions demand their complete separation. Calvisius, like all his contemporaries, therefore believed that the music of the human voice was God-given, at Creation; that instrumental music, beginning with Jubal, "the father of all such as handle the harp and the organ," came afterward;[12] but that the sounds of Nature's instruments "invented" and perfected by man are worthy to rank with vocal music in the praise of God.

This, as we shall see, came to be contrary to Roman and Puritan theory, so that later histories argue interminably over the "priority" of vocal over instrumental music, for all sorts of reasons — theological, mythological, esthetic, and anthropological.

Calvisius goes on to name, in chronological order, the various "inventors," theorists, and innovators through whose *labor* and *industry* the art of music was developed. He quotes Horace's *Art of Poetry,* which is probably one of the earliest applications to music history of the theory of progress from simple to complex.[13]

---

annotavero ad Musica Theoremata & praecepta explicanda commodius accedemus.

Praepotentem Deum, omnium bonarum artium in vita hominum necessarium, datorem esse, non solum sacrae literae ostendunt, sed etiam qui apud profanos atque. . . ." (pp. 74, 75).

[11] See [30] for a long list of titles on this subject.

[12] Calvisius quotes Luther as adding also that *von dem (Jubal) sind gekommen die Geiger und Pfeiffer.* The use of the choir combined with orchestra and organ in the Lutheran service has always been a conditioning factor in the fostering of German musical arts.

[13] For a modern translation of the passage from Horace, see T. A. Moxon's, in Everyman's Library, No. 901, pp. 67–68. In this passage Horace shows the develop-

It has already been noted that Calvisius followed Martin Luther's desire to "*simplify and popularize* the music of the church." But this did not prevent him from writing eight-part motets and advanced treatises on the scientific aspects of music. And just as Luther had admired that master of polyphony, Josquin des Près, so did Calvisius. Josquin, Clemens non Papa, and Orlandus Lassus are mentioned by Calvisius with great admiration. He mentions these dominating figures of the century previous, in fact, as proof of his belief that Pope John XXII had been entirely wrong in condemning figured music (polyphony) in 1324–1325.[14]

In short, Calvisius was interested not merely in the ancient beginnings (*initio*) of music, but in its meaning for him as a practical musician, composer, and teacher. He was willing to accept the theory of music's divine origin in the first vocal utterance of man, at Creation, but was able to see progress in a continuous series of men who had inherited accumulating musical tradition, and who had passed them on with worthy contributions of their own. There is reason to believe that Calvisius was led to use this genealogical method because of his work in chronology. Joseph Justus Scaliger (1540–1609), the great Huguenot chronologer, was only sixteen years Calvisius' senior; his *De Emendatione Temporum* had appeared in 1583, just seventeen years before Calvisius' historical treatise. In the latter, Scaliger is quoted as authority for the date of the fall of Troy (2769), on pp. 81–82. But Calvisius himself, among mathematicians, is best known as a chronologer,[15] so it is not surprising that he should be the first to write a history of music in chronological order.

In his genealogical résumé of the subject, Apollo, inventor of the cithara, or lyre, is, as always, the first and foremost of the "inventors," followed by Mercury, Terpander with his added strings, Pythagoras, John of Damascus of the Eastern Church, and Guido

---

ment of the simple flute with a few holes to the new instrument, "bound with brass," which rivals the trumpet. This development correlates with the change in the audience, beginning with simple rustics and ending with sophisticated crowds in larger cities, for whom strings were added to the lyre, and "dancing and wanton gesture to the simple art of old." But this did not mean "decadence," because "daring eloquence rivaled the pronouncements of Delphi."

[14] [1], pp. 129–131. Calvisius prints part of the original text of the edict. For a modern translation of this papal edict from Avignon, see [301], pp. 108–109.

[15] His *Opus Chronologicum* (Leipzig, 1605, 7th ed., 1685) was based upon records of 300 eclipses, and was followed by proposals for calendar reform in his *Elenchus Calendarii Gregoriani* (Frankfort, 1612).

d'Arezzo, "inventor of modern music" according to some, and of notation and counterpoint according to others. The disagreements between Aristoxenus and the Pythagoreans as to whether music is for the ear or for the reason as a science of numbers is dealt with (pp. 91, 92) and citations appear from Boethius' *De Musica*,[16] as in every treatise of the day.

But Calvisius condenses these conventional items with admirable brevity to get down to an explanation of the different methods of metrical music and of solmisation. He gives not only Guido's hexachord system with the syllables *Ut, re, mi, fa, sol, la* at the beginning of each line of the famous hymn to *Sanctus Johannes* (repeated in nearly every history of music to this day), but also a system for singing syllables for the major scale, for treble voices in the G clef, our most common clef today (then just coming into favor). These predecessors of the "movable *do*" system were *Bo, ce, di, ga, lo, ma, ni, Bo,* and are used in transposition (pp. 121-122).

At the end of this little treatise, which covers much ground in a few pages, Calvisius says that these matters discussed show that "from the beginning of the world to our own times," *Musica* has progressed from very small beginnings, little by little, thanks to the labors of men who have added so much to it to make the art that we enjoy today.

Then follows the usual benediction, in which the heavenly choirs are anticipated, in the perfection of music beyond this life:

> perfectissimae illius musicae in vita coelesti, ab universo
> triumphantis Ecclesiae & beatorum Angelorum choro,
> propediam inchoendae, et per omnem aeternitatem
> continuandae
> FINIS

It is obvious that this pious scholar did not have to wait until the nineteenth century to survey his subject from "a lofty point of view." The Idea of Progress, at the end of the seventeenth century, came to mean something more than successive additions and development of possibilities, but among Baroque music histories Calvisius' method was unique. No one else attempted to make a similar survey until nearly a century later.

---

[16] Boethius (c. 470-525 A.D.) was the chief source of data on Greek musical theory for medieval and Renaissance theorists. The legends of Pythagoras, who left no writings whatever on music, stem largely from this philosopher's work.

Calvisius, as already pointed out, found merits in the older, complex, many-voiced music of the Renaissance, but knew how to adapt
himself to modern methods in an age that was beginning to prefer
simple monody.[17] Some other men were more apt to condemn polyphonic music. Père Mersenne, for instance, who will be discussed
in the next section, is quoted as follows:

" It seems that the art of composing in parts, which has been practiced
only for the last one hundred and fifty or two hundred years, had been
invented merely to supply the defects of air (melody), and to cover the
ignorance of modern musicians in this part of *melopoeia,* or melody, as
practiced by the Greeks, who have preserved some vestiges of it in the
Levant, according to the testimony of travellers, who have heard the Persians and modern Greeks sing. . . . The beauties of a trio cannot be so
easily discovered and comprehended as of a *duo;* as the mind and ear
have too many things to attend to at the same time." [18]

Calvisius was a sober scholar who found little, if any, place for
fancy, hearsay, and superstition. He accepted Biblical traditions, as
did everyone else, but gave no space to pictures of Pythagoras " discovering " ratios with the hammer and anvil,[19] or for legendary
accounts of the bewitching and curative powers of music. It seems
curious that the importance of his historical *Übersicht* should have
been overlooked by modern lexicographers.[20] In point of volume,
it is a mere mite in the extensive publications of a versatile scholar,
composer, teacher, astronomer, and mathematician (see Riemann's
Lexicon for a list of Calvisius' compositions); but with respect to
method, his few pages of *Historia* are of great importance.

Like Johann Sebastian Bach, who came a century later, Calvisius
was born in Thuringia and died in Leipzig. Another native of
Thuringia, fifteen years younger than Calvisius, was Michael Prae-

[17] Hugo Riemann, an authoritative historian of music theory, supports this statement by naming Calvisius as one of those who were most successful in transforming
the study of counterpoint into that of harmony. [107], Vol. I, p. 269.

[18] As translated and quoted by Charles Burney. [26], Vol. I, pp. 147–148.

[19] Burney, in discrediting the wild speculations of older writers, says that " hammer and anvil have been swallowed up by ancients and moderns, and have passed
through them from one to another, with an ostrich-like digestion." [26], Vol. I,
Chapter V.

[20] Grove's *Dictionary* is the only one found that lists the *De initio* at the beginning of a list of histories of music. Riemann mentions the *Exercitationes duae* as a
theoretical work only; Moser does not mention it at all.

torius (1571–1621). Praetorius began publication of his great *Syntagma musicum* in 1615, the year of Calvisius' death.[21]

The technical information contained in Volumes II and III of the *Syntagma* has proved so interesting and worth while that both volumes have been made available in modern reprints, as noted. But for the purposes of this inquiry Volume I is, like the much less voluminous effort of Calvisius, extremely important. Few commentators have noted the fact that this volume, much larger than the other two, is in many and unusual respects a true *history of music*. There is probably much more historical information in its 459 pages than in the three histories that are usually said to be the first. (See Section III of this chapter.) But it evidently does not count as a history for modern historiographers because it shows complete disregard for chronological order. As a matter of fact, *Volume I of the Syntagma is a history in terms of use and function, not of progression* from one stage to another in the development of the art.

For Praetorius, like most of his contemporaries, there was no such thing as *one art of music*. Riemann in his *Musiklexikon* states that he sought out "all the expressive forms of his day," in order to transplant and assimilate them. The list of his enormous musical output (1,244 songs in his *Musicae Sionae* alone) shows that he composed for all sorts of functions — church, concert, civic, and intimate. The Venetian styles were absorbed for church music, the French for dance music, and the German folk styles for all sorts of occasions.

Praetorius was interested in the music of all ages, and frequently juxtaposes old and new music for his purposes. He was, as already indicated, interested in instrumental music — such an authority on the organ, in particular, that he is now regarded as one of the "boldest sound-architects of all time." However, his compositions are

[21] *Praetorius* is also a Latinization (of Schultheiss, according to Moser; or Schulz, according to Riemann). The *Syntagma* was originally planned to comprise four volumes, of which three were completed. Modern editions of Vol. II, *De organographia* (1619) were published in 1929 as Vol. 13 of the *Publ. der Gesellschaft für Musikforschung,* also in facsimile as the first *Publikation der hist. Section des deutschen Orgelrats,* Gurlitt, Kassel, with the original illustrations. The latter was in connection with the post-war revival of the Baroque organ, a movement which has spread also to American organ building. In the *Nachwort* of this edition Praetorius is hailed as one of the *Kühnste Klangbaumeister aller Zeiten.* Vol. III, ed. by Ed. Bernouilli, was brought out in a revised edition in 1916 (Kahnt, Leipzig). This contains quantities of information about music and musicians of the author's own day.

primarily for voices; and he is not known as an historian because he did not " clearly apprehend " the idea of " progress," because he did not attempt to survey the pageant of history as "unity," from "a single lofty point of view! " Praetorius, in other words, had a pluralistic point of view that is evident in the title to Volume I: *Syntagma Musicum ex Veterum et Recentiorum.*

In other words, music in his everyday environment was a mixture of ancient heritage and recent innovation; the lengthy title speaks of *Polyhistorum consignatione, variarum linguarum notatione, hodierni seculi usurpatione, ipsiusque Musicae artis observatione; in Cantorum, Organistarum, Organopoeorium Caeterorumque Musicam Scientam amantium tractantium gratiam collectum,* . . .

In all the other music histories with which this inquiry attempts to deal, no such toleration of differences has been found on a title page, with the possible exception of Printz' history in 1690. Praetorius made use of these differences by organizing his history as follows:

Part I deals with *Sacred Music,* and is dedicated to the clergy.

Part II is entitled *Historia de Musica extra ecclesiam,* and is dedicated to the Elector of Saxony and the Duke of Brunswick. The subtitle in the German register is *Eine Historische Beschreibung der alten politischen und weltlichen Musik, welche ausserhalb der christlichen Kirchen nur zur Luft und Kurtzweil in freyem loblichen Gebrauch jederzeit vorblieben.*

Out of the 151 pages in Part I, 67 are devoted to instrumental music in the church, a section entitled *Theoria Organices Sioniae,* full of information, mingled though it is with the speculative comments typical of Baroque investigation.

As for the origins of music, the divine origin of psalmody is probably taken for granted, but little is said about it, even in Part I. But the scientific interests of the day are apparent in Part II, at the beginning of which he finds the origins of music in Nature, "the mother of all things and the mistress of all the arts " (*rerum omnium mater et omnium artium Magistra,* p. 167). This part goes on to explain the functions music serves in society, its usefulness in peace and war, in triumphal celebrations, in physical education, and so on.

Place is found for genealogy, the great-man theory, in Section II of Part II, devoted, as the register promises, to *Anfängern und*

Vorstehern aller zusammen stimmenden Harmoney und Gesangen,
and is dedicated to Apollo and the muses. But utter indifference to
chronology is shown elsewhere. Discussion of the Lutheran *Missa,*
in Part I, Section I, is carried back to the elements in Hebrew music
that the Lutherans wished to preserve, but no attempt is made to
begin with Hebrew music, then to progress through that of the
Greeks and Romans, in order to get down to the seventeenth century. It may be that Volume I of the *Syntagma* is not to be called
history, if this lack of order is the final criterion. But since Benedetto
Croce has called for the need of history as "contemporary history,"[22] it may yet be admitted to the fold.

Then came the Thirty Years' War. Music and scholarship suf-
fered with everything else. The next German researcher in music
in point of time fled from his native land to France, but belongs in
the following category of Catholic scholars. Father Athanasius
Kircher, the Jesuit, had nothing to do with the Lutheran pioneers
in this field, and his works are of a different order. He did, however, have great influence on the third and last of the Lutheran
historians of the seventeenth century, Wolfgang Printz von Waldthurm, whose work, in 1690, is usually hailed as "the first history
of music."

Printz is far removed from Calvisius and Praetorius, and his
Historische Beschreibung der edlen Sing- und Klingkunst will be
discussed in detail under "the Nationalists," in Section III of this
chapter. It should be pointed out, however, that he, like the two
pioneers at the beginning of the century, was a Lutheran, with the
German point of view that instrumental music was as worthy an
art as vocal music (as indicated by his title). He, like them, was a
layman; he studied theology in his youth, but came into conflict
with Catholic teachers because of his militant Protestantism.[23] Like
his two predecessors, Printz found twofold origins and more for
his many-sided *Sing- und Kling* art. It was of divine origin, to be
sure, and music had its first duty to perform for *die Ehre Gottes,*
but it was most decidedly of natural origin and human invention
also, an art to make life merrier and happier. More concerning
Printz' work will be discussed later.

[22] *History, Its Theory and Practice,* tr. by Douglas Ainslie, N. Y., 1923, Chapter
I, and p. 135.
[23] According to Riemann's biography in the *Musiklexicon.*

II. THE CATHOLIC SCHOLARS

Unlike the men who have just been discussed, the Catholic leaders in seventeenth-century musical research were priests. Lutheran clergy, during this era, evidently showed little interest in music. Praetorius, in his long dedication to the clergy, found it necessary, evidently, to bring up an amazing mass of symbolism, esoteric references to the breastplate of the High Priest, and so on, to interest them in his subject.

The three priests who should be mentioned are Dom Pietro Cerone, the Italian who wrote in Spanish (1566–c. 1613); Père Mersenne (Marinus Mersennus), the French Minorite (1588–1648); and Father Kircher, mentioned above, the German Jesuit who died in Rome in 1680 after living there for 45 years. These men did not write histories, but provided a great mass of materials for future historians.

Cerone spent years in Spain, and published *El Melopeo y Maestro* in Naples in 1613.[24] After that date very little is known concerning his career. His interests were primarily ethical and technical. Like Calvisius, he was interested in precepts, but not the *nova et facillima* — rather the good old conservative precepts of discipline, temperance, and virtue. At the beginning of his work the use of the term *Historia* has nothing in common with the sense in which Calvisius used the term. He admits the necessity of dwelling upon *digressions, Historias, fabulas y sentencias,* but shows no intention of writing a history. For Cerone there is no connection whatever between the ancient music and modern music since Guido. There is no persistence of Hebrew tradition as for Praetorius, and no genealogical chain *ab initio mundi ad praesens tempus* as for Calvisius. Ancient music had its inventors (Vol. II, Ch. XVII) but they have nothing to do with *la nuestra musica* (II, Ch. XVIII). Ancient music was simple, with no instruments, and had no *variedad de bozes — come agora se haze* (I, p. 239). Nature may have inspired their music, but not our modern art (I, p. 227). Cerone accepts the old legends of the music of the spheres, carefully repeats the old reasons why we cannot hear it (II, Chs. XII, XIII), and finds the

---

[24] The work is in two large volumes. Copies are in possession of LC and NY. Vol. I is entitled *Tractado de musica theorica y pratica,* in which Cerone is interested in what makes *un complido Cantante, y un perfecto Musico.* Vol. II is for composers, with *Avisos necessarios para mayor perfección de la Compostura.*

three great "divisions" of music accepted by medieval theory (see Chapter 2 of this book). His training in hierarchized thinking leads him to set up comparisons, scales of value, the significance of which in this inquiry will become evident in later chapters. The ancients held music in better respect than the moderns (I, Ch. LIII); the Italians are better *professores* of music than the Spanish (I, Ch. LIII), and the heresies within the church of God *impede* the development of the art (I, Ch. LXVII). In other words, music is divided into fixed categories that can only be compared, not connected.

However, with all his conservatism in these fields, Cerone ranks as one of the great theorists of his day, especially in the field of vocal counterpoint. Book Twenty-one, in Volume II, is devoted to instruments and their tuning (pp. 1037–1072). To devote any more space to Cerone in connection with music histories would only anticipate the subject matter of the next chapter.

The outstanding contributions of the other great Catholic theorist, Père Mersenne, date from the decade 1627–1637. In 1627 the first complete statement of his musical philosophies and researches appeared in a small volume entitled *Traité de l'Harmonie universelle où est contenu la Musique Théorique et pratique des Anciens et des Modernes, avec les causes de ses effets, enrichi de raisons prises de la Philosophie, et des Mathematiques par le Sieur de Sermes (nom de plume)*, Paris, 1627. NY.[25] Mersenne belongs, properly speaking, to the history of musical theory, and the musical world is indebted to him for researches in the realm of acoustics, musical intervals, and tuning.

But a study has yet to be made of the philosophical bases of Mersenne's work, and their influence upon music theory, musical science, and music education ever since. It might be shown, after thorough investigation, that Mersenne's place in the musical sciences is comparable to that of his colleague, Descartes, in the physical sciences.[26] Suffice it to say here that the tenets of Cartesian dualism do seem to be manifest in the work of Mersenne, combined with persistent

---

[25] This work is not to be confused with Mersenne's greatest work, *Harmonie universelle, contenant la théorie et la pratique de la Musique*, 2 large folio volumes, Paris, 1635, 1636. LC. In these latter years Mersenne also published another folio volume, with the 12 *Harmonicorum Libri*. For a complete analysis of Mersenne's ten works on theology, mathematics, philosophy, and music, see Hellmut Ludwig, *Marin Mersenne und seine Musiklehre*, Halle, 1934.

[26] After the publication of Mersenne's treatises, Descartes also took up the subject, among the many that excited his interest; the *Compendium musicae* appeared in 1650.

adherence to medieval theology. Just as Descartes distrusted sensory evidence, so also Mersenne condemned the sensual aspects of music. While the Lutheran scholars were practical musicians, in touch with and sympathetic to all uses of music, sacred and secular, Cerone and Mersenne, not practical musicians at all (except that Cerone had participated in choral singing), lived primarily in the realm of theory; as priests, furthermore, they were somewhat out of touch with secular interests in music, save for those that were scientific.

Theology had its place for the Lutheran pioneers, so long as sacred music was under discussion; but for Cerone and Mersenne it was still the queen of the sciences, never to be left out of the picture for a moment. For Mersenne, *Harmonie universelle* was completely dominated by the *first* " cause of its effects," God himself.[27] Cerone and Mersenne were not interested in Protestant research into Old Testament chronology; for them all the phenomena of musical science were contained in a great Triunity, timeless as all creation. For example, in Mersenne, the three great *genera* of music — the diatonic, the chromatic, and the enharmonic — constituted a Triunity comparable to the Holy Trinity.

The Father is represented by the diatonic, because this mode with its whole steps and half steps includes the two other modes, just as God contains within himself the Son and Holy Ghost principles. The Son parallels the chromatic mode (which takes its name from the Greek word *chroma*); both represent beauty, equality, and wisdom. Thus the Son and the chromatic mode proceed from the Father and the diatonic, respectively; the enharmonic proceeds from the chromatic and diatonic, just as the Holy Ghost proceeds from the Father and the Son. Beyond the Holy Ghost and the enharmonic no further development is possible.[28]

Similar uses of analogy are found in Mersenne's second book of the *Traité*. This is entitled *Des Paralleles de la musique*. Here he proposes to show the relationships which *intervals* bear with " rhythm, meter, and verse; also with colors, tastes, figures, geometrical forms, virtues, vices, sciences, the elements, the heavens, the planets, and several other things."

In the parallels with poetry, the hexameter is comparable to the

---

[27] See Hellmut Ludwig, *Marin Mersenne und seine Musiklehre*, p. 5.

[28] The passage summarized here is in Part I of the *Traité*. [4], pp. 60–61. In modern parlance, the enharmonic scale would be a scale having divisions or intervals smaller than half steps, the chromatic one consisting entirely of half steps.

octave, because one has six feet and the other six whole steps, or twelve half feet to the octave's twelve half steps. " The smallest meter, which has one and a half feet, corresponds to the smallest consonance, which has a tone and a half tone [the minor 3rd]." (Bk. II, *Theorème II,* p. 311.)

Similarly, consonances and dissonances are comparable to taste and colors. Black and white are dissonance and consonance, and chromatic intervals give " color." This analogy is still current and useful, but Mersenne finds that in taste, the 5th has a *saveur grasse,* the 4th a *saveur salé,* the major 3rd a *saveur astringente,* and the minor 3rd a taste that is " insipid." (Bk. II, *Theorème II.*)

In astronomy, Mersenne follows Kepler, who found parallels between the interval ratios and the distances between the planets.[29] Mersenne concludes that a " concert of the planets" would involve a spacing of distances between the planetary voices that go to make up the " music of the spheres," or " world music," as it was called during the Baroque era. Thus the bass would be assigned to Saturn and Jupiter; the *taille* (tenor) to Mars; the *haute-contre* (the alto) to the Earth and Venus; the *dessus* (soprano) to Mercury.[30]

Mersenne also found hierarchical analogies between the numerical ratios of intervals and the hierarchical stages of Being in scholastic philosophy. The lowest audible fundamental corresponded to the earth itself, the ground-tone, as the bass is still called. Living beings are " higher " forms of life in the same sense that " higher " notes are represented by higher numbers. Inaudible high notes beyond the reach of computation are comparable to the nine orders of invisible angels that surround the Holy Trinity. The twelve modes, as he says, on his last page, are comparable to the twelve pearly gates of the Celestial City. In other words, all of the esthetic beauty of medieval scholastic theory is bound up with the musical theory of Père Mersenne.[31]

[29] Kepler had published his *Harmonices Mundi Libri V* in Linz, Austria, only seven years before, in 1619.

[30] Bk. II, *Theorème VIII,* p. 381. For similar use of this analogy in Romantic philosophy, see the quotation from Schopenhauer, in Chapter 10 of this book.

[31] It is significant to note that an infinite divisibility of color in the spectrum scale is just as easily demonstrable as the infinite divisibility of tone in the musical scale. Yet while the latter has inspired such theological analogies as those of Mersenne noted here, the writer knows of no such analogies applied to the color scale. At any rate, compared with histories of music, histories of art have been free from analogy. See the Introduction to Part Two of this book for further discussion of this matter.

As for music, Mersenne's basic principle is that there are two objects of study, the *material* and the *formal*. *Le son est le principal objet matériel* (Bk. I, *Theorème VII*) and *Les raisons des sons les uns avec les autres, et la manière de s'en servir aux chansons, et en toutes sortes de compositions, sont l'objet formel de la Musique* (Bk. I, *Theorème VIII*). At the very beginning of the work he states that "Music is a part of mathematics, and consequently a science which shows the causes of its effects, the properties of tones and intervals (*des sons*), melodies (*des chants*), chords (?) (*des concerts*), and everything connected with them."

Man and his use of music as communication is left out of the picture, just as surely as man and his senses were shut out of Cartesian Nature.

The dualism postulated by Mersenne seems to have been perpetuated in the following assumptions that have been persistent for three centuries:

1. That *harmony* is the universal term for theoretical study in music and that basically it is a mathematical discipline; *counterpoint* is a secondary discipline, to be studied later. Here Mersenne differs from Cerone, for whom counterpoint was the essential discipline. Mersenne's dislike for counterpoint has already been cited above, in Burney's translation.

2. That *tone* is the primary element of interest in theoretical study. This was not the case with Cerone, Calvisius, and Praetorius, who gave great attention to metrics and rhythm. Mersenne's interests in meter and rhythm are, again, purely scientific. They only touch upon experience by analogy, *not in communication*.

3. *Analogy* itself continues to be a useful tool for inquiry. Music is to be understood only by means of analogy with theology, mathematics, taste, color, mechanics, and geometry. (For modern uses of analogy, see Chapters 11 and 12.)

4. *Division* is the only concept by which one can understand unity. The word *tone* is often synonymous with *interval*. The importance of this position will become apparent in later chapters, in connection also with scales of value suggested by the hierarchical concept.

And yet, in his personal relationships, and in his recognition of the worth of his contemporaries, Mersenne shows no narrowness of judgment. Even today his work is regarded as "an inexhaustible mine of historical information." [179], p. 103. He was an indefatigable correspondent and an outstanding figure in this remarkable era of scientific inquiry.

The third of the great trio of Catholic scholars under discussion was Father Athanasius Kircher, mentioned at the end of Section 1 of this chapter. As already noted, Kircher, born in Germany, forms a link between two interesting points of view. In him meet the Germanic interest in folklore and the Old Testament and the interests involved in Mediterranean culture. Kircher's travels carried him far and wide,[32] and he became much more secularized in his interests than either Cerone or Mersenne. He therefore had more in common with his young and admiring contemporary, Printz von Waldthurm, the Lutheran.

One of the absorbing activities of seventeenth-century scholars was the foundation of museums.[33] The collecting of antiquities was what might be called a laboratory phase of humanistic research. One of the most active scholars in this field was Kircher himself. He was an indefatigable collector, and his museum was bequeathed at his death to the Collegium Romano.[34] He was an authority on Egyptian hieroglyphics, and even published a work on *China illustrata* in 1660. The works chiefly devoted to music are the *Musurgia universalis* and the *Phonurgia nova*.[35]

The *Syntagma* of Praetorius and, to a lesser extent, the *Harmonie universelle* by Mersenne, might be termed at least partially encyclopedic in arrangement, but Kircher's *Musurgia* is museographic, full of curiosities and legends as well as of useful information. In addition to the text, which is a veritable musical museum,[36] the numerous plates, with pictures of birds, with attempts

---

[32] After being driven from his university post in Würzburg in 1630 by the ravages of war, he took up temporary residence in Avignon. After various wanderings he settled in Rome in 1635, where he remained until his death in 1680.

[33] See "Museums," *Encyc. Brit.*, 14th ed.

[34] See "Kircher," *Encyc. Brit.*, 14th ed.

[35] *Musurgia universalis sive ars magna consoni et dissoni, in X libros digesta,* Rome, 1650, 2 v. Extracts, in German, were published by Andreas Hirsch, Laidingen, 1662, 375 pp. The original volumes are 690 and 492 pp.

Phonurgia nova sive conjugium mechanico-physicum artis et naturae, 229 pp., Rome, 1673. This appeared in German, in 1684, under the title, *Neue Hall-und Thon-Kunst; oder, Mechanische Gehaim-Verbindung der Kunst und Natur, durch Stimme und Hall-Wissenschaft gestifftet.* This work treats at length of the echo, laws of acoustics, and of instruments. This subject evidently came to be well understood by Bach's day, for when Johann Sebastian visited the newly built opera house in Berlin, he was able to describe peculiar acoustic effects after superficial observation and before testing.

[36] The first Russian history of music, in 1831, is entitled a *Lyric Museum* [46].

to put their calls into notation, diagrams and designs by competent draftsmen, and fine engravings, provide a wealth of illustration typical of Baroque interests in natural science, mechanics, and acoustics.[37]

The chapters of the *Musurgia* most pertinent to music history are Books I and II. *Anatomicus de Natura soni et vocis* treats of the nature of tone as such. Book I, *Philologicus de sono artificioso sive Musica, eiusque prima Institutione, Aetate, Vicissitudine, Propagatione,* discusses the origins of the art, or rationally organized sound.

The magnificence with which both works were published in Rome contrasts significantly with the cheap, limited character of the translations issued afterward in Germany. Kircher's works appeared after the Peace of Westphalia. Although Germany had been ravaged by war and pestilence that were more devastating, proportionately, than the World War, musical life persisted and interest in scholarship seems to have increased.

One other research scholar, Marcus Meibomius, needs to be mentioned, not for original investigations, but for his important edition of classical texts concerning music.[38] Until this service was performed the frequent quotations from old sources were apt to be from second- or third-hand, and none too reliable sources.

Thus we find musical research of various sorts going on in several countries during this early part of the Baroque era, a designation given to a period in which music and art displayed an amazing variety of musical forms, but all characterized by a tendency toward an expansive, buoyant, lusty sort of style. Paul H. Láng has compared the music of the Baroque with that of the Rococo, or Classical eighteenth century, as follows:

" It appears that the basic stylistic feature of the music of the Baroque period is *continuous expansion*. Totality of a closed form is achieved by an uninterrupted ' discursive ' development of the given musical material. Opposed to this style stands the musical idiom of the so-called classical period. Here we have to deal with *organizations of sections into a whole.*" [39]

[37] These arts of engraving appear also in the folio publications of Mersenne.

[38] *Antiquae Musicae auctores septem,* 1652, containing Greek and Latin texts, including Aristoxenus, *Harmonics;* Euclid, *Introductio harmonica;* also works by Nichomachus, Alypius, Gaudentius, Bacchius Senior, and Aristides Quintilianus. Modern reprint, ed. by Karl von Jan, 1895.

[39] *Bulletin of the American Musicological Society,* No. 1, June, 1936, pp. 2–3.

FROM KIRCHER'S "MUSURGIA," VOLUME I

This comparison of Baroque musical style with that of the Classical eighteenth century is also appropriate for the analysis of music histories in both centuries. All of the treatises discussed so far are highly discursive. Even Calvisius, who glimpsed the possibilities of chronological history, wrote an " uninterrupted " history that is not divided into sections. There are *libri,* chapters, and sections in all the other works, Catholic and Protestant, but each one is written in this continually expansive and discursive manner.

Beginning with Printz' history in 1690, however, there is a tendency to organize *sections into a whole.* This was made possible because of the four factors of chronology, language, nationality, and new economic conditions.

Chronology was developed still further during the seventeenth century by such men as Bishop James Ussher, with his *Annals of the World,* who found Seven Ages in world history from Creation (4004 B.C.) to the Destruction of the Temple in the " Year of the World " 4079; and the Catholic chronologer Cardinal Baronio, whose computations are quoted by Mersenne.[40] Chapter 3 in this book will begin, therefore, with the Old Testament chronology which came to be used by Catholics and Protestants alike, well into the nineteenth century.

Latin, the language of the learned, was used exclusively by Calvisius and Kircher, except for occasional quotations. But Praetorius wrote his indices in German for Volume I of the *Syntagma,* and Volumes II and III entirely in the vernacular. But when he gets particularly discursive, the extensive quotations from the Greek and the Hebrew make his history hard going for the modern student. Mersenne vacillated between his native French and his theological Latin, and Cerone used the language imposed upon the Kingdom of Naples by Spanish invaders.

But with the rise of independent organization of *national* " sections into a whole," the use of borrowed language ceases. The internationalism of Latin is abandoned; separation and division come to be the keynotes of investigation in the eighteenth century.

---

[40] Baronio's *Annales Ecclesiastici,* in 12 folios, appeared in 1588–1607, and Ussher's work was published in London in 1658.

III. THE THREE FIRST HISTORIES IN GERMAN, ITALIAN, AND FRENCH

The three first books to bear the general description *History of Music* (aside from Volume I of Praetorius' *Syntagma*) appeared within a twenty-five-year period (1690–1715). One is in German [6], the second in Italian [7], and the third in French [9]. Then, after 1715, there is little use made of the term until the latter part of the century.

Printz was a well-trained church and court musician. His book is the first historical treatise on music written in German. This is noteworthy, not only because Latin was still the favored language of the scholar, but also because of the domination of French culture in aristocratic Germany. Voltaire, even a half century later, could write from the court of Frederick the Great, who despised the language himself, that German was necessary only in traveling and in talking to servants.[41] Parts of the *Syntagma* by Praetorius were written in German, as we have seen, and Kircher's works had been translated in popular editions, all of which attests that music was an essentially popular art. In the petty courts of Germany music was an imported luxury and German music was as thoroughly despised as was the language; but in the family and in civic life music was cultivated as one of the home-made necessities of life.

Studies of the rise of the spirit of national unity in Germany must recognize the French influence in aristocratic circles and the factors at work among the common people. Inspired by C. J. H. Hayes of Columbia University,[42] another study has just been made of this subject,[43] describing the part played by Pietism in the development of enthusiasm for the *Vaterland*. None of these studies, however, refer to the part played by music in this connection, except to mention briefly folk music and the chorale.

The German musician had two avenues of employment open to him in the late seventeenth and early eighteenth centuries. He could don livery in the *Residenz,* mingling with Italian and French musicians, or serve as organist and cantor in the *Stadtkirche* and the church school. By working alternately or simultaneously in both fields, he was in contact with all ages and all classes of society.

---

[41] Robert Ergang, *Herder and Modern German Nationalism*, N. Y., 1930, p. 26.
[42] C. J. H. Hayes, *Essays on Nationalism*, N. Y., 1926.
[43] K. S. Pinson, *Pietism as a Factor in the Rise of German Nationalism*, N. Y., 1934.

Such musicians laid the foundations for a musical culture that conquered all Europe (and America) during the nineteenth century.

Printz, author of this first history in German, Heinrich Schütz
before him, and J. S. Bach after him, were among those who had
employment alternately with both court and church. In one environment a musician could absorb the fashionable French and Italian
styles in vogue, and in the other he could continue the great folk
traditions in music that had helped sustain Germans through the
Reformation conflicts and the devastating Thirty Years' War.

So Printz, as said before, shows the same variety of interests that
the other German scholars displayed before him. He also accepts
the theory of divine origins, without allowing it to conflict with
other theories. In his first chapter, the following origins are all
deemed possible: (a) man's powers of reason; (b) irresistible natural impulse; (c) the accents and inflections of the voice under
emotion; (d) the wind in the trees, and other sounds of nature;
(e) the ambition to outdo others,[44] and many other psychological
origins. For Printz *all* these theories had validity. His genial
sense of humor might have made him very appreciative of the
quest for origins conducted in nineteenth-century histories of music.
The "lofty, single point of view" brooks no pluralistic sources.
(See Chapter 9 of this book.)

Printz is probably regarded as the "first" music historian because
he is the first one of these scholars to attempt systematic biographies
in chronological order, beginning with Jubal. According to *der
seelige Herr Luther,* Jubal was father of all such as handle *all* instruments, not merely the harp and organ (p. 5). In direct line of
genealogical descent, Apollo was the inventor, not merely of the
cithara, but of the flute as well.

After Luther, one of the most frequently quoted authorities is
Father Kircher. Whole pages are quoted, occasionally, but in all
cases Printz cites his authority — which is more than Kircher did.
Kircher is his authority for the statements that the Egyptians were
the first to "restore" music after the Flood (p. 8), and that the
Greek inventors Linus, Orpheus, and Amphion inherited all they
knew from David and Solomon.

[44] Here Printz shows that his origin theories are not mere speculation. He points
to actual Nature music then in vogue, for voice and instruments, and to the new
developments in wind instruments themselves, as much as to say, "Lucretius is right
today." And certainly the ambition of music-patrons " to outdo each other " was the
actual origin of much music.

A large proportion of Printz' work is devoted to contemporary musicians and those of a previous generation, and evidently Lutheran taste of his day could still look back with admiration upon the complicated polyphony of earlier centuries, as Luther's encomium of Josquin des Près is repeated.[45]

Chapter XIV carries out specifically, in few words, the thesis of Praetorius — that music is for *use*. The notion of *Unterschiedlicher Gebrauch* in his title is amplified in Chapter XIV, entitled *Der Musik Endzweck und mancherley Gebrauch*. There are two classifications, of course, sacred and secular: the first is the *Äusserste und Gemeine*, for the glory of God; and the second is the *Äussere und Eigene*, for the *Bewegung des menschlichen Gemüthes*.

Barely three pages are necessary for the discussion of the sacred functions music has to perform. But the others are so numerous, from the assuagement of grief to Horse Ballet, that twenty-one pages are required (173–194). Printz may have figured that Sunday, though important, is only one day in seven.

Chapter XVI, on "the enemies of music," is one of the most fascinating of all. Anyone who does not love *all kinds of music* is an "enemy of music." There are three classes:

1. Those who hate all kinds of music. Several figures in Roman and Turkish history are mentioned, also François I of France. He adds that there are some still living, but that he needs mention no names.

2. Those who approve only certain kinds of music. Plato heads the list, together with the Lacedaemonians, who permitted no innovations. Aristotle and other Athenians who did not like the flute; Zwingli, who permitted no music in church; and all those who do not like brass instruments are included.

3. Those who despise hard-working *Musikanten*, and only bestow their favors and rewards on virtuosi. God has not given equal ability to everyone, but music is impossible without the efforts of all musicians. The lowly ones should not be so exploited and so woefully underpaid.

No history of music since that time has had a chapter like that, but it is a timely one at all times. Although no music historian could conceivably belong to the first group, there have been many, unfortunately, who could be placed in the second category. Interests

---

[45] " Josquinus ist ein Meister der Noten; diese haben thun müssen, wie er gewollt; andere Componisten thun wie die Noten wollen." (p. 117).

and prejudice have not only dictated the selection of the materials which are deemed important, but, in addition, some hierarchized scale of value is provided. All historians, since Printz, until the Marxian interpreters discussed later in Chapter 8, have tended to ignore the third group of "enemies." Since the Baroque era very few histories have been dedicated to the "Friends of Music," the patrons of the art, as old custom demanded. In a "democratic" desire to "free" the musician from "servitude," the very important items of patronage on one hand and exploitation on the other have been overlooked. Their significance today is discussed later in Chapter 8 under "Music and Technology." The methods of Printz and earlier Lutherans like him will be referred to again in Chapter 13, in conclusion.

Bontempi's *Historia musica* [7] makes no contribution worthy of note, except for the fact that it is the first history of music in Italian. The use of the vernacular in Italian literature on music was nothing new, however, as the sixteenth-century works on theory were largely in the vernacular. Bontempi merely perpetuates the scholastic treatment of the subject as a mathematical discipline. History, therefore, is presented in a series of *corollaries* and *demonstrations* which compare the *divisions* of music and the respective merits of ancient and modern music. The controversial background of these questions is examined in Chapter 2 of this book.

Although the work has none of the humanistic qualities of the German texts, Bontempi himself, like the Lutheran scholars, was a practical musician: a church singer and opera composer. In his travels he was a co-worker with Schütz in Dresden. Hawkins, in 1776, criticizes this author for his rationalistic bias, alleging that

" *an unjustifiable partiality for the country where the author was born distinguishes this work; for among the moderns whom he has taken occasion to mention, the name of any musician not an Italian scarcely occurs.* In a word, the information contained in the *Historia musica* is just sufficient to awaken that curiosity which it is the end of history to gratify." [27], II, p. 656.

The first history in French [9] is a motley compilation, the work of three men. Jacques Bonnet merely finished the book and published it. His uncle, the Abbé Bourdelot (Pierre Michon, 1610–1685), had assembled the materials; and his brother, Pierre Bonnet, had begun to put it together. The *Histoire* frequently appears under the name Bourdelot.[46] In 1726 a new edition appeared in Amsterdam, with two additional volumes which contained a reprint of the *Comparaison de la musique italienne et de la musique françoise,* by Le Cerf de la Viéville (1704). This work aimed to show *quelles sont les vrayes beautez de la musique.*

The text of the history, perhaps the easiest to read of all the histories discussed in this chapter, is written in a facile, journalistic style, with no attempt at erudition. But the date, 1715, explains the change. Bonnet was a contemporary of Joseph Addison, whose articles in the *Spectator* a few years earlier were so influential in molding English musical opinion. In other words, this history belongs, not to the Baroque, but to the Classical era, when the history of music began to be the concern of men of letters as well as of musicians and theologians and scientists. So further discussion of Bonnet is reserved for later chapters.

For similar reasons, the first histories of music in English, dating from the second decade of the eighteenth century, belong in a later chapter, on the Enlightenment (Chapter 5).

The "single, lofty point(s) of view" for Baroque research were provided by theology, by the chronologies worked out by theological historians, and the ethical precepts of Cerone. The "telescope" of biography was a crude instrument at the beginning of the century, although it had been used successfully long before by Vasari in the history of art (as will be shown in the next chapter). But although Calvisius observed only a score or so of past peaks of musical achievement, Praetorius and Printz located many more. Printz classified them in orderly chronological succession, in concise thumbnail sketches, and for most histories that genealogical method has been the favorite ever since.

The "microscope" of mathematical, scientific research is found in the work of Mersenne and in the general scholastic tendency to divide music into its simplest parts — scales and intervals — in order to begin "history." This is still considered by many the proper introduction to the subject.

---

[46] Another posthumous work by Bourdelot appeared in 1724, an *Histoire de la Danse, sacrée et prophane, ses progres et ses revolutions depuis son origine jus qu'a present.* This work is a significant indication of the French interest in ballet during the Baroque era. A supplement was added to this volume on music history, with a *Paralele de la peinture et de la poesie.* This feature is prophetic of the modern French tendency to study music in relation to other phases of culture.

But, as stated before, many Baroque scholars were not satisfied with these views, or these tools. They had not yet acquired the importance that has been vouchsafed to them since; consequently their works, with few exceptions, are also concerned with the events and problems of their day.

On the other hand, when men in this period, like others who have followed them, became immersed in pure theory, credulity was only matched by indifference to the various kinds of music being produced all about them — folk song, folk dance, the music of pageant, opera, ballet, masque, and ceremonial. The seventeenth century began with Peri, Monteverde, and their colleagues writing opera in Italy, with the Gabrielis bringing forth colorful antiphonal music for choirs and orchestras in the churches of Venice, with Frescobaldi drawing throngs to St. Peter's to hear his organ playing, with music occupying a unique place in Elizabethan society, both in the church and in the home. Jesuit priests from the *Collegium germanicum* in Rome were bringing the Passion Music of the Spanish monk Victoria into Germany, to be passed on to Heinrich Schütz, Hassler, Bach, and others. Jesuits were also making use of opera and ballet as counter-attractions in connection with Counter Reformation. And yet some writers about music were still prone to debate matters of classification in musical theory, and even into the eighteenth century many a history opens with a dry disquisition on the *modes* and *genera* of ancient as compared with modern music.

Before continuing, as Chapter 3 does, with the separation of the religious from the naturalistic tradition, and the historical survey of eighteenth-century research in later chapters, it is necessary to pause and survey the controversial backgrounds of sixteenth-century origin. In Chapter 10, III, further discussion of the spirit of the Baroque era will endeavor to show how influential beliefs in progress affected philosophies of music history, beliefs that emerged from these controversial backgrounds.

CHAPTER 2

THE CONTROVERSIAL BACKGROUND

WITH the exception of treatises on counterpoint, collections of new instrumental compositions, manuals of instruction, and other practical works, sixteenth-century literature on music had been largely controversial. There were five subjects, all interrelated, that were bitterly disputed, and no understanding of the early literature on music history is possible unless these subjects are analyzed briefly. It was in these five fields that *division* was a basic problem, and almost as many definitions of the musical term *division* emerge in the literature. Even into the early nineteenth century, history frequently began with the words: "Music consists of . . ."

I. THE DIVISIONS OF MUSIC

Today we speak of theoretical and practical, or applied, *branches* of music study. But medieval and Renaissance classifications gave independent reality to "inspective" or "speculative" music as something quite apart from "active" music. And these were fixed and independent divisions of a larger division. Roughly, there were three great kinds of music: first, the mystic "world music," the music of the spheres, which, as shown in Chapter 1, was so important to the Catholic scholars Cerone and Mersenne; second, human music; and third, instrumental music. The second had to do with the ethical phases stressed by Cerone. All Baroque research was interested in the third, which was divided into "harmonical" and "organical" music. Theory and practice were both parts of "harmonical" music. There were various and different schemes of classification,[1] and the order of superiority or inferiority was apt to vary with the interests of the writer on the subject. This is the scheme proposed by Ornithoparcus, whose *Micrologus* was trans-

---

[1] Grassineau mentions 45 different kinds of *Musica* [14], pp. 153–157.

lated by John Dowland, the famous song writer and singer of the Elizabethan era:[2]

"The world's Musicke is an Harmonie, caused by the motion of the starres, and violence of the Spheares. . . . Now the cause wee cannot heare this Sound, according to Pliny is, because the greatnesse of the sound doth exceed the sense of our eares.

"Humane music is the concordance of divers elements in one compound, by which the spirituall nature is joyned with the body, and the reasonable part is coupled in concord with the unreasonable, which proceedes from the uniting of the body and the soule. . . . Every like is preferred by his like, and by his dislike is disturbed. Hence it is, that we loath and abhor discords, and are delighted when we heare harmonicall concords, because we know there is in ourselves that concord.

"Instrumentall Musicke is an Harmony which is made by helpe of Instruments. And because Instruments are either artificiall, or naturall, there is one sort of Musicke — the Philosophers call Harmonicall; the other Organicall. . . . Organicall Musicke is that which belongeth to artificiall instruments: or it is a skill of making an Harmony with beating, with fingering, with blowing. . . . Yet such Instruments as are too voluptuous, are by Coelius Rodiginus rejected.

"'Harmonicall Musick' is divided into Inspective Musicke, a knowledge censuring and pondering the Sounds formed with naturall instruments, not by the ears, whose judgment is dull, but by wit and reason: and Active Musicke, which also they call Practick (as St. Augustine in the first Booke of his *De Musica* writeth), the knowledge of singing well."

From the above it is evident that Ornithoparcus and his translator were both interested in "Active Musicke . . . the knowledge of singing well," and that they looked down upon instrumentalists with undisguised scorn. They, however, were looked upon with equal contempt by pure theorists who argued for the supremacy of "inspective," or "speculative Musicke."

"It seems as if theory and practice were ever to be at strife, for the man of science, who never hears music, and the musician, who never reads books, must be equally averse to each other, and unlikely to be brought to a right understanding. . . ."[3]

[2] Andreas Vogelmaier (Ornithoparcus), *Musice active micrologus*, Leipzig, 1517. The English version is entitled: Andreas Ornithoparcus, his *Micrologus, or Introduction, Containing the Art of Singing*, digested into foure Bookes, not only profitable, but also necessary for all that are studious of Musicke. London, 1609.

[3] Burney [26], Vol. I, p. 116. For a discussion of the theorists' resistance to innovations from the time of the Greeks to the Present, see Otto Kinkeldey: "The

As early as Plutarch we find this question raised:

"'Whether the masters of music are sufficiently capable of being judges of it.' The priest of Apollo averred the negative, 'for it is impossible to be a perfect musician and a good judge of music by the knowledge of those things that seem to be but parts of the whole body, as by excellency of hand upon the instrument, or singing readily at first sight, or exquisiteness of the ear, so far as this extends to the understanding of harmony and time.'"[4]

In sixteenth-century Spain, learned savants of music had been referring contemptuously to practical musicians as "slaves of music," whose "barbarous and venomous tongues" should no longer be permitted to spread "musical heresies that contradict Boethius and other authorities in the practical and speculative domains of this mathematical science."[5]

Spain, during the sixteenth century, had led the rest of Europe in university music, carrying on medieval traditions in education with the same zeal with which Philip II battled to retain the purity of Gregorian chant. But Morales, Victoria, Guerrero,[6] Cabezón and others were "slaves of music" who are known today while the pure theorists have been forgotten. Illustrious achievements had also been recorded by the Netherlanders, led by Josquin des Près (c. 1450–1521), a favorite in the most magnificent courts of Europe; the Tudor school of composers was under royal patronage in England; Palestrina was at work in Rome, and Wagner was being anticipated in the daring harmonic innovations of Carlo Gesualdo (c. 1560–1614) and other madrigalists, particularly of the Venetian School. French contemporaries, until recently not so well-known, included Pierre de la Rue, Goudimel, Jannequin, Claude le Jeune, and Costeley.

Sixteenth-century music was an international art, and the achievements of these masters, not slaves of music, make the theoretical arguments of the day seem rather puerile.

Harmonic Sense, Its Evolution and Destiny," in *Proceedings* of the Music Teachers' National Association, 1924.

[4] Plutarch's *Morals,* "Concerning Music," 36, ed. by W. W. Goodwin, N. Y., 1870, Vol. I, p. 129.

[5] See Henri Collet, *Le Mysticisme Musical espagnol,* Paris, Alcan, 1914, p. 178.

[6] These three were the outstanding composers of sixteenth-century religious music in Spain. Cabezón (1510–1566), "the Spanish Bach," was court organist to Philip II.

II. PARTIALS, PARTS, AND HARMONY

There can be no possible controversy over the "partial tones" that can be heard in the fundamental tone, say, of a vibrating string, and partials that are inaudible are mathematically demonstrable. For that reason, music, in the medieval *Quadrivium,* was studied as a mathematical science.

But when simultaneous tones of equal strength are sounded, there can be and has been ample controversy over the combinations that are agreeable. And when groups of singers (or players) are divided into different parts, the choice of concord and discord is an important matter. The permissibility or esthetic acceptability of certain intervals from the partial or overtone series varies from age to age, and from place to place.

In the early Middle Ages, the simplest ratios — the octave, fifth, and fourth — were the only ones allowable in part singing, or *organum,* as the first polyphonic efforts were called. But by the eighteenth century, the third and the sixth had become the favorite intervals in academic counterpoint, and to this day conservative theory looks askance at consecutive perfect intervals, excepting the octave.

Two analogies based on harmony have been of great service to philosophers seeking to explain the fundamentals of political science; first, that of a leader holding and guiding his singers, with their different parts, in a harmonious ensemble; second, the notion of the power of the fundamental tone, to which all the partials are subordinate. The first concept was stated by Aristotle thus:

"The single harmony produced by all the heavenly bodies singing and dancing together springs from one source and ends by achieving one purpose, and has rightly bestowed the name not of 'disordered' but of 'ordered universe' upon the whole. And just as in a chorus, when the leader gives the signal to begin, the whole chorus of men, or it may be of women, joins in the song, mingling a single studied harmony among different voices, some high and some low; so too it is with the God that rules the whole world. . . .

"As is the steersman in the ship, . . . the law in the city, the general in the army, so is God in the Universe; . . . he moves and revolves all things, where and how he will, in different forms and natures; just as the law of a city, fixed and immutable in the minds of those who are under it, orders all the life of a state."—*De Mundo,* ch. 6, 399a, 400b, in *Works,* Vol. III, ed. by W. D. Ross, Oxford, 1931.

The second analogy is illustrated by a remarkable passage written in the late sixteenth century. Jean Bodin concluded his *Six Books of a Commonweale*[7] with a statement of "Harmonicall Principles," in which the traditional preferment for perfect intervals is referred to as a means of unification of differences. Bodin proposes that Harmonicall Justice will be preferable to Geometrical Justice, as the latter would merely reward the leaders in each particular field:

"We must also, to make an harmonie of one of them with another, mingle them that have wherewith in some sort to supply that which wanteth in the other. For otherwise there shall be no more harmonie than if one should separat the concords of musique which are in themselves good, but yet would make no good content if they were not bound together; For that the default of one is supplied by the other. In which doing the wise Prince shall set his subjects in a most sweet quiet, bound together with an indissoluble bond one of them unto another together with himself and the Commonweale. As in the first foure numbers to be seene; which God hath in harmonicall proportion disposed to show unto us, that the Royal estate is harmonicall, and also to be harmonically governed. For two to three maketh a fift; three to four, a fourth; two to foure, an eight; and againe afterwards, one to two maketh an eight; one to three a twelfth, holding the fift and the eight; and one to foure a double eight or Diapason; which containeth the whole ground and compasse of all tunes and concords of musicke beyond which he which will pass into five, shall in so doing marre the harmonie, and make an *intollerable discord*."

Every harmonic innovation, in the past, has been met by theorists and historians with statements similar to the last phrase above.

Choral music, in the Baroque era, when histories of music first appeared, was often divided into many parts — even as many as forty. Richness of harmonic coloring became a prime desideratum in those days when the old fifteenth-century concept of independent voices was being superseded by the harmonic concept of chords governed by fundamental bass tones, with one prominent melodic line above. Hence, Hugo Riemann, in 1905, refers to the Baroque era as the "General-Bass Period." So another meaning of division survives today, in the word *divisi,* a term which directs orchestral instruments that ordinarily play in unison to play in separate parts.[8]

[7] Tr. by Richard Knolles, London, 1606, pp. 790–794.
[8] As in the divided first violins in the *Lohengrin Vorspiel,* and the divided 'celli in Rossini's overture to *William Tell.*

III. DIVISIONS OF THE OCTAVE

It was not in the realm of vocal music that the disputes were most bitter. Instruments were being perfected; people in all walks of life had been using them, and composers were beginning to write for them independently of voices. In Germany, Italy, and Spain, the organ was becoming increasingly popular, and recent researches by Otto Kinkeldey, H. J. Moser, Schering, and others have brought to light Reformation and even pre-Reformation organ music of great interest.

Problems of tuning had been disputed throughout the Middle Ages, but they became more acute at this time, because of the necessity for having fixed scales for keyboard instruments. At any rate, this became the major subject of debate between the theorists, who appealed to the authority of the ancients, and the practical musicians, who used their ears. One sixteenth-century pedant berated the organists for

" groping in the dark and without any agreement as to the *division* of the organ diapason into tones and semi-tones . . . and that is why they can never succeed in making an organ with all the perfection it should have; no matter what they do, whether they tune, put out of tune, put on, take off, shut or close the pipes, their organs are never perfect, and the only cause is their ignorance of that which they should know, and which they could learn by going to those who know, and could teach them." [9]

Ramis de Pareja, Andalusian theorist and later professor of music at Bologna, was one of the first to propose that the octave be divided into twelve equal parts. This he did in 1482, in his *De musica tractatus sive musica practica.* His propositions to change the character of the interval of the third let loose a storm of protest among foreign music savants, because he had dared to criticise the eleventh-century system of Guido d'Arezzo. But in 1558 the cudgels were taken up by a still more capable person. Gioseffo Zarlino was not only a theorist, but a practical organist, composer, and choral director. He put the argument for equal temperament into clearer terms and continued Ramis' appeal for a return to a scale which

[9] As quoted by Collet, *Le Mysticisme Musical espagnol,* p. 180.

had been proposed by Ptolemy in the second century A.D., a scale approximating our modern major.[10]

From the foregoing it is apparent that some agreement was necessary concerning the division of the octave. *Division* came to be defined as " the dividing of the interval of an octave into a number of less intervals." [14], p. 65.

The disputes over the *genera* (scales) have already been mentioned. The *genera* of Greek music were supposed to have been three in number: *diatonic*, with two kinds of divisions; *chromatic*, in half-step divisions, and *enharmonic*, with divisions of the octave into intervals smaller than the half step. Modes were the functional scales possible within the diatonic *genus*. Since these modes came to be recognized as either major or minor, only two modes, one major and one minor, were needed by those who were adopting the new concept of harmony. The result is well-known: the tempered scale proposed by Ramis in 1482 and again by Werckmeister in his *Musikalische Temperatur* (1691). Bach and other practical musicians tuned the half-step divisions of the keyboard as equal intervals, thereby making music possible in all major and minor keys. *The Well-Tempered Clavichord,* Vol. I, was composed in 1721, proving that by means of compromise a B flat could do the work of an A sharp. But so great was the controversy, and so great was the tenacity of those who argued for " pure " intervals, that British piano manufacturers did not adopt this tuning until about 1845. The organ builders were even more reluctant.[11]

Still another definition of *divison* arose as a result of running scales in virtuoso instrumental passages. The definition now found in all modern dictionaries states that it is the name of an English form of *Variation* popular in the seventeenth and eighteenth centuries. Grassineau's definition cited above goes on to say that " To run a division is to play or sing after the manner above-mentioned, i.e., to divide the intervals of an octave into as many parts, as agreeably as possible."

But here again, there is controversy. There are always those who maintain that *coloratura*, decorative virtuoso music is an " inferior "

---

[10] Zarlino's two outstanding treatises are *Institutioni harmoniche*, Venice, 1558, 1562, 1573; and *Dimostrationi harmoniche*, Venice, 1571, 1573.

[11] See " Tuning," in Grove's *Dictionary of Music and Musicians*, 1910 ed., N. Y., Vol. V, p. 180.

form of art.[12] And if inferior, it may even be damaging to morals. Pope John XXII complained that singers were "depraving" the melodies with discants (*discantibus lubricant*), and that "voices are incessantly running to and fro, intoxicating the ear, and not soothing it."

Future histories have an interesting task ahead, not yet well-explored, that of tracing back the sources of our esthetic and ethical prejudices in music. We wonder at the medieval ban on the major scale as the "modus lascivus," but the widespread notion that the minor mode is sad only goes back to the Romantic period. And we still feel that with small chromatic divisions as close as possible to the enharmonic *genus* of the Greeks, "the melody becomes more moving" (Grassineau, on "Enharmonic"). Yet the Chinese and Hindu musical classics, with finer divisions of the octave than we can use, get with these scales effects of calm, contemplative serenity.

Finally, there has also been controversy about musical notation. To record tones of different pitch, space was divided, on paper, to represent "high" and "low" tones. The old *tablature* gave a picture of the fretboard (as of a lute — now revived for the ukulele) to show where notes should be played;[13] the modern staff may have been suggested by strings of instruments. These marked a great improvement over the neumes of the Middle Ages; shifting clefs on the four-line staff (still used in Gregorian hymnals), and the secular five-line or the Great Staff for keyboard music have made possible a workable system which still defies all sporadic attempts to discredit it.

Some of the bitterest controversy over pitch relationships has

[12] "The right measure will be attained if students of music stop short of the arts which are practiced in educational contests, and do not seek to acquire those fantastic marvels of execution which are now the fashion in such contests, and from these have passed into education. Let the young pursue their studies until they are able to feel delight in noble melodies and rhythms, and not merely in that common part of music in which every slave or child and even some animals find pleasure."— Aristotle, *Politics,* VIII, 7–9, tr. by B. Jowett, Oxford, 1885, Vol. I, p. 253.

"With genuine Orientals the love of unmeaning decorative ornamentation is excessive. . . . This is generally a sign that the technical or manipulatory skill is far in excess of the power of intellectual concentration. . . . When mental development and powers of intellect and perception are too backward . . . the human creature who is blessed with facility of execution expends his powers in profusion of superfluous flourishes."—C. Hubert H. Parry, *The Art of Music,* 5th ed., London, 1894, p. 63. (Known in later editions as *The Evolution of the Art of Music* [126].)

Schopenhauer's opinion was the opposite. See Chapter 10, III, 2, B, for his defence of coloratura melody as the supreme embodiment of the will.

[13] [301], pp. 87, 113.

been with reference to the *sol-fa* syllables accredited to Guido. First used as a mnemonic aid, these syllables have risen to increasing importance ever since. There are at least three systems of solmisation in use today, and two are debated in some quarters even now, namely, the system of "movable *do*" for teaching tonality, and the French system which fixes *do* on C.[14]

IV. THE DIVISIONS OF TIME

The history of notation must take cognizance of two phases — the notation of relative pitches and also the notation of rhythm with symbols indicating the relative time-duration of sound.

Pope John XXII did not complain of scale divisions alone. His edict also says that "ecclesiastical music is now performed with semibreves and minims, and pestered with these short notes" (*in semibreves et minimas ecclesiastica cantantur, notulis percutiuntur*). From this it is apparent that the division of long notes into those of shorter value offered difficulties.

The date of this Papal bull, 1324–1325, marked the time when great debates were raging over the *ars nova*. This new art was essentially a style in which duple division was being urged as a means of expression. This is the most common form of division today, but was revolutionary for Western music then, since triple division was the only type of metrical division approved by medieval practice in church music.

The Greeks had needed no rhythm notation, because music was wedded to poetry, and singers sang in declamatory style. Similarly, medieval plainsong was dependent upon the text, with very smooth, flowing rhythms which called for little variation in note values. But in the thirteenth century two forms of art were being widely cultivated which made rhythm notation necessary: (1) dance rhythms and measured song, such as carols; and (2) polyphonic music.

In the system worked out at first[15] a long note equalled three of shorter value. In 1309 the *prolations* were introduced by Marchettus of Padua, permitting duple division. John of Muris (fl. 1321–50) was the conservative defender of ancient tradition in his *Speculum*

---

[14] See J. J. Rousseau on the subject, in *Emile;* also articles on Tonic-Sol-Fa in any musical dictionary, for information concerning staffless notation in Great Britain.

[15] For details on these systems see [210], pp. 86–90; [300], Chapter VIII; [301], Chapter 9.

musicae, while Philippe de Vitry (c. 1290–1361), Bishop of Meaux, and Guillaume de Machaut (1300–1377) were the chief sponsors of the new style. As for dance music employing this duple rhythm, the earliest examples date from this time (c. 1300).[16] Yet modern German historians are endeavoring to locate the origins of duple measure, "analogous to the heartbeat," in the origins of unrecorded primitive German music in the dawn of history. (See Chapter 8 of this book.) Metrical music, therefore, is a comparatively modern art, as far as is known, and the bar line which too often confuses *rhythm* with *measure,* in the minds of modern students, did not come into use until the seventeenth century.

Modern music histories, as already noted, give excellent summaries of research into the early history of notation, but, again, future studies may perform a needed service by tracing the history of our present-day musical habits on through the eighteenth century, when duple division became so fixed as the natural pattern that even music in triple measure falls into duple phrase patterns of four to form what the average man calls a tune.

V. THE DIVISIONS OF HISTORICAL TIME

In Chapter 3 it will be shown that histories of music adopted the time-divisions suggested by the Old Testament; but the dichotomy ancient and modern was the historical octave. Later historians recognized a middle (medieval) division, and the attempts to subdivide these segments have caused as much division of opinion as the rival schemes for dividing the eighth, the simple ratio 1:2. The division most important to a history of music history, however, is, at this point, the partisan division of opinion regarding the superiority or inferiority of ancient as compared with modern music. The partisans themselves came to be called "Ancients and Moderns."

1. THE QUARREL IN ITALY — SOLUTION BY COMPROMISE

Study of the literature on music indicates that this famous quarrel, which was at its height in literary France during the later years of the seventeenth century, and which is usually regarded as an exclusively literary quarrel, began in Italy one hundred years

[16] See Pierre Aubry, *Estampies et danses royales,* Paris, 1907.

earlier, and that music was one of the principal arenas. Gioseffo
Zarlino has been mentioned for his work in theory, but Zarlino
appears not only as a defender of a theory, but also as a defender
of contemporary music. Just as new conceptions of rhythm had
been demonstrated by Philip de Vitry, exponent of the *ars nova*,
against Johannes de Muris, defender of ancient tradition (*ars an-
tiqua*), so Arnold Schönberg is such an exponent today, in his ad-
vocacy of new principles, by theory and by example.

A reply to Zarlino was made by Vincenzo Galilei in 1581, in
his *Dialogo della musica antica e della moderna*. His was a defense
of the Ancients, and the battle was on.[17]

These opponents in the controversy were not historians in any
sense of the word. They, like other disputants in literature and
social theory, made use of historical data, but only to compare the
condition of arts and sciences in ancient times with the conditions
obtaining in their own day. But the important fact is that certain
notions were formed concerning the study of music which have
continued to influence musical taste, musical criticism, music history, and music theory down to the present.[18]

Now for the correlation between this quarrel and the development of opera. We are told that the Florentine innovators were
trying to revive Greek drama, but the reason for their desire is not
clear until we realize that Italian humanists had been reviving the
glories of antiquity for nearly two centuries. But during this quarrel we find two opposing sides comparing past with present conditions. The question raised in music was: Did the Greeks have
this elaborate, many-voiced harmony, or were they content with a
single line of melody? [19] Italian admirers of the simplicity and
grandeur of antique art and literature were repelled by what
seemed to them to be the dry, quasi-scientific quality of much of
the Flemish polyphonic vocal music, an art very influential in Italy,
which had reached a degree of complexity never equalled since,
except in modern orchestral scores. After deciding that the Greeks
had practiced no such complicated, scientific art, the aim of the

---

[17] And yet, J. B. Bury, in *The Idea of Progress*, 4th ed., 1928, p. 80, finds no
comparison between Ancients and Moderns until 1620!

[18] See Frederick John Teggart, *Theory of History*, Yale University Press, New
Haven, 1925, p. 80.

[19] Burney has a section in Book I on "Whether the Ancients Had Counterpoint or
Music in Parts."

Ancients became the "restoration" of a simple, monodic declamation of the text, a setting which would give more opportunity for enunciation of the words and interpretation of their meaning.

So on one hand the protagonists of the Ancients succeeded explicitly in opera, in bringing poetry back into its own in musical recitative, or declamation, although the old contrapuntal forms (madrigals) were still retained for the chorus. On the other hand, however, the defenders of the Moderns presented their arguments implicitly in their novel and empirical experiments with the orchestra. The implied argument on this side of the controversy is that the Moderns should take advantage of all these new inventions, unknown to the Greeks, that were making life so much more interesting than it could possibly have been of old.[20]

It is possible that some extremists on the side of the Ancients might have been content with monotonous declamation of the text, with negligible accompaniment on reconstructed Greek instruments revived for the purpose. It seems reasonable therefore to regard the *dramma per musica* of Monteverde and his colleagues as a synthetic compromise. The so-called *stile nuovo* was based upon current conceptions of the antique only so far as the dramatic recitative was concerned; the victory for the Moderns that had great promise for the future was in the instrumental accompaniment. The demand for the latter had been insistent for three centuries, since the days of the *ars nova*.

2. THE QUARREL IN FRANCE

With the prodigious musical activity that Italy displayed in opera and oratorio during the seventeenth century, there was almost complete cessation of her literary battles over musical science. G. B. Doni made a last stand for the Ancients in 1647 (*De praestantia Musicae veteris*):[21] However,

"His writings and opinions were much respected by the learned, though but little attended to by practical musicians, on which account most of his treatises are filled with complaints of the degeneracy and

---

[20] Even two hundred years earlier, Marsilio Ficino, a fifteenth-century commentator on Plato's *Timaeus*, "asserts that the Platonists could not have understood music so well as the moderns, as they were insensible to the pleasure arising from thirds, which they regarded as *discords* . . . the most grateful of our concords, and so necessary that without them our music would be destitute of its greatest ornament, and counterpoint monotonous and insipid." [26], I, p. 115.

[21] Published in Florence and dedicated to Cardinal Mazarin.

ignorance of the moderns, with respect to every branch of music, in theory and practice." [22]

Spain was completely silent on the subject, but John IV, King of Portugal, in 1640, wrote a *Defensa de la Musica Moderna contra la errada opinion del obispo Cyrillo Franco* which was published anonymously.

So instead of Spain and Italy, we find France, England, and Germany the principal centers of interest, respectively, in the seventeenth century. The quarrel of the Ancients and the Moderns first shifted to France, and became identified with literature, while music was relegated to a secondary place. Out of this, the most famous phase of the quarrel, emerged the Idea of Progress, in the late part of the century, with its concept of orderly, continuous, necessary, and gradual change.[23] In France the concept of Authority, so important in the controversy in all its phases, was Roman rather than Greek. Authority won out in the absolutism of the throne and the academies, while the concept of Progress became identified more with the social sciences than with artistic expression. No synthesis was possible such as the Italians had created in music drama. Possibly this is one reason why the music of Italy became the envy of her neighbors.

The quarrel did not reach England until the latter part of the century. By this time Italian music had become associated with all of the desirable virtues that the Ancients possessed, but eighteenth-century England accepted or rejected Italian music with no such attendant disturbances as the *Guerre des buffons* and the quarrel of Gluckists vs. Piccinnists. *The Beggar's Opera* (1728) laughed Italian opera off the boards, but the ideals of Italian melody remained as models.

To return to France: Hubert Gillot points out that the quarrel involved the two principles of Authority and Progress, supported by two radically opposed elements. One element finds that classic traditions had been preserved just as faithfully in the University of Paris as among the Italian humanists, and that France, moreover, had her own heroes worthy of emulation — Charles Martel, Godfrey of Bouillon, Charlemagne, and others. Comparing them to Augustus, Gillot says " the French made war to succor the weak;

---

[22] Burney [26], Vol. I, p. 116.
[23] See Bury, *The Idea of Progress,* Chapters IV, V; Teggart, *Theory of History,* Chapter 8.

the Romans to conquer the oppressed and subjugate the oppressor. France conquers civilization in order to teach her, in order to establish the reign of law." [24]

The upholders of the concept of Progress pointed to the advances made in modern culture, in exploration, science, and communication of ideas. The modern age succeeds centuries of gross ignorance. Antiquity herself "teaches the moderns to defy authority." With Authority centralized in the person of the king, literature, music, painting, and that favored art, the dance, became more or less subservient. The concept of Progress is expressed not so much in these arts as in philosophy and the sciences. Gillot points out, in this connection, that French arts and poetry were set on the road to academicism by Malherbe (1555–1628).

Richelieu and Mazarin had to struggle against independent resistance in art and literature just as much as in national politics.[25] But with the absolutism of Louis XIV " *via* the control of the Académie and the Protectorate of Richelieu, art and literature set out for the absolutism of a Boileau, a Le Brun, or a Lulli."

The first academy in France, *L'Académie de Musique et de Poésie,* was founded by de Baïf, under the protection of Charles IX. The academies founded under Louis XIV in the next century, however, were quite another story. The dominance of the court and Roman ideals of authority and amusement demanded, even of de Baïf's humanists, that the lyric-dramatic revival must be in the form of ballet rather than of opera. The court's fondness for Italian importations began with Baltazarini (adopted name, Beaujoyeulx), who was prominent in the notoriously extravagant *Ballet de la Reine* (1582), ten years after the Huguenot massacre. The climax came with the rise to power of Lulli, the Florentine, under Louis XIV, who enjoyed a royal monopoly on operatic production never granted to any other one man before or since. Gillot refers to the early Academy of de Baïf, mentioned above, as a " respectful subordination to power," showing a desire to *illustrer la nation* by working for the progress of the arts, which latter, however, must serve the glory of France by glorifying her representative, the king.

Thus arose, in France, the institutions described by Walter Bagehot (*Physics and Politics,* 1904) as " asylums of the ideas and tastes

[24] *La querelle des anciens et des modernes en France,* Paris, 1914, pp. 28, 29.
[25] Corneille's struggles against the fetters of " classic " authority exemplify this.

of the last age. . . . Out of their dignified windows (the academicians) pooh-pooh new things."

As a result, under Louis XIV the young Frenchman with musical ability, unless favored at the Parisian court, was not free to
further the progress of musical art in his own country. Italians
and Germans seem to have been free enough, though deprived of
the blessings of centralized national prestige and patronage. This
does not mean, however, that there was any dearth of music in
Paris, or of discussions concerning it. Music was a topic of constant
concern with philosophers, and figured very prominently in the
famous quarrel. But music was dominated by Italians imported
by Cardinal Mazarin and later courtiers. The discussions came to
be debates over the relative merits of French and Italian music.
The latter was upheld by the protagonists of the Ancients as em-
bodying all that was truly "natural" according to the principles
revealed by antiquity. It may be of interest to examine a condensation of one such typical discussion. This unpublished manuscript
by Claude Perrault, one of the brothers who defended the Moderns
with great zeal, is placed by Gillot at the end of his work [26] and
shows the importance of music in current arguments of the day
(1681, just one hundred years after Galilei). It is a Preface to a
Traité de la Musique. The dialogue recounts a conversation overheard at a Paris theater: —

Paleologue says that the same difference between the divine and inimitable works produced by antiquity, compared with what his century is
capable of, exists between what pass for sciences and art among the
Italians and the French.

Philalethe recalls the production of a purely French opera nearly one
hundred years before, from having seen an old program, names on
which — actors, engineers, etc.— were all French. He argues further that
the supporters of the Ancients talk in such glib, general terms of the
"divine and inimitable" works of antiquity but, when pressed for details, are obliged to admit the superiority of modern artists in many details, technical or otherwise. And Michelangelo, so revered at present,
himself had to argue with his own contemporaries, who could see no
good in modern achievement. He cited Michelangelo's stratagem in bury-
ing his statue so it would be dug up by the savants, then producing the
arm he had broken off, after getting the savants to praise the statue as
far superior to anything modern.

[26] *La querelle des anciens et des modernes en France.*

Two reasons for praising the Ancients are cited by Philalethe: first, to avoid praising contemporaries and competitors; second, to appear more intelligent than the rest: to seem to perceive in the beauties of ancient art something hidden from the crowd.

After the opera, which both enjoyed greatly, Philalethe mentions a treatise written by a friend which shows that the Greeks, with all their admirable qualities, could have had no knowledge of the finest development of music — singing and playing in parts.

The author himself appears and gives the substance of his treatise, but Paleologue is still unconvinced, although mollified, saying that, after all, nothing is proved *pro* or *con*.

The further significance of this controversy with relation to the philosophy of Progress in music histories will be discussed later, in Chapter 10, III.

These disputes over historical division still go on, even among laymen who argue for the superiority of " classical " as opposed to " modern " music. But in the meantime the old dichotomy of historical periodization has given way to finer divisions which are subjects of debate among the learned.

" In their ' periodizations,' our historians still dispose their periods in a single series end to end, like the sections of a bamboo-stem between joint and joint or the sections of the patent extensible handle on the end of which an up-to-date modern chimney sweep pokes his brush up a flue. On the brush-handle which our contemporary Western historians have inherited from their predecessors as part of their stock-in-trade, there were originally only two joints — the ' Ancient ' and the ' Modern,' corresponding to the ' Old Testament ' and the ' New Testament ' of the Bible and the dual back-to-back reckoning by years ' before Christ ' and by ' years of our Lord ' in our traditional Janus-faced system of chronology." [27]

" As time has gone on, our Western historians have found it convenient to extend their telescopic brush-handle by adding a third section, which they have called ' medieval ' because they have chosen to insert it between the other two. They have not yet realized that they are the victims of a malicious trick. If they would remove their heads from the chimney for a moment and take a walk around the house, they would observe that the builder is at work all the time on the roof and that he is heightening the chimney-stack faster than they are adding fresh sections to the handle of their brush." [28]

[27] Arnold Toynbee, *A Study of History,* 2nd ed., Oxford, 1935, Vol. I, p. 169.
[28] *Ibid.,* p. 170.

Chapter 11, on the "evolution" of music, will endeavor to show, however, that the triple division, in music history at least, is not due to "insertion" of a medieval period. Other considerations arising from the use of analogy seem to be involved.

The foregoing pages have attempted to describe briefly some of the fields of musical art and science that have provoked controversy, from the Renaissance down to the present. The very nature of music, an art and a science and a means of communication, involves complexity. It involves many factors, calling as it does for much division of tone, time, and tuning, much grouping of persons and parts, for all sorts of functions, sacred and secular, public and private, for voices and instruments, in all countries. With people divided by language and custom, the music of western Christendom has served roughly as an international means of communication. But with international communication made infinitely easier today, quarrels over music in modern histories of the art are being resumed where Paleologue and Philalethe left off, not only on esthetic grounds, but as a result of bitter national rivalries. (See Chapter 8, III, of this book.)

Summarizing these five fields of division in a different order, we find that the quarrels over theory and practice began in Spain, between the clerical theorists, on the one hand, and the practical, experimenting "slaves of music" on the other. The continuation of these quarrels in Italy, however, took on different premises and new objectives, being waged between those who wished to revive the pagan arts of the Greeks with all their apparent simplicity and dramatic truth, and those who felt that music should profit by the addition and development of modern instruments and modern harmonies that were superior to any the Greeks had known. Compromise was found in opera and oratorio.

In the meantime, the other matters of division, in rhythm, meter, acoustics, composition, and performance, were hotly debated, but the establishment of academies in France and the rise of academic schools in other countries provided centers where these matters became settled, and canons of good taste became as binding as the laws of Nature so eagerly sought at the same time. At any rate academic writers who could write up the history of music objectively were rare, particularly in the sixteenth century, when these controversies were at their height.

VI. THE HISTORIES OF ART BEGIN EARLIER

Giorgio Vasari's *Lives of the Artists* (1550) marks an event in the history of art that has no parallel, unfortunately, in the history of music. With all the controversies that may have arisen over art techniques, we find no fourteenth-century theorists scoffing at the discovery of perspective as an impious revolt against authority, nor were painters called "slaves of art" because of devotion to their craft. In the sixteenth century, while all these disputes were being waged over musical problems, little or no effort was made to preserve biographical data concerning the musicians of the day. But Cardinal Farnese commissioned Vasari to collect material for "some kind of treatise" tracing the "history of all who had been famous in the arts of design, beginning with Giotto and coming down to our own day," saying that "by so doing you would confer a benefit on these arts of yours." [29] It is to be noted here that the interest in art history, on the part of Cardinal Farnese, began with an interest in the art of his own present, and that he only suggested going back to the pioneer in Italian art — Giotto. No interest was manifested in the "Origins of Art," not only because no examples of ancient painting were at hand, but also because no theoretical treatises existed telling what materials were used. Furthermore, no mystic notions obsessed the minds of men concerning the "color of the spheres" in connection with divine cosmogony, and the "divisions" of art provided no analogies for sociological theory.

Vasari does desire "that this book may be complete in all its parts, so that the reader shall not need to seek anything beyond it," so he adds

"part of the works of the most celebrated ancient masters, as well Greek as of other nations, the memory of whom has been preserved even to our own days by Pliny and other writers; but for whose pens that memory must have been buried in eternal oblivion, as is the case with many others. And perhaps this consideration also may increase our desire to labor truly; for, *seeing the nobility and greatness of our art,* and how, by all nations, but especially by the most exalted minds, and the most potent rulers, it has ever been honored and rewarded, we may all be the more influenced and impelled to adorn the world with works, infinite as to number and surpassing in their excellence — whence, embellished by our

[29] As quoted from Vasari's autobiography in R. W. Carden's *Life of Giorgio Vasari,* New York, 1911, p. 73.

labor, *it may place us on that eminence* on which it has maintained those ever admirable and most celebrated spirits." [30]

It may be pointed out that Vasari was an ardent nationalist, but he may well be pardoned, in view of the facts. The essential point for this study is that there is no hint of the ancient-modern quarrel so prominent in music literature of the period. As an ardent biographer, Vasari seeks as much material as possible from the past, but only to support his belief that the present and future "may be the more influenced and impelled to adorn the world with works, infinite as to number and surpassing in their excellence."

Such confidence in the future was rare in Vasari's day, and was worthy of the more optimistic seventeenth century. The sixteenth century had begun with Machiavelli and his reactionary belief that a return to ancient Roman ideals of order through force, if necessary, was essential in a disorderly society torn by corruption. But the Machiavellian tyrants of the fifteenth and sixteenth centuries were the most lavish patrons of the arts, and Vasari's optimism is that of one who was sheltered from the "stern realities." The path of the musician was more difficult. It was beset with the bitter controversies just noted, and there had been less incentive for the rank and file of composers to put the results of their art in permanent form. The history of painting begins to be written a half century before that of music, and the extant editions of Renaissance music are pitifully few in contrast to the riches of painting and sculpture. But the assertion, found in most histories, that music was the "slowest of the arts to develop" proves in the light of modern research to be uncritical guesswork, if not entirely false.

"Historians of culture, and even historians of music, have often suggested that when any notable movement affects the arts, music is always the last to show the influence of the new ideas. From a musician's point of view there is not the slightest ground for such an assumption. There is no reason why the new ideas should not have been expressed in terms of music even before they were expressed in terms of the other arts." [81]

[30] Vasari, *Lives,* tr. by Mrs. Jonathan Foster, London, Bohn, 1855, pp. 7–8.

[81] Edward J. Dent, "The Relation of Music to Human Progress," *The Musical Quarterly,* XIV, 1928, p. 311. For further comments on this theory of slow development and Ambros' theories on this score, cf. "The Renaissance Attitude Towards Music" by Hugo Leichtentritt, *ibid.,* Vol. I, 1915, pp. 604–622. See also P. Sorokin, *Social and Cultural Dynamics,* N. Y., 1937, Vol. I, *Fluctuation of Forms of Art,* Ch. 12, also Ch. V, p. 209.

CHAPTER 3

RELIGIOUS, NATURALIST, AND ETHICAL TRADITIONS

I. BIBLICAL PERIODIZATION AND ETHICAL CLASSIFICATION

THE purpose of this chapter is to show that churchmen and moralists dictated the fundamental bases of early music histories, that certain secular concepts were debated by them from the first, and that in spite of the preponderance of secular theory today, occasional texts still appear which show the persistence of old traditions.

For the early schemes of periodization in music history, evidence is first brought from Bonnet's *Histoire* [9], cited at the end of Chapter 1. His periods were as follows:

I. From the Divine Origins at Creation to the Flood.
II. From the Flood to King David and Solomon.
III. From King Solomon to Pythagoras.
IV. From Socrates (3600 years after Creation) to the Birth of Christ.
V. From the Birth of Christ to Gregory the Great.
VI. From Pope Gregory to St. Dunstan.
VII. From the Eleventh to the Sixteenth Centuries (Chap. X and XI).

Chapter XII is devoted to seventeenth-century musicians, and Chapter XIII to musicians of the author's own day.

Supporting the theory of Aristides Quintilianus, Bonnet divides music into *Musica Mondana* (music of the spheres), *Musica Humana* (a harmony of the one and the other in man, made by the body, and controlled by the mind), *Musica Rhithmica* (the consonant harmony one feels in prose), *Musica Metrica* (music of verse), *Musica Politica* (the harmonious organization of the State), and *Musica Harmonica* (musical science and theory).

Bonnet, although a priest, shows less concern with Christian tradition than the laymen, stressing rather the Greek *ethos* of music so important in didactic music history.

In 1757 Dom P. J. Cassiaux wrote an *Essai d'une histoire de la musique* [17], but the unpublished manuscript, in the *Bibliothèque Nationale,* Paris, is inaccessible to an American student. The Benedictine author follows the traditional periodization, but from the titles seems to have been much more interested in secular music than his contemporaries mentioned here.

In that same year Padre G. B. Martini, Italy's most learned scholar, began publication of his *Storia della musica* [19]. Beginning with a presentation of evidence from the Holy Scriptures, and deductions therefrom, no attempt is made to go beyond the music of the Greeks. The epochs of Biblical history are as follows:

I. Music from the Creation of Adam to the Flood.
II. Music from the Flood to the Birth of Moses.
III. Music from the Birth of Moses to his Death.
IV. Music from the Death of Moses to the Reign of King David.
V. Music from the Reign of David to that of King Solomon.
VI. From the Reign of King Solomon to the Destruction and Rebuilding of the Temple.

Vol. II begins with a chapter on the origins of music according to the ancients, particularly in Greece.

In 1774 Martin Gerbert published *Di cantu et musica sacra a prima ecclesiae aetate usque ad praesens tempus* [25]. This work, by a learned and active Benedictine monk, although a history of sacred music only, is perhaps the most important German music history of the eighteenth century. Gerbert, as shown by his correspondence with Martini, expected to collaborate with the latter; Martini was to write the introduction and general summary, with a discussion of secular music, while Gerbert reviewed sacred music.

Gerbert had a zealous purpose in writing his history of sacred music. The abbot saw the dangers to theology from the Enlightenment and tried to stem the tide with an appeal to history. Theology, for him, was divided into three categories: first, dogmatic theology, in its historical development; second, moral theology, concerning the Christian life; third, liturgical theology, including music. Gerbert strenuously opposed the mixing of secular elements in sacred music, and demanded a return to simple, severe plainsong and chorales. Instruments were recommended only for support of the voices, and instrumental music independent of the service was condemned. No *coloratura* singing was to be permitted.[1]

---

[1] On account of the association of florid singing with operatic arias, Gerbert chose to disregard the florid elements in medieval Alleluias. See [25], Vol. II, p. 408.

Music itself must be *sacra* (in contrast to the Protestant view that music is sacred or profane, depending on the spirit with which it is performed). As a basis for this in history, the divine-origin theory is inevitable. Gerbert's history begins with the creation of Adam and Eve, therefore, not because of mere concession to convention, but as a basis for theoretical "proof." Music, for Gerbert, began with origins in special creation, then showed steady progress, slowly, but surely, through the ages, up to Palestrina. Since that great master's period, the art has steadily declined. The three periods are given the terms now used so frequently: Ancient, Medieval, and Modern. In this case the periodization is used, however, to denote growth, maturity, and decay.

Gerbert contributed much to musical research. His collections of medieval documents [2] and accounts of his travels in Germany, France, and Italy would have made him famous, even if he had written no history.

Martini was more tolerant of secular music than Gerbert, but equally conservative in matters of musical science. In this respect he came into conflict with another priest, the Spanish Jesuit Eximeno [24], who had settled in Rome. Eximeno was less interested in ecclesiastical tradition than in musical theory. He made some remarkable proposals, for that day, some of which anticipate Wagner. He inveighed against the dry teaching of counterpoint, and wanted to apply rules of prosody to musical composition. He was also one of the first to advocate a basis of national folk music in musical art, advice that has been followed in all countries of Europe except his own (until very recently). Needless to say, like Wagner, he met with a storm of criticism.

II. WAS MUSIC REVEALED, IMITATED, OR INVENTED?

In 1754, J. A. Scheibe, a German *capellmeister* in the service of the Danish king, wrote his *Abhandlung vom Ursprung und Alter*

---

[2] *Scriptores ecclesiastici de musica sacra potissimum* (1794), 3 v. Reprinted, 1905. This collection contains about forty works, dating from the fourth to the fifteenth centuries. The development of notation is traced from St. Isidore (seventh century), who denied the possibility of preserving melodies otherwise than by tradition. Notable works include the *Musica enchiriadis,* and treatises by Guido d'Arezzo, John Cotton, Franco of Cologne, Johannes Muris, and Adam de Fulda.

For further analysis of Gerbert's work, see Elisabeth Hegar [290]. Miss Hegar points out the ways in which Gerbert was a pioneer in evolutionary treatment.

der Musik (NY), in which he expressed the notions that had long been current. Adam and Eve must have lifted their voices in grateful song on the day of their creation, so vocal music was *erfunden* by the first human beings, in Paradise. As in all early histories, Jubal is mentioned as the inventor of instrumental music, " the father of all such as handle the harp and organ " (Genesis 4:21), but Scheibe explains that instrumental music, man's invention, became separated from vocal music before the Flood, on account of the godless race of Cain. After the long abuse of instrumental music, due to the Fall of Man, the two branches of the art remained separated, until united in the service of God by Moses. The question still raging as to the priority of vocal or instrumental music was thus settled very simply.

There has always been a conservative element in the Christian tradition which has looked with disfavor on " invented," " artificial " instrumental music.[3] Although much of this may have been due to the association of instruments with the pagan rites of Greece and Rome, it is possible that this prejudice is rooted in this theory of music's twofold origin and separation.

At any rate, the evidence of music histories shows conclusively that whenever the historian recognizes a long, proud tradition of religious music, the divine-origin theory survives, even today, in modified forms. Following the ecclesiastical tradition down to modern times, we find it thinning out into esthetic, linguistic, and psychological theories in England and Germany and among philologists of France and Italy. But with some writers, the church traditions persist in all their vigor, especially in France, Italy, and Ireland.

Romanticism also brought about English and German revivals of divine-origin theories, with modifications. For example, in 1823, Isaac Nathan says,

" The earliest music, as reason and nature point out, must have been entirely vocal: devotion was its exclusive accompaniment." [40], p. 2.

In Germany, this explanation of genius was vouchsafed in 1830:

" There are individual men, in whom the divine (the Godlike) works in constant revelation. But even they cannot withstand fatigue and

---

[3] Medieval musical theorists were all churchmen, who believed that music's sole purpose was that of enhancing and emphasizing the sacred text. Certain papal edicts condemn all other music.

change, while the being and remaining in constant touch with the divine is not long to be endured. Hence the persistence in giving out these revelations cuts their earthly existence short, as in the case of Raphael, Schiller, or Mozart. Even they feel, at times, the need to partake of the human element in life. So they look, in the sphere of the finite, for materials in which the form of their eternal ideas may be mirrored. Hence the necessity for pictures, myths, art, and culture." [43], p. 2.

In the same year, the English Protestant, William C. Stafford [45], finds a place for natural causes, without entirely abandoning Biblical authority:

"It is almost lost time to search for the origins of any of those arts which have been handed down to us from the remote ages of antiquity. . . . *Natural causes* may, however, sufficiently account for its (music's) origin, without referring to a miracle (of the gods) for the event . . . instruments, without doubt, owed their origin to the observation of the effects flowing from the natural causes . . . such as the whistling of the winds in reeds, and the sonorous singing of hollow bodies when struck."

These speculations led the author into discussions of Comparative Music, the first third of the book being devoted to exotic systems. (American music is discussed on pp. 110–111.) The author's piety and reverence for Scripture lead him to approve with critical reservations the Martini theory of origins:

"Padre M. in his *Storia della musica*, imagines, with a great show of reason, that Adam was instructed by his Creator in every art and science, and that knowledge of music was of course included — a knowledge which Adam employed in praising and adoring the Supreme Being. The learned Italian, however, subsequently attempts to prove that Jubal was not only the inventor of instrumental but vocal music; a position inconsistent with the idea that Adam derived the knowledge of the latter from the Most High, and which is not borne out by the sacred text, where Jubal is mentioned as the inventor of instrumental music only. . . ."

Stafford, like many of his contemporaries, accepted Bishop Ussher's date for Creation (4004 B.C.), and followed the usual Biblical chronology:

"Though the records of the state of music in the antediluvian period are so scanty, *we shall not be wrong in supposing that in the 1600 years and upwards which elapsed between the Creation and the Deluge, considerable progress was made in the science* . . . though the Deluge swept away all the glory and grandeur of the antediluvian world, yet we cannot suppose that Noah and his family were ignorant of the arts and sciences taught before that event. . . .

" The Egyptians are generally looked upon as the fountain from whence the arts and sciences were diffused over the greater part of Europe. To them the invention of many arts, amongst others, music, is ascribed . . . all tradition points at Ham, or one of his sons, as the first who led a colony into Egypt, and some writers suppose that Noah reigned there, identifying that patriarch with Osiris, to whose secretary, Hermes Trismegistus, Apollodorus ascribes the invention of . . . this enchanting art; and though the art itself certainly did not owe its origin to the encounter of Hermes with the tortoise, it is not improbable that the invention of the lyre may be attributed to some such adventitious cause."

In linking the history of Noah and his family to Egyptian tradition, Stafford quotes the following account of the naturalistic origins of instrumental music, taken from Apollodorus (an old legend which appears in every early history):

" The Nile having overflowed its banks at the periodical period for the rise of that wonderful river, on its subsidence to its usual level, several dead animals were left on the shores, amongst the rest, a tortoise, the flesh of which being dried and wasted in the sun, nothing remained within the shell but nerves and cartilages, which being tightened by the heat, became sonorous. Mercury, walking along the shore of the river, happened to strike his foot against this shell, and was so pleased with the sound produced that the idea of the lyre suggested itself to his imagination. The first instrument he produced was in the form of a tortoise, and was strung with the sinews of dried animals."

In 1838, William M. Higgins, in his *Philosophy of Sound and History of Music,* quotes Lucretius on the origin of music; it is the same passage referred to in Chapter 1.

" Through all the woods they hear the charming noise
Of chirping birds, and tried to frame their voice
To imitate. Thus birds instructed man,
And taught them songs before their art began.
And whilst soft evening gales blew o'er the plains
And shook the sounding reeds, they taught the swains:
And thus the pipe was framed, and tuneful reed." [4]

[4] A very free translation. See Lucretius, *De rerum natura,* Book V, 1379–1412.

Much earlier, Charles Henri de Blainville, in 1767, had said in his *Histoire générale, critique et philologique de la musique* [21] that " the breathing of the wind, the whistling of animals, must have given the idea of Flutes to our ancestors." A century later an Italian historian avers that

" Music is not an invention; it is *natural;* but the rules are really fixed laws, fruits of centuries of observation. . . . Vocal (natural) music preceded instrumental music. The songs of birds may have indicated various inflections of the voice copied by men." [54], p. 1.

These theories have not figured extensively in modern music histories; they were only used by Romanticists, for whom Nature was the keyword in all esthetic and social theory.

But the arguments as to whether music was " natural " or " invented " were parallel with even more heated arguments over the invention of language. Adam Smith, in his *Origin of Languages,*[5] had argued that language was an invention of men who had to find tools to meet their needs. De Bonald, leader of the Catholic reaction against Napoleon, had condemned such free-thinking. He branded the belief in the invention of language as

" An untenable theory, as these philosophers understood perfectly well that language is inseparable from thought and social life. Men could never have invented language, had they not already lived in society; and they never could have lived in society had they not already possessed language. You cannot, Bonald claims, get out of this circle, unless you admit this marvel (for language is no less marvelous than the organism of living beings) to be a gift from the Creator to rational beings." [6]

But the " Nature " theorists left little room for belief in the inventive powers of primitive vocalists. Some assigned the belief in invention to legend, maintaining that music and harmony were in Nature itself, therefore in man's nature.[7] Imitation, not invention, was therefore the secret.

[5] Published with the *Theory of Moral Sentiments* (2nd ed.).

[6] Lucien Lévy-Bruhl, *History of Modern Philosophy in France,* London, 1899, pp. 312–313.

[7] " Harmony seems a part of nature, as much as light and heat; and to number any one of them among human inventions would be equally absurd. Indeed nature seems to have furnished human industry with the principles of all science; for what is *geometry,* but the study and imitation of those proportions by which the world is governed? *Astronomy,* but reflecting upon, and calculating, the motion, distances and magnitude of those visible, but wonderful objects, which nature has placed before

The Romantic trend toward naturalistic rather than divine origins was also evident in a work by William Gardiner, entitled

The Music of Nature, or, an attempt to prove that what is passionate and pleasing in the art of singing, speaking and performing upon musical instruments is derived from the sounds of the animated world. London, 1832.

But all these naturalistic theories were very repugnant to good churchmen: F. Marcillac, also an historian of literature, maintained that the origins of music are as ancient as those of man himself. It was by no means a result of the imitation of nature; according to Marcillac, our music begins in the church. [94], p. 1.

Jean Baptiste Labat, a cathedral organist interested in church-music reform, and also a royalist who is pleased with the " regeneration " of France after the restoration of monarchy, says, in 1852, that

" Music, since the beginning of time, since the foundation of religions, has been wholly identified with them, with an essence wholly divine." [64].

Labat found two periods of music history:

I. From the Origins and Greek Music to Palestrina.
II. From Monteverde to the Music of the Bourbon Restoration.

His royalist belief in the divine right of kings may account for the emphasis, in treating of secular music, upon the glories of court music, particularly under the French kings.

An Italian writer, in 1867, appealed, as Padre Martini had, to the authority of St. Thomas Aquinas, who said that the first man had knowledge of all things by means of the species infused into him by God . . . a knowledge not acquired. [77].

History, for Trambusti, is divided into these epochs:

I. From Jubal to Pythagoras.
II. From Pythagoras to Guido.
III. From Guido to Palestrina.
IV. From Palestrina to Rossini.

---

our eyes? *Theology,* but contemplating the works of the Creator, and adoring Him in his attributes? " [27], Vol. I, pp. 195–197.

According to J. H. Mees, a Belgian writer, " It is a gross error to think that there are different music systems. The songs of the most barbarous people can be written with our signs. . . . Music is not an invention . . . it is *in Nature,* but the rules are established laws, the fruit of centuries of observation. Vocal music came first,·as the result of imitating birds. Franco of Liège was the first master in music." [42]

The same view is taken by Father L. F. Renehan, in the only Irish *History of Music* [65]:

"It does not appear that Music can justly be reckoned among the results either of chance or industry: for, it seems to be *coeval with man himself* and *the bountiful gift of his Creator*. . . . That music made considerable progress before the deluge, is manifest from the earliest invention of musical instruments, and from its being then of sufficient importance to be made a profession."

In other words, it must be admitted that man invented instruments, but not that he invented music.

In 1846, an anonymous *Manual of Music* [57] "containing a Sketch of its Progress in all Countries," began as follows:

"Music *did* originate with that great Being who endowed the man he had created with speech and thought — and gave him, in the sense of hearing, and the love of the agreeable and the beautiful, the faculty of perceiving and appreciating the concord of sweet sounds. This faculty is universal. . . ."

In 1869, an Inaugural Dissertation at the University of Rostock, *On the History of Music down to the End of the Seventeenth Century,* was delivered by the Rev. Charles Booker [80].

Booker begins with divine origins, and closes thus:

"I have now accomplished the task which I proposed to myself . . . tracing most imperfectly, yet with some degree of precision, the rise, spread, progress and perhaps perfection of music as a science . . . hoping that even so imperfect a sketch of this noble science may cause us to feel thankful that we live in an age when it has probably reached its highest pitch, and may each of us in our several stations and callings endeavor to praise our Creator on earth as the archangels do in heaven."

These examples offer only a few instances of the concern felt over the secularization of church music. There was a tendency to view with extreme alarm the departure from "purity" in church music, with the attendant danger to morals. Men were being asked to choose extremes — to believe in progress or degeneration; evolution or special creation, and there were many who looked upon the introduction of "artificial" instruments into the church as a concession to Beelzebub. The "origins" of "pure" sacred music were in Gregorian chant; church music must not be contaminated with any worldly elements. The puritanism of the *motu proprio*

has much in common with the Calvinistic attitude toward adorn-
ment in music.'[8]

Puritanism in church music also favored the development of the
a cappella myth. At the present time most choral directors are
under the mistaken impression that all sixteenth-century music, for
instance, should be sung unaccompanied, in order to preserve the
proper tradition. As Leichtentritt's researches showed, thirty years
ago,[9] the only tradition preserved is that of nineteenth-century surmise. Since the music did not carry specific instructions for instruments, it was assumed that they were not used. But the myth aided
the campaign for purity in church music, and the campaign has
kept the myth alive, although research exposed it long ago.

Two translations appeared in England of Thibaud's *Reinheit in
der Tonkunst* (1825). One is inclined to wonder whether the hesi-
tation to adopt equal temperament was not due to some deep-
seated ethical desire to preserve the original purity of just intona-
tion. The suspicion grows that clerical theories of the origins of
music, especially as formulated in the eighteenth and preached in
the nineteenth century, may have made us forget what the processes
were by which early Christian music, early *organum,* Flemish and
French motets, and Reformation chorales were actually created.
The interaction of " sacred " and " popular " factors in the creation
of our great church music is an historical fact.

Even within this generation, some purists still support the ecclesiastical theory of origins. For example, a French textbook for schools
[105], originally in the form of a *Chronologie musicale,* says the
Scriptures attribute the invention of the first instruments to Jubal,
but that vocal music was probably " born " about the same time as
the spoken word.

Félix Clément was an organist and director of church music,
historian of the fine arts, and author of *Histoire générale de la
musique religieuse* (1861). He asserts that *musique humaine* had
the same origins as those of language, that the principal sounds
(intervals), those of the tetrachord and the octave, were revealed to

---

[8] For the purist's viewpoint in modern American music, see Archibald Davison's
Protestant Church Music in America.

[9] Hugo Leichtentritt's study revealed the scarcity of pictures showing singers
alone, in comparison with the numerous pictures of instrumentalists, with or without
singers. The article referred to is *Was lehren uns die Bildwerke des 14–17 Jahrhunderts über die Instrumentalmusik ihrer Zeit?* in *Sammelbände der IMG,* 1905–
1906, pp. 315–364. (NY).

man by the Creator, at the same time that an articulate language was vouchsafed to him. The idea of origins in the imitation of Nature is repugnant to Clément: " One would not be able to reproduce Nature in servile fashion without degrading this human art from the high rank it occupies in Creation." (pp. 1–2).

For a Belgian writer, late in the century, the origin and first expression of music was in the hymn of recognition of the Creator by his creature. . . .

" A people that sing are a believing people, aspiring for liberty." [132].

Another elementary text, *pour les jeunes,* by Mlle. Gabeaud, professor at the Schola Cantorum and pupil of Vincent d'Indy, teaches that musical art, the origin of which is lost in the darkness of time, is revealed to man in two forms: (1) *l'art du geste ou de la danse, expression de la joie populaire;* (2) *art de la parole chantée, venu de prière et du recueillement.* [262].

III. THEORIES CONCERNING THE ETHOS OF MUSIC

The Greeks recognized the value of music (which for them included all phases of mental culture) in the education of youth; thus we find Plato greatly concerned with music's origin in the soul and its effect on the individual. Although Plato recognized and stressed the great value of mathematics, he started a more humanistic view of the nature of music, a view developed also by Aristotle and Aristoxenus. Plato ridiculed the Pythagoreans for their theory that the essence of music was number:

" they act just like the astronomers, that is . . . they investigate the numerical relations subsisting between these audible concords, but they refuse to apply themselves to problems, with the object of examining what numbers are, and what numbers are not, consonant, and what is the reason of the difference." To ascertain the latter would be " a work useful in the search after the beautiful and the good." (*Republic,* VII, 531.)

Later, when the church became responsible for the morals of her children, it was inevitable that ecclesiastical recorders of medieval music should ignore the raucous, immoral *modus lascivus* of the common folk, to leave for posterity only the music approved by authority. (Hence the one-sided nature of earlier music histories, especially those works written in ages of piety by men who accepted both the theories of musical origins in the soul of man, and the theories of divine creation.) Thus the church has remained for many, even until recently, the final arbiter of taste concerning music, the "handmaid of religion." In 1887 Louis S. Davis could say, "Music is but one effect of the great cause, the Christian Church, and upon its rituals and institutions depended the fate of the whole tone-system." [10]

IV. A MODERN REVERSAL OF CAUSAL THEORY

Cyril Scott has presented the point of view of theosophy in *The Influence of Music on History and Morals, A Vindication of Plato.* For Scott, music is the first cause, not a mere result of natural causes or of human effort:

"Throughout the ages, philosophers, religionists and savants have realized the supreme importance of sound. In their most ancient scriptures, the Vedas, it is stated that the world was brought into manifestation through the agency of sound. . . . The writer of the Book of Joshua must have possessed some knowledge of the power of sound, otherwise it is unlikely that he would have written the story of the Fall of Jericho." [253], pp. 3, 4.

Handel's music was largely responsible for the characteristics of the Victorian Era:

"It was, in fact, his exalted mission to revolutionize the state of English morals; it was he who came to be responsible, so to speak, for the swing of the moral pendulum from one extreme of laxity to the other of almost undue constraint." (p. 11).

Scott then goes on to argue that the music of Bach made the Germans more profound and that Beethoven made people more sympathetic, and "made possible the introduction of the science of psycho-analysis to a baffled and horrified public." (p. 32). As for the modern age,

"It is regrettable that a type of 'music' which is so popular as *Jazz* should exercise an evil influence, but such is the occult truth. Jazz has been definitely 'put through' by the Black Brotherhood, known in Christian tradition as the Powers of Evil or Darkness, and put through

[10] *Studies in Musical History,* N. Y., 1887, p. iv.

with the intention of inflaming the sexual nature and so diverting mankind from spiritual progress. . . .

"The question may be asked: Then why have the Higher Powers permitted Jazz to 'come through'? — it is because Jazz-music makes that lesson (of sexual control) rather more difficult, and consequently renders the learning of it the more deserving of merit." (p. 153).

Reversing the old hypothesis, in a sense, Scott believes that music is the Great Cause in history:

"It may seem extravagant to say that *through music the first conception of God was aroused in the human mind,* yet when primitive Man came, deemed his prayers (sung) were heard, he naturally came to conceive of a Being higher than himself. . . . Hitherto his conceptions had been entirely phallic . . . but after he had discovered song, he conceived the idea of the great Mother. . . .

"*The next stage in the evolution of religion* is common knowledge; when once the idea of the Great Mother had been formulated, Man fashioned her image in wood and stone. . . . *Finally,* having fashioned his idols, he appointed someone to guard them; and in this manner the office of priest originated. It was the priests who discovered that if certain notes were reiterated, definite emotional results could be obtained and definite powers brought into action. Thus music became associated with ceremonial magic in the very earliest ages of Mankind. . . .

"One of the effects was to increase religious fervour, with the result that men began to sway with their bodies, and to clap their hands. In the course of time the most elementary form of drum was invented to accentuate the rhythm; this led to the invention of other instruments and so to the actual birth of music as an art." (pp. 157–158).

The effects of music on nations are described as follows as a causal explanation of history:

1. The Indians, with quarter-tones, became subtly wise, but lethargic.
2. In Egypt, the third-tone was characteristic, "one degree less subtle than that of India, with the result that instead of working on the minds it stopped short at the emotions." (p. 163).
3. With Greece we come to the half-tone and to European music, all of which affected the material or physical, rather than the emotional or mental. (p. 172).
4. In Rome, martial music energized the body and affected practical results, but degenerated into love of power, brutality and sensualism.
5. Music practically re-commenced with the monks — again associated with religion. Once more men were induced to think.
6. Folk song brought about the feeling of *patriotism.*

7. Polyphonic music made communities susceptible to "give-and-take."

8. Music of the Catholic Church, having made people think, brought on, ironically enough, the Reformation and Protestantism.

9. Palestrina and his contemporaries brought back purity of emotion into Church music.

10. Polyphonic music, as a whole, was indirectly responsible for early scientific discoveries: "its vibrations, by affecting the mentality, helped to render the minds of philosophers, inventors and scientists more receptive to ideas, and the minds of humanity to accept them." (p. 215).

11. The Neapolitan melodies of Scarlatti "made religion more attractive" and thus "co-ordinated church and the home" (p. 217) but this was followed by effects of effeminacy and degeneracy, especially in France, where the Revolution came as a result.

Finally, prescriptions for the future which will mean spiritual and mental progress: "The appearance of the quarter-tone would greatly spiritualize the Western peoples. . . . It would endow them with wisdom without depriving them of their practicality. Again the third-tone, through its specific effect on the *emotional* body and its power to loosen that particular sheath of the soul, would aid Mankind in deriving first-hand knowledge of the Emotional Plane, as it so aided the Egyptians. . . . So far, with our earthly music we have only been able to imitate the faintest echo of the music of the Spheres, but, in the future, it will be given us to swell the great Cosmic Symphony."

CHAPTER 4

LEXICONS, DICTIONARIES, AND ENCYCLOPEDIAS

"Every other author may aspire to praise; the lexicographer can only hope to escape reproach; yet even this negative recompense has yet been granted to very few."— Samuel Johnson.

SEVERAL of the seventeenth-century treatises cited in Chapter 1 were encyclopedic in size and scope, but not in arrangement. As if to remedy that defect, the few important music treatises of the early eighteenth century are nearly all in the form of dictionaries. There had been little or no activity along that line since 1474, when Tinctoris, one of the numerous Flemish musicians in Italy, had put out his *Terminorum Musicae diffinitorium*,[1] not only the first musical dictionary, but one of the first printed books on music. In 1703 Brossard's *Dictionary* came out in Paris, to be translated by James Grassineau in 1740 [8, 14]. In the latter year Walther and Mattheson presented the first two of a long series of lexicons which have been monuments to German thoroughness ever since [12], [15].

Mattheson (1681–1764), contemporary of Bach and Handel, was their equal in indefatigable versatility, leaving over 8,000 printed pages of history, criticism, biography, journalistic comment, etc., in addition to much music written during an active professional career. He was evidently a progressive supporter of innovation, especially in the field of changing orchestral styles. The work of Walther and Mattheson was continued later in the century by Ernst Ludwig Gerber [31]. The activities of these men are linked up more or less with musical criticism, and to understand them fully it would be necessary to study the development of societies and journals for music research.

Brossard's *Dictionary* came out shortly after the first edition of the Academy's *Dictionary of the French Language* (1694). The history by Bonnet-Bourdelot followed, in 1715. J. J. Rousseau's

---

[1] Reprinted in Forkel, *Allgemeine Lit. der Musik*.

immensely popular *Dictionnaire de musique* appeared in 1767, not so dependable as a source of information but important in the history of the controversies over the *Encyclopedia*.

Dictionaries are not the only signs of the classificatory activities of this era. The botanical and zoological work of the Enlightenment was descriptive and taxonomical, as for example in the *Systema naturae* by the Swedish botanist Linnaeus. The first edition of this work appeared in 1735. It embodied a system of classification based upon a belief in the fixity of species. This belief was reflected in the proverb, "God created, Linnaeus arranged."

The exact contemporary of Linnaeus was Buffon (1707–1778). His *Natural History* (1749–1779) employed a system of arbitrary classification directly opposed to that of Linnaeus, and as a curator his interests roamed far and wide. What Linnaeus attempted in botany, and Buffon in zoology and geology, Réaumur tried in entomology with his *Mémoire de servir à l'histoire des insectes* (1734).

The inorganic world was just being mapped and classified, also.[2] Many details of geography were just being revealed by new explorations, and pioneer geologists were becoming aware of such details as strata and fossils.[3]

The simultaneous appearance of classificatory works in various fields seem to indicate something more than coincidence, for the main emphasis at this time appears to be directed toward atomistic types of philosophy and investigation. The sensualist concepts of Locke,[4] leading to the atomistic phases of psychology, the "selfish" philosophy of Mandeville,[5] and certain features of Rousseau's social theories all provided subjects for debate concerning the individual, particularized elements that went to make up the concept of the whole.

In Rococo art, lavish attention was given to minutiae and embellishment of detail. In English literature, short poems, hymns, essays, odes, and comedy replace the epic drama and poetry of the seventeenth century. New ventures in journalism create new needs for concise thumbnail sketches.

---

[2] Jaillot, *Atlas Nouveau contenant toutes les parties du Monde* (1689). Hermann Moll, *The Compleat Geographer* (1723).

[3] Woodward, *Essay toward a Natural History of the Earth* (1695).

[4] *An Essay Concerning the Human Understanding* (1690).

[5] *Fable of the Bees* (1729).

In music, conventionalized opera had departed from the ideals of Peri and Monteverde to become a "concert in costume," consisting of arias and concerted numbers without any organic unity. The instrumental suite, likewise, was a collection of dances linked in a musical chain by the device of writing them all in one fixed key. The sonata form, with its highly organized, rational scheme of "development" is a later event in the century. J. S. Bach (1685–1750) lays solid foundations for it at this time, but his sons and the contemporaries of Kant, viz., Mozart and Haydn, were among those who perfected it.

Rameau published his *Traité de l'harmonie* (1722), in which chords were treated as "absolute and independent entities, detachable from all content, devoid of any melodic implications and susceptible of scientific analysis and classification." [246], p. 161.

I. THE DICTIONARY AND ITS USES — HISTORY OR CRITICISM?

Classification and reference were not the only ends involved in the compilation of dictionaries. In 1697 a new French tendency, represented by Pierre Bayle, with his *Dictionnaire historique et critique,* set out to combat superstition, belief in miracles, and many orthodox traditions.[6] Even earlier a *Grand Dictionnaire Historique* by Louis Moréri had appeared (1674), and, much later, the *Philosophical Dictionary* by Voltaire, with its satirical treatment of conventional dogma.

Purification and fixation seem to have been the objects in dictionaries of French and English. The Académie was bent upon

"purifying the language of the filth which it has gathered either in the mouths of the people, or in the mob in the Palais de Justice . . . or by the abuse of writers and preachers who say the right thing in the wrong way."

In England "it was imagined by men of letters — among them Addison, Swift, and Pope — that the English language had then attained such perfection that further improvement was hardly possible, and it was feared that if it were not fixed by lexicographic authority deterioration would soon begin. Since there was no English 'academy' it was necessary that the task should be entrusted to some one whose learning

---

[6] Helmuth Osthoff observes that the first French history of music by Bonnet-Bourdelot followed Bayle's lead in this respect, singling out problems to be clarified in essays, instead of presenting an array of chronology [292].

would command respect, and the man who was chosen was Samuel Johnson.[7]

" The first effective protest in England against the supremacy of this literary view was made by Dean Trench in a paper on ' Some Deficiencies in Existing English Dictionaries,' read before the Philological Society in 1857. ' A Dictionary,' he said, ' is *an inventory of the language* . . . it is no task of the maker of it to select the *good* words . . . the business which he has undertaken is to collect and arrange *all* words, whether good or bad, whether they commend themselves to his judgment or otherwise. . . . *He is an historian of the language,* not a critic.' " [8]

That statement raises a very important question in the field of musical historiography, for ever since the eighteenth century historians have had the notion that they should be critics. A general historian of music, according to this theory, must select from the great mass of available material only that which is " important." Unfortunately, however, the importance of the material can be determined only by the esthetic judgment of the critic-historian. And few historians were interested in the present, consequently the criterion is always based upon a standard set up by some authority in the past. The tendency, too frequently, is to forget that " the business which he has undertaken is to collect and arrange (and compare) *all* (works), whether good or bad, whether they commend themselves to his judgment or otherwise." In this case it should be added that the *significance* of music in relation to the society in which it emerges is of vastly greater importance than the esthetic judgment of the historian concerning that music. All music becomes important when this question of significance is raised, but its significance becomes apparent only when it is compared with contemporary developments in other arts, philosophy, science, and politics.

The latter half of the eighteenth century yielded a great amount of esthetic speculation. Diderot, Hogarth, Burke, Rousseau, Schiller, and Schelling are only a few of the contributors. Winckelmann's *History of Ancient Art* (1764) perhaps did more than any other work to fix certain misconceptions of Greek art in people's minds.

[7] *Dictionary of the English Language, in which the Words are deduced from their Originals and Illustrated in their different significances by examples from the best writers,* London, 1755.
[8] *Encyc. Brit.,* 14th ed., article " Dictionary."

But it will be apparent that the influence of French and English esthetics was very profound in music histories, also.

To trace fully all of these influences upon the formation of taste and the writing of music history would demand a complete volume. It must suffice here to point out (1) that during the Era of Classification Rameau worked out a system of harmony that was used as a basis for determining what was "correct" and "permissible" in music; (2) that Rousseau's nature philosophy is contemporaneous with Rameau's theories, both being influential in the work of Dr. Burney, one of the many historians who felt it necessary to be a critic; (3) that the eighteenth-century decisions as to what was truly "natural, beautiful, graceful, and in good taste" were influenced by Italian models which were regarded as revivals of antique beauty; (4) that these decisions as to what constitute "universal" [9] beauty and logical, correct harmony affected nineteenth-century criticism and music teaching as strongly as Greek theories had affected the Middle Ages.

II. MODERN FRENCH ENCYCLOPEDISTS

French pioneers in public education [34], criticism, and women's literature [38], contributed to this list in the first quarter of the nineteenth century, but very little appears in either France or Germany until the new dispensation in both countries after 1870. The first impetus to modern French musicology was given by the Belgian scholar, Fétis, whose monumental *Biographie universelle des musiciens* began to appear in 1837.[10] By 1864 eight volumes had appeared (and in 1873 a second edition, to which supplementary volumes were added in 1878 and 1880 by Arthur Pougin). Fétis had applied to the French government for aid in the printing, but the committee refused it on the ground that the history was not in narrative form. Fétis therefore wrote his *Résumé philosophique* as preface to this first edition, to show that he did have a picture in view. Curiously enough, although the biographies are of European musicians, the *Résumé* is largely concerned with exotic music. The question of Differences was suggested to the author by the report of Villoteau, of the Bonaparte expedition in Egypt.

[9] For the concept of "universal" beauty see Hegel's *Aesthetics,* and Tolstoi's *What is Art?*

[10] [51, 86]. See also Ch. 6, III, for Fétis' elementary work in 1830.

Fétis maintained that a history or encyclopedia of music should be organized by one man, in order that the work should possess unity. This was disputed by Francis Hueffer, who pointed out, in 1883, that Fétis, " the arch-blunderer," could not possibly verify all of his assertions, and that one man's errors were easily copied and passed on.[11] This opinion is expressed by several modern scholars, in theory and practice.

Cesari, the most recent opponent of Fétis' theory, states his belief in the principle of " division of labor," as proved, in his opinion, by the incomplete histories of music of a previous century, works that were too ambitious in scope to be finished by any one man, with the load of centuries on him. As he points out, musicological research in the nineteenth century has, therefore, made definite progress by confining studies to particular areas and periods [270]. In the realm of biography, furthermore, it has been proved that complete collections of a composer's works must be available before any story of his life can have full significance and adequate historical value. This was proved by Carl von Winterfeld, for instance, in the 100-volume collection made to supplement his study entitled *Giovanni Gabrieli und sein Zeitalter.* More than a hundred volumes of this composer's works were unearthed, and are now available in the Berlin Library, in Winterfeld's own hand.

No more historical lexicons appeared in French, even after interest in research was revived after 1870, with the exception of a two-volume work by a Parisian playwright [108]. But Alfred Lavignac began a distinguished career as lexicographer in 1895, with *La musique et les musiciens,* a book widely used in England and America [131]. Lavignac's crowning achievement has been the *Encyclopédie de la musique et dictionnaire de la Conservatoire,* in ten volumes [190]. After Lavignac's death, in 1916, the direction of the work was carried on by L. de la Laurencie. It is the most comprehensive work on music ever attempted. Among the 130 collaborators are 27 conservatory professors or members of the superior council, 20 philologists and *savants,* a physician, a physiologist, 21 musical critics, journalists, littérateurs and estheticians, 37 instrumentalists, including 8 organists and choir directors of different cults, 6 instrument

[11] *Italian and Other Studies,* London, 1863, p. 162. " Arch-blunderer " seems a harsh term, but is mild, in view of the notorious fact that when Fétis could not find a date, he invented or guessed at one. For Fétis' influence on evolutionary history, see Chapter 6.

makers, and 15 foreign correspondents. Lack of adequate indexing, however, makes this great work difficult to use.

Michel Brenet (1858–1918), with her posthumous *Dictionnaire pratique et historique de la musique,* added a worth-while contribution to a long list of achievements in musical research.[12]

III. GERMAN LEXICONS

Half a century elapsed before German lexicographers took up the work started by Walther, Mattheson, and Gerber. In 1870, Hermann Mendel began publication of a 12-volume *Musikalisches Conversations-Lexicon,* which enjoyed great favor. His assistants were David, Dorn, Naumann, Paul, and Tiersch. The important and neglected works of Gustav Schilling, published 1830–1842, are discussed later in Chapter 6.

Hugo Riemann began a new chapter in German music lexicography in 1882, with his *Musiklexicon, Theorie und Geschichte der Musik* [107], one of the most useful works of its kind, and followed it up with a *Katechismus der Musikgeschichte,* Leipzig, 1888 [120]. This versatile scholar and teacher was also the first to put out a music history containing nothing but musical examples, including old music ordinarily inaccessible to the average student.[13]

Others have supplemented this material since with similar collections.[14]

In the meantime, Robert Eitner had assembled a monumental 10-volume work that is indispensable for the musicologist as a mine of information concerning source material [145]. Erich H. Müller made a fine contribution in 1929 [259] and then Hans Joachim Moser carried on in Riemann's footsteps from 1932 to 1935. Moser's is, therefore, the indispensable volume for those who want information on living musicians [287].

Another graphic form of music history for ready reference has been developed in Germany, with chronological tables. This had been tried first by the piano teacher Karl Czerny, in 1851 [60], and in 1909 by an English writer [176]. Hans Dauter took it up

---

[12] Enlarged by A. Gastoué, Paris, 1926. Michel Brenet was the *nom de plume* of Mlle. Marie Bobillier.

[13] *Musikgeschichte in Beispielen,* Leipzig, 3rd ed., 1925.

[14] Alfred Einstein, *Beispielsammlung zur Musikgeschichte,* 4th ed., 1930. Arnold Schering, *Geschichte der Musik in Beispielen,* Leipzig, 1931, 4to, 481 pp., 313 examples from the Seikolos Melody to Gluck.

in 1932 [279], but the most successful of all is the system adopted by Arnold Schering [197], whose parallel columns indicate contemporary events in other fields of culture.

IV. DICTIONARIES IN ENGLISH AND OTHER LANGUAGES

England's contributions to music dictionaries and encyclopedias are headed by Sir George Grove's *Dictionary of Music and Musicians* [99]; but A. Eaglefield Hull's *Dictionary of Modern Music and Musicians* is also a highly esteemed work, having reached a German edition in 1926, edited by Alfred Einstein. A *Cyclopedia of Music and Musicians* by Champlin and Apthorp (1888–1890, 3 vol.) also deserves mention. In 1879 Grove could say that

" The limit of history has been fixed at A.D. 1450, as the most remote date to which the rise of modern music can be carried back. Thus *mere archaeology* has been avoided, while the connection between the medieval systems and the wonderful modern art to which they gave rise has been insisted upon and brought out wherever possible." (Editor's Preface to original edition.)

This statement shows just what the limits of music history were before the dawn of the twentieth century. Historical research is no longer dubbed " mere archaeology." Its contributions, which have opened up four centuries of music unknown to Grove, are beginning to be appreciated.

Two extensive encyclopedic efforts have appeared in the United States, combining dictionaries, biographies, and essays on various musical subjects. The first of these appeared in 1908 [168] and the second in 1915 [201]. Less voluminous, but useful works have been done by Theodore Baker [205], Waldo S. Pratt [228], and Oscar Thompson [315].

For a complete account of this type of literature, see " Lexika," in Riemann's *Musiklexicon*. No attempt has been made to give an exhaustive list; only those which have been consulted with reference to the study of *music histories* have been included. Significant works by Lichtenthal in Italy, and those by Spanish, Swedish, and other compilers have been omitted, but enough has been included to indicate the persistence of a long line of lexicographers who have made possible the syntheses discussed in the following chapters.

CHAPTER 5

EIGHTEENTH-CENTURY HISTORIES: THE ENLIGHTENMENT

IT IS now time to pick up the thread dropped at the end of Chapter 1. The last history discussed under Baroque research was the compilation, by the Bonnet brothers, in 1715, of the Abbé Bourdelot's *Histoire de la musique.* The same work was mentioned at the beginning of Chapter 3, to show that it continued, in form, the Biblical type of chronology favored by the religious tradition; and the scholastic "divisions" which had been passed on by Boethius. It will be quoted again to show the nationalistic fervor of the author (Chapter 8, IV). In the Preface, *Music* is personified as running to the French monarch for protection — a dramatic touch, which seems to contradict the continuation of scholastic "divisions." This personification of music has a double significance: in one sense, it illustrates the journalistic tendency in Bonnet's work, and on the other hand it emphasizes the possibility of considering music as *one art,* which has developed in the course of time. Calvisius, in 1600, had treated music as *an* art to which successive great men had added parts, to build up and develop it to perfection. This method is the foundation of the biographical form of treatment, which comes to be the favored approach throughout the eighteenth century.

The method of biographies in a genealogical chain and the tendency to treat *the* art of music in terms of its "inventors" completely shoved the pluralistic methods of Praetorius out of the eighteenth-century picture. The ethical interests of Cerone also came to be forgotten as a basic consideration until Cyril Scott's work, discussed at the end of Chapter 3. In that same chapter it was also noted that during the eighteenth century the religious tradition came to be separated entirely from the naturalistic legends of music's origins. The frontispiece, from Printz' *Historische Be-*

schreibung, showing Orpheus charming the birds and animals down on the ground while Gabriel is blowing his trumpet up above, is a picture that later historians of music could not include. Those who believed that music was of divine origin found the theory of natural origins repellent; the catholicity of the Lutheran historians came to be forgotten.

With the increasing secularization of music during the Enlightenment, all interest in celestial music disappeared, but the concerns over "invention" and the mathematical bases of music continued. As we have seen, one historian of church music complained of this secularization, but on the whole the change was a stimulating one.

I. MODERN MUSIC HISTORIOGRAPHY BEGINS IN ENGLAND

The Scottish work by Malcolm, cited on the next page, appears to be the first music history in English. A few years later, an imitator of Grassineau made a brief summary,[1] but both of these treatises merely illustrate the fact that history is, for the early eighteenth century, merely a continued effort to compare " Antient " with " Modern Musick."[2] To understand the eighteenth-century

[1] " Music has been always esteemed one of the most agreeable and rational Diversions Mankind cou'd be blest with, and is now become so general throughout the greatest Part of Europe, that almost every one is a Judge of Fine Air and True Harmony: —

" To render the Work compleat I have collected a short History of Music showing its Rise and Progress with several Remarkable Incidents, wherein I flatter myself, I have given some Satisfaction to the Learned and all others who are desirous to Know the Origin of this Noble Science, and what Esteem it has met with from all Nations in all Ages.

" The most Ancient System of Music that we have any account of, is reported to have been invented by the Greeks, about two Thousand Years after the Creation." [13].

After twenty pages of theoretical discussion culled, as the title confesses, from old authors, the compiler concludes as follows: " Many more important observations might be made upon this Subject, but I think this Sufficient to show what the Ancients meant by their Moods, and how We ought to reason about them, according to the Practice of Modern Music."

[2] One exception may be noted. In 1728, the Hon. Roger North wrote his *Memoires of Musick* [11]. This work was not published until 1846, but Dr. Burney had access to the manuscript and quotes it frequently in his *General History* [26]. North seems to have been the first to recognize the merits of old English musicians whose works had been neglected. He finds the Quarrel futile, because " in matters of taste, there is no criterion of better or worse " (p. 3). He found origins, not in legendary invention, but in the use of spoken language (p. 7). He feels very certain, however, that the first interval was that of the perfect fourth; that in " early times the cycle of all the alterations was confined to that interval."

A N
O D E

ON THE
Power of MUSICK,
Inscrib'd to
Mr. MALCOLM,
AS A
Monument of Friendship,
By Mr. MITCHELL.

I.

WHEN *Nature* yet in *Embrio* lay,
  Ere Things began to be,
 The ALMIGHTY from eternal Day
  Spoke loud his deep Decree:
The Voice was tuneful as his Love,
 At which Creation sprung,
And all th' *Angelick* Hosts above
 The Morning Anthem sung.

    a 2   II. At

FROM A LAUDATORY PREFACE TO ALEXANDER MALCOLM'S "TREATISE OF
MUSICK, SPECULATIVE, PRACTICAL AND HISTORICAL," 1721

literature, brief reference is necessary, therefore, to some Latin treatises of the century previous.

One year before the birth of Purcell, in 1657, Dr. John Wallis published his *Tractatus elenchticus adversus Marci Meibomii dialogum de proportionibus.* In 1662 he published his *Appendix* to Ptolemy's *Harmonies.* His comparison of modern and ancient music favored the former, supporting Zarlino. The Ancient-Modern Quarrel was slow in coming to England, but once arrived it goes on well into the eighteenth century. It even supplies the motive for Sir John Hawkins' history, in 1776.[3] Two seventeenth-century writers in particular aroused the ire of Hawkins and spurred him to write in defence of the Moderns. The first was a Hollander, Isaac Vossius, who died in Windsor during the year of the Bloodless Revolution (1688). In 1673 he published *De Poematum cantu et viribus rhythmi,* in which he attributes the efficacy of ancient music to its rhythm.

"According to this opinion there was no occasion for mellifluous sounds, or lengthened tones; a drum, a cymbal, or the violent strokes of the Curetes, and Salii, on their shields, as they would have marked the time more articulately, so they would have produced more miraculous effects than the sweetest voice, or the most polished instrument." [4]

Long before Hawkins, Alexander Malcolm, in his *Treatise of Musick,* had also taken issue with Vossius thus:

"That it (Rhythm) gives life to Musick, especially the Pathetick, will not be denied . . . but to make it the whole is perhaps attributing more than is its due: I rather reckon the Words and Sense of what's sung the principal Ingredient; and the other a noble Servant to them, for raising and keeping up the Attention, because of the natural pleasure attached to the Sensations." [10], p. 602.

The second defender of the Ancients was Sir William Temple. On the first page of Hawkins' history, Temple's own words are quoted to prove that when it came to an argument over the merits of ancient music, there was no historical data available. Sir William's lament, often quoted from his "Essay on Ancient and Modern Learning" (1690),[5] runs as follows:

---

[3] *A General History of the Science and Practice of Music* [27], London, 1776, 4 v.; 2nd ed., London, 1875, 2 v.

[4] [27], Vol. I, p. xxxiii.

[5] Reprinted in Spingarn's *Studies in the Seventeenth Century.*

"What are become of the charms of Musick, by which Men and Beasts, Fishes, Fowls and Serpents were so frequently Enchanted, and their very Natures changed; By which the Passions of men were raised to the greatest height and violence, and then as suddenly appeased, so as they might be justly said to be turned into Lyons or Lambs, into Wolves or into Harts, by the Power and Charms of this admirable Art? 'Tis agreed by the Learned that the Science of Musick, so admired of the Ancients, is wholly lost in the World, and that what we have now is made up out of certain Notes that fell into the fancy or observation of a poor *Fryar* in chanting his Mattins. So as those two Divine Excellencies of Musick and Poetry are grown in a manner to be little more, but the one Fidling, and the other Rhyming; and are indeed very worthy the ignorance of the Fryar and the barbarousness of the Goths that introduced them among us."

"What have we remaining of Magick," etc.

For a confident answer to all this, recall the title of the first history of music written in German, in the same year, by Printz, already cited:

"Historical description of the noble art of singing and playing in which the origin and discovery, progress and betterment, different uses, wonderful effects, many enemies, and the most famous exponents of the same are related and put forth in the shortest possible space, from the beginning of the world, down to our own day." [6].

Bach, Handel, Domenico Scarlatti, and Bishop Berkeley were then five years old, and Purcell had five more years to live. By 1721, Malcolm's treatise brands Temple's dictum "the poorest thing ever said." Malcolm goes on to say of the Quarrel:

"The fault with many of these contenders is that they fight with long weapons; I mean they keep the argument in generals, by which they make little more of it than some innocent Harangues and Flourishes of Rhetoric." [10], p. 570.

Hawkins' answer to Temple was as follows:

"Sir William Temple . . . has betrayed his ignorance of the subject in a comparison of the modern music with the ancient . . . notwithstanding that Palestrina, Bird, and Gibbons lived in the same century with himself." . . .

"The natural tendency of these reflections (on the miraculous powers of ancient music) is to draw on a comparison of the ancient with modern music; which latter, as it pretends to no such miraculous powers, has been thought by the ignorant to be so greatly inferior to the former, as scarce to deserve the name. In like manner do they judge of the characters of men, and the state of human manners at remote periods, when they compare the events of ancient history, the actions of heroes, and the wisdom of legislators, with those of modern times, inferring from thence a depravity of mankind, of which not the least trace is discernible." [27], "Preliminary Discourse."

Swift's satire, *The Battle of the Books,* written in 1697 and published in 1704, was another work inspired by Temple's essay. And as late as 1778 the question is of sufficient interest to warrant translation of a Spanish work on the subject.[6]

Meanwhile the Quarrel, in France, continued to be focused on the problems of opera, and the relative merits of French and Italian opera at that. In England opera came to be a matter of little importance. With the rising popularity of the ballad opera, Italian opera lost its hold on the public. This was partly due to the attitude of Dryden, Pope, Addison, Chesterfield, and others who ridiculed opera as a serious art form. It was also due to the tremendous concern over religious and moral problems, and the still-powerful Puritan influence. So while the French carried on the War of the Buffoons and the Gluckist-Piccinnist controversy and continued to write volumes[7] on opera, the English literature on music was more didactic in character, with arguments over the degeneration or progress of church music.

In 1706 Arthur Bedford published *Temple Musick, Or an Essay concerning the Method of singing the Psalms of David in the Temple: Wherein the music of our cathedrals is vindicated as con-*

---

[6] Feijos y Montenegro, Benito Jeronimo (1675–1764). *Three essays or discourses on the following subjects, a defence or vindication of the women, church music, a comparison between antient and modern music.* Translated from the Spanish of Feyjos; by a gentleman (John Brett), London, 1778.

[7] In addition to works by Voltaire and Rousseau already cited, see François de Castagnères, Abbé de Chateauneuf, *Dialogue sur la musique des anciens,* Paris, 1725. NY.

Other French works included: Pierre Jean Burette (1665–1747), *Dissertation, ou l'on fait voir, que les merveilleux effets, attribuez à la Musique des anciens, ne prouvent point, qu'elle fust aussi parfaite que la notre.* In *Académie des inscriptions et belles-lettres, Paris, Memoires.* Paris, 1729, tr. into Italian, Venezia, 1748. An *Essai sur la musique ancienne et moderne* [28] was compiled under the auspices of de la Borde, one of the *fermiers généraux* who was guillotined in the Terror. Among the contributors were Beche, one of three brothers in the King's Band. Abbé Roussier did the theoretical portion. Chapters VIII–X, Vol. III, on French musicians, include Lully and constitute one source of information on music in France in the seventeenth and eighteenth centuries. NY.

formable, not only to that of the primitive Christians, but also to the practice of the Church in all preceding.

After arguing that plainsong is identical with the music of the Jewish temple, he expounded his views on degeneration (1711) in *"The great abuse of Music: containing an account of the use and design of musick among the antient Jews, Greeks, Romans, and others; with their concern for and care to prevent the abuse thereof. And also an account of the immorality and profaneness, which is occasioned by the corruption of that most noble science in the present age."*

The question even came up as a pathological problem, as evidenced by Richard Brocklesby's *" Reflections on antient and modern musick, with the application to the cure of diseases. To which is subjoined, an essay to solve the question wherein consisted the difference of antient musick, from that of modern times."* London, 1749. The Rev. John Brown's important *Dissertation* (1763) is discussed later.

These and other minor works are only preludes to the first and most ambitious narrative histories ever attempted in English. These two remarkable items in classical English literature appeared in the same year (1776): *A General History of the Science and Practice of Music*, by Sir John Hawkins [27], and the first volume of Dr. Charles Burney's *A General History of Music* [26]. From each of these quotations have already been used.

These two works stand near the top of every bibliography of music history, and have been the models for all of our narrative histories since that time. No student of English letters in the eighteenth century should neglect them, because those who are captivated with the sonorous prose of Gibbon, the pompous style of Johnson, and the writings of the Scotch philosophers will enjoy the equally fascinating volumes of these two very different men.[8]

Burney's approach to music and its history was, at first, through the conventional channels — choir boy, organist, Doctor of Music at Oxford, and composer of some pieces in the accepted Italian style. But, unlike most of his colleagues, he enjoyed traveling. Thus,

---

[8] It is difficult to imagine, at this day, the tremendous interest in these two books. The popularity of Burney's history and the pun in the catch which condemned Hawkins to oblivion ("Burn 'is history!") is almost incredible until one realizes how seriously Londoners took literature of merit, and how vehement was popular partisanship. The complete reversal of the popular verdict was, again, as extreme as the latter was unjust.

in his trips to the continent, he got away from the narrow musical routine of the English cathedral organist. Burney's observations were published in two volumes entitled *The Present State of Music* in the countries visited. During all these travels his interest in the present state was leading him to gather all the materials he could find for study of the past.[9]

Burney's fundamental concept of music was vastly different from that of Hawkins. The former's assertion that music is " at best, but an amusement," ties in with his *dictum* that he would " rather be pronounced trivial than tiresome, for the labor of intense application should be reserved for more important concerns"!

On the other hand, Hawkins was author, lawyer, magistrate, biographer of Dr. Johnson, editor of Walton's *Compleat Angler,* and patron of the arts. He avows

" an early love of music, and having in his more advanced age not only become sensible of its worth, but arrived at a full conviction that it was intended by the Almighty for the delight of his rational principles, and a deduction of the progress of the science . . . another end is the set-tling music upon somewhat like a footing of equality with those, which, for other reasons than that, like music, they contribute to the delight of mankind, are termed the sister arts."

In contrast to Burney's aim " to fill up a . . . chasm in English literature," Hawkins desired to

" reprobate the vulgar notion that its [music's] ultimate end is to excite mirth; and, above all, to demonstrate that its principles are founded in certain general and universal laws, into which all that we discover in the material world, of *harmony, symmetry, proportion,* and *order,* seem to be resolvable."

Burney, on the other hand, believed that music is an

" innocent luxury, unnecessary indeed, to our existence, but a great grati-fication and improvement of the sense of hearing. It consists at present of Melody, Consonance, and Dissonance." I, xiii.

As for the origins of music, Burney believed that

" It is vain to endeavor to trace music from a higher source than the history of Egypt: a country, in which all human intelligence seems to have sprung. . . .

[9] See *The Present State of Music in France and Italy,* London, 1771–1772. Also, *The Present State of Music in Germany, the Netherlands, and the United Provinces,* London, 1773.

"The origin of every people . . . is involved in darkness, which no human light can penetrate; so that the fables which national vanity has given birth to, and the poetical fictions . . . are all the materials which high antiquity has left us to work upon. . . . However, as the fables . . . and wild imaginations have employed the wisest and most respectable writers of modern times, to digest into system, and to construe into something rational and probable, I shall not wholly neglect them." (Vol. I, 253–256).

The origins of song are "coeval with mankind. . . . This primitive and instinctive language (the voice of passion, weakened and made unintelligible by invention of words) is still retained by animals, while our artificial tongues are known only to the small part of the globe, where, after being learned with great pains, they are spoken." (Chap. VI).

From the foregoing it is apparent that Burney agreed with his contemporary Adam Smith that language was invented. He also paved the way for the Wagnerian disparagement of mere speech as an expression of emotion. But while denying the Holy Word, he retained respect for Holy Writ:

"It is not so much from the hope of being able to throw any new lights upon the music of this ancient people (the Hebrews) that I dedicate a chapter to the subject, as out of respect for the first and most venerable of all books, as well as for the religion of my country, and for that of the most enlightened part of mankind, which has been founded upon it."

Burney fought the eighteenth-century attitude which, in England and France, put poetry above music.

"When harmony was first cultivated . . . verse was so rude in the new and unpolished languages that it wanted some such sauce as harmony to make it palatable." . . . "And at the revival of letters, when poetry began again to flourish, *melody was so Gothic and devoid of graces* that good poets disdained its company or assistance; and we find that the verses of Dante, Ariosto, and Tasso supported themselves without the aid of music, as musical compositions in counterpoint have done without poetry. It was the cultivation of the musical drama that once more reconciled the two sisters; however, their leagues of friendship are but of short duration."

Here Burney took issue with Rousseau, who wrote in his article "Harmony" in the *Dictionnaire de la Musique:*

"When we reflect, that of all the people on the globe, none are without music and melody, yet only the Europeans have harmony and chords, when we reflect how many ages the world has endured, without any of the nations who have cultivated the polite arts knowing this harmony: that no animal, bird, or being in nature, produces any other sound than unison, or other music than mere melody; that neither the Oriental languages, so sonorous and musical, nor the ears of the Greeks, endowed with so much delicacy and sensibility . . . ever led that enthusiastic and voluptuous people to the discovery of our *harmony;* that their music, without it, has such prodigious effects, and ours such feeble ones with it; in short, when we think of its being reserved for a Northern people, whose coarse and obtuse organs are more touched with the *force* and *noise* of voices, than with the sweetness of accents, and melody of inflexions, to make this great discovery; it is hard to avoid suspecting that all our harmony, of which we are so vain, is only a Gothic and barbarous *invention,* which we should never have thought of, if we had been more sensitive to the real beauties of the art, and to music that is truly natural and affecting." (Tr. in [26], I, 146–147).

Burney seemed to prefer the Tudor Cathedral School to the Elizabethan madrigalists. Grudgingly he granted the merits of these compositions, which were "in nothing inferior to those of the best contemporary productions of the continent." But

"taste, rhythm, accent, and grace must not be sought for in this kind of music; indeed we might as well censure the Greeks for not writing in English, as the composers of the sixteenth century for their deficiency in these particulars, which having then no existence, even in idea, could not be wanted or expected." (III, 144).

Elizabethan instrumental music

"seems to partake of the pedantry and foppery of the times; eternal fugues upon dry and unmeaning subjects . . . dull divisions, and variations in which the change was generally from bad to worse. . . . Handel was perhaps the only Fughist exempt from pedantry. . . . Sebastian Bach, on the contrary, like Michelangelo in painting, disdained facility so much, that his genius never stooped to the easy and graceful." (III, 110).

It is in just such passages as the above that Burney voiced the dogma of eighteenth-century taste. Melody, if "Gothic," was "devoid of graces." And when polyphonic music was pitied for its want of "taste, rhythm, accent, and grace," he referred to the taste, rhythm, accent, and grace of the Italian metrical aria.[10] Roger

---

[10] For a discussion of eighteenth-century notions of symmetry in music, see pp. 221–222.

North had complained that sixteenth-century polyphony had no
" variety," or " air." Because it did not have marked accent at the
beginning of each measure, it was for him all " plain-song musick,"
comparable to the "confused singing of birds in a grove," something "monstrous and insupportable" if sung or played for a
whole evening ([11], pp. 70–72).

But Burney sought for regularity, not only in meter and measure
(which he and many others since confused with rhythm) but also
in " The Scale of Nature," the major scale. Thus he was puzzled by

"those wild and irregular melodies which come within the description
of *National Music* . . . if not more ancient than the scale ascribed to
Guido, (they) were certainly formed without its assistance, as we may
judge by the little attention paid to Keys, and the awkward difficulties
to which those are subject who attempt to clothe them with Harmony.
This kind of artless music is best learned in the nursery and the street.
Real music arises from a complete scale [11] under the guidance of such
rules of art as successful cultivation has rendered respectable and worthy
of imitation." (II, 220).

After such judgments, therefore, it is not surprising to find
Baroque music condemned for violation of eighteenth-century rules:

"Monteverde's ' violations of fundamental rules and prohibitions ' and
his ' anticipations ' are beyond my comprehension." (IV, 28–29).

Volume IV was devoted, largely, to the glories of Italy. Here we
have the old British attitude toward music as something luxurious,
a commodity to be imported:

"The ancient Romans had the fine arts and eminent artists from
Greece; the modern Romans, in return, supply the rest of Europe with
painting, sculpture, and music. This last is a *manufacture* in Italy, that
feeds and enriches a large portion of the people; and it is no more a
disgrace to a mercantile country to import it than wine, tea, or any
other product from remote parts of the world (p. 221) . . . but the
vocal music of Italy can only be heard in its perfection when sung in
its own language and by its own natives."

In this connection, note Burney's English inferiority complex,
with reference to Handel:

[11] See the discussion of " Origins in Scales " on pp. 217–221. Also note that to
Burney " National Music " means folk music.

"we must take a melancholy leave of his regency; (after he ceased writing operas) for after this period, having no concern in the composition or conduct of Italian opera, he never set any other words than English, and those wholly confined to sacred subjects." Burney shows no appreciation of Handel's oratorios.

Brief mention is made of the Mannheim School, and the *Symphonies,* showing Burney's interest in " The Present State of Music " on the continent:

"a new species of compositions . . . at which there was an outcry, as usual, against innovation, by those who wish to keep music stationary. . . . But . . . the variety, taste, spirit, and new effects produced by control and the use of crescendo and diminuendo . . . had been of more service to instrumental music in a few years than all the dull and servile imitations of Corelli, Geminiani, and Handel had been in half a century."

This last paragraph is an improvement over the treatment of contemporary music by Hawkins, who ended his book with Handel and Geminiani, with no reference whatever to the new developments in Germany at that time. Hawkins stated that in view of music's

" pre-eminence over many sciences and faculties, we are convinced of the stability of its principles, and are therefore at a loss for the reasons why . . . novelty in music . . . or the love of variety should so possess the majority of hearers, as almost to leave it a question whether or no it has any principles at all." [27], I, 83.

Thus, Hawkins, who claims to be upholding the Moderns, has no interest whatever in the novelty and variety of music produced in his own present. No mention is made of the important developments going on in Germany, very little of Bach, and nothing concerning the sons of Sebastian. That is curious to us today, for whom the word "moderns" means contemporaries, but references to *Modern Music* still meant what they had meant in the sixteenth century, namely, music made since the Dark Ages, music distinct from the music of antiquity. As for Burney, he was trained to regard the harmony instruction founded by Rameau in the shadow of French absolutism as an infallible guide to the evaluation of the music of the past. And as a critic who loved " grace and elegance, symmetry, order, and naturalness," he was thoroughly representative of eighteenth-century taste.

II. THE COMPARATIVE CLASSIFICATION OF CULTURAL STAGES

In discussing Père Lafitau's *Manners of the American Savages Compared to the Manners of Primitive Times* (1724), Preserved Smith says that this eighteenth-century theorist "with really brilliant insight compares the Indians to the people of the Age of Homer and of Moses," and that he deserves the praise of having been the first to point out the real parallel between ancient and contemporary barbarism.[12] In the first place, grave doubts may be cast upon that "real parallel," and in the second place, Lafitau was not the first to point it out. Thomas Hobbes (*Leviathan,* 1651) seems to have accepted the validity of such a parallel, and John Locke, in 1690, had said that America "is still a pattern of the first ages in Asia and Europe."[13]

But one might readily believe in Père Lafitau's priority, because his influence was great, particularly in the realm of music history and musical ethnology. In 1763, strongly influenced by Lafitau, John Brown published the first "complete" picture of music history printed in English: *A Dissertation on the Rise, Union and Power, the Progressions, Separations, and Corruptions of Poetry and Music* [20]. The fundamental assumption, borrowed from Lafitau, is stated at the beginning:

"Whatever is founded in such Passions and Principles of Action as are common to the whole race of Man, will be most effectually investigated, as to its *Origin and Progress,* by viewing Man in his savage, or uncultivated State." (Sec. IV, pp. 36–46).

Thirty-six stages are traced, from the early unity of melody, dance, and song in one person to its perfection in Greek society; then downward, by degeneration, to the complete separation of melody, dance, and poetry at the present day.

Brown's dissertation offers an excellent example of an eighteenth-century history written according to the "fixed species" concept of an atomistic developmental series, in a Chain of Being. "Modern" historiography, later on, was hailed as a great improvement when each stage was seen, in the light of "evolution," to be an unfolding

---

[12] *A History of Modern Culture*, N. Y., Holt, 1930, Vol. II, p. 105.
[13] In *Of Civil Government,* in his *Works,* Vol. 4 (12th ed.), London, 1824, pp. 399, 402. Fontenelle, Père Alexandre, and de la Créquinière are also cited as having worked on this theory before Lafitau. See Teggart, *Theory of History,* as cited, pp. 88–91.

from the one previous. One hundred and twenty-five years later, another clergyman, Rowbotham, is to show how this takes place, according to the biological analogy.

Brown's own observations on the state of music in colonial and conquered societies are of more value than his theory of stages. His dissertation was quite unique and more scholarly than a later work, also by a divine, Richard Eastcott. The latter shares Brown's theory of origins, but states frankly that

" These sketches are by no means intended for persons of science; for otherwise, if they should induce the juvenile reader to peruse works of real character and known respectability, his end will be fully answered . . . those young ladies, who receive their education at public academies, may have an opportunity of being slightly acquainted with the history of an art, in which many of them spend a considerable part of their time in endeavoring to excel. . . .

" Among the ancients, the priest, the prophet, the poet and the musician were frequently united in the same person.

" The miraculous and medicinal powers attributed to music, and its effects on the human passions, and on the animal world, have been subjects of the author's inquiry, and though investigation may in a great measure check the enthusiasm of hyperbolical praises, yet he doubts not of establishing its utility upon a foundation not to be overturned by the flashes of ill-timed wit, or the arbitrary decisions of cynical severity."— From the Preface [33].

III. PROGRESS AND POETRY

Evolution was an eighteenth-century theory formulated in poetry as well as in science, while some histories of music were still assuming cosmic origins. It is not surprising, therefore, that the first Romantic historian in Germany, J. N. Forkel [30], should develop the theory already current in England concerning the original and organic union of poetry and music. Forkel lived in the *Sturm und Drang* period, was an ardent admirer and biographer of Bach, and a Doctor of Philosophy at Göttingen. The latter fact probably explains his rationalization of the divine-origin theory and his implicit belief in progress, an idea manifest in the Göttingen school of historians.[14]

---

[14] Forkel's interests in music and poetry are contemporaneous with the researches of Eximeno [24], whose work has already been discussed in Ch. 3.

Music, the language of the emotions, has a history that is exactly parallel to that of language, and the origins of both are identical. "Music is inborn in man, and is as necessary a part of his system as language."

Forkel finds two great divisions of music modifying the medieval tradition: grammar and rhetoric. Musical grammar has further divisions. But progress is observable in three periods, defined in terms of psychology and esthetics, rather than in historical time. The highest culmination of musical grammar is *harmony;* the peak of rhetoric's development is the fugue. Progress is as real in music as in Nature's movement from source to lake, river, and ocean, and it can be observed, as in the ages of man. (For further discussion of Forkel's periodization, see pp. 263–264.)

Forkel would probably have regarded Bach as the greatest composer, at this peak. Having reached Bach, it would have been interesting to see what sort of movement he would have traced from Bach to Haydn. That may have bothered him. At any rate, the *Allgemeine Geschichte der Musik* gets no farther than the first half of the sixteenth century.

Forkel was also a biographer of Bach, and was one of the few writers of the day who recognized that master's genius. Many have wished that he had spent more time on this task than on the theories developed in his history. Another contribution was his great bibliography, previously cited.

Forkel was no such dilettante as Brown or Eastcott, and condemns Burney for regarding the divine art of music as an innocent amusement. But, with Burney, he shares the eighteenth-century abhorrence of the Gothic "barbarities" of composers he did not understand, except as products of an early stage.

In 1825 Zelter wrote to Goethe as follows:

"Forkel was Doctor of Philosophy and Doctor of Music at the same time, but all of his life long came into direct touch with neither of them, having begun a history of music and then stopped right at the point where history, for us, can begin."

The journalistic type of historiographical writing associated with Mattheson was carried on in the mid-eighteenth century by F. W. Marpurg. His *Beyträge* [16] were originally published in thirty brief installments, and contain much information about the music of his own day. His history, *Kritische Einleitung* [18], deals only with ancient music and much attention is given to the old question as to whether the Greeks practiced harmony.

A new departure was initiated by the pedagogue Kalkbrenner, at the end of the century [32]. His little condensation of music history was the first of many new instruction texts to be written for young people. But whereas Calvisius had written his brief sketch in 1600 for theory and composition students, this new type, of presentation was for students of instrumental music. Kalkbrenner endeavored to inspire the latter with biographies of great musicians, with a leaning toward the sacred-origin theory. The relationship between the great-man theory and the divine-origin theory will be discussed in the next chapter as one of the manifestations of the Romantic period.

But at the beginning of the nineteenth century Burney and Hawkins loomed so large that the history of music seemed to be a subject that had been exhausted. For a long time many a new history of music was a mere scissors-and-paste job, in which writers did not always bother to say " according to Burney " . . . or " according to Hawkins." Nor was the insatiable curiosity of eighteenth-century writers duplicated for many years to come. No musicological research worthy of the name was carried on from Forkel's history in 1788 to Kiesewetter's in 1834 — roughly equivalent to the period of Beethoven's creative life.

Eighteenth-century histories of music were on the whole objective studies which attempted rational classification into neat divisions or stages. They contained very little of the mysticism that was to color nineteenth-century works, but laid down emphatic dogma as to what was " natural and simple and graceful." The continuance of these notions gave rise, as we shall see, to nineteenth-century conflicts over the definition of beauty.

The English legacy included some unfortunate prejudices. Percy Scholes[15] has indicted the puritanism of the English gentlemen who kept music down more effectively than did the Puritans themselves. Charles Burney's puritanism was of this harmful sort. Romantic music was to come from countries where composers were encouraged at home.

[15] *The Puritans and Music*, Oxford Press, 1934.

CHAPTER 6

THE ROMANTIC ERA (1800-1850)

I. THE GREAT-MAN THEORY

" Puissant Palestrina, vieux maître, vieux génie,
Je vous salue ici, *père de l'harmonie!*
Car ainsi qu'un grand fleuve ou boivent les humains
Toute cette musique a coulé de vos mains."— Victor Hugo

SOME nineteenth-century histories have already been cited, in Chapter 3, to show the persistence of ecclesiastical traditions which upheld the theory of music's divine origins. In the early part of the century, most of the general histories are influenced by this theory; none could ignore it entirely. This was only natural, during the Romantic period, at a time when Christianity was being rehabilitated by Chateaubriand and other apologists who found beauty, as well as truth, in religion.[1] It cannot be emphasized too strongly that the mainspring of the Romantic movement was the restoration of Christian belief. Rationalism had resulted in revolution and terror; faith in revelation began to take its place.

In music histories which were inspired by purely secular interests, the divine-origin theory survived as an explanation of the origins of genius. Mueller's history has already been quoted on this score, and many similar examples could be cited.

Eighteenth-century rationalists had extolled early musicians as *inventors*,[2] men who had advanced the art and science of music because of their reasoning powers, and as a result of their conscious

[1] " The appeal (of Chateaubriand's *Génie du Christianisme*) did not lie in its logic, it lay in the appreciation of Christianity from a new point of view. He approached it in the spirit of an artist, as an aesthete, not as a philosopher, and insofar as he proved anything he proved that Christianity is valuable because it is beautiful, not because it is true."— Bury, *The Idea of Progress*, 4th ed., 1928, pp. 264–265.

[2] For frequent use of this term, see Burney [26], especially in early chapters of Vol. I. But Burney decries efforts to trace back an invention to one single man: " Few persons who speak or write on the subject of the present system of music

efforts. But with the revival of belief in a revealed, rather than an invented, word, historians began to return to supernatural explanations. G. Baini, in 1828, referred to Palestrina as "the amanuensis of God," [3] and frequent references to "God-given genius" were not figures of speech, but statements of "historical fact." At any rate, the history of music began to be written more and more in terms of great names, those of the leaders in musical thought upon whom the gods or the muse had smiled at birth. In short, the great-man theory was the guiding concept for the music histories of this period, just as it was the inspiration for other forms of art. At the Paris Opéra, virtuosi were depicting the heroes of history — Wilhelm Tell, Rienzi, The Huguenots, The Prophet (John of Leyden), Masaniello, Cortez, Vasco da Gama, and hosts of others; Sir Walter Scott had increased the vogue of the historical novel; Thomas Carlyle had fired the imagination with his vivid word-picture of the French Revolution, and Victor Hugo had just opened the militant phase of the Romantic movement with his *Cromwell,* when Georg Kiesewetter wrote his *History of the Modern Music of Western Europe.* [4] For Kiesewetter, the great man dictated the epoch. He took issue with older schemes of historical division, and refused to allow that the history of musical art had anything to do with the history of anything else:

"The different authors who have hitherto devoted their labors to the history of music have generally divided it according to historical periods, or to the periods of the reign of native kings; some also according to countries and provinces, and partly to the so-called schools. I am of opinion that *the art in its own changes ought to form historical periods for itself,* which usually differ from those of universal history, and have, in fact, nothing in common with the particular periods of various states: that *music, a general blessing to mankind, has no connection with the political divisions of kingdoms;* and that the divisions of it into schools of art . . . would prove, in the history of music, to be the most useless and deceitful of all. . . .

---

express the least doubt of *Counterpoint* having been invented by Guido. . . . But there is nothing more difficult than to fix such an invention as this upon any individual; an art utterly incapable of being brought to any degree of perfection, but by a slow and gradual improvement, and the successive efforts of ingenious men during several centuries, must have been trivial and inconsiderable in its infancy; and the first attempt at its use necessarily circumscribed and clumsy." (Book II, Ch. II.)

[3] *Memorie storie-critiche della vita e delle opere di G. Palestrina,* Rome, 1828.

[4] For Kiesewetter "modern" music still meant music since the late Christian era.

"But even the division into certain great periods of the art does not appear to me to be a very happy one for its history. . . .

"The system, therefore, which appeared to me to be the best was the division of the history of music into *epochs,* not only as being the best attested, but as the most simple, natural, and authentic. *Each of these epochs should be named after one of the most celebrated men of his time* — of him, for instance, *who possessed the greatest influence* over the taste of his contemporaries in their cultivation of the art, and who . . . may have demonstrably promoted the art to a higher degree of perfection." [47], English ed., pp. 26, 27.

Now when Kiesewetter claims "that the art in its own changes ought to form historical periods for itself," he evidently refers implicitly to the supernatural origins of music, because at the very beginning of his work he settles the ancient-modern controversy on a religious assumption:

"The ancient Greek music may be described as having died in its infancy, a lovely child indeed, but incapable of reaching maturity; and so far as mankind was concerned, its decay was not a loss to be deplored.

"Modern music — if at its origin it may be so termed — had arisen unnoticed in lowly huts and secret caves, . . . *It formed itself* in the assemblies of the early Christians . . . who had a natural horror of everything connected with the heathen." (pp. 1–3).

In other words, music given to the Greeks by their gods was necessarily short-lived; but music which formed itself in the worship of the Christian God was destined to progress to perfection, with the aid of divinely inspired genius; at the end of Kiesewetter's history, the author could state his belief that

". . . this fairest of the arts has, through a series of epochs, with slow, yet certain progress, gradually arrived at that perfection which we all believe that it has now attained." (p. 248).[5]

Victor Hugo, in his *Preface to Cromwell,* in 1827, had explained the demise of Greek religion and birth of Christianity in the following passage:

"A spiritual religion, supplanting the material and external paganism, makes its way to the heart of the ancient society, kills it, and de-

---

[5] Chapter 10 will study the meaning of "progress" as "development." The concept of progress through epochs is as old as St. Augustine. It had been revived for Kiesewetter by such men as Condorcet (*Sketch for an Historical Picture of the Progress of the Human Mind,* 1794) and Herder (*The Destiny of Man,* 1800).

posits, in that corpse of a decrepit civilization, the germ of modern civilization." [6]

Thus progress was, for the Christian nations, a necessary and inevitable process of development of inborn potentialities. For Kiesewetter, the law of progress is demonstrated by the succession of epochs advocated above, each named after a composer, the greatest of his period, and greater than the leader of the epoch preceding.

One difficulty lies in the fact that historians do not agree as to who these leaders are. For Kiesewetter, the epochal composers included Willaert, Carissimi, A. Scarlatti, Leo, and Durante. Bach and Handel, not mentioned as leaders at all, are now placed far above Leo and Durante in modern histories; Kiesewetter's favorites, on the other hand, have sunk into an oblivion which they do not deserve. Romain Rolland says, truly, in extolling the merits of old musicians long forgotten, that

" History is the most partial of the sciences. When it becomes enamored of a man, it loves him jealously; it will not even hear of others." [223], Ch. V.

Since Kiesewetter the great-man theory has ruled in many cases that, somehow, " Genius alone is absolute; everything else is relative, impermanent, unessential." [246].

But although we can never get entirely away from the great-man theory, the Romanticists went too far in treating it as an absolute.

The great *Biographie universelle*, by Fétis, has already been cited; this author took issue with Kiesewetter's attempt to select leaders of epochs, and set out to provide data concerning *all* composers deemed worthy of mention. At the front of this dictionary of biography, Fétis placed a *Résumé philosophique* which aims to make a summary of history, prefatory not only to this particular work, but also to the labors on his history which appeared years later.

When Fétis used the term *philosophique,* he did so merely to differentiate this historical *résumé* from the main body of his work,

---

[6] *The Harvard Classics,* N. Y., 1909, Vol. 39, p. 364. Hugo also supplements the great-man theory by showing why modern genius is superior: " It is of the fruitful union of the grotesque and sublime types that modern genius is born, so complex, so diverse in its forms, so inexhaustible in its creations, and therein directly opposed to the uniform simplicity of the genius of the ancients . . . as a means of contrast with the sublime, the grotesque is, in our view, the richest source that nature can offer art."— As cited, p. 366.

which consists of biographies in alphabetical order. This *résumé* was written to show that he had some complete picture in view other than the discrete facts treated by a dictionary.

Fétis' absorbing interest in the music of extra-European nations indicates that he would probably devote all his time to comparative musicology, were he alive today. About two thirds of this *résumé* is devoted to primitive and exotic music before he embarks upon a review of medieval music. Only the last forty pages are devoted to "The Modern Era" (from the sixteenth century).

Fétis' contribution here marks a step in advance, if we remember the eighteenth-century contempt for the "barbarous" music of non-Europeans. He cites Villoteau, who found, when a member of Bonaparte's staff in Egypt, that music which sounded "out of tune" was, in reality, an art product which utilized entirely different divisions of the octave, intervals obtainable on instruments of novel construction.

Fétis feels somehow that these differences make history, but he makes no attempt to link them together in "stages of development." His contemporary, Comte, was working on his formulation of the comparative method at that time, and in the Preface to the second edition, in 1873, the influence of this becomes fully apparent.

Biography, at any rate, became the keystone of music history; but there were those who began to see that this necessary ingredient was not enough, that a biography is inadequate unless the composer's music is available — hence the great credit that is due men like Carl von Winterfeld, already mentioned. Winterfeld was an historian of church music, but spent his efforts in collecting the actual music of the past, without romantic biography for its own sake, and without speculations concerning origins.[7]

All in all, the general dependence on the great-man theory is understandable in view of the new status of the musician. Beginning with Beethoven, composers had to make their own way in the world as never before. Aristocratic patronage of music ceased after the Revolution and the composer came to be more dependent upon the favor of the public and upon engagements and commissions. The successful composer really was a great man in the popular sense and may still be so regarded. There are also inexplicable

---

[7] Carl G. A. von Winterfeld, after another study of Palestrina in 1832, published *Johannes Gabrieli und sein Zeitalter* (1834) and his great 3-vol. work, *Der evangelische Kirchengesang und sein Verhältnis zur Kunst des Tonsatzes*, in 1843–1847.

factors in genius which elude analysis. The great-man theory will never be entirely superseded. Further discussion of genius theories will be found later in Chapter 9, III.

II. THE ORGANIC HYPOTHESIS AND TRIUNE THEORIES

Objecting to the type of historical approach undertaken by Kiesewetter and Fétis, another school was attempting to formulate a philosophy of history which would see the subject as a whole, with individual men and single events sinking into insignificance. Hegel had pictured the march of the human spirit across the centuries in his lectures at the University of Berlin, during the first quarter of the century.[8]

"The theory was finally to emerge that art and literature, like laws and institutions, are an expression of society and therefore inextricably linked with other elements of social development — a theory which, it may be observed, while it has discredited the habit of considering works of art in a vacuum, dateless and detached, . . . leaves the aesthetic problem much where it was." [9]

In other words, the organic hypothesis, while glimpsing a fundamental truth, was too vague and mystic to make this truth helpful to the science of history. It is true that arts, customs, and institutions are interdependent, but the demonstration of that truth is only possible after minute research into comparative histories. The Romanticists merely proclaimed the truth, and the demonstration was purely logical, rather than scientific. Their logic was based upon premises derived entirely from analogy, one of the most dangerous of our useful modes of thought.

Pascal had said, in 1647, that

"the whole succession of men, throughout the course of so many centuries should be envisaged as the life of a single man who persists forever and learns continually." [10]

This dictum was of the greatest importance in Romantic philosophies of history; Auguste Comte made this biological analogy the cornerstone of his system, in an attempt to delineate the progress

[8] *Lectures on the Philosophy of History*, tr. from the 3rd German ed., by J. Sibree, London, 1894, 1900.

[9] Bury, *The Idea of Progress*, pp. 124–125.

[10] From a "Fragment of a Treatise on the Vacuum," among the *Opuscules*, in *Works*, Vol. II, tr. by O. W. Wight, N. Y., 1859.

of knowledge, and so did Hegel in his philosophy of history. For Hegel, " each particular national genius is to be treated as only one individual in the process of universal history," and " a single principle " is to be attributed to each of the people chosen to be " dominant for a given epoch in the world's history." [11]

For Hegel " the history of the world travels from east to west, for Europe is absolutely the end of history, Asia the beginning." The childhood of the human spirit was in the Orient, therefore; the boyhood, in Central Asia; adolescence was reached in Greece, manhood in Rome, and maturity and full strength in the German state of the early nineteenth century.

Auguste Comte, in his *Philosophie positive* (1830–1842), adopted a similar method, but instead of five ages of man, he postulated a great Law of Three Stages in his organic " view of the progressive course of the human *mind,* regarded as a whole ":

" From the study of the development of human intelligence in all directions, and through all times, the discovery arises of a great fundamental law . . . the law is this: that each of our leading conceptions, each branch of our knowledge, passes successively through three different theoretical conditions: the *theological,* or fictitious; the *metaphysical,* or abstract; and the *scientific,* or positive." [12]

But even before Comte made this Law of the Three Stages the cornerstone of his new science of sociology, it had appeared in the philosophies of music history, and of the history of literature. In 1827, there appeared Victor Hugo's famous *Preface to Cromwell,* and a music history by Karl Christian Friedrich Krause [41]. This history is now forgotten, but it is based upon the same assumptions used by Hugo and Comte. According to Krause, the three ages of man are analogous to the three periods of music history — Ancient, Christian, and Modern. And the three kinds of music that evolved in those periods, respectively, were melody, polyphony, and harmony.

In antiquity, the childhood of music, only simple, unadorned melody was known, as is the case today with such people as the Hindus, Chinese, Persians, and Arabs, who have not yet progressed beyond the childhood stage.

[11] Hegel, *Grundlinien der Philosophie des Rechts,* tr. as *Philosophy of Right,* by S. W. Dyde, London, 1896, pp. 346–347.

[12] *The Positive Philosophy,* freely translated and condensed by Harriet Martineau, 1853, Vol. I, Introduction, Ch. I.

In the Christian era, the youth of music, religion came into its own, with many-voiced praises to God, the organ, and other instruments. Late in the second period, the glories of music came to fruition in individual genius.

Now, in the manhood of music, our music expresses the "budding harmony of the whole life of mankind." (pp. 44–47).

This is perhaps the first work to draw parallels between artists and musicians. Handel is likened to Michelangelo, but Beethoven is worthy of that honor in even higher degree, since he "has led music to heights which cannot be surpassed unless new realms and media of expression are opened up."

Victor Hugo's *Preface,* that same year, the year in which Beethoven died, made use of this same Law of Three Stages, and the analogy is not stated as such, but as a fact:

"Let us set out from a fact. The same type of civilization, or to use a more exact, though more extended expression, the same society, has not always inhabited the earth. The human race, as a whole, has grown, has developed, has matured, like one of ourselves. It was once a child, it was once a man; we are now looking on at its impressive old age.— Behold then three great successive orders of things in civilization, from its origin to our days. Now as poetry is always superposed upon society, we propose to try to demonstrate, from the form of its society, what the character of the poetry must have been in those three great ages of the world — primitive times, ancient times, modern times." [13]

In spite of the "fact" that "poetry is always superposed upon society," the poet declares that

"In primitive times, when man awakens in a world that is newly created, poetry awakes with him. In the face of the marvellous things that dazzle and intoxicate him, his first speech is simply a hymn."

This word-symphony [14] then goes on to demonstrate further "facts"— that the three stages of social evolution, patriarchal, theocratic, and national, are marked by three corresponding types of poetry: *lyric, epic,* and *dramatic.* About twenty different applications of this Law of Three Stages appear in a few pages: the three ages of history, corresponding to the three ages of man, witness the prog-

[13] Hugo, *Preface to Cromwell,* Harvard Classics, Vol. 39, p. 356.

[14] The historical-esthetic parallel that comes to mind here is the development of Romantic program music. Analogy plays a part in this type of music, with its literary suggestion which goes beyond the Classical ideal of form. The Tone Poem of Liszt was an attempt to paraphrase or reproduce poetry in musical language.

ress of the family and community to the tribe and to the nation; of the lake to the stream and to the ocean; of literature from the Bible to Homer and then to Shakespeare; of art from crude beginnings to the monumental and then to the decorative and grotesque, and so on.

And while Comte was writing his great work, J. M. Fischer explained the evolution of the art in these terms:

"Just as the evolution of Humanity from the state of Nature only progresses gradually, by stages, up to civilization, so also progress Art and Science, the outstanding manifestations of that Progress. . . . Similarly the principal evolutionary periods of Music coincide with the most noteworthy Epochs in the History of Mankind." These three Epochs are:
1. Antiquity — Simplicity — Pure melody.
2. The Christian Era — Harmony — Brotherhood (*Gemeinschaft*).
3. Modern Era — Many-sided union of Harmony and Counterpoint [50].

So firmly entrenched is this organic explanation of the history of music, that it still appears on the opening pages of the *Oxford History of Music* [146]:

"The phenomena may be seen as arranging themselves in three main divisions or periods . . . first in which the beauty to be obtained from the material is perceived only as consisting of consecutive simple sounds; second . . . a new beauty to be obtained by combining individual utterances simultaneously . . . separate melodies preserve a relative independence; the outcome is a complete union maintained upon the principle of absolute equality . . . this is Polyphony.

"The third, or strictly harmonic period, in which we now·are, represents the phase in which the principle of equality between the individual and the collective elements has been abandoned . . . melody . . . is entirely controlled by harmonic considerations." (Intro., Vol. I).

The great confidence placed in the division of history into three parts was not merely an attempt to get away from the vague divisions of Ancient and Modern. Laws of three, the fundamental significance of the triad in nature, and the doctrine of unity in a trinity are old and familiar, and their revival in the Romantic period need not occasion surprise:

"As the Pythagoreans say, the world and all that is in it is determined by the number three, since beginning and middle and end give the number of an 'all,' and the number they give is the triad. And so, having taken these three from nature (so to speak) as laws of it, we make further use of the number three in the worship of the gods. Further, we use the terms in practice in this way. Of two things, or men, we say 'both,' but not 'all'; three is the first number to which the term 'all' has been appropriated."— Aristotle, *De Caelo,* Book I, 1. (Oxford ed.; Vol. II.)

The triad thus became the basic concept of social classification, as in Plato's *Republic.* Not only three classes, but three powers in the individual and social body are to be reconciled; and three virtues are to be realized through the use of reason. The number three also offers the most convenient suggestion of choice between extremes. (Note the Platonic-Aristotelian studies of the three forms of government, and Aristotle's insistence upon the value of the mean, or middle course, in states and in education.— *Politics,* IV, ii; v. 9; VIII, 6, 7.)

A summary of these concepts of the triad, applied to social science, is found in the last paragraphs of Jean Bodin, *Six Books of a Commonweale,* tr. by Richard Knolles, London, 1606:

" And as for the motion or moving of the celestiall spheres we see that God hath made one motion equall, which is the swift motion of the superiour sphere: and another unequall, which is the motion of the planets (contrarie unto the former) and the third the motion of trepidation, which containeth and bindeth together both the one and the other. And so if we should enter into the particular nature of other worldly creatures also, we should find a perpetuall Harmonicall bond, which uniteth the extreames by indissoluble meanes, taking yet part both of the one and of the other. Which coherence is neither agreeable unto Arithmeticall nor Geometricall, but even proper unto the Harmonicall proportion onely; wherein the sweetnesse of the consent consisteth in tunes aptly mixed together; and the harsh discord, when as the tunes are such as cannot fitly be mingled together. So we see the earth and stones to be as it were joyned together by clay and chaulke, as in meane betwixt both; and so betwixt the stones and metals, the Marcasites, the Calamites, and other divers kinds of mineral stones to grow. So stones and plants also to be joined together by divers kinds of Corall: . . . Betwixt plants and living creatures, the Zoöphytes, or Plantbeasts, which have feeling and motion, and yet take life by the roots whereby they grow. And againe . . . those which they call *Amphibia,* or creatures living by land and water both: . . . so betwixt men and beasts, are to be seene apes and munkies; except we shall with Plato agree, who placed a woman in the middle betwixt man and beast. And so betwixt beasts and angels God hath placed man, who is in part mortall, and in part immortall: binding also this elementarie world, with the heavens or the celestiall world, by the ethereall region. . . ."

". . . And as he himselfe being of an infinit force and power ruleth over angels, so also the angels over man, men over beasts, the soule over the bodie, the man over the woman, reason over affection: And so every good thing commaunding over that which is worse, with a certaine combining of powers keepeth all things under most right and lawful commands. Wherefore what *the unity is in numbers,* the understanding in the powers of the soule, and the center in a circle: so likewise in this world that most mightie king, in unitie simple, *in nature indivisible,* in puritie most holy, exalted farre above the fabrike of the celestiall spheres, joining this elementarie world with the celestiall and intelligible heavens: with a certain secure care preserveth from distruction *this triple world,* bound together with a most sweet and harmonious consent."

The Trinitarian concept of Three in One is stated by Plato thus:

" It is not possible for two things to be united without a third; for they both need a bond between them which shall join them both. The best of bonds is that which makes itself and those which it binds as complete a unity as possible; and the nature of proportion is to accomplish this most perfectly. . . .

" God accordingly set air and water betwixt fire and earth, and making them as far as possible exactly proportional, so that fire is to air as air to water, and as air is to water water is to earth, thus he compacted and constructed a universe visible and tangible."— *Timaeus,* ed. by R. D. Archer-Hind, London, 1888, pp. 97–98.

The significance of these triune theories in connection with the evolutionary periodization of history will be discussed more fully in Chapter 11.

Lorenz Oken, in 1810, in his curious speculations on " Triunity," says:

" As the complete principle of mathematics consists of three ideas, so also does the primary principle of nature, or the Eternal. The primary principle of mathematics is Zero; so soon, however, as it is actual, is it $+$ and $-$; or the primary idea resolves itself in being at once into two ideas, each of which resembles the other in essence, but differs from it in form. Thus it is here one and the same essence under three forms, or three are one. Now that which holds good of mathematical principles, must also hold good also of the principles of nature. The primary act is manifested, or operates under three forms, which correspond to the 0, $+$ and $-$."—*Elements of Physiophilosophy*, tr. by Alfred Tulk for the Ray Society, London, 1847, p. 17.

In 1859, J. M. Fischer, in another forgotten work [66], attempted to correlate the history of harmonic resources with the development of individual and national character, morally, spiritually and intellectually. These three phases are illustrated in the composition and *evolution of the triad:*

" The fundamental, unison, prolonged ground-tone is the healthy, masculine element in moral life; the life of the soul appears in the feminine Third, stronger in Major than in Minor . . . and the bright, determined Dominant stands for the intellectual supremacy of to-day." (p. 10).

The triad is often out of tune, just as the " pure temperament" of human relations is often disturbed by social disharmony.

The unity and harmony of family life brought about by the power of music in the home is contrasted with the disunity that keeps members of the German family, as a whole, apart. The ideal of organic unity is symbolized by the four-tone chord (with the octave), and the organic character of the classical four-movement sonata (*Ibid.,* p. 184).

III. TEXTBOOKS FOR CONSERVATORIES

Between these two opposing schools of thought, but borrowing assumptions from each, are found compilations of history for music students in conservatories and other schools.

The conservatory teacher found the great-man theory useful for students of piano, composition, singing, and so on. " Lives of great men all remind us" that one should practice and study hard to become famous, and this is the incentive for music histories made during the vogue of the success-theory in nineteenth-century education. At the same time, it was necessary not to frighten students who might gaze upon greatness and become discouraged; so just as Calvisius had sought for *praecepta* that were *nova et facillima,* so also the nineteenth-century student was told, " Music is not difficult, but easy to learn; man invented it." [15] At the same time the

15 Gustav Schilling [44] started his work in 1830 with an elementary text; so did Fétis, with *La musique mise à la portée de tous*, Liège, 1830; as " Music explained to the world," it appeared in Boston in 1842. The London edition (1846) was wrongly entitled *The History of Music*.

organic hypotheses were used to show that music, in its origins and essence, was a natural phenomenon, in spite of the mechanical drill it took to master it. During this period of great musical activity, Germany, for the first and only time, borrowed a few little histories, in translation, for popular use. In addition to Mme. Bawr's little history for the ladies, translated from the French [38], two English compilations were done into German [36, 37].

Two translations from the English in one year may offer evidence of the influence of English esthetics on German thought at that time. However, it may have been due largely to German admiration for the great works by Hawkins and Burney, in particular. The latter were too bulky for translation, so evidently the Germans took up these condensations instead. The German translator found Jones somewhat biased, and deemed it necessary to fill the gaps made in the omission of many "Heroes of Music." The numerous mistakes are also said to be corrected.

In the original, "The Progressive History of Music" is confined to pp. 288–316, the remainder being given to discourse on theory and instruments. Whereas Busby frankly acknowledges his debt to Burney and Hawkins, Jones fails to do so, except in a few references. Jones believes the climate has great influence on national music. The warm climate of Italy accounts for their superior music, and the lack of English national music is thus explained: "They have no leisure to exhale their character in songs!"

In 1821, Franz Stoepel published a short outline [39]. In the career of this author and teacher, the influence of England appears again and the musical interests of the day are manifest. Stoepel was sent to England in 1821 to investigate a sensational system of piano teaching then in vogue. Bernard Logier had invented his "chiroplast," a machine for guiding arms and fingers at the keyboard,[16] and Stoepel reported so favorably that the king of Prussia invited Logier to introduce his system into Germany.

These events illustrate the fact that the new and dominant interest was in the pianoforte and that, for many, music study was becoming synonymous with the technical drill necessary to become a brilliant virtuoso. Two other teachers of piano figure in the history of music histories — in these cases, histories for conservatory students, texts to be read between hours of practice. Christian Kalkbrenner, father of Friedrich Wilhelm, teacher of Chopin, had

---

[16] See the article "Gymnastics," Grove, *Dictionary of Music and Musicians.*

written a short history which has been mentioned at the end of the previous chapter. Half a century later, Carl Czerny rounded out his career as a piano pedagogue by publishing his *Umriss der ganzen Musikgeschichte* (Mainz, 1851). Czerny followed the lead of Kalkbrenner and Müller, cited in Chapter 3, by pointing to the divine origins of music in genius. Czerny, in some chronological tables, found twenty-two epochs of music history, named after great musicians, beginning with Apollo, and ending with Alexis Lvoff, composer of the old Russian national anthem. Czerny's history was also translated into Italian, and his chronological chart is found in Engel's *Musical Myths and Facts*. (See Chapter 12 for further discussion of Engel's use of this chart.)

IV. A NEW DEFINITION OF MODERN MUSIC

The old definition of modern music as that which had begun in the early Christian era persisted, as far as can be ascertained, until 1841. In that year Gustav Schilling asserted that the *eigentliche Geschichte der modernen Musik* did not begin until 1600. So although his title [53] is similar to Kiesewetter's, the organization is along different lines. As a matter of fact, Schilling's history is different in nearly every respect from those of his contemporaries. In matters of opinion he reflects, of course, the taste and prejudices of his day, but he deserves especial mention for these reasons:

(1) No mention is made of origins, divine or natural.

(2) The great-man theory is not the basis; men and works are treated, and occasionally used, as chronological markers but not as defining epochs.

(3) It is one of the very few histories of music at this time which does not employ the biological analogy, and pays no attention to the current craze for three stages of development. (The periodization employed is cited later, in Chapter 11.)

(4) It is the first history of music, as far as has been ascertained in this study, to envisage music and its changes in relation to political events and cultural changes in general.

It is the work of a writer intensely interested in the problem of his own present. Denying the *dictum* of Kiesewetter, that the history of music had nothing to do with other affairs in history,

Schilling gives over a hundred pages at the close of his book to political events and their bearing on musical life.

Beethoven is held up as the protagonist of the spirit of freedom. The ideals symbolized in his music went down to defeat, according to Schilling, because of (1) the growing supremacy of the State; (2) the separation of art from the life of the people; (3) the revival of Italian supremacy as symbolized by the triumphs of Rossini. [53], p. 729 ff.

Inquiry is made into the social phenomena known as music festivals, and the reason for their popularity in Germany and England, and not in France; earlier, the question is raised, "Why did Handel turn to oratorio? "; and the social as well as the esthetic reasons are discussed. In other words, Schilling was interested in the history of musical and other *ideas*. He came to the conclusion that the word *modern* had its root in *mode* [53], pp. 28–29; therefore that modern music began with the new modes of scientific thought that can be traced back to 1600. His knowledge of music before 1600 was uncertain, and yet he did not condemn it merely as an immature stage of development. Schilling also pointed out that in every period, each one modern at the time, many diverse styles emerge; that these styles can only be understood with reference to the environment.

Schilling was director of the Stoepel Piano School in Stuttgart, so it was natural for him to rejoice in the development of instrumental music as an independent art. But his enthusiasm for all kinds of music pervades everything that he wrote.

The *Einleitung* is entitled *Über den Begriff der Modernen in der Musik,* and attempts to establish the historical bases for classical concepts of form. The *Überschau* at the beginning of the popular edition [17] is devoted to a discussion of music's relation to the other fine arts, and its various functions in society.

The development of the author as an independent thinker, in one decade, is apparent when one examines his first publication [44]. The historical preface in this follows a tradition as old as Calvisius' *De initio*. Schilling, almost after the pattern set by Calvisius, has a few paragraphs on the origins of music, and lists a

---

[17] *Die schöne Kunst der Töne, oder heutige Musikkunst, zur Orientierung über ihr gesammtes inneres und äusseres Wesen, für Jedermann . . . historisch-praktisch dargestellt,* Stuttgart, 1847, 2 v. Vol. 1, 518 pp., is, except for the new preface, an abridgement of the *Geschichte.*

few contributors to the history of theory. But origins are not in one source alone; man invented it as a result of both inner and outer compulsion. Jubal, however, should be credited with the invention of musical art, if he really made natural sounds in some artistic form. (pp. xvii–xix).

This indefatigable teacher and writer did the bulk of his work in lexicographic form. A *Musikalisches Conversations-Handlexicon,* in two volumes, appeared in 1841–42, but his great work (with the able assistance of A. B. Marx and others) began in 1835 and ran to seven volumes. In fact, this *Encyclopädie der gesammten musikalischen Wissenschaften oder Universal-Lexicon der Tonkunst* [49] was the only German music encyclopedia published during the first half of the century. It stands out like an island of research in a sea of romantic speculation. But it was evidently so far in advance of the thought of the time that F. S. Gassner reduced it to one volume in 1849. In the introduction, Gassner mentions the original collaborators, but omits Schilling's name. Evidently the abridgment was done without Schilling's approval. The object of this version, so it was stated, was to reduce the cost and the difficulties for the average reader. Gassner cut down on the biographies except for the *Heroen und Verewigten* (p. 11). Some very valuable articles and information (e.g., the article on *Ballet,* and data on music and instruments outside western Europe) were lost thereby.

Political difficulties forced Schilling to emigrate to New York in 1857, then to Montreal, and finally to Nebraska, where he died, forgotten, in 1881.

V. MISCELLANEOUS ENGLISH AND FRENCH CONTRIBUTIONS

In England, the first historical summary of the century is a very brief one, made in 1818 by a cultivated man of letters, again on the subject of Ancient *vs.* Modern music, but this time with a plea for the restoration of plainsong in the church [35]. The only other work, besides that of Stafford, already cited, is that of a very capable journalist and critic, George Hogarth, who leaves a very clear picture of the taste of his day, and of the revival of interest in a church music that should be free from secular influences [48]. It is important also as the first history of music to be published in an

American edition. Taking issue with older historians, Hogarth points out that

"The music of a country can be handed down to a remote posterity only by the preservation of actual compositions, by means of a notation which is . . . adequate . . . and intelligible." (p. 11).

The danger of subjective opinion in historical writing is illustrated by the following:

"Music of an original character is never appreciated at first . . . the earlier compositions of Beethoven, which are now in general favour, were in their novelty, looked upon as strange and extravagant. The extreme simplicity and naturalness of Beethoven's melody is a peculiar feature of his most admired works . . . no music is more easily comprehended, and more powerfully felt." Then —" There is no analogy between the case of the compositions in question, and the latest works of Beethoven. The truth appears to be that in consequence of his total exclusion from the audible world, his mind must have been deprived of that constant supply of new ideas, derived from the hearing of actual sound, but the ideas accumulated during his earlier years must have faded from his memory." [48], pp. 352–353.

This echoes a similar judgment on Beethoven's later works pronounced by William Gardiner in his *Music of Nature*:

"During the last ten years of his life he was completely deaf, during which his compositions have partaken of the most incomprehensible wildness. His imagination seems to have fed upon the ruins of his sensitive organs. What must we say to his posthumous quartets? Who dares, at the present day, avow himself equal to the task of unravelling the hidden mysteries they contain? " (p. 15).

Three other French writers, in addition to those already mentioned, belong to this period. A distinguished scholar and traveler, Adrien de la Fage, projected a general history of music and the dance [56], but it was never finished. The two volumes treat only of the music of China, India, Egypt, and the Hebrews. A. L. Blondeau's two-volume history, in 1847 [58], is the only " complete " French narrative of the story of music during this early half of the nineteenth century. In 1852, two curious works indicate the fascination that music history had, first for the moralist (Labat [64], already quoted), and second for the vocalist. A. Debay [63] was one of the very few to include an historical summary in a work on voice culture. He also wrote a history of physiology.

Altogether, this romantic half century was a comparatively sterile period in the history of music histories. There was a vague feeling that the history of music could be envisaged as a whole, as has been shown in discussing "the organic hypothesis." But with the acceptance of the evolution doctrine, the organic becomes an organismic hypothesis. Biographies of great men are replaced with histories of musical form; a new cosmology replaces the theology of old.

It is interesting to note that the triune theories of Père Mersenne [18] were not mentioned in eighteenth-century histories of music. They were foreign to the spirit of that secularized period known as the Enlightenment. This chapter has shown how these theories reappeared with the Romantic revival of Christianity. Ensuing chapters will describe their persistence in Richard Wagner's philosophy of music history, also in contemporary schemes of "periodization." Curiously enough, mystic obscurity is to accompany the demand for the "clear view." [19]

[18] See pp. 16–17.
[19] See pp. 263–265, 267, 274.

CHAPTER 7

REVOLUTIONISTS AND EVOLUTIONISTS

BETWEEN 1850 and 1900, there appeared as many histories of music in Germany alone as had appeared in all the years previous in all countries. But during this period there was still a comparative dearth of lexicons. Scholars, instead of devoting themselves to atomistic activities of this sort, preferred to formulate historical pictures that possessed the prime desideratum of the age, that of organic unity. The doctrines of Progress and Development were basic in nearly all these works.

I. A NEW INTEREST IN THE PRESENT AND FUTURE: PRESCRIPTIONS FOR PROGRESS

In 1848, two important documents appeared: the *Communist Manifesto,* by Marx and Engels, and Richard Wagner's essay on "Art and Revolution," prelude to his *Art of the Future.* Marx and Engels pictured the separation and struggle of classes in a human society that had once been united, in primitive society, for the common good; Wagner, like John Brown, deplored the separation of arts that had once been united in one great art, the musical drama of ancient Greece:

"With the Greeks, perfected dramatic art was . . . in an intimate historical sense, the nation itself, conscious of itself, enjoying itself at public representations for a few hours of the noblest pleasures. . . .

"With the subsequent downfall of tragedy, art ceased to be an expression of the public consciousness. *Drama became separated into its component parts:* rhetoric, sculpture, painting, music, etc., left the ranks in which they had marched in unanimity before; each to go its own way, each to find independent, but lonely, egoistic development. . . .

"Each of these single arts, nursed and cultivated luxuriously for the entertainment of the rich, has filled the world lavishly with its products; great minds have accomplished wonders; but . . . the perfect art-work, drama, tragedy, . . . has not been *re*-born. It must be born *anew*, not born *again*.

"Only the great Revolution of Mankind can win this art for us, an art that shall bring back a profound sense of beauty to all." [1]

For Wagner, revolution had a romantic ideal by which the nation was to recover a common consciousness and enjoyment of beauty that had been lost since the downfall of Greek tragedy.

For Karl Marx, revolution meant a call to action that would tend to level national barriers that Wagner's theories helped to strengthen.

The theory that in the evolution of the individual arts each had been brought to perfection led to the belief that future progress was only possible with an organic unity of all of them. It was no mere accident that this sort of theory should develop at a time when a divided Germany was longing intensely for *national* unity. Writers and lecturers on the history of music included men like Schilling, who were interested in the whole sphere of culture and politics.

These men made frequent references to the significance of Liszt and Wagner. Liszt, the great cosmopolitan, represented an enlightened tradition that was being extinguished by the fires of national patriotism; Wagner, as is well known, became the exponent of German nationalism. But Wagner's supporter, the historian Franz Brendel, saw beyond the immediate ideal of national unity to the dream of a united Europe,

"the goal of European evolution, in which single states and nations would co-operate spiritually, to constitute a great Whole, a whole wherein the national element would be preserved only as a matter of *Schmuck*, or individual color." [2]

Then the author points out, as do many of his contemporaries, that the first necessary stage in that desired evolution is the unification of Germany herself, culturally and politically.

It is necessary to look into this book on the music of the present and the future unification of the·arts to understand the guiding impulse back of Brendel's extremely popular *History of Music in Italy, Germany, and France* [62], which appeared two years earlier. But although the author did have the distant goal of European unity in mind, that has been forgotten. The influence that this work

[1] Wagner's *Gesammelte Schriften*, Leipzig, 1872, Vol. III, pp. 37–39.
[2] *Die Musik der Gegenwart, und die Gesamtkunst der Zukunft*, 1854.

has had, together with that of Wagner's music, so vigorously defended by Brendel, has been to accomplish only the immediate objective, the stimulus of German nationalism and the love of supremacy.

F. Stade, in the Preface to the fifth and sixth edition, speaks of the " epoch-making significance " of Brendel's *History:*

" All contemporary criticism, consciously or unconsciously, is under its influence . . . for the first time a synthesis appeared of material which formerly had only external unity, showing the history of music as a great, self-evolving whole under the control of law. . . .

" Dr. Brendel was a professor of history and aesthetics, lecturer, and, most important of all, a critic who was vitally interested in modern music, an active defender of Liszt and Wagner. As editor of the *Neue Zeitschrift für Musik,* he followed in the footsteps of Robert Schumann in defending the music of his Present, with a zealous ardor for New Paths, Reformation, and Regeneration.

" ' Music is the sovereign art of the present.' With this introduction, the author aims: first of all, to show an arrangement and grouping of the material which would place before the reader a picture of the evolution that has taken place up to this time.

" Second, to state the general points of view, the categories under which the chief epochs and principal manifestations are to be grouped.

" Then, I have tried to link the History of Music to the most important manifestations of general culture.

" Finally, the chief goal of my efforts was the revival of the masterpieces of past centuries."

Two of Wagner's aims are very suggestive, reflecting, as they do, similar efforts in other fields of activity. In the first place, Wagner's " Art of the Future," calling for an organic unity of arts that had heretofore been developed individually, was in line with the Romantic demand for syntheses in science and the philosophy of history. As already indicated, Comte's application of the methods of biology to the social sciences was contemporaneous with the Romantic belief that painting, music, and poetry were each individual aspects of one art, and that one could, to some extent, do the work of the other. Wagner's synthesis was a logical culmination of this Romantic attitude.

In the second place, Richard Wagner was the most consistent German nationalist of his day. The exile imposed upon him by mistaken authorities put no damper on his Germanic zeal. As a matter of fact, his Swiss asylum became a center for Count de Gobineau [3] and Houston Stewart Chamberlain,[4] whose theories, eagerly adopted by the Germans, have become the basis of Nazi ideology today.[5] Nietzsche, in spite of his influential theories of the superman, made no application of the same to the German " race," and broke with Wagner, very largely on this account. Nietzsche even went into self-imposed exile rather than live among his imperialistic countrymen. In a letter written from Turin in 1888, he says, "Wagner's stage requires but one thing — *Germans!* The definition of a German: an obedient man with long legs. . . . There is a deep significance in the fact that the rise of Wagner coincides with the rise of Empire. . . . Never have people been more obedient, never have they been so well ordered about. The conductors of Wagnerian orchestras are worthy of an age which posterity will one day call with timid awe *the classical age of war.*" [6]

II. THE RETURN TO THE PAST

In summing up the foregoing, we find, during the Liszt-Wagner era, a series of music histories written by men vitally interested in the music and events of their present. This constitutes a remarkable phenomenon in the history of music histories, for very rarely since that time have histories been inspired by interest in contemporary music. After the victory over France, in 1870, scholars settled down to one of two different tasks: to write lexicons or pedagogical textbooks, or to plunge into musicological research. The latter was done in two branches of study: one the history of musical genres by means of paleography and style criticism, and the other in the field of musical ethnology. In the first field, serious scholars recognized the fact that the materials of music history were all too scanty, that without them all the talk about organic syntheses was day-dreaming. In the second field the spur came from the anthropologists, as will be seen. Textbooks came to be

[3] *The Inequality of Human Races,* N. Y., 1915, tr. by Adrian Collins. (First ed. 1853.)

[4] *Foundations of the Nineteenth Century,* tr. from the German by John Lees, London, 1921, 2 v.

[5] For reply to these theories, and an account of Wagner's part in their dissemination, see Friedrich Hertz, *Race and Civilization.*

[6] See " The Case of Wagner," in Nietzsche's *Works,* ed. by Oscar Levy, London, 1911, Vol. VIII, p. 34.

written in nationalistic terms but always with reference to a glorious past. The glowing ardor for the present died down, possibly because Brendel and his contemporaries had been too grandiose in their dreams for the future.

Before proceeding to list the numerous histories published in the second half of the nineteenth century, special mention should be made of the work of Fétis and Ambros. F. J. Fétis has already been cited as the leading lexicographer of the early nineteenth century, but his other lifework, a general history of music, did not begin to appear until 1869, and was never completed [81]. One other Belgian history had appeared in 1862 [68].

By 1873, Fétis, in the second edition of the *Biographie universelle* [51], had absorbed current evolutionary doctrines sufficiently to enable him to explain, to his own satisfaction, progressive change in music history, disparaging, in a sense, all his collected and carefully arranged data concerning *events*.

But the crux of the argument is in the two points of view for the history of music, one from the general, evolutionary standpoint and the other from the vantage point of criticism and value judgment.

" The first point of view is therefore that which envisages the art in itself, *creating itself, developing itself,* and *changing itself by virtue of various principles which are unfolded,* each in its turn. Each one of these principles bears *all its consequences within itself,* and *these are discovered periodically, by men of genius, in a logical order which nothing can prevent.* . . . This history has been the object of labor and study the greater part of my life, and of more meditation than labor, always seeking conclusions that were clearer, simpler, and more general.

" The second point of view concerns the *value* of works of art — and the part that each artist has had in the changes of the art. This other part of history is the object of the *Biographie universelle. Authority* for such a task demands *connaissance de tout ce qui est du domaine de la musique.* The layman may have impressions from art works which may satisfy or repel him, but such impressions have no value as judgments." [7]

---

[7] The weaknesses in history that tries to be criticism are apparent in Fétis' comments on the music of his own day: " The noise, the increasing fracas of exaggerated forces with which our ears are assaulted these days is decadence, nothing but decadence, far from being progress." (vi). The " new school," beginning with Mendelssohn and Schumann, needs to go back to eighteenth-century ideals. Modern music is too obscure, overloaded, etc. Our artists are skillful enough, but social conditions are responsible: there have been more extraordinary events and revolutions

The great Bohemian contemporary of Fétis, August Wilhelm Ambros, was apart from the circle of historians interested in Liszt, Wagner, and politics. But in spirit he had much in common with them, believing that the history of music was closely bound up with other phases of art and culture.[8] Unfortunately he also did not live to complete his lifework [67], for had he done so, he would probably have left some illuminating comments on the music of his day. His aim, always, was to get at the inner meaning of music in the light of the culture that produced it.

The interest in the present, so remarkably manifest in Schilling and in Brendel, was only an incident. In the same decade in which Brendel's history appeared, Darwin's *Origin of Species* came out in England. This, together with Herbert Spencer's theories, became the most potent influence upon the writing of histories in England and France. Interest turned back to origins, and epochs of growth as exhibited not in the lives of men, but in the organisms known as musical form. So even though historians learned to respect facts, the evolutionary treatment turned them back to analogy.

---

during the last seventy years than in ten centuries previous. Music is too nervous — too dramatic. The French opera writers of the late eighteenth and early nineteenth centuries are held up as models — Méhul, Philidor, Grétry. They excelled for " good taste, exquisite sensibility, elegance, grace," etc. The modern system (Romanticism) " is contrary to the destination of music." [51], pp. x, xi, xii, xiv.

[8] Although Ambros achieved his early education under great handicaps, he became the leading musicologist of his day, possibly of the nineteenth century, until Hugo Riemann. As a result of this work he became Professor of *Musikwissenschaft* at the University, also in the Conservatory of Prague. In 1872 he was Professor at the Vienna Conservatory.

He was a nephew of Kiesewetter, mentioned above, and was a native of Prague. He combined musical teaching, writing, composition, and playing with his duties in the Attorney-General's office after his graduation from Prague University with the degree of Juris Doctor. After promotion to Vienna he was able to give all his time to musicology. This work, incomplete, has had its vicissitudes.

Ambros makes a distinction between the origins of music among ancient peoples and the origins of European-Christian music. The latter, he believed, had its origins in folk song based upon ancient tradition. No sympathy is shown for theories of Byzantine origins, or for Byzantine art of any kind.

" There can be no discussion of any real musical art among the peoples of northern Europe. What we know of their poetry and song indicates that there was aptitude, but no art." [67], II, 20.

In the introduction to Volume III, interesting parallels are drawn with learning, art, and architecture.

III. EVOLUTION FROM THE SIMPLE TO THE COMPLEX

In 1850 Herbert Spencer had published his *Social Statics*, in which he asserted that "advancement is due to the working of a universal law." [9] In 1854 he included an essay on "The Origins of Music" as one of the *Illustrations of Universal Progress*. In 1859 Charles Darwin in *The Origin of Species*, applied the Law of Progress to biology, and in 1862 Spencer follows up the Wagnerian demand for synthetic art with his *Synthetic Philosophy*. In eleven volumes devoted to this great enterprise,[10] Spencer makes much of the theory that society evolves as an organism.

In his *First Principles*, Spencer restates Von Baër's law as a basis for his principle of evolution:

"Evolution is an integration of matter and concomitant dissipation of motion; during which the matter passes from an indefinite incoherent homogeneity to a definite coherent heterogeneity; and during which the retained motion undergoes a parallel transformation." (p. 145).

Spencerian laws of progress and evolution gave some music historians a new solution to their problems. Music history need not be a mere chronicle of men and events; to be scientific one need only envisage music as an evolving organism "creating itself, developing itself and changing itself by virtue of various principles which are unfolded, each in its turn."

So if, as Fétis continues, men of genius need only discover these principles "in a logical order which nothing can prevent," then the historian need only fix upon the logical order. Unfortunately, however, there has been as much division over "the logical order" as there had been formerly over modes and genera, and logical methods of tuning.

One of the first music historians to adopt Spencer's fundamental assumptions, in an attempt to arrive at the logical order, was John Frederick Rowbotham [113], a poet and clergyman, like John Brown a century earlier, and amateur musician.[11] He was trained

---

[9] Part I, Ch. 2, Sec. 4.

[10] *First Principles*, 1862; *Principles of Biology*, 2 v., 1864–1867; *Principles of Psychology*, 2 v., 1872; *The Study of Sociology*, 1873; *The Principles of Ethics*, 2 v., 1879–1891; *The Principles of Sociology*, 3 v., 1876–1896.

[11] Other works by the same writer include: "How to Write Music Correctly," "How to Enter the Musical Profession," and "How to Vamp: A Practical Guide to

at Oxford, where he must have come into contact with logicians,[12] ethnologists, and evolutionists. At any rate, Rowbotham's "Law of Development" shows the influence of the doctrine of fixity of species when he maintains that the *Drum Stage,* the *Pipe Stage,* and then the *Lyre Stage* appear in that positive order in prehistoric times. His evidence, gleaned from primitive ritual and mythology, offers sufficient "proof" of "facts" as positive as those brought forth by Hugo. (But Richard Wallaschek [127], by using the same methods, "proves" that the "pipe must have antedated the drum.")

The following passage from Rowbotham [113] seems to show the influence of the Darwinian concept of gradual, progressive change and the Spencerian law quoted above. It is prefaced by reference to the old psychological theory mentioned in the eighteenth century by Burney, and later by Spencer, in his "Essay on the Origin of Music":

"The Origin of vocal music must be sought in impassioned speech." The first and most important influence in changing from the latter to the former is the Story: "Whether it were that the unity of subject in the narration would engender unity of vibration in the tone, or whether the wish to avoid fatiguing the voice were the reason, or the desire to make it carry it farther, men gradually acquired the habit of confining the voice to one note.

"First, men were contented with one note. . . . A long time must have elapsed before tone itself would come to be looked upon as a subject for objective treatment. The very first musical note ever heard in the world was G, and for a very long time indeed the whole musical art lay in embryo in that note. The living illustrations of the primitive period are those people who are generally looked upon as in the lowest stage of human development, the natives of Tierra del Fuego, etc.

"The practical effect of chanting an impassioned speech would be ever more and more to isolate the tone from the words: and the struggling into being of the one note would bring the isolation before men's minds. So that we may expect that the next step would be to treat the tone objectively, to make it the subject matter of art. . . . A one-note period would be succeeded by a three-note period . . . if these people (Samoans, etc.) can be content nowadays with two notes in their songs, we may see that there is nothing improbable in the assumption that

the Accompaniment of Songs by the Unskilled Musician." The art of vamping is also divided into three stages!

[12] For the logician's defense of the comparative as the "historical" method see Joseph's *Introduction to Logic,* Oxford, 1906. For discussion of this method see Chapter 10, 1.

there was a period, probably a very long period, in the history of primitive man, when the whole resources of vocal music consisted of two notes. One more note was added to the compass of the chant, and, as was natural, it was the next above. And now there was the prospect of many more melodic changes being rung. For the feeling of melody came later than that of rhythm, and was making itself felt now. Next stage: The Pentatonic scale formed by the Great (3-note) scale, with the Little (2-note) scale above: G A B-D E.

" There is one song of the Fuegians in which they get beyond their one note. By this it is clear that even the Fuegians are emerging from the one-note period in Music."

The above is an extreme statement of the evolution theory as applied to music history, and Rowbotham's work is now out of print. But, in a less naive form, some of the assumptions are still to be found in current histories, and the author is still mentioned as a dependable pioneer in the field of musical ethnology.[13]

The first French history to do away with composer biographies in order to show the evolution of musical forms, was by Henri Lavoix, librarian of the *Bibliothèque nationale* [110]. The preface states that

" Sound, rhythm and timbre are the principal characters in this history, in the form of melody, harmony, measure and instrumentation. . . . We shall try to find the bonds which unite ancient to modern art, for — do not be deceived, there are no gaps [14] in history — there are only ignorances. If the links in the chain appear broken, it is because the historians have not known how to unite them. . . . This is a history of music, not of musicians."

Sir C. Hubert H. Parry, the English historian, was the next to take up the evolutionary history of musical forms [126]. This influential composer and scholar felt also that the biographical method had been carried too far, and that the inquiry should be directed not so much to the evolution of genius, which is individual, but to the evolution of the art as a whole.

[13] See Robert Lach, " Die Musik der Natur-und orientalische Kulturvölker." [224], p. 5.

[14] This significant quotation from Leibnitz appears only twenty-five years after Darwin's use of the same assumption. In the *Origin of Species*, Darwin says, " As natural selection acts solely by accumulating slight, successive, favourable variations, it can produce no great or sudden modifications; it can act only by short and slow steps. Hence the canon of *Natura non fecit saltum*, which every fresh addition to our knowledge tends to confirm, is on this theory intelligible." p. 447 (Everyman's Lib.).

Parry's method was to trace the evolution of musical forms as objective manifestations of spiritual activity. The various phases of spiritual activity belong in another category, to which only incidental reference is made. Parry and his followers are fearful of getting into the morass into which a purely subjective treatment of the subject can lead, so the focal point of interest is in the changes that take place in musical structure. The dependence of Parry upon Spencer's Law of Progress is stated thus, in speaking of " The Rise of Secular Music " in the seventeenth century:

" The progress of this somewhat immature period shows the inevitable tendency of all things from homogeneity towards diversity and definiteness." [15]

An attempt to find a " logical order " is found in the chapter on scales; the history of musical structure must decide the sequence in which man progressed from " simple " intervals to definite, heterogeneous melodies and scales:

" It is quite certain that human creatures did exist for a very long time without the advantage of a scale of any sort; and that they did have to begin by deciding on a couple of notes or so which seemed satisfactory and agreeable when heard after the other, and that they did have to be satisfied with a scale of the most limited description for a very long period. What interval the primitive savage chose was very much a matter of accident.". . . And yet,

" Of all these intervals there are two which to a musician seem obviously certain to have been the alternatives in the choice of a nucleus. As has been pointed out, sixths, thirds, sevenths and seconds are almost inconceivable. They are all difficult to hit without education. . . . There remain only the intervals of the fourth and the fifth, and evidence as well as theory proves almost conclusively that one of these two formed the nucleus upon which all scales were based; and one of the two was probably the interval which primitive savages endeavored to hit in their first attempts at music." (pp. 16–19).

And in describing the evolution of harmony, in the chapter on incipient harmony, Parry is even more specific:

" The early phase of the progress of harmony from homogeneity to heterogeneity is distinctly traceable in this respect. In the first stage there is no variety at all; all are fifths or fourths consecutively. A slight variety appears when fourths are mixed up with one another and with octaves. . . . When the force of circumstances drove composers to use the less perfectly consonant combinations of thirds and sixths . . . their materials became more heterogeneous . . . ultimately the composers with the higher instincts learnt to use the qualities of the different consonances . . . and then going a step still further, composers at last found out how to use real discords." . . .

A summary of Parry's evolution doctrine is also found in an Introduction written for an American publication [199], in 1915:

" The way complication has been built upon complication may be easily grasped by observing the successive stages of art for which organization had to be provided. At first it had to serve for a single melodic line; then, in the period of ecclesiastical choral music, for two or more combined melodic lines; then composers combined more and more melodic lines as they found out how it could be done, and this caused their minds to be almost monopolized by what may be called linear organization. . . . The highest outcome of this was the fugue."

Parry then proceeds to show what organization of new forms evolved when men " began to feel the harmonies which were the result of combined melodious parts as entities in themselves," etc. (p. xxxviii).

Now this procedure is linked up to another series of stages in man's subjective experience, which is only mentioned as a starting-point.

" Mankind, like the individual, passes through *three stages* in his manner of producing and doing things. The first is unconscious and spontaneous, the second is self-critical, analytical, and self-conscious; and the third is the synthesis which comes of the recovery of spontaneity with all the advantages of the absorption of right principles of action. . . . It is in the last phase that the greatest works of musical art are produced," etc.

This statement of the Idea of Progress in music is followed up with the delineation of another series which is deemed a necessary prelude to his main theme — the evolution of forms.

" There are two phases of organization. The first is the organization of terms, signs, methods, materials, some of which must be found before art begins, but most of which is found as it evolves. The second is the organization of the individual works of art." (pp. xxxii–xxxiii).

Here we have in a few pages three sets of stages: (1) in the realm of human experience, (2) in the evolution of art, (3) and in the phases of its organization, ideal progressions which are set up for comparison by way of explanation of men's activities in music. But the breaks with the past, due to changes in men's ways of thinking, cannot be explained in these continuous series.

IV. DEVELOPMENT FROM SAVAGERY TO CIVILIZATION

The foregoing pages have cited evidence to show that the old notions of divine origins of music at Creation were completely discredited by leading scholars, but that equally dogmatic assumptions were substituted. Briefly summarized, these assumptions were

(1) that music "created itself," like other organisms.
(2) that the various "divisions" of music were at first united.
(3) that this unity was that of undifferentiated homogeneity.
(4) that progressive evolution took place to the definite, clear-cut forms of modern art.

The Wagnerian belief that the arts were to be united in an art of the future was not, however, the basic concept in music histories at the end of the nineteenth century. A new interest was making itself felt, namely, the concern with musical ethnology. Spencer agreed with Wagner's theory and speaks of " the co-ordinate origin and gradual differentiation of poetry, music, and dancing." But Spencer's conclusion is radically different from Wagner's:

"Rhythm in speech, rhythm in sound, and rhythm in motion, were in the beginning parts of the same thing, and have only in process of time become separate things. Among various primitive tribes we find them still united." [16]

Wagner was interested in his present and future, and so was his protagonist, Brendel. Wagner was primarily interested in making new music; his synthetic work was undertaken in the spirit of the creative artist. Explanation was secondary. Spencer's *Synthetic Philosophy* may also have been inspired by the urge to create a new and esthetically satisfying system of thought, but the primary objective was explanation. Spencer, like many of his contemporaries, was content to show how man had progressed, from primitive savagery to modern European civilization, and to formulate " laws

[16] From *Illustrations of Universal Progress;* first essay, " Progress, Its Law and Cause."

of nature" by which this progress had taken place. For revolutionists like Wagner and Marx, something new had to be done; for
evolutionists like Spencer, nothing need be done, for fear of interference with natural progress. For Wagner the unity of the arts
was something to be recaptured with a supreme effort; for Marx,
the classless society had to be reachieved by turning society upside
down; but for Spencer united arts and classes were merely characteristics of "primitive tribes" at the "lowest stage of development."

Parry's history has been quoted at length, first, because it is the
only history of music mentioned so far which is still in general
demand and widespread use; second, because it offers so clear a
statement of the evolutionary method of explanation. Unlike Rowbotham and other evolutionary music historians, Parry was a great
leader in music education, a prolific, though conventional composer,
and an impartial critic of his contemporaries.[17] He agrees implicitly
with Kiesewetter that the history of music has nothing to do with
contemporaneous events, but makes no complaints, as did Fétis,
concerning the decadent tendencies of his own day. To have done
so, in fact, would have been contrary to his belief in progress, that
"the long story of music is a continuous and unbroken record of
human effort to extend and enhance the possibilities of effects of
sound upon human sensibilities. . . ."[18] He concludes with a tribute to Wagner, not with the older romantic eulogy of genius, but
merely for the success with which Wagner developed the resources
of musical art:

"His (Wagner's) personality, and the particular subjects that he
chooses, and the manner in which he looks at them, affect different
people in different ways; that is a matter apart from the development
of resources or the method of applying them. Of the method itself it
may be said that it is the logical outcome of the efforts of the long line
of previous composers, and the most completely organized system for
the purposes of musical expression that the world has yet seen." [126],
p. 363.

To a self-styled revolutionist, that is more epitaph than tribute.
Wagner was sure that his method was no mere "logical outcome."

[17] The extent to which both Parry and Rowbotham have influenced American
music education will be apparent in Chapter 8, III, on "Evolution in the Classroom," and in Chapter 12, II, 2, B.
[18] This tolerant spirit is not carried on by H. C. Colles, editor of the 1935 edition,
who calls many modern composers "impostors."

Like Marx, he believed that there had been progress up to the present in certain particulars, but that future evolution could only become progressive by means of a new and radical effort. For them, future evolution meant revolution.

Parry, like Spencer, was no revolutionist. For both of them, great men were important, but, as the Law of Progress was a cosmic principle, the genius was merely the actor who was assigned a part in the great drama. For them evolution meant development of potential resources. They fostered the belief that

"Inspired by the great doctrine of the nineteenth century, the doctrine of evolution, first formulated by biology, but immediately applied to all realms of knowledge, we read in events a continuous movement, a coherent growth, a vast and single process. For us, individual men and events sink into insignificance in comparison with the great drama of which they are only acts and actors." [151], p. 4.

V. OTHER GENERAL HISTORIES

I. IN GERMANY

It has been noted that the only two English histories ever translated into German appeared in the same year (1821). The tables are turned, however, with the translation of Kiesewetter, as noted above, in 1848. In 1865, the translation of another general history of music, by Schlüter [73], came, significantly enough, after two decades during which German musicians had been flocking to England in great numbers. Schlüter shows more than average interest in Bach, is distrustful of Wagner, and closes with this statement so typical of the classicist in all ages:

"No one living has been able to replace Mendelssohn: were *he* living, we should certainly never have heard all this talk about new theories. We therefore await patiently the resurrection of *real genius* — such as shall put to silence the disputes which distract the musical profession in Germany. Another springtime of music, another classical epoch in music we may scarcely hope to see. The tendency of the age is a different one; there is less scope for imagination in these days; and instead of Art, political, national, and material interests principally employ the minds of men. For this reason, the artist who reveres the immortal Past will cherish the element in which its greatness consisted — the beautiful Ideal, that it may continue to set forth all that is noblest and best in men."

But of the three nineteenth-century German texts that have been translated, the most popular and helpful has been the two-volume *Illustrated History of Music* by Emil Naumann [100]. The doctrine of Progress, which has always tended to discredit the achievements of the age previous, is apparent in Naumann. Just as the eighteenth century abhorred the " Gothic barbarities " of the Middle Ages, so did the nineteenth century piously rebuke the " extravagances " of the seventeenth- and eighteenth-century Baroque. Naumann shows romantic interest in the Middle Ages, but his information was meager. Then, too, his prejudices make it impossible for him to present Bach and his predecessors objectively. *Zopf* is the term of contempt for the Rococo influences which were so harmful, and yet he does not realize what stimulating effects *Zopf* had on serious German musicians, and how the German classical tradition refined and perfected many of these *Zopf* forms which were so popular. This prejudice was applauded in Victorian England, and the translator accentuates it, if anything. Information regarding the new nationalistic tendencies in the latest edition is given later.

But with all the prejudice, there is a quantity of interesting information, and Naumann's is important as having been the first foreign text to become well-known in England and the United States. One popular textbook in this country contains paragraphs which are lifted bodily from Naumann.

Wilhelm Langhans published his *History of Music in 12 Lectures* in 1879 and these were translated also, during the next decade [98]. The writer was a violinist, with practical experience as performer and teacher. In common with his contemporaries he believed that the discussion of an artist still living and creating among us in the same line with the masters of the past is on principle not allowable, because to his contemporaries is denied a general survey of his work, and it must therefore be left to a later time to determine its value. And this was only a few years after Brendel had fought so hard for recognition of the living artist.

The success of these lectures, intended, as the author says, to increase our " understanding, not only of near-by epochs, but of the evolutionary development of the whole," was so great that Leuckardt, the publishers, asked him to finish the incomplete work of Ambros [67].

An array of rather dull textbooks completes Germany's contribution to this field of literature in the late nineteenth century. But the titles show the trend toward progressive, evolutionary explanation of music's "Development;" lectures on *Fortschreitende Entwickelung der Musik* [104]; *Die Hohenzüge der musikalischen Entwickelung* [119] and *Die Musik in ihrer kulturhistorischen Entwickelung und Bedeutung* [93]. The latter item consists of three lectures delivered at Bayreuth by a Protestant theologian. The Rev. Kraussold agrees with Kiesewetter, who had maintained that Occidental music could never have developed from the Greek system. The tremendous importance of music in the folk culture of ancient Greece is matched by the importance of the music of the present in German culture, a music that has evolved from early Christian music. The history of the latter parallels the history of the church. Each nation came to develop its own national characteristics in music; but just as Luther triumphed over the papacy, so also Germany, formerly only a geographical term, has triumphed over the musical empire to the south. Hence "all lines of evolution meet in Wagner, with Liszt at his side. In the Catholic Liszt, and the Protestant Wagner, it is hoped that the old cleft between the two cultures will be closed. Wagner's *nationalism* is of a *universal* sort, since universality is one characteristic of German national feeling." [93], p. 102. Wagner may not have been discreet in his anti-Semitism, but Kraussold did not think that he distorted the truth.

Lutheran clergymen who wrote music histories in the nineteenth century seem to have made no effort to perpetuate the ecclesiastical traditions discussed in Chapter 3. The trail blazed by the seventeenth-century pioneers was still a wide one which gave equal importance to sacred and secular music. This is even true in the work of the Rev. Köstlin [89]. But none of these conservatory-lesson texts could make the subject as interesting as Praetorius and Printz had made it long before, and as exciting as it was yet to be, under the nationalists. As far as can be ascertained, the first music historian who began to find significance in early Northern music archaeology was Adalbert Svoboda, in 1892 [125]. He discusses the *lur* and the bronze bells found in Scandinavia, which are now made so prominent in modern Nazi theories of the Germanic origins of music. (See pp. 162–164, 209–210.)

But the most important fact concerning German research in the late nineteenth century is the seriousness with which it was done.

Whereas Gustav Schilling and Von Winterfeld stand out among the few German musicologists worthy of the name in the early nineteenth century, as noted in the previous chapter, there is a host of them for this chapter. Brendel in his own way and Naumann in his set a high standard for what might be called journalistic, descriptive history. Mendel and Riemann, as already noted in Chapter 4, took up the task of lexicography once more, and Ambros set an example for careful scientific work in style criticism, free from prejudice.

It was the decade of Ambros, the 1860's, when other scientific work of a high order appeared. Joseph Fröhlich did a worth-while task with his study of documents [78], and so did Arrey von Dommer, with his *Handbuch der Musik-Geschichte* [79].

Von Dommer maintains an objective position with reference to the question of origins. He is interested in the connection of music with the practices of religion, and believes that Christendom was the soil from which music came up as a new growth, enriched by the practices of the Greeks and the temple music of the Hebrews.

But as regards primitive origins, the current theories concerning the inborn sources of the art in the religious impulses of man are severely criticized. "Music received from Nature nothing but inorganic sound; the first step was for man to get concepts of fixed pitch, and then organize different sounds into certain relationships to each other. All this had to be done before the raw material could have any artistic significance."

Although the work came out in 1867, it is carried no farther than Beethoven. In 1914 the completely revised edition came out, under Arnold Schering, who selected it as the best of the nineteenth-century histories. Even in this edition, however, the scope was carried no farther; but the addition of the results of twentieth-century research has made it a more useful work.

In 1885–1886 Franz Xaver Haberl, with his *Bausteine zur Musikgeschichte* [115], provided, like Von Winterfeld before him, one of the first collections of rigorously scientific investigations of certain phases of music history. Haberl was a great authority on polyphonic church music, and held a papal patent for the publication of the *Edition Medicaea* until the researchers at Solesmes demonstrated its errors.

2. IN FRANCE

Some of the best work in musicology of the nineteenth century was in religious music. A historian of sacred music, Clément (see Chapter 3), made some observations which were unique for that day and age:

"I do not believe it necessary to drag the reader into anthropological and ethnological theories in order to explain the differences in musical culture among various peoples.— All men without exception are endowed with the same senses; that of sight gives knowledge of form, while that of hearing gives knowledge of sound. As for results, they depend upon the degree of culture and civilization here and there.— One can not imagine a Raphael in the Malay peninsula, or a Mozart among the Zulus." [111], p. 3.

". . . Musical art is sociable by nature; thus mutual influences and exchange of ideas contribute to its progress, as to the progress of other forms of knowledge." (p. 7).

"If Méhul had stayed in Givet and Haydn in Rohrau, no matter how great the talent, it would never have come to its full development.

"The former found in the Abbey of the Prémontrés a favorable intellectual environment . . . and opportunity to emulate genius, under Gluck, in Paris. Haydn had been impressed with the religious harmonies in which he participated as a choir boy in the Vienna Cathedral. But later was he not carried away by Italian melody at the little court of Prince Esterhazy?

"Mozart doubtless studied hard at Salzburg, under his father's direction, but when, at the age when impressions are the strongest, from fifteen to nineteen years of age, he accompanied, in Rome and Milan, the principal singers in Italian theatres, was this not to his advantage, in learning how to write supple melodies for the voice?"

Reflecting the traditional French interest in literature and music, Clément reminds the reader that

"when we come to discuss taste and dramatic intelligence we must not forget that Mozart kept a volume of Metastasio constantly by him, in his coat pocket. Music being of all the arts that in which imagination and feeling have the greatest part, *exterior influences play a prominent role in the direction of ideas and the conception of great works.*"

But as soon as Clément gets to the subject of origins, he returns to fundamentalist theory:

"The alphabet, like the scale, was a medium of revealed language; signs, whether mute, painted or sculptured, do not constitute language." (p. 10).

In order to prove the communal origins of the seven-tone scale, it then becomes necessary to bring up many examples from exotic cultures, all of which fill 150 pages.

The academic prejudices of his day are notable: Brahms is barely mentioned in a list of names in the appendix, but Franck is omitted entirely, although Saint-Saëns is included. Wagner possessed "consummate knowledge" but had no taste; "harmony of proportions was unknown to him . . . his sterility of imagination explains his banishment of pure melody." (pp. 777, 778).

If the reader turns back to Chapter 3, he will note that several Catholic writers of this later ninet~enth-century period were quoted there. In that chapter France, Italy, and Ireland were represented as well as Protestant England. There are consequently only two more French writers to be mentioned: Louis Lacombe's *Philosophy of Music* [133], in which the author is interested in the origins of speech music, popular songs, and patriotism; and a work by Albert Soubies [144], which offers a unique example, i.e., short histories of all European countries except that of the author. Soubies, however, wrote extensively on special phases of French music, especially in the field of opera.

3. IN ITALY: BEGINNINGS OF CHAUVINISTIC HISTORIES

After Bontempi [7] and Martini [19], Italy was as silent concerning music history in general as she was productive in composition. The only attempt made in the early Romantic period was the little pamphlet by Celoni [54] already cited in Chapter 3. But the Risorgimento stirred Italians to some historical activity, and they immediately began along the nationalistic lines that have been so bitterly drawn in recent years. It will be shown in the next chapter that Italian and German rivalry in music often breaks into very bitter dispute. Hence we find in the 1860's, that most fertile decade for histories of music, that the first extensive work since Martini was a *Storia della musica* [76] — but *specialmente dell'italiana*. This work concludes with the modest claim that *il nostro paese nella scienza e nelle arte sopravenza ogni altri nazioni*. In the fateful year 1871, Galli [84] makes this slogan prominent: *Accettiamo il progresso, ma restiamo italiani.* And after 1871, with the progressive movements in state education in Italy as well as in France, there were teachers and writers who felt that

"Italy, the most eminent musical country, the classic land of harmony, the mother of the greatest masters in sound, song, and melody, has very few books which tell the story of music to the people." [87].

So G. Frojo took the stand that since many books have been written in the north, by nations that have their own music history, he would merely try to sketch a picture of Indo-Mediterranean culture as he saw it, in a work which was also entitled *principalmente italiana.*

It becomes apparent that these new Italian histories were passionate protests against the rise of German romanticism, from the country which had enjoyed supremacy in the musical world for so long. These were climaxed in 1886 by a book which claimed to be a history of music from the standpoint of social philosophy [114]. Fiorentino, a violent anti-Wagnerian, claimed that

"The universal language of song and our modern national language arose in Tuscany, in the same land, and at the same time . . . thus (we see) Italy mistress of the world in everything." (p. 282).
"Orlandus Lassus was Flemish by birth, but Italian in life, studies and breeding." (p. 28). Mozart was *l'italiano dei tedeschi,* etc. (p. 25).

The general argument is that when Rome fell to the barbarians, music disappeared also, to be revived in Christianity. The Roman missionaries carried music and other civilizing influences to the barbarians of the north. Schools of barren harmony and counterpoint developed in the north, but the breath of life so vital to the art was infused by Italian, *natural* melody in spite of barbarian invaders ("Wagners") in every century. Therefore true music is Italian music: *"Musica é la musica italiana."*

But evidently the outstanding successes of Verdi and younger Italians in the operatic nineties made such protests unnecessary; no more history of music was written in Italy until Bonaventura's praiseworthy work in 1914, except a popular narrative history by Untersteiner [128], a Tyrolean who died in Austria during the World War as an interned Italian.

Bonaventura's history of music [192], which has gone through many editions, makes a very sensible plea for composer-resistance to German influence, condemns undue worship of foreign gods, but without any spirit of offensive chauvinism. This did not reappear until after the World War, until the emergence of the Fascist histories to be discussed in the next chapter.

4. IN ENGLAND

The opposite of chauvinism appears in English histories of music during the Victorian era. The worship of the German gods, Handel, Mendelssohn, and Brahms, was as devout as Burney's conviction that music was a luxury to be imported from Italy. This situation made the British historian of music more detached, more apt to view differences not from a nationalistic, but from a world point of view. We have noted this tendency in the work of Rowbotham and Parry, who followed in the methodological paths of Comte and Spencer, and their works were dwelt upon at length because of their influence upon the teaching of music history today in this country.

With the exception of the rather truculent work published by Chappell in 1874 [88], all of the music historians of this period were connected with education, directly or indirectly. John Pyke Hullah, the very successful lecturer and pedagogue, was the outstanding figure in the 1860's, the decade of Ambros and so many others. Hullah seems to have been one of the first to follow Schilling's definition of modern music as having begun in 1600. The British interest in Progress as a matter of world differences is illustrated in this passage from Hullah's *History of Modern Music* [70]:

"What we now call music, that which completely realizes our idea or answers to our definition of music, has come into being only within comparatively few years; almost within the memory of men living. . . . Composers and performers of the eighteenth and nineteenth century have been too much occupied in making history to study it. . . . Although it would be inexcusable to omit from the baldest outline of it certain grand forms which loom out of the darkness of the earlier centuries of our era, yet we shall find little demanding precise attention until the eleventh, and little of what we now understand by music, until the fifteenth century. Moreover, the history of modern music is altogether European." As for the Orientals . . . "How can there be music acceptable to one comparatively civilized people and altogether unacceptable, unintelligible even to another? The answer is to be found in the different nature of their musical system. . . . It is difficult enough for an ear trained in the nineteenth century to reconcile itself to the various modes used in the fifteenth and sixteenth centuries. But to reconcile itself to another system seems impossible. Happily it is not in the least necessary. The European system, though the exigencies of practice prevent its being absolutely true, is nearer the truth than any other."

All of this, while showing interest in world-wide systems, evinces no disposition to enjoy differences or to understand them. Belief in Progress made it essential to prove the " truth " or " superiority " of European music and the " higher " development of the modern as compared with the ancient. At another point Hullah betrays the insular point of view and that of the borrower in a paradoxical judgment on Bach:

" The Well-Tempered Clavichord will probably outlive all existing music. . . . But is Bach the Handel even of Germany? Does he enter into the musical life of his countrymen as Handel does into ours? Surely not. *Handel's music is an oak* which has struck its roots deep into English soil. . . . *Bach's,* so to speak, *is an exotic, even in Germany;* blooming no doubt in the *Conservatorium* and the *Akademie,* but unfit, as yet at least, for open-air life. Whether many specimens of it will ever be acclimatized anywhere remains to be proved." (p. 136). (A footnote in the second edition acknowledges growth of Bach's popularity.)

Hullah was admittedly a popularizer, but a skillful one, who probably interested many laymen in music and its history. His *Transition Period of Musical History* shows in some respects a more sympathetic treatment of seventeenth-century music than is accorded it in some later works in which the evolution theory was more definitely basic.

Other popularizers included Nancy R. E. Bell [103], who attempted a synthesis of art histories, Sir George MacFarren [112], and Henry Davey [123]. Davey urged the rather surprising advice that composers " steer clear of the rock of conventionality on which nearly every British composer has been wrecked." Davey's book, like Hunt's text, went through several editions. Hunt [95] frankly says his book is *not* " readable, but written for systematic students, not for entertainment." Hunt was also one of the first to include chronological charts.

Perhaps the most serious Victorian history of music aside from Parry's was that of William S. Rockstro [117], contemporaneous with and comparable in some respects to the *Illustrated History* by Naumann [100].

The climax of Victorian music historiography was reached in the *Oxford History of Music* [146]. It continues the evolutionary philosophy of Parry, as already noted, but as it comes after 1900, it will be treated among modern texts on the subject.

In 1896 Edward MacDowell returned from an eleven-year sojourn abroad. Acknowledged leader among American composers, his every word was heeded with great interest by eager students. The next chapter will show how his casual acceptance of the prevalent theories of Rowbotham and Parry influenced the teaching of music history in this country.

5. IN THE UNITED STATES

As already stated, the first histories of music in this country were reprints from abroad [45, 48]. The first text published in this country was Joseph Bird's *Gleanings from the History of Music,* in 1850 [59]. This volume was to have been followed by a second. Acknowledging his debt to Burney and Hawkins, the author says,

" From these two works we have taken what seems to us most useful and pleasing, trusting that what was most so to us would be so to others." (p. iv).

The first work by a trained scholar of the German school was by Frédéric Louis Ritter [83]. Ritter, an Alsatian by birth, came to New York in 1861, and was made Professor of Music in Vassar College in 1874. This pioneer work in American music history writing was inspired, as most American texts have been, by the practical exigencies of the classroom. Music-library materials were practically nonexistent in the average American city of Ritter's day and his bibliographies are evidently lists of the books that he had brought with him.

There are no speculations on origins and no guesses, but evidence is given of a sound grasp of his subject, and of high ideals in presenting it. He condemns the superficiality of the average person's notions of music, but scores no less severely the " one-sided education of our musicians . . . in general . . . their whole attention is directed toward the technical side of musical art." To offset this, he urges that musicians equip themselves with training in the humanities, philosophy, history, and esthetics. Ritter also left a history of American music.

William J. Henderson was the first in this country to make a summary of the subject from the standpoint of the journalist and musical critic [121, 139]. All the others, until 1900, and most since that time have been compilations from foreign summaries, and of course it could not be otherwise until our libraries and librarians were equipped to offer the necessary access to original sources.

It is important to note, however, that none of these texts are concerned with speculations concerning the "origins" of music, or with cosmic or nationalistic philosophies concerning its "progress." The method is merely the old genealogical chain of biographies.

CHAPTER 8

HISTORIES OF MUSIC SINCE 1900

I. PRELIMINARY SURVEY OF LITERATURE IN CURRENT USE

THE FIRST pre-war decade and a half of this century might be called
the Voluminous Period. Ten authors and editors began or completed works of more than two volumes each, which now total
seventy-three volumes in all. Three of these were German, three
were French, while England and America each produced two.
First the *Quellen-Lexicon* of Eitner [145] began to appear, then
the *Oxford History of Music* [146] and then Hugo Riemann's
Handbuch [150]. The last marked a new epoch in the literature.
The author was one of the first theorists and practical musicians
to take up music historiography since Calvisius and Praetorius.
After years of lexicographic and other research,[1] Riemann approached this task with a vast store of erudition and insatiable
curiosity concerning the hitherto unknown. Erudition is attested
not only by his Lexicon, but by his *History of Music Theory*
(1898); and curiosity by his original research on the mid-eight-
eenth-century music of the Mannheim School, to name one item
alone. But Riemann's *Handbuch* is for these reasons a formidable
work, for advanced students only, and his interests as a theorist
dominate his whole concept of history. The seventeenth century,
for example, now studied as the Baroque era, was styled by Riemann "the general-bass period," because of the technical use of
the figured bass as the basis of ensemble music at that time.

The *Oxford History of Music* was initiated three years before
Riemann's, consequently the first edition came too early for inclu-
sion of modern data unearthed by continental research. It is hard
to understand why the second edition was not brought up to date
in this respect. However, in explaining the necessity for the Intro-

---

[1] See Moser's *Musiklexicon* for a partial but staggering list of Riemann's works.

ductory Volume,[2] the editor, in the preface, shows that the original volumes by Wooldridge on the medieval period employed a method that was,

"to a large extent, too one-sided. The student of his volumes is liable to gather the impression that throughout the Middle Ages music was in a state of chaos, and that the great men were those who nursed the art through its growing pains and infantile complaints, steered it through shoals and quicksands, and slowly and painfully forged a medium in which we can now express ideas which are moving and profound. But are we justified in assuming that for centuries musicians felt themselves to be struggling in the dark after something dimly conceived to be possible, never imagining that they had attained to a means of expressing the human feelings of joy and beauty in a form felt, at the time, to be entirely adequate? It is an axiom of the modern historian that, however backward the development of any branch of human life may seem when scrutinized by a later generation, to its own contemporaries it is always ' modern.' "

All this refutes Parry's notions of evolution and progress in music, with all its "stages" of "development" that appear in "logical order."

Just as Parry felt that mere biography does not make music history, so also men today are beginning to realize that the evolutionary explanation of historical processes has its difficulties. This introductory volume now comes as an effort to make a new beginning for a work that began, in 1901, with a disquisition on Greek music as a "stage" preliminary to the "development" of polyphonic music. The new Volume I now begins with early Christian music, gets as quickly as possible to the first notated compositions, and leaves the discussion of Greek music, at least of Greek scales and theory, to an introductory volume.

In 1905, a new type of organization was introduced, a collection of independent volumes, edited by Hermann Kretzschmar, each volume devoted to a different form or style — Lieder, Opera, Oratorio, Symphony, and Suite, and so on [153]. The distinguished list of contributors includes several who have other histories recorded in this bibliography.

The other voluminous works to which reference was made above were the Hubbard compilation in this country [168], the prize Histoire by Woollett [177], Mason's Art of Music [201], Colles'

---

[2] A new work, not published until 1929 [257].

Growth of Music [185], Jules Combarieu's great history [189] and the colossal *Encyclopédie* of Lavignac [190], described in Chapter 4. But while these works were in preparation, some smaller works came out which have had even greater influence on the continuity of philosophies of music history in education. So during the "Voluminous Period" there came to be, more than ever, a Babel of argument.

Eighteen texts appeared in 1907–1908 in different countries — the beginning of a veritable flood of new material to meet the increasing demand for information about music, in schools and conservatories, colleges and universities. In the United States, Winton J. Baltzell, in his *Complete History of Music* [152], initiated the evolutionary gospel of music history in 1905, after hearing MacDowell's lectures, which he edited in 1912 [186].[3] In 1907 Edward Dickinson warned Americans that the "origin of music is a speculative and not a historical question, since records must be lacking," and that "the history of music cannot be led back to a priority of either melody or rhythm."

But in that same year powerful support came for the evolution theory, from Jules Combarieu [158] in France, who was strongly influenced by Wagnerian and Darwinian theories of evolution,[4] and from Thomas Whitney Surette and Daniel Gregory Mason, whose pioneer work on *Music Appreciation* made basic use of Parry's theories.[5]

It was in 1907 that Waldo Selden Pratt [162] published the first syllabus draft of his history for American college students, a sober work after the fashion of the German *Handbücher*. But it was in the same year that a work of the opposite nature appeared in Paris, by Riciotto Canudo [156], author of *Mon âme pourpre*. This impressionistic-symbolist interpretation of the history of music shows the extremes to which the evolutionary theory could carry an enthusiast. According to Canudo, primitive man and woman learned *mouvement extatique* by bodily contact in " nights illumi-

---

[3] Baltzell's preface is entitled " What We Learn from Ethnology," and states the assumption of Rowbotham [113] and Parry [126]: that the primitive people of the world today occupy a *stage* similar to that of the primitive races from which the civilized folk of Western civilization have sprung; that from primitive origins history can trace the development of the art germ up to the product we now know.

[4] Lavignac's *Musical Education* had taken the same lead a few years earlier [147]. Both the Combarieu and the Lavignac texts were translated into English almost immediately; [158] is one of the most frequently quoted sources quoted in Part II.

[5] See Chapter 12, pp. 289–305 ff.

nated by the amorous eyes of the stars;" and they learned *mouvement orgiastique* from elements let loose by the tumultuous rhythm of the storm (that is, "in repeating, with their furious bodies, the movement of the trees, in order not to be vanquished and annihilated"). Primeval song burst forth for the same reason, "in order to surpass with their own cries the cries of Nature." After tracing music's evolution through the cosmic upheavals represented by church and state and man, the series is carried through the usual "stages."

In the following year (1908) William Wallace, M.D. [172] attempted to discuss the art of music in relation to other phases of thought, and to trace, through its history, the cerebral processes concerned in its own development, concluding that "music is the youngest of the arts," because the human brain has only developed the complex qualities necessary for real music within the last two centuries! (See pp. 154, 257 of this book.)

On the other hand, Frederick J. Crowest, at about that same time, maintained that "Music is not the 'youngest and greatest,' but the 'oldest and grandest' of the arts;" furthermore, that moderns should be omitted from history, because "the last word in music worth hearing has been spoken for many a long period, and this by the masters dealt with in my small space." [148], Intro. And simultaneously there appeared a title which takes one back to the eighteenth century: "The Rise of Music, being a Careful Inquiry into the Development of the Art from its Primitive Puttings Forth in Egypt and Assyria to its Triumphant Consummation in Modern Effect." [167].

In 1908, the first of the German chauvinistic histories of music [161] appeared, in which it is exultantly stated that no genius in France has ever reacted upon Germans as Wagner has upon the French.

By 1910 a French text, by Paul Landormy [179], is ready for the nationalistic combat for culture supremacy, and in the English translation it becomes a potent antidote for pre-war beliefs in native German supremacy. Karl Storck retorts in kind from Stuttgart [181], but puts out a more amiable work in 1911 [181A], which shows the history of music with the aid of caricature and satire.

In the meantime, patient scholars like Wolf, Ludwig, and others were deciphering medieval and Renaissance notation, and bringing to life the glories of Gothic music and the *ars nova,* thus extending the frontiers of music history for future enjoyment and knowledge of the past. A vast gulf yawned between the musicologist and the popularizer who was intent upon simplifying the " Story of Music," while between the two was the field of argument, battles over the priority of rhythm or melody, the historical order of the pipe, lyre, and drum, and whether vocal music came before any of them. Then came the World War, and the cultural battle between the nationalists has been intensified ever since.

During the war, production of music histories almost ceased, as might have been expected. Arnold Schering completed his revision of Von Dommer [196] and his interesting *Tabellen* by 1914 [197], and Alfred Einstein's popular book [204] first came out in 1917. Stanford and Forsyth, and Tapper and Goetschius, started a vogue for joint authorship [199, 203], and a Polish history of music emerged [202]. But the most interesting developments in the whole history of this literature have taken place in the post-war period.

Post-war is an unfortunate term, of course, as war still rages. At any rate, after the Armistice, diametrically different tendencies appeared in histories of music. One was a humanistic and the other an ideological trend; one tended to broaden and the other to narrow the outlook of the student of music history; one sought to find correlations between music and the other arts, to keep music and its history entirely hospitable to interesting changes, while another was conservative and suspicious of the unusual. These trends were not at all new, but the texts manifesting them began to appeal to lay as well as to professional and student readers.

Several short summaries have had international circulation; four liberal continental texts have been taken up in translation, in at least four other countries. The authors are Einstein, Bekker, Wolf,[6]

---

[6] Alfred Einstein [204] is the editor of Riemann's *Musiklexicon* (1929 ed.) and is now in this country. Paul Bekker [238], driven from Germany after 1933, made his home in New York until his death in 1937. Other works of his known in English are *The Changing Opera, Beethoven,* and *The Story of the Orchestra.*

Johannes Wolf [261], of the University of Berlin, is particularly noted for his valuable work on the music of the Middle Ages. This explains the preponderant emphasis upon medieval music. The Baroque period is briefly treated, but with a complete disappearance of nineteenth-century prejudice. The Age of Enlightenment, in its two divisions, is treated more at length, and in both periods the author shows an international outlook, giving more information than one might expect in so small a compass concerning the lesser individuals that went to make up the groups which were so important.

and Karl Nef [210].[7] Nef's book, like the other three, is free from the virus of nationalism, and the translator's Foreword mentions the " fair and impartial manner " in which this outline is presented, from the traditionally neutral Swiss point of view. Furthermore, the author has endeavored, as he said in his own original Foreword, to provide " not merely a reference book, but a book for the general reader as well." For the serious student the extensive bibliographies and musical illustrations are particularly valuable.

Although Romain Rolland has not written a general history, his *Musical Tour through the Land of the Past* [223] contains some observations very pertinent to the subject. For example, Rolland believes that the greatest artistic personalities are not always the pioneers of the future. . . . (Intro.) He even asserts that Wagner laid waste the future of German music; that Kuhnau quietly foreshadowed the future destinies of German art and the achievements of his successor, J. S. Bach. The greater (German) composers of the eighteenth century received a liberal education; they studied jurisprudence, and often hesitated before becoming musicians professionally.

Two English critics have had a large reading public in the United States among students and laymen as well: Cecil Gray [246] and George Dyson [280]. Gray makes no attempt to write a complete history, but discusses music history in its relationship to other phases of culture. It is a series of essays, in which many traditions are questioned, among them the exaggerated importance of Greek influence and the Idea of Progress.

There is much concern over the matter of relative genius; frequent use is made of the words " great," " greater," or " greatest." The picturesque language of analogy is brought in to support value judgments; Okeghem is " the Karl Marx," Josquin " the Lenin," and Wagner is " the Napoleon " of music. The author brings some artists to the fore that had been neglected by nineteenth-century

---

[7] The work of this Swiss scholar has been translated into French, Norwegian, and now into English for American students.

It is Number One in a series inaugurated by the Columbia University Press, entitled *Studies in Musicology*. " The choice of the first volume of the series was dictated by the desire to provide an introductory manual which would be of interest to the beginner in musical history, since a scholarly view of the development of the art must be the foundation of scholarly research into special problems." (Otto Kinkeldey, in the Prefatory Note).

historians, notably Mussorgsky, with appreciation of his great significance.

The Spengler influence is manifest. In both books music is seen to be evolving in some way from classic to romantic values:

"All romantic art is a swan-song, the final expression of a civilization, the rich autumn tints of decay, the writing on the wall, the flaming comet heralding the approach of anarchy and dissolution." (*A Survey of Contemporary Music*, p. 18).

George Dyson provides a series of essays on music (1) in "The Church," (2) in "Castle and Chamber," (3) on "The Stage," and (4) in "The Concert-Hall," with one, in conclusion, on "Men and Machines." The procedure is to discuss musical activities in these various fields in relation to the social environment:

"Bach was in truth himself a provincial organist, and had not provincial organists at that time been composers as well, there would have been no Bach. Wagner, at the time his ideas were germinating, was a provincial conductor, who, like his fellows, also wrote operas. Neither Bach nor Wagner could claim any peculiar status; they did what all their contemporaries were doing. . . . The reason why our present-day organists and conductors are not writing music is simply the lack of demand. These men hold, between them, nearly all the most influential musical appointments. We have ceased to expect them to be creative as well. We ask them for high specialization of performance, and we get what we seek. . . . A few specialist-writers producing a few specialist works are no sufficient substitute. . . . *The supply of potential genius does not fail. . . . What fails is the power of a society, mainly engrossed in reproducing the past, to provide for present arts and crafts.* Had the eighteenth century behaved as we do, what should we know of it? What will our successors know of us? " [280], p. 233.

This is the sort of statement that has been rare since the Baroque histories. (See Ch. 1.)

Cyril Scott's theosophical interpretation [253] has been discussed in Chapter 3. Other histories are better known, e.g., the educational texts of Percy Scholes [234, 252], the tiny history in reverse by Percy Buck [255], and the suppressed work by Eaglefield Hull [244].

Buck begins with the present, and works back through the Romantic, Viennese, Contrapuntal, and Renaissance periods to the *Infancy of Music*. There are frequent references to "stages of development" and the "continuous progress" of the art. The author, in his Preface to the Oxford Introductory Volume [257], gets away from this. It would seem as if this little book were an earlier work.

In the Preface it is claimed that "It is a history of music, not of musicians," but Beethoven is credited with the invention of orchestration, Chopin with the invention of piano technique, Wagner with the invention of orchestral color.

The post-Armistice production of music histories has been prolific, but only two editors have brought together histories comparable to those of the "Voluminous Period" prior to 1914. These two musicologists are Guido Adler [224] and Ernst Bücken [260], each representing a different school of thought, but each with his distinct contribution.

Whereas Adler's work is more concerned with music as a particular art, with unique problems of its own, that of Bücken seems to be more in agreement with Bonaventura, who said, in 1914, in his Introduction [192] that

"The study of the history of music, to be truly profitable, and successful, cannot remain isolated, but must be correlated with history in general, and the other arts in particular. . . .

"Thus, for example, we must know the intellectual conditions during the early Middle Ages, when religious fanaticism had taken hold of men's minds, to really understand the essence of Gregorian chant, and of the later vocal, sacred polyphony of our great sixteenth-century masters; similarly, knowledge of the seventeenth-century society, particularly in the France of Louis XIV, is most necessary, in order to get the spirit of a gavotte, or of a minuet. . . . And certainly the state of mind in the epic and glorious period of our political Risorgimento, made its impression upon the early works of Verdi."

The ten *de luxe* volumes edited by Bücken, with lavish illustrations in color, are apt to make the two large volumes in Guido Adler's *Handbook* appear drab and sober in comparison. But both works, staffed by brilliant writers, place the results of modern historical research within easy access.

Bücken and Adler have always been diligent students of historical method. They have brought to the compilation of these works intelligent ways and means of improving upon the works of their predecessors. Bücken is strongly influenced by the line of humanist historians from Forkel and Ambros on, rather than by the analytical group, from Fétis to Riemann and Adler. Bücken seems to be one of the few commentators who have recognized these two schools of historians and their opposing tendencies.[8]

So while Adler treats the history of music as a phenomenon to be studied by and for itself, Bücken treats it as only one of the interrelated ways in which man expresses himself, not to be understood without some knowledge of pictures, architecture, sculpture, and letters. Adler would not neglect these matters, but recommends caution. He believes that *inner* resemblances between music and architecture hold good, but that temporal manifestations of the spirit of the age are not always parallel, and that even when they are, they assume different forms. In other words, Adler is more particular about periodization than Bücken; the former's position is that technical analysis of music alone, its form (melody, harmony, polyphony, key, subjects, tone-color, etc.) together with its intellectual and psychological content, must provide the basic criteria. Time, place, and composer are the historical facts that must be calculated on these bases alone. In the first place, according to this theory, the date of a given composition can be determined by comparing it with the typical styles isolated as characteristic of certain periods. These periods must first be arranged in historical order. The place is determined by examination of folk music and national characteristics, also with reference to that which is typical. The highest task of style criticism concerns itself with the work of the composer. The typical must always be isolated, not, as in the older school of biography, with subjective, psychological examination of personality traits, but with technical comparisons of individual styles and idioms.

For those who may find Adler's *Methode* [207] too formidable, a brief summary of his theories is available.[9] In this he refers to the fact that his first work (*Der Stil in der Musik*, 1911) appeared simultaneously with and independently of *Style in Musical Art* (London, 1911), by Sir C. Hubert H. Parry. But Adler and Parry have little in common when discussing style. As in *The Art of Music*, already cited, Parry is more interested in "higher" or "lower" phases of style than in objectively studied style periods.

[8] See *Grundfragen der Musikgeschichte als Geisteswissenschaft*, in *Jahrb. der Musikbibliothek Peters*, 1927, pp. 19–30.

[9] "Style Criticism," in *The Musical Quarterly*, XX, 2, Apr., 1934, tr. by Oliver Strunk.

There were music historians in France, also, who treated the subject with emphasis upon concepts of independent, abstract form, but the general tendency has been to agree with Bücken and Bonaventura. In 1911, Maurice Emmanuel, in his *Histoire de la langue musicale* [183], began as follows, with the evolutionary theory of form history:

" This book is an attempt to write history in which neither artists nor works occupy the foreground, but in which the successive epochs, abstractly individualized, form the natural divisions of the treatment . . . scales, harmony, notation, rhythm, and the forms are studied and summarized — reduced to their principles."

But four years later this same author, also a composer, authority on Greek music, and teacher, wrote a preface commending A. Dandelot [200] for including names and dates from other fields of history in the margins, with this remark: *L'excessive spécialisation des études est un grand danger.*

Another follower of Lavoix was Paul Bertrand, who stated, in his *Précis d'Histoire de la musique* (Paris, 1914), that the *principles générateurs des formes musicales* are:

1. Unitary — implying mere existence.
2. Binary — implying action.
3. Ternary — implying knowledge, equilibrium, and symmetry, the complete expression of life.

Each form is catalogued with its characteristics and its evolution. The above tri-partite classification is found everywhere, reminding one of the Romantic use of three in the previous century. Music is discussed according to epochs and schools, as well as the forms just mentioned:

The " Ancient Epoch " divides into (a) Antiquity, (b) Middle Ages, and (c) Renaissance. The " Modern Epoch " into (a) Classic, (b) Romantic, and (c) Modern.

The principal schools are Italy, Germany, and France. Italy, influenced by Antiquity, puts melody above everything, and, as in the plastic arts, develops music on the surface. Germany, of much more recent national origin with basic harmonic concept, aims at expression and inner depth. France, " predestined to receive the impressions of other races and to co-ordinate them harmoniously," is a sort of arbiter between Italy and Germany. Other nations are treated as secondary growths.

In 1928, Armand Machabey pursues the *Histoire et évolution des formules musicales du Ier au XVme siècle de l'ère chrétienne,* to find that the perfect cadence of the classicists was formulated so successfully by the fifteenth century that musicians have used it ever since and that it has received positive consecration in the textbooks of musical theorists [250].

So although the abstract study of musical forms found adherents in France, it appears in various guises, thanks to the intellectual vivacity of the Gallic scholar. And for the most part French and Italian historians are in agreement with the Ambros-Bücken school, for they very frequently find ways and means of linking up the arts by means of interesting correlations.

"The development of harmony parallels that of Occidental civilization . . . certain synchronous parallels can be pointed out, even though one must allow for the particular conditions under which various arts are developed." [10]

Before citing these works in detail, however, it may be appropriate to discuss the problem of correlation, with review of some contemporary thought on the subject.

II. MUSIC AND THE OTHER ARTS

I. MUSIC, LANGUAGE, AND POETRY

It has been pointed out that the rationalization of the theory of music's divine origin emphasized its simultaneous origin and parallel development with that of language. A phrase used over and over in Romantic histories is "Music is coeval with mankind." When Hugo says that poetry awoke with man and that primitive man's first speech was a hymn, he formulates in Romantic terms the basic argument of the earlier ecclesiastical histories. This argument was an inference from Genesis, asserting that man's first vocal utterance was a hymn of praise to his Creator. Romantic historians interested in vocal music primarily, whether for dramatic or liturgical uses, have always agreed that poetry and music were originally united, and that they became separated in a sort of degenerative process.[11]

---

[10] *L'histoire de la musique et l'histoire générale,* in *Gand Artistique,* Ghent, 8me Année, No. 3, 1929, by Paul Bergmans, author of *La musique et les musiciens,* Paris, 1901.

[11] See discussions of John Brown and Forkel, in Chapter 5.

Too often, studies in the origins of music or of language deal with psychological speculation concerning unorganized sound or exclamation. The Darwinian and Spencerian theories relating music to sexual selection and impassioned speech illustrate this confusion. Music is, in one sense, a language, an art which communicates tonal ideas in organized form. The study of sound, *per se,* whether vocal or otherwise, is a branch of physiology or physics that may have nothing whatever to do with art. A writer on linguistics has already stated the case admirably, and every word of his remarks can be applied to music as well as to language:

"Language, as it really exists, as an instrument for the communication of thought, only exists in the form of complete sentences, and therefore any further analysis of the sentence into words, syllables and sounds is, whatever its value as a grammatical exercise, purely artificial. The century-long tradition of analyzing the sentence into its component parts, combined with the more modern practice of investigating sound changes, has obscured the recognition of this fact. Concurrently the belief has grown up that the sound or the word is the unit of language, even though a moment's reflection would show that neither sound nor word exists independently in language except in a few exclamations and commands." [12]

The foregoing considerations may well be kept in mind whenever the parallel histories of music and language come up for discussion.

"The Boundaries of Music and Poetry" were well defined, in the mid-nineteenth century, when such definition was badly needed, by Ambros.[13] Ambros' little volume treats of these boundaries in the field of esthetics, with a sensitive appreciation of values that inspired his *magnum opus* (1862). Treating, as it does, of poetry and music from Shakespeare to Beethoven, it makes the reader regret that Ambros' history never reached the periods in which his esthetic reflections would have been of the greatest value.

In more recent years, treatises by Torrefranca [165] and Combarieu [158, 175] are illustrative of Latin interests in the subject. Both are philologists, one interested in a typical Italian theory of the origins of music in alliteration, and the other in a theory of

---

[12] E. Claasen, " A Theory of the Development of Language," *Modern Language Review*, XII, 1917, p. 2.

[13] See the English translation, *The Boundaries of Music and Poetry*, by J. H. Cornell, Schirmer, New York, 1893, 187 pp.

music's beginnings in magic and ritual. It is inevitable that such theories should be stressed in France and Italy, both great centers of music history from the early Christian era until the Renaissance. The beginnings of our system in Gregorian monody and Gothic polyphony and the glorious traditions of folk and operatic song in both countries have made it obviously necessary to study music and poetry together. The weaknesses of those theories which attempt to go beyond historical records into the unknown past will be pointed out in a later section on "Nationalism in Music Histories." Obviously, the history of recorded poetry can go back much farther than the history of recorded music, hence the reams of theory into which the latter is stretched, in a Procrustean effort to parallel the former.[14]

Wagner's theories are in a class by themselves, to be discussed later.[15] Torrefranca, since 1918, has been the stormy petrel of Italian nationalism, but Combarieu died during the World War, after leaving a general history, perhaps the most exhaustive discussion of music history from the social standpoint [189]. The *Histoire* of Combarieu was originally in two volumes, ending with the death of Beethoven; the third volume was added in 1920, having been finished by others after Combarieu's death.[16]

Combarieu takes a middle position between the types of historian represented by Bücken and Adler. There are important parallels for him, but the art of music has more relationship to the arts of rhythm (poetry and dance) than to those of design. The preface begins with an inquiry into the neglect of music by French writers who claimed to write the history of art, and the place of the "arts of rhythm" (music and poetry) in contrast to the arts of space and design:

"Only the arts of rhythm are of the people. They can become very erudite if they choose, but they alone can attain a high degree of beauty

---

[14] This sort of history is well illustrated by the initial chapters of Moser's *Geschichte der deutschen Musik* [209], in which the characteristics of pre-historic German music are *deduced* from extant fragments of old poetry.

[15] In Chapter 11.

[16] Combarieu came into contact with German scholarship in 1887, under Spitta, in Berlin. This experience evidently made him more sensitive to the lack of musical instruction in the French schools. He became general inspector of choral singing, founded two musical reviews, one, the *Revue Musicale,* devoted to research. His interests led him to write on esthetics, and his *Music, Its Laws and Evolution* [158] is a statement of the sociological and psychological theories upon which his history is based. (See Chapter 9 of this book.)

when remaining near their source, that is, near to the poems and songs of illiterate peoples." (A debatable assumption, to be answered by the admirers of other folk arts.) " The arts of space are, on the other hand, aristocratic, luxurious and costly. . . . The History of Musical Art is a branch of philology . . . its method is none other than that of the classical histories: study of original documents, deciphering of old works, comparison of authorities, classification of the literature, and, *when gaps have to be filled, discreet conjectures."* (Preface, Vol. I, p. viii).

More recently, Wilhelm Dilthey has managed to discuss music and poetry without even " discreet conjectures" about origins.[17] He begins his historical references with the data available in Tacitus and other writers. Except for passing mention which may be lip service to national myths, no attention is paid to theories of " Indo-German" origins. No attempt is made to ascertain what old German music "must have been; " Dilthey is content to begin his discussions of music with *Anfänge der grossen deutschen Musik* in the eighteenth century (p. 194). The reader is given a picture of the sort of society that demanded music and poetry. With this picture drawn, another is sketched which compares the art of Bach, Haydn, Mozart, and Beethoven. These comparisons show clearly the relationship which their music bore toward poetry, illumined by light from the social background. Both Combarieu and Dilthey have made helpful interpretations of masses of material showing how both music and poetry may be guides to the understanding of our habits of communication.[18]

2. MUSIC AND THE VISUAL ARTS

Visual arts, while having no such vital connection with music as is possessed by poetry and the dance, offer, nevertheless, many suggestive possibilities. These were first appreciated by Ambros, who has been cited in connection with poetry:

"When, in his Athenaeum, Schlegel called music architecture in a fluid state, and architecture frozen music, this was by no means a trivial play with antitheses. In like manner, Sebastian Bach's profound yet fantastic tone-tissues have been compared to the miracles of Germanic architecture. Of a truth, music, with its symmetrical repetition of parts,

---

[17] *Von deutscher Dichtung und Musik,* from *Studien zur Geschichte des deutschen Geistes.* Leipzig and Berlin, Teubner, 1933, 467 pp.

[18] Recent American texts, by Finney and Ferguson, have good chapters on this correlation, but much remains to be done.

with its tone-members harmonizing and standing in intellectual relation one with another, offers in its formal part the most decided analogy
with architecture. . . ."

This paragraph indicates one of the major interests in Ambros'
historical research. He stands quite apart from other nineteenth-
century historians on account of this interest in the parallels between music and the fine arts of design.

Curiously, it did not occur to Ambros to include pictorial repro-
ductions which might have illustrated his text effectively. The first
to adopt this procedure was Naumann [100], who simply followed
the example set by Father Kircher. (See Chapter 1.) Illustrated
histories, with pictures of contemporary painting, sculpture, and
architecture, have been common ever since, but in the last decade
there are several which have endeavored to emulate Ambros in
discussing the spirit common to music and the fine arts. Henry
Prunières, for instance, in Volume I of his new history [293] includes pictures of thirteenth-century sculpture in an attempt to
give his readers a hint of the underlying genius of Gothic art, in
view of the rarity of Gothic music in actual performance today.
Another able Parisian has published another work, attractive for
the same reason [294].

Among the Italian histories, that by Enrico Magni-Dufflocq relies
extensively on pictorial aids [258],[19] and one American text, at
least, has introduced interesting material for study of artistic and
historical parallels.[20]

At least one history has been attempted with pictures only.[21]

[19] This *Storia della musica*, by Magni-Dufflocq, is by far the most interesting
Italian work, and of great interest to the lover of *de luxe* books. The binding is in
vellum, and the plates, both in color and in photogravure, are as distinguished as
the selection is admirable. Pictures include many scenes from the stage and opera
house, as well as examples from the masters. *The Theatre*, from Greco-Roman days,
and the development of instruments are among the subjects given most attention.

The text would need only one modest volume, were it not for the illustrations,
and is intended for the layman rather than for the professional, as explained in the
Preface.

The work begins with chapters on exotic, extra-European systems, as examples
of " primitive " music. Contemporary and late nineteenth-century music is given
extensive treatment in Vol. II. The chapter on Russia is unusually adequate. No
music of the western hemisphere is mentioned.

[20] Howard McKinney and W. R. Anderson, *Discovering Music; A Course in
Appreciation*, with a supplementary chart, *The Arts against the Background of
History*, New York, American Book Co., 1934.

[21] Georg Kinsky, *A History of Music in Pictures*, Leipzig and London, 1930.

Some of these examples may indicate nothing more than the authors' desire to make their books attractive with pictorial illustration. But the study of art correlations in music histories have two serious phases that are worthy of recognition. In the first place, research has gone to ancient, medieval, and Renaissance art for information concerning musical life and the use of instruments. In the second place, analyses of music and pictorial art have sought to define the fundamental characteristics that appear in all great art during a given period.

Paintings and bas-relief have furnished source material for music history from time immemorial. The evidence gleaned from these sources has sometimes disproved certain assumptions that had been common previously. Edward Buhle [22] assembled some interesting data from medieval miniatures, in 1903, and important conclusions came out of the research made by Hugo Leichtentritt two years later. The theory that Renaissance vocal music was entirely *a cappella* had to be discarded thirty years ago, as a result of Leichtentritt's studies.[23]

In the late nineteenth century, musicians and painters seem to have begun to realize, more than before, how much they have in common. In Germany, this may have been due to the Wagner-Liszt tradition, which had upheld the ideals of " tone painting " and " orchestral color." In France, the association of Symbolists and Impressionists with musicians had its effect. New preoccupation with light went hand in hand with " atmospheric " effects in tone. Since Cézanne and Renoir more artistic terms have been put into circulation, such as " color orchestration " and " planes of sound." In art history, H. Wölfflin [24] seems to have been one of the first to recognize parallels in past periods. At least his are the discussions which have occasioned most comment in musical journals. Three articles in the latter give a clue to the concepts which have made the terms Renaissance, Baroque, and Rococo as meaningful, lately, in music as in art history. As pointed out in Chapter 1 of this volume, the term Baroque, until the late nineteenth century, was a term of contempt. But Wölfflin, in *Renaissance und Barock* (1888),

[22] *Die musikalischen Instrumente in der Miniaturen des frühen Mittelalters,* Leipzig, 1903.

[23] As cited in Chapter 3 of this book.

[24] See *Principles of Art History,* tr. from the 7th German ed. of *Grundbegriffe der Kg.,* London, 1932.

pointed out that the music of Wagner's day had certain qualities which related it to the Italian Barocca. His observations coincided with the appreciation, by a few *connoisseurs,* of certain neglected beauties in seventeenth- and early eighteenth-century art, an appreciation which is still increasing. Some musicologists were quick to recognize the fact that this period, so important in the history of modern music, should be an ideal period for comparative art studies. The first to take up Wölfflin's suggestions was Curt Sachs,[25] who picked up several of the former's *Grundbegriffe* to show, with musical quotations, how and in what respects the musical and pictorial styles of the Baroque were identical. This article was followed, in 1927, by another from Theodore Kroyer,[26] who continued the comparison initiated by Wölfflin. Still more recently, Erich Schenk[27] has endeavored to fix the boundaries of these periods and concepts, equally convinced of the validity of these parallels, at all times.

3. MUSIC AND THE DANCE

Curt Sachs and others are rendering a great service to students of music who are interested in the dance.[28] Until recently, this vitally important art, in its relation to music history, has been neglected. Much yet remains to be done in the study of the history of our rhythmical habits, of our bodily responses to music, and of the numerous ways in which bodily movements condition the forms and styles of music favored by a given community at a given time.

Two prevalent attitudes toward music have probably contributed to the neglect of dance rhythms and their history in general treatises. In the first place, church-inspired histories were often written by men who had prejudices against dance music, for its vulgar, worldly associations. Hence the necessity for giving priority to vocal music. But when popular forms of church music adopted metrical

---

[25] " Barockmusik," in *Jahrb. der Musikbibliothek Peters,* 1919, pp. 7–15.
[26] " Zwischen Renaissance und Barock," *ibid.,* 1927, pp. 45–54.
[27] " Über Begriff und Wesen des musikalischen Barock," in *Zeitschr. für Musikwissenschaft, Jahrb.* 17, *Heft* 9/10, 1935, pp. 377–392.
[28] *Eine Weltgeschichte des Tanzes,* 1932, is now available in English. *A World History of the Dance,* tr. by Bessie Schönberg, Norton, N. Y., 1937. See also Kinney, *The Dance, Its Place in Art and Life,* N. Y., Stokes, 1914, 1924; Tudor Pub. Co., 1935, 1936.

patterns, certain religious groups took to singing dance music without realizing it.[29] Religiously minded historians found two courses open: either to ignore religious dance music or to condemn it. Prejudice often kept them from seeing a third and middle method of interpretation, which could see the intermingling of vocal styles and dance forms as one of the common processes of music history. To an unprejudiced mind, " good " music is that which fits appropriately the time, the place, the mood, and the function. Dance music is no longer necessarily "inferior" to church music, and instrumental music is no longer an " artificial " aftermath of sanctified vocal music.

On the other hand, and in the second place, the modern sanctification of symphonic music goes to another extreme. The study of musical form as an evolving organism, from folk dance to suite, sonata, and symphony, has too often, in courses on appreciation, neglected the element of physical response necessary in listening. "Listening lessons" have become, too often, mere exercises in contemplation of formal structure, thematic development, and so on. On the other hand, the overpowering magnificence of modern orchestration can often act as a stunning soporific that may paralyze, temporarily, the rhythmical response in the listener. Too often, today, the admonition is, " Sit still, children, and hear some *good* music." One modern historian and leader in the music-appreciation movement has even admonished a teacher for having students dance to " good " music as a means of vital appreciation, even when the pieces in question were minuets, gavottes, and other classical dance forms.[30]

Nietzsche, in condemning the music of Wagner, complained that it compelled the hearer to submit to the sensuous elements of music.

---

[29] This is particularly true in evangelical churches, with militant marches (as with Sullivan's "Onward, Christian Soldiers"), minuets (as in "Come, Thou Almighty King," and Handel's "And the Glory of the Lord," from the *Messiah*), pastorales (as in "Rock of Ages," sung to *Toplady*), and waltzes (as in gospel hymns, such as "Oh, that will be glory for me"). It would appear, from the exuberant movements of devotees in camp and street meetings, as if dance music, when excluded as an amusement, will find vent in religious observance.

[30] For further comments on this difficulty, see *The Challenge of Education*, by the Stanford Education Faculty, McGraw-Hill, New York, 1937, Ch. XI, by Warren D. Allen; "The Challenge to the Teacher of Music," pp. 154–155, also "The Rudiments of Music," by Warren D. Allen, *Music-Educators' Journal*, March, May, 1937, pp. 23–25 in No. 5; pp. 30–31 in No. 6.

"In older music . . . one had to do something quite different, namely, to dance. . . . Richard Wagner wanted another kind of movement — he overthrew the physiological requisite of previous music. Swimming, hovering — no longer walking — dancing." [31]

This may explain a classroom difficulty today, to get an average group of students to want to dance to a Mozart minuet. Reverence for the classics is carried so far that the origins of our symphonic literature, in older forms of dance music, are forgotten.[32]

Curt Sachs, therefore, made a contribution to the general history of music, and he was able to do so because of his interest in all kinds of music, sacred and secular, and because of his researches into the practices of extra-European "pagan" peoples.

New developments in modern ballet are also bound to have healthy results in music histories and music education. Leading historians are no longer so sure of strict and narrow classifications of "sacred" and "secular," the "good" vs. the "popular;" we are getting away from attempts to distinguish "superior" from "inferior" phases of musical art in an evolutionary series. This means no abandonment of a belief in standards, however; on the contrary, appreciation of music will be on a higher plane when we learn to recognize sincerity and vitality in musical art, regardless of classification, function, or epoch.

4. MUSIC AND DRAMA

The art of worship is essentially a dramatic art; the history of liturgical music is closely bound up with the history of dramatic music, and vice versa. This is apparent with reference to the civic-religious music dramas of the ancient Greeks and it is equally obvious in the liturgical dramas of the medieval church, in which both plainsong and metrical music came to be used. The oratorio and the opera of the early seventeenth century were both music drama, to begin with, the only difference being in the subject matter; and the employment of ballet and opera by the Jesuits during the Counter-Reformation is an item worthy of more notice

---

[31] "Nietzsche contra Wagner," in *Works,* ed. by Oscar Levy, London, 1911, Vol. VIII, p. 68.

[32] Wagner's theories are of fundamental importance here. He said: "The farther gesture departs from her definite, but . . . most straitened basis,— that of the dance . . . so much the more manifold and delicate become the tone-figures of instrumental speech." [61].

than it has received.[33] It is difficult to distinguish the operatic music of Handel from that of his oratorios; neither he nor J. S. Bach had any compunctions concerning the revision of a secular composition for a sacred work, and the history of hymnology shows numerous instances of the adoption of secular tunes for churchly use.

Today, certain sections of Wagner's *Lohengrin* and *Parsifal* are deemed worthy of acceptance at sacred concerts, since Wagner went so far as to introduce the Holy Eucharist itself into a " sacred festival stage-play." In so doing, he merely reversed the procedure adopted by Theophrastus, who, during the Iconoclastic Controversy, introduced the theater into the Eastern Church.[34]

The terms " sacred " and " secular " do have objective meaning when used with reference to the function music is called upon to perform, and with reference to certain musical material deemed appropriate and fitting for certain occasions. But tendencies to keep these separate, as fixed categories, have been noticeable in countries and at times when there has been strong anti-theatrical feeling among churchmen and moralists.

France has been singularly free from puritanical opposition to the theater. Even when a modern member of the Schola Cantorum finds room for the sacred-origin theory, place is found for the instinct for pleasure as well as for the impulse to devotion.[35] Above all, Combarieu, in his *Histoire de la musique* [189], gives a great deal of attention to the comparative histories of dramatic music, in liturgy before the congregation and in music drama before the audience. His work is, therefore, of more value than most to studies of music in relation to society.[36] Combarieu went so far, however, in his interests along these lines, that he came to find the origins of *all* music in magic and ritual, a theory discussed in Chapter 9 of this book.

In Germany and England, however, the voice of the moralist has been heard frequently, in condemnation of the theater in general and of opera in particular. In 1763 John Brown, in his *Dissertation* [20] found opera " an Exhibition altogether out of Nature, and

[33] René Fülop-Müller, *The Rise and Power of the Jesuits,* tr. by F. S. Flint and D. F. Tait, New York, Viking Press, 1930.

[34] See Tunison, *Dramatic Traditions of the Middle Ages,* Chicago, 1907.

[35] See Chapter 3.

[36] P. Sorokin, in *Social and Cultural Dynamics,* American Book Co., N. Y., 1937, quotes Combarieu exclusively for his musical data.

repugnant to the universal Genius of Modern Customs and Manners." [20], pp. 201–202.

The oratorio comes in for equal condemnation, but

"*The Messiah* is an exception to this. . . . Though that grand musical Entertainment is called an Oratorio, yet it is not dramatic; but properly only a collection of *Hymns* or *Anthems* drawn from the Sacred Scripture. . . ." [20], p. 218 n.

Brown believed that music and poetry, beginning in Rome in a weakened or borrowed state, thereafter degenerated, and when modern opera appeared in Florence and Venice it came about as a revival of decadent Roman tragedy:

"Sulpitius, an Italian, speaks of the musical Drama, as an entertainment known in Italy in the year 1490. . . .

"History traces the rise of the Opera no farther; but a circumstance mentioned by Sulpitius may seem to lead us up to its true Origin. . . . We have seen that the Tragedy of the ancient Greeks was accompanied by music; that the same union was borrowed and maintained through the several periods of the Roman Empire: if, therefore, we suppose . . . that the Form of the ancient tragedy had been still kept up in some retired part of Italy which the Barbarians never conquered, we then obtain a fair account of the rise of the Modern Opera, which hath so confounded all inquiry.

"As Venice was the place where the Opera first appeared in splendor, so it is highly probable that there the ancient tragedy had slept in Obscurity, during the darkness of the Barbarous Ages. For while the rest of Italy was over-run by the Nations from the North, the Seas and Morasses of Venice preserved her alone from their Incursions; hence History tells us, the People flocked to Venice from every part; hence the very form of her Republic hath been maintained for thirteen hundred years, and from these views of security it was necessary for the helpless Arts to seek an Asylum within her Canals. . . ." [20], p. 201.

Modern research shows, however, that the musical entertainments in vogue in Venice were not at all the re-awakening of "helpless Arts" which had sought "Asylum within her Canals." One modern and simpler explanation is that after the fall of Constantinople, in 1453, Greek refugees began introducing types of musical entertainment which had been cultivated in Byzantium for centuries. It is even pointed out now that mystery plays and liturgical drama were not introduced until after the Crusades,[37] thanks to returning soldiers who heard and saw such things in Constantinople.

Modern histories of music may do well, therefore, to follow the lead of histories of drama which are discovering the importance of historical events and of new cultural contacts, also the fact that the history of our Western forms of music has neglected the East. Furthermore, the modern emphasis upon instrumental music and the worship of the symphony conductor should not loom so large as to obscure the importance of music and words in dramatic forms of communication.

Now that our technical means of communication have undergone vast changes, another new factor enters into the making of music histories.

5. MUSIC AND TECHNOLOGY

A. The Phonograph

The phonograph has been the greatest single aid yet devised for the teaching of music history. A new literature is necessary, therefore, to classify recorded music for teachers and schools of music. One modern move has been to provide selected histories with phonograph records; among these are the following:

Percy A. Scholes, *The Columbia History of Music through Ear and Eye,* Oxford Press and Columbia Graphophone Co. In 5 parts, 1930–39. Explanatory text accompanies each album of 10 in. records.

Curt Sachs, *Two Thousand Years of Music,* Parlophone, London, 1931, 12 records.

Curt Sachs, *Anthologie Sonore,* Paris, 1935–   4 vols. to date.

Hornbostel, *Musik des Orients,* Parlophon-Odeon, Lindstrom, Berlin.

No music history is now complete without adequate lists of records for illustrative material. Finney and Ferguson, in their very recent American texts, previously cited, include excellent lists. *The Gramophone Encyclopedia* of recorded music, N. Y., 1936, is, thus far, the most complete source of information, but should be sup-

[37] See Tunison, as cited, p. 64. Tunison's authority for these statements is Constantine Sathas, a modern Greek historian whose researches, in 1878, brought to light hitherto neglected facts concerning ecclesiastical drama in Byzantium.

plemented by the monthly lists released by Victor and Columbia in this country, and those given out by foreign companies. See also a French text centered about the use of the phonograph [271].

B. The Radio

Only in pre-Nazi Germany did it ever occur to an official of a national broadcasting company to write an esthetic, musico-historical-sociological treatise on the relation of radio to music culture, and to begin with a history of the " concert concept " from its origins to the present. The author was not a German, but a Hungarian-born cosmopolitan, A. A. Szendrei [274]. *Rundfunk und Musik-pflege* is a book that deserves to be better known, as a healthy, optimistic antidote for chauvinism. The general unity of human destiny is a postulate. In reality mankind has always been divided into greater and lesser groups, but the desire for unity has never lost its strength entirely, even in the mistakes and sufferings of the World War.

Thus Szendrei saw the radio as an important weapon in the battle which present-day civilization must wage against the ever-increasing tendencies which separate nations and societies. Consequently it would certainly be a one-sided viewpoint to look at the radio only as a technical achievement. Parts Two and Three are full of information concerning present-day radio practice and possibilities for the future. Part One is of interest to this study because of the history of the *Konzertbegriff*.

Although " in primitive times there are no listeners, only participants," Szendrei debates the common assumption in most histories that the existence of a listening public is not to be found until the eighteenth century. The modern concert, in our sense of the word, comes into vogue at that time, but one can find pictured evidence of esthetic pleasure in listening to others as far back as the ancient Persians and Assyrians. The difference that must be noted is that in earlier times music had significance not merely for itself alone, but also as a representative experience arising from such inner necessity.

The zenith of music's power over entire populations was reached in the great Greek festivals; the Romans, with interest only in political, practical matters, brought about a decline in music's prestige which was only revived in Christian culture.

A well-documented history of musical listening serves as a prel-

ude to the main thesis: that radio has brought about a " Panto-
nomie " in musical culture that has no parallel since the days of
Greek festivals. Radio's responsibility is therefore very great. Keeping in mind the Greek realization of music's power in culture,
radio can and should be a force for the highest good.

C. The Sound-Film

Prophecy enters into a recent book by Carlos Chavez [307], who
urges " constantly greater use of the media at our disposal " (p. 180).
First radio and now the sound-film are reaching far more people
than can be reached with other forms of reproducing instruments,
even the phonograph. But because these media are so common there
is a tendency to underestimate their possibilities:

" The general notion has been that the present is commonplace. We
must purify this concept. . . . The present age, with its fertile agitation,
its incredible social injustices, its portentous scientific development, is
perfecting, in electricity, its own voice. This, clarified and matured, will
become the legitimate art of our era." (pp. 15–16).

Chavez sees an entirely new stage of evolution ahead. His argument is based upon a philosophical appeal to the past, in Chapter I,
entitled, " Seeing the Present in Perspective." The old theory of
the priority of vocal music is accepted to postulate a first stage of
development. In the second stage, newly-invented instruments conditioned new kinds of music. Then the invention of notation made
it possible to preserve the music improvised in performance; today
the writing of music must precede performance, under our complex conditions. But Occidental music writing contains no possibilities for future development; electrical instruments do. In their
first stage of development, electrical instruments were only used
for reproducing old music; now they offer possibilities for new
forms of musical composition. For the first time in history there is a
possibility for creating " music of fixed values unalterable in successive performances." (p. 62). So far, music for films has been only
" musical salads," made of old materials, "arranged " by clever artisans.

The author's case would be just as strong without a philosophy
of history, and without the value-judgment on music now being
written for the films.[38]

---

[38] Composers of music for the European film include Honegger, Shostakovich,
and many other leaders. Erich Korngold, Sigmund Romberg, Oscar Straus, Ernst

The facts are simple: (1) the phonograph has not yet com-
manded new music for that medium, and will not until there seems
to be money in it; (2) the Esterhazys of radio may yet have to
have staff composers, as well as orchestras and arrangers, rather
than pay tribute to the owners of copyrights; (3) the makers of
films have already been forced to engage composers, partly because
of royalty fees on old favorites, partly because of the demand for
novelty.

Chavez calls attention to a fact too seldom recognized in older
histories; namely, that the great masters recognized contemporary
media and their possibilities, and wrote for the media and social
functions of their day.

A great event in the history of music occurred, in 1926, when
music and pictures were combined for the first time. There can be
no doubt that Richard Wagner would have been interested in such
a medium had it been available. New syntheses of the arts are yet
possible.

III. EVOLUTION AS A BASIC EXPLANATION

Even with all these new contributions, in research and correlation, the doctrines of development and evolution continue to be
applied to the interpretation and teaching of the history of music.
This application is found in four different fields:

(1) as a means of describing changes in abstract musical form;
(2) as a mystic, poetic explanation of music in the cosmos and
in human psychology;
(3) as a basic educational method, in which students are made
to go back to primitive exercises and work through the assumed " stages " of music's development through the ages;
(4) as a basis for nationalistic music history.

I. THE EVOLUTION OF FORM

In the first category, the French historians Emmanuel and
Machabey have already been cited, also the Oxford history and
other texts in English which follow the Parry tradition. One of the

---

Toch, and others have been brought here for the purpose, while Werner Janssen,
Frank Churchill, Leigh Harline, and the late George Gershwin are not to be dismissed lightly.

latest attempts is by Margaret H. Glyn [295], who aims to supply the missing links in the evolutionary scheme.

" The evolution of the types of form that we know is all that can be attempted, for lack of evidence of the great past. In tracing these types back to their origins we are dependent upon the present practice of primitive peoples, on traditional melodies handed down, on ancient statuary, and on the recovery of actual musical instruments from which scales and possibly chords may be inferred. Of absolute certainty there can be none until the historical period is reached." But absolute certainty seems to be postulated, in this later statement: " As we grope back into the dim past, two things present themselves as essential to the music of primitive man. He must have exact repetition, and he must have noise. All other musical factors were at first non-existent." (pp. 25-26). In summarizing, the author claims: " We have traced the various styles of music to their roots in the working of these principles, and assigned them their place in the evolutionary order. We have seen that the bulk of the actual tone-material (apart from instruments) comes into being at an early stage, and the development of music consists thenceforward of the use of the materials as units of recurrence." (p. 253).

In the Appendix an attempt is made to show an evolutionary series of classification in modern notation of examples ranging from an Australian monotone to folk and art music of the Renaissance (pp. 258-299).

2. PSYCHOLOGICAL EVOLUTION

The second sort of evolutionary interpretation is dominated by a desire to explain the history of music in terms of psychology. Scientific psychologists may testify that some of these histories are too vague and impressionistic, but they make interesting reading. One extreme illustration [156] has already been quoted.

At least one American writer [247] has presented music history in similar terms:

" Before the universe was anything else, it was a great, roaring, singing musical instrument. When it split into other parts, it created other musical instruments. . . .

" There were birds who twittered, and animals who expressed themselves in tones. Then man was put upon the earth.

" And before he could speak, he could sing, and before he could sing, he could dance in pantomime.

" And thus is written the Genesis of Music.

" The baby of today reproduces in rapid order the gradual evolution of the savage's musical possession.

" His love-making sang with the music of a cat. . . . Then he began clapping his hands . . . and he danced with hand-clappings . . . etc." [247], Chap. X.

As early as 1908, in England, William Wallace, M.D., attempted to discuss the art of music in relation to other phases of thought, and to trace, through its history, the cerebral processes concerned in its development. To show the " utility of music " in answer to the " Scientific Attitude ":

" The thing is there, in an intense state of activity. . . . Its existence proclaims its utility, and the vital weakness lies not in the music, but in the man who cannot grasp this phase of mental energy." [172], p. 13.

" I believe that, viewed in correlation with man's other faculties, music is still in its infancy." (p. 17).

" In order to arrive at an understanding of its progress from a primitive state towards its present development, we may take the other arts as a basis for comparison. *Music is the youngest of the arts.*"

" Of the scale, how it originated and passed into the form which the Greeks recognized as a determinate fact, we can only make *deductions based upon our experiences of music still young in its development, such as we gain from the study of other races.*" (p. 31).

In describing the cosmic processes envisaged by the Idea of Progress, the author says that

" The whirring of the fibre in its socket, the moan of the wind and the whip of the rain, awakened in man those powers of mimicry which no assault against the facts of evolution can counteract or destroy, for the infant of three months old throws back at every turn to an unrecorded ancestry. Then man for the first time sang." [172], p. 267.

Music has " no history to look back upon, no interminable pedigree to be traced . . . its ancestry is of yesterday. . . . What music has accomplished it has done in the last two centuries; sculpture, on the other hand, is not far from where it stood in the Golden Age of Pericles." (p. 32).

In other words, there is no sympathy with older forms of musical expression. Only in the last two hundred years has " the movement of thought " become continually swifter and more fertile (p. 148).

The most extensive attempt to write a psychological history of music is *Musique et la vie intérieure* [215]. The authors, Bourguès and Denéréaz, explain in the *Avant-propos* that

" What we have attempted is a history of psychological phenomena of a musical order; a study of successive metamorphoses of sound, mentally and temporally. It is a double history, in fact, of the human emotions revealed by music and of the sonorities that reveal these emotions.

" So while one of the parallel parts of this work is devoted to the history of musical art, to the origin and development of sonorities, the other is concerned with the tendencies, emotions, sentiments, passions (collective and individual) which arouse the former in the course of time."

The study of origins begins, for these authors, in "Dynamo-genesis." Reliance is placed upon the older school of English associationist psychology, and Bain's Law of Diffusion is "the point of departure for all explanations which follow." (p. 7).

" Pleasure is nothing more than the consciousness of dynamogenesis." (p. 9). (Since it is said below this that pleasure and dynamogenesis are synonymous, this sounds suspiciously like Molière's famous explanation of the " dormitive " virtue of opium.)

" Every musical piece determines in the organism of the auditor a ' global ' dynamogenetic rhythm, which is at every moment the sum total of all dynamogenetic factors, intensities, pitch relationships, tone-durations, tone-production and timbres, combined simultaneously and reacting successively." (p. 17).

Aside from this dynamogenetic rhythm as a whole, two other rhythms are generated in music — the motor rhythm (*kinesthésie*) and the emotional rhythm (*cénesthésie*). The latter sets up visceral activities in the listener, " thrills up the spine."

The origins of *esthétisation* are sought in ancient legend, but the gaps in the psychological history are considerable, between the preliminary theories above and the discoveries in " phonoaesthetics " described on pp. 37–69 (conceptions of tone relations as we know them). Some of these suggest some decidedly original hypotheses, such as the *three dimensions of sonority*. In this theory "the harmonic sense is based upon the *triad* of the perfect chord, just as the spatial sense relied upon *three dimensions*. To what may we attribute this tendency toward the Trinity,[39] as common in the domain of sound as in space? Is it not due to habit contracted by the functioning of the *three semi-circular canals* . . . in the inner ear? " (pp. 60–61).

[39] See Chapter 6 in this book, on explanations involving the Trinity, also Ch. 11, IV, I.

After the above preliminaries, the history proper begins with the vicissitudes of the musical spirit in the Orient, Greece, and Rome. The *prototype of the suite or sonata in Greece* was the "Pythicon" of Sacadas (c. 600 B.C.). "Like a J. S. Bach, *Sacadas sums up the past and contains the future in embryo*. If the sonata of Sacadas had been followed by other sonatas, pure music would have reached inconceivable splendors in Greece; but at that moment, it was drawn away and absorbed by tragedy."

We are informed that Simonides of Keos was the prototype of C. P. E. Bach, Pindar was the prototype of Haydn, Damon was the prototype of Mendelssohn, and of course the tragedy operas of Sophocles and Euripides were the counterpart of Wagnerian music drama.

The first chapter on the Middle Ages is entitled *Eclosion du sens harmonique*. Instead of being content with many worth-while comments on medieval music, it is deemed necessary to search for the origin of this harmonic sense among analogous practices in the use of *organum* among Fijians, Samoans, Hottentots, et al.

From this point (p. 112) the illustrations of musical examples are numerous, together with "filiation" charts, indicating that the efforts of many are summed up in one great genius, who passed the torch on to many others.

Riemann's esthetic theories concerning consonance and dissonance are quoted occasionally, *pro* or *con,* and much space is given to the evolution and transformation of *formulas:* "While borrowing the phono-esthetic formulas of his predecessors and contemporaries, Bach completes, changes, multiplies and enriches them, so that they are no longer recognizable."

The attempt to write a "psychological history" from this point onward depends largely upon adjectival description of the motives, powers, dynamogenetic forces, excitability, "emotional tensions," etc., of individual composers, and the psychological effect of certain harmonies and rhythms on the auditor.

The supplement to this work, the *Arbre généalogique,* a *Planche hors texte,* is an amazing chart showing on a sheet about twenty feet long the extent to which the evolutionary treatment of music history can be carried. The roots of the tree are three in number: Protoplasmic Excitability, Will to Power, and Vital Rhythms. Modern branches, continuing into the upper, invisible Beyond, are labelled Schönberg type, Debussy type, and so on. The French trunk has a bright red bark, making it the most glorious flowering of the organism.

3. EVOLUTIONARY RECAPITULATION IN THE CLASSROOM

The third category of texts is very important, and bears so closely on the educational implications involved in this study that further discussion will be found in Chapter 12. This is the place for introduction of the materials and a brief statement concerning their contents.

Vincent d'Indy's contribution to the evolutionary method of teaching composition will be discussed in Chapter 10, under the examination of the concept of " development " dating back to medieval theology. The American trends have been oriented more in the direction of Victorian anthropology.

As already pointed out, MacDowell's lectures at Columbia University were attended by students who have since become leaders in music education. These stimulating lectures delivered by the leader of American musical thought at that time are very important in the history of music histories in America. Here, as everywhere else, the evolutionary explanation was received gladly, because it made the picture so simple. MacDowell had lived abroad for over ten years, and was thoroughly steeped in the traditions of European Romanticism. Believing that national music must have its " roots in primitive, native folk music," he turned to the Indian theme for much of the inspiration of his American music, also to the Nordic elements of folk art made popular in Germany by Wagner.

MacDowell's theory of history may be summed up as follows:

" The origin of music is attributed to the whole range of human emotion." [186], p. 7.

But instead of accepting the pluralistic view, MacDowell asks,

" Now what is mankind's strongest emotion? . . . The soul of mankind had its roots in fear. . . . In groping for sound symbols which would cause and express fear far better than words, we have the beginning of what is gradually to develop into music." . . . (p. 2). Then, " some savage . . . completed the first musical instrument known to man, namely, the drum." (p. 4).

"Vocal music began when the first tone could be given clearly; that is to say, when the sound sentence had amalgamated into the simple musical tone." (p. 23).

This original note was not G, as Rowbotham claimed, but F. (p. 19). MacDowell quotes Rowbotham, however, and accepts Rowbotham's principal conclusions: the origins in impassioned speech, and the "invariable sequence" beginning with the drum. Since these lectures were given, American students have been given little hint of the disputes over this sequence; the drum has won a complete victory over here. (For discussion of the arguments over this sequence, see p. 195 of this book.)

In this country, therefore, the evolutionary approach to the study is a commonplace, as far as titles are concerned. The "origin," "growth," "development," "progress" and "evolution" of music are familiar to hosts of students and teachers who have never been concerned with the thought patterns which these terms suggest. Most school texts begin with chapters on "primitive" or "ancient" music, sometimes with a combination of the two, but occasionally the compiler states the European source of the evolutionary assumptions used. Rowbotham's influence first became apparent in this country in Baltzell's *Complete History of Music,* as already noted, but in recent years Satis N. Coleman [220] has applied Rowbotham's philosophy of history to a theory of music education which has become very influential in American education:

"A musical historian (Rowbotham) brings much evidence to prove that the history of vocal music commenced with a one-note period . . . followed by a two-note period, and later the third note above was added. . . . Rowbotham's theory suggested to me the plan of following that order in both the singing and the playing of little children, and the results indicate that . . . the order fits the natural development of the little child to-day and allows musical beginning to take deep root in him. . . . (p. 106).

"Being little savages, they can understand savage music. I shall find the child's own savage level, and lift him gradually up to higher forms; and he shall understand each stage as he reaches it. . . . The natural evolution of music shall be my guide in leading the child from the simple to the complex, and we, with guidance, may probably often discover and cover in one lesson things that required generations for man, without guidance, to learn. . . . (p. 29).

"Everything that a primitive savage can do in music, children can do. . . .

"Beginning at the drum stage, my children shall be little savages who know nothing of music, and then shall dance primitive dances and beat upon rude drums and shake rude rattles until they discover some way of making tone." . . . (p. 30).

These statements bristle with assumptions borrowed from nineteenth-century philosophers of music history, but the critical examination of them is deferred to Chapter 12, where the implications of these assumptions for modern education will be discussed at length.

Since the publication of the above work, Robert W. Claiborne [241] has children begin with primitive drum music in Indian games, then a great skip is made to "some really great drum music," drum parts from Beethoven, Wagner, and MacDowell. Chapter V relates that once upon a time there was a primitive savage down by the river, cutting reeds to make shafts for his arrows. . . . This led to the invention of Pan's pipes; so the children make a seven-tone scale with the Pipes of Pan. Furthermore, "All the very earliest songs we know have bird-calls in them." So the first folk songs to learn are cuckoo songs, etc. Thus the child is led through the "stages of development" worked out in Romantic history. (Then the youngsters go home and turn on the radio.)

Assuming that everything in music is a "logical outcome" or "growth" from a previous stage, the chapter headings of another elementary text are as follows: From Shouting to Song — From Hollow Stump to Drum — From Ram's Horn to Trumpet — From Pipe to Pipe Organ — From Bowstring to Violin — From Songs to Symbols — From National Traits to Tunes — From Bards to Bands — From Church to Theatre — From Patchwork to Pattern.[40]

IV. MUSIC HISTORY AND NATIONALISM

In Chapter 3 it was noted that histories of music were dominated for a long time by ecclesiastical authority, Biblical chronology, and the theory of divine origins. It was also shown that these influences have dwindled practically to the vanishing point in present-day histories.

New religions have now arisen, and the greatest of these is Nationalism. Again, an oft-quoted statement comes to mind:

[40] Fannie R. Buchanan, *How Man Made Music,* Follett Publishing Co., Chicago, 1936.

"Historic art has everywhere reached its highest state of development amongst nations who have had to hold their own *vi et armis* against neighboring tribes." [41]

If this be true, we may not be surprised to find occasional "monuments of boasting" [42] in the music histories of rival European nations.

The first French music history (Bonnet, as cited in Chap. 1) begins as follows, with a dedication to the Duc d'Orléans:

"Music is a heroine, who, after having run her course for four thousand years, in all the courts of the world, comes to give an account of her conquests to her Protector, the most enlightened Prince in Europe.

"The favorable asylum you have given her, Monseigneur, will forever be a monument to the esteem and taste you have showed her and will mark the time during which French Music has equalled, nay, possibly, surpassed, that of other nations, due to the great Progress she has made since the establishment of l'Académie Royale de Musique in this flourishing kingdom." . . .

One hundred years later, during days of stress and depression, another historian says, speaking of the contemporary French school:

"It holds a much more distinguished rank than is admitted by foreigners blinded by national pretensions . . . the inferiority in which she finds herself at the present moment is the result of circumstances which, at other times, would have produced the same effect on the nations which are better situated today. History shows that at certain epochs she has obtained over these same nations a general supremacy, and she can do so again." [34].

Today, a modern French conclusion is that

"French music continues to hold her place as the educatress of the world (*d'éducatrice du monde*).

"European, Occidental musical art, *the only one which has evolved until now,* seems to be extending on all sides. Numerous artists from all countries, *even from America and Japan,* are coming for instruction to the older countries, especially to France. They will, perhaps, take away European knowledge and ideas to erect a new art." [262].

Henry Prunières can even say, on page 108 of his *Nouvelle histoire de la musique* [293], Vol. I, that up to that point it had been possible to make no mention of any music made outside of France,

41 Yrjö Hirn, *The Origins of Art,* London, 1900, p. 179.
42 *Ibid.,* p. 181.

as all of the composers from other countries who had done anything in polyphonic music had been identified in some way with
the school of Notre-Dame! Prunières also adds that after the missionary work done by France, other nations were able to go ahead
with their own. But in England, R. Vaughan-Williams can rejoice
in the accusation that British music possesses "smugness," because
that may mean that English composers have some secret which is
at present for their ears only.[43]

Thus English and French scholars, thanks, possibly, to more favorable political circumstances than those in Germany and Italy
since the World War, need not argue about music history; they
need only tell about it. Both point calmly and dispassionately to
records of early achievement; England to the account given by
Giraldus Cambrensis, in the twelfth century,[44] of part singing in
the British Isles; and France to the music of the troubadours and
trouvères with which the history of the secular art usually begins.
John Dunstable is also the stand-by for English claims for priority
(in spite of the fact that he spent most of his life on the continent)
and the Reading rota, "Sumer is icumen in," is an indispensable
beginning for every history of counterpoint. But thanks to German
research,[45] the center of thirteenth-century activity in polyphonic
music proves to have been in the great scholastic center in Paris
and Notre-Dame, as Prunières is able to claim.

The plan for historical recognition of a primeval German music
is not new. Back in 1821, Stoepel's obscure little history [39] began
thus:

"Our forefathers knew and practiced music, even before their hordes
overran the South, the provinces of imperial Rome. However completely
the old and accustomed, which had therefore become dear and precious,
was suppressed by the new, even though that were better, nevertheless
there has certainly always been a pure German music. The first goal of
a *German History of Music* should be to establish this idea . . . that
the divine (spark of) music is our own peculiar heritage, and not a
strange plant on foreign soil. However, we have formed the habit of
thanking the Greeks and the Romans for music, as for all other arts."

It is easy to sympathize with this patriotic point of view, and to
recognize the one-sided nature of a music history that follows tra-

43 Ralph Vaughan-Williams, *National Music*, Oxford Press, 1934, p. 116.
44 *The Itinerary through Wales*, New York, Dutton, 1908.
45 See Ludwig's article and Bibliography in [224], 1924, Vol. I, pp. 214–295.

dition in finding the origins of music in the Mediterranean area.

The right on the side of the German argument is (1) the recognition of the neglected folk element in music history, (2) the disproportionate treatment given to Greek theory in former histories, and (3) the theory that all European music "grew" out of Gregorian plainsong.

The wrong is the extreme to which the nationalistic pendulum has swung. The disturbing fact about the arguments on both sides is that they are symptomatic of the increasing separation of peoples in the modern world. All fail to recognize that great art, like great ideas in all realms, has never been developed in complete national isolation.

Even in the days before the World War, when most German histories were at least objective if not international in their treatment, occasional notes of nationalistic contempt for others were heard: some evidence of this has already been noted in histories by Fischer and Grunsky, and in 1904 there appeared a strongly nationalistic history, which made much of Nordic and old German origins [181]. The high development of music among modern "primitives," like the gypsies, was cited in proof of the theory.

But in 1914 there appeared an article that is very significant in view of the new German histories of music that are now appearing under the imprimatur of the Nazi *Kultusministerium*.

Moser's lecture on the subject of "The Major-Minor Idea (*Durgedanke*) as a Problem in Cultural History" [195] presents a theory of history that is based upon the Chamberlain notion of "irreconcilable conflict" between the Nordics and a Mediterranean culture of Oriental, Semitic origin. By the term *Durgedanke*, Moser means the concept of major and minor as opposed to the musical concepts fostered by the use of the melodic Greek and ecclesiastical modes. He asserts that according to the evolutionary concept of history, the major-minor scales and the church modes present *a priori* such radically different aspects that a development of one principle out of the other is "ontologically unthinkable."

The argument then, in substance, is as follows: There is an irreconcilable conflict between the major-minor system and the modal system which cannot be explained by any historical materials older than the thirteenth century. We only know there was a strong folk idiom opposed to the art music of the church. Then Moser goes on to claim that Houston Stewart Chamberlain has proved the existence of an equally irreconcilable conflict between North and South, "German" and "Mediterranean" culture. In both music and culture in general it was a matter of internationalism *vs.* nationalism, communism *vs.* individualism, *Völkerchaos* vs. *Germanentum*. One statement is repeated over and over in modern German histories of music, namely that only in the free cities of *Northern* Italy, strengthened as they were by *germanisches Volkstum* could the Renaissance proceed unhindered.

Curiously enough, the assumption that the German represented individualism as opposed to communism does not interfere with the next argument, namely, that the feeling for harmony is, essentially, a German concept. The *sine qua non* of major and minor is the feeling for the third and then for the triad — I, IV, V, I [46] in contrast to the stepwise *melopoeia* of the Gregorian, with its rare jumps to the fifth and fourth.[47] Evidence for this in early German music is found in the ancient *lur,* a large bronze instrument found usually in pairs, upon which a skilled player can blow twenty-two partial tones of a soft trombone-like timbre. The Germans must have blown these instruments (and in major and minor thirds) long before the Christian era.

In 1930, Moser, evidently seeing how far his theories are being carried, warns, in his *Epochen der Musikgeschichte* [263], that this evidence must not be taken too seriously, since similar old instruments are found in Tibet. And even in his early lecture on the subject Moser has no sympathy with those who claimed, as had Willy Pastor, that the penetration of Christian music into northern and middle Europe was unfortunate. He says, rather, that this very struggle and the resulting enrichment of both inimical cultures was responsible for bringing our Occidental music to its present heights; that the conflict has ended with the final victory of the major-minor concept, but since the tendency to harmonic superficiality is all too apt to influence our folk-consciousness, our composers must reach back, for refreshment and enrichment, to the treasures of church modal music as two great German masters have done before them, namely Bach and Brahms [195].

Having thus conclusively disproved his own theory of "irrecon-

[46] These Roman numerals are symbols for the triads on the first, fourth, and fifth notes of the scale, known as the "primary triads" because they are all major chords.

[47] These skips, to be sure, are not so rare as Moser implies, as one may note by examining the Gradual, though they do generally occur at the beginning or the end.

cilable conflict," Moser had a great opportunity to initiate an objective, international method of presenting historical materials, showing how music has developed as a result of friendly interchange of artistic thought, and how changes in musical form have come about through modification and enrichment of each culture in contact with the others.

Moser's experiences in the World War, however, evidently put notions of an international outlook out of his head, for in 1920 his history of German music [209] came out, with the Chamberlain theory of Germanic superiority at the core of Volume I. In this work the methods and assumptions of comparative musicology are utilized to bolster a remarkable theory of primitive harmonic origins in a pure German race. Among all the varied theories of the origins of music advanced by pseudo-scientific speculation, Moser accepts, as best suited to his theory, the conclusions of Carl Stumpf, who maintains that music originated in signal calls from hilltop to hilltop.[48] In this heroic process, the early "Indo-Germans"[49] must have come to an inevitable use of the octave. Thus these sturdy heroes came to develop war songs and folk dances in which the melodic line consisted of skips to the intervals of the common chord. Hence the fundamental assumption in his work (Vol. I, p. 11), that "The ear of the Indo-German race has, out of inner necessity, from the earliest times on down, demanded the harmonic division of the octave"— *never* into the "subtle, dwarfish" divisions of the half-step, or even stepwise melody. "Our" music is healthy, springing, and daring (p. 10).

The corollary to this theory is that since Germans *feel* music with their whole being, consequently one of the elements that makes German music what it indubitably is, is its *rhythm*. This leads to the conclusion that only among the Aryans, and strongest of all among the Germans, can one find music organized with strong and weak pulses similar to those of the heartbeat, and music organized into four-measure phrases.[50]

The most extreme application of Moser's theories is in the anti-Semitic argument, as found in *Musik und Rasse,* by Richard

---

[48] See Chapter 9, III, 3 of this book.

[49] Note the assurance with which this term, originally used to denote a family of ancient languages, is now accepted as a racial term in German anthropology.

[50] The fallacy of this claim is apparent when one examines some of the earliest dance music known (of French origin). See Pierre Aubry, *Estampies et danses royales,* Paris, 1907. Little German music of this period (c. 1300) has been found.

Eichenauer [281]. Eichenauer's summary of the Chamberlain-Moser theories, applied to a philosophy of music history, may be outlined briefly, as follows:

The two races that have struggled for supremacy in European music are the Aryan and the Oriental. It is a case of virile, diatonic, metrical music of " Indo-German " origin, coming down from the Hindus, Persians, Greeks, to the Germans of today, *versus* a measureless, florid, sensuous music of Oriental origin handed down to us by the Hebrews and the early Christian heirs of a decadent Roman culture.

The debatable assumption that Gregorian chant was principally evolved from Jewish liturgical music is thus linked with the old Chamberlain theories and the equally bold assumption now appearing in all late German histories, namely, that " great " Occidental music had its origin in the heroic folk music of the Nordic " barbarians." This latter assumption is the logical reply to traditional historical theories that have always asserted that our music " evolved " from Greek and Gregorian sources. The masterpiece in rationalization is found when the author's theory has to face the facts involved in the cases of Mendelssohn, Wagner, and Mahler. The explanation hinges upon the " ill-advised " emancipation of the Jews at the turn of the nineteenth century, which resulted in a great deal of mixed blood. The result was that a few gifted individuals, even though somewhat " tainted," grew up under hereditary or environmental conditions that impressed them so vividly with the strength of the German tradition that they themselves were able to write in the true Nordic manner. Mendelssohn had the weaknesses of the typical Jewish virtuoso, and the Hebrew strain was so marked that he was destined never to achieve true greatness; Wagner, a storm center for hereditary and esthetic reasons, passes muster because the racial traits in his music and his outlook are so strongly " Dinaric." Mahler must be admitted to the elect because of his undying love for German folk song.

Portraits of the masters carry descriptions of their racial characteristics; e.g., Monteverde is *nordisch-dinarisch,* Rameau is *vorwiegend nordisch,* while Mendelssohn is *vorwiegend orientalisch mit vorderasiatischen Einschlag.*

Altogether the book provides an illuminating sidelight on the methods by which the paganization of Germany is sought, in opposition to a Christian tradition of suspect Jewish origin.

The histories that have appeared in Germany since 1933 all bear the stamp of these nationalistic theories. The first instance of music history rewritten for ideology's sake is that of Anton Mayer's *Geschichte der Musik* [291]. The original edition of Mayer's book came out in 1928 — a simple, conventional text beginning with the music of the Greeks. This edition, completely made over to suit the present régime, makes no mention of the original edition.

The Greeks are dismissed as of little importance to the history of music, except for the significance assigned to the art in civic life. With little if any reference to Plato himself, it becomes apparent that the National Socialist authorities are fully alive to the dangers of subversive music in the ideal state. So the essential concept of the place of music in the totalitarian state is made clear in the last chapter, on contemporary music. One of Germany's foremost composers, Hindemith, whose music is now under the ban, is dismissed as "an excellent viola player, who writes a good melody occasionally in his chamber music." Expressionism and Impressionism are condemned as "Marxian" in their implications. Stravinsky and Schönberg are, of course, beyond the pale, and the only contemporary mentioned with any approval is a George Vollerthum (sometimes spelled Vollerthun), who wrote the preface. This preface, an adulatory paean in praise of the Leader, is rewarded in the final pages with a reprint of a banal page by the composer, who is hailed as the "musical representative of that newly-awakened folk consciousness which has led all the great masters to their fame and the glory of the art."

A very significant title is that of a book by Hans Mersmann, *Eine deutsche Musikgeschichte* [297]. The author refers to the "facts" about primitive German music as revealed by comparative musicology and archaeology, but is particularly interested in the "struggle" between Latin Christendom and Germanic Kultur.

The latest example of complete rewriting is that of Emil Naumann's *Illustrierte Musikgeschichte* [100, 298]. Although intended for popular consumption, like all of the Nazi-inspired works, this does not go so far as some of the others. The core of the new argument, however, appears on p. 17 — in italics — under the heading, *Musikkultur in germanischen Norden,* which states, in substance, that *Occidental music would never have developed into an art peculiarly different from other systems without the stamp put upon it by the Germans.* (Scandinavians, Britons, and Icelanders are included among Germans, *im weitesten Sinne des Wortes.*) The arguments for this statement will be discussed later and traced back to their origin.

Finally, one of the most objective and international of German scholars, Ernst Bücken, in *Die Musik der Nationen* [306], turns ardent nationalist, the same Bücken who edited the 13-volume *Handbuch* [260], one of the finest achievements in this field in Germany after the World War. As already indicated, its humanistic, internationalistic point of view made it a model of its kind. This new work, however, is devoted to nationalistic comparisons, often with the fairness for which the author has been noted, but too frequently with a forced effort to exaggerate German influence, as on Orlandus Lassus (p. 61), and in the treatment of the Mannheim School. In this connection, Bücken maintains that Germany won a great " victory," in the classical period, over mixed and international styles (p. 6). The anti-Semitic bias is also very strong.

Thus German histories foster the belief that Germany has been the " guiding star " for both the other leaders in music, France and Italy [219].

But Italy, as noted at the end of the chapter previous, has been combating that statement ever since the Risorgimento. Italy was once content to create and enjoy music, writing epoch-making treatises on musical theory, without writing up its history; she is content to do so no longer. Not only the commanding position of Germany in the nineteenth century, but also the world-wide recognition of French and Russian music, since the beginning of the twentieth, have spurred Italy to historiographical activity.

Now the Fascist cry is for more histories, for texts which shall only call attention to the old supremacy of Italy, not only in opera and song, but also in *every* field of composition. The battle is a bitter one.

The situation in music, as in politics, is rather complicated, when one studies the Italian dependence upon Germany on one hand, and the desire to be free from German influence on the other. This dependence is deplored by critics and historians like Alfredo Untersteiner, who complained, just before the World War,[51] that new works from Germany received an immediate hearing in Italy, but that the reverse was not the case.

But Italian dependence upon Germany did not and does not stop with music. A casual glance at Pareto's *Mind and Society* (Vol. IV) will show how frequently German militarism is mentioned with envious approval. This fundamental philosophy of the Fascist state, seeking to review the Machiavellian gospel of order

---

[51] In *Harmonia,* an Italian musical periodical.

by means of force, holds up the Prussian ideal on one hand, while at the same time the Italian concert halls go in for German Romanticism.[52]

This is not the whole story, to be sure, for earnest Italian scholarship has built up contributions to music history without any external urging other than the love of music and the zest for research. But even the most disinterested research cannot disguise a certain justifiable pride in *la patria*. That this pride is now being exploited for ultra-nationalistic ends is plainly evident in the literature.

The most aggressive of all the Italian nationalists, in musical circles, is Fausto Torrefranca, whose theories concerning Italian priority and supremacy in instrumental music have made him a thorn in the flesh of German savants for some time. In 1930 he attempted to show that the Italians were the original creators of all the great instrumental forms for which Germans have claimed so much credit in history [268]. Teutonic "artisans" are accused of having no originality of their own, merely imitating their gifted neighbors, and producing quantities of good-enough music by dint of patience and industry. In this work and on other occasions, Torrefranca has hailed Sammartini as the "inventor" of the symphony, thereby going back to a favorite theory of "origins" in music history. Forsaking his previous theories of philological origins, as being of merely academic interest, Torrefranca provides material for the more pressing demands of Fascist historiography.

The first evidence of official Fascist interest in modern music is found in the third series of *Quaderni dell'Institute Nazionale Fascista di Cultura,* a booklet (107 pp.) entitled *Il Rinnovamento Musicale Italiano,* by Adriano Lualdi, who was elected to Parliament in 1929 as a representative of the Fascist Syndicate of Musicians. Mascagni is quoted, at the beginning, in a violent diatribe against modern music, the evils of jazz and discordant harmony. The reply to Mascagni made by A. Casella is quoted with approval and made the basis of a discussion which upholds modern artistic developments in Italy. Mascagni is accused of judging all modern music by the aberrations of foreign artists; except for certain extremists,

---

[52] For a point of view that is rare in Italy today, see an article entitled *Le tre razze Europee in conflitto e la loro musica di guerra* (*Harmonia, Revista italiana di musica,* August-September, 1914). G. Bastianelli contrasts the "legitimate ideal" of national independence, in Verdi's music, with the imperialistic desire for economic expansion in Wagner's. Mussorgsky differs from both, however, in that his martial music reflects a sympathy for down-trodden humanity, regardless of nationality.

modern Italian music needs to be better known and encouraged. The tendency in Italy has been to look, too often, outside her own borders for all great music except opera. But Italy has been the source of all kinds of music, at all times. Foreign countries are awakening to the beauties of the music of Palestrina, Frescobaldi, the Gabrielis, and others; so Italians need to do the same.

The most vociferous demand for one-hundred-per-cent Italianism in music history comes from Pietro Pecchiai, who says militantly, " The history of music must be rewritten." [299]. Just how far Italian scholars will follow this call to arms remains to be seen. Thus far their texts have not gone so far as the Germans. The Italian arguments have two merits: First, they seek for origins in the documents of history, rather than in the unfathomable depths of pre-history. Second, they do call attention to the one-sided nature of a music history that concentrates attention upon a few great figures (most of them in Germany) to the neglect of groups and individuals without whose labors the giants could never have risen to eminence. Torrefranca frankly says, and with great justice, that his aim is to revive " ancient, continuous, and glorious musical traditions " that have been shamefully neglected, even by Italian students.

But one-sidedness is never corrected by swinging to the other extreme. The modern Italian forgets, too, that Rome is noted for being the great borrower in history. A truly objective international study would probably reveal secrets of Italian musical greatness other than inborn Italian genius. It might be found that her commanding position, geographically, culturally, politically, and in religion, had much to do with it. And for any music history to put the stamp of pure nationality upon most of the great music made in Italy from the fourteenth to the sixteenth century, is to overlook the fruitful, fertilizing efforts of visitors and foreign residents. Many of the singers in the papal choir throughout this period were Spaniards, and Flemish singers were numerous from the Avignon Papacy onward. Several of the greatest names in music history, familiarly known in their Italian forms, were Spanish or Flemish composers, as, e.g., Victoria (Vittoria), Adriano Willaert, Cipriano de Rore, Clemens non Papa, Orlandus Lassus, and others.

Now if Spain could establish an *entente cordiale* with the Arabians, another very interesting theory concerning Hispanic-Moorish origins of European music could be developed, with the aid of English and other scholars.[53]

In the United States, as in the Scandinavian countries, there are as yet no nationalistic theories, as an international point of view is taken for granted. American music histories have had a pedagogical purpose, and although many are only compilations of European materials, the laudable aim has been to acquaint large numbers of students with the historical facts necessary for what is called appreciation. So in closing this discussion, it may bring the point of it home by trying to imagine what would happen here if this hyper-nationalistic virus were to creep into future studies.

The history of music in America has been shamefully neglected in our own general histories of music, so far. But it is to be fervently hoped that no Fascist dictatorship, in a future attempt to get composers to create music that is one-hundred-per-cent American, will ever go to such extremes in nationalistic history. Such history could stress the sturdy character of early New England music, under such men as Billings, and the zest for life found in the folk songs of our mountain and frontier life. But it could go farther and ban the jazz idiom on account of the Semitic influence, and all the subversive tendencies inherent in "inferior" Negro culture. The "Stars and Stripes Forever" could thus be held up as the highest flower of American music evolution.[54]

However, apropos of this question of nationalism, O. G. Sonneck, late Chief of Music Division, Library of Congress, in addressing the Music Teachers' National Association in 1916 [214], made some comments on the study of history which are of great significance. Although he was pleading for needed research into neglected areas of the history of American music, his remarks are applicable to general history as well. As he said, the history of American music

"lies in the lowlands. . . . There is little room for hero-worship." But nevertheless, " *the history of music* in America *is not at all uninteresting, or unworthy of consideration by the* American *scholar if it be approached in the proper spirit and from the proper angle.* . . . *Our books*

---

[53] See Henry Farmer, *Historical Facts for the Arabian Musical Influence,* also his *History of Arabian Music to the Thirteenth Century.* Also Ribera-Hague, *Music of Ancient Arabia and Spain,* Stanford Press, and J. B. Trend's *Music of Spanish History to 1600,* Oxford, 1926.

[54] This statement is not to be construed as in any sense derogatory of Sousa and his vital contribution to American music. In this connection, see Ch. 12.

deal more with the history of music and musicians in America *than with the history of* American *musical life."*

If the words in italics be re-read, omitting reference to America specifically, the indictment of most general histories of music will be complete. The "lowlands" have been disregarded; "hero-worship" has reigned supreme, and in the craze for "music appreciation" many interesting phases of the history of musical life have been neglected as if they were unworthy of the scholar. The librarian is in a position to know not only books, but human beings. The latter come to him frequently with questions that can only be answered by delving in the out-of-the-way corners, with queries that the general histories do not answer, inquiries that cut across the lines of vertical, linear development that are followed as a rule. Such questions as these, for instance, are often well answered in periodicals and special studies, but not in any general history: "What music, from overseas, was most influential in the life of the American colonies?" "What were the contrasting social conditions in Italy, Germany, France, England, and Spain that made part-singing appear in so many different forms? What social mingling brought about an internationalization of French and Flemish technique?" "Why do the Italians and the Spanish have such totally different attitudes toward art music and folk music, and what has been the result of these different tendencies?" and so on.

V. THE MARXIAN INTERPRETATION

The rival gospel of the day, opposed to that of chauvinistic nationalism, is that of communism, so there are those who feel that any attempt to discuss the social aspects of music history must somehow be identified with Marxian theory. Only one general history of music has endeavored to present the subject from the standpoint of economic determinism. That has been written by a Russian communist [240], whose aim is to show that music, like religion, has so far in European society been a means used by capitalistic ruling classes and the bourgeoisie to keep the exploited worker content with his lot. This is to be the "first history of music written from the sociological standpoint." The argument was first published by Dreizin, in 1921 [216]. The main thesis developed later by Chemodanoff appeared in this volume, which was No. 1

in a series of outlines of the history of art in the light of Marxian-
·ism. Dreizin voices the desire for universal development of culture
in the Soviet Union, and presents his economic theory with the
statement that the hungry cannot enjoy, much less create, art.

The argument is that the forms of music, its character, and contents, depend on the forms of the economic, social, and political
structure of society.

To prove the argument, recourse must be had to some theory of
origins, so this communist theory maintains that music originated
in the rhythms of work, in the struggle for existence. This theory,
proposed in 1896, in Karl Bücher's *Arbeit und Rhythmus* [136], is
discussed in the next chapter.

Through the courtesy of Ashley Pettis, the English title and table
of contents is given herewith:

History of Music in Connection with the Class Struggle

I. The sociological method in music. The origin of *music as the
result of the process of the struggle for existence*. Ancient musical
culture. [Mr. Pettis' translation of this chapter appeared in *The
New Masses,* April, 1936.]

II. The Middle Ages. The music of the feudal classes and folk music.
The development of polyphony.

III. The struggle of two cultures. The decline of feudal music. " The
new art " of the bourgeoisie. The development of homophony.

IV. The struggle of two cultures (continuation). The origin and rise
of the musical drama. Handel's and Bach's oratorios.

V. The period of the growth of the bourgeoisie. The flourishing of
symphonism. The heroic and naturalistic opera: Haydn, Gluck,
Mozart.

VI. The music of the revolutionary bourgeoisie. Mass songs during
the period of the great French Revolution. Beethoven.

VII. The epoch of the Restoration. The school of the Romantics. The
flourishing of the Italian opera. Opera in France.

VIII. The music of feudal Russia. The dilettantes and Glinka. Dargo-
mizhsky and Serov.

IX. Western music in the period of capitalistic development. Liszt and
Wagner. Wagnerism and the anti-Wagnerian trend in Germany.

X. Western music in the period of capitalistic development (continuation). The Italian opera. Music in France. Western schools. Music
in other countries.

XI. The music of the Russian bourgeoisie. Westernism and populism.

Rubinstein and Tschaikowsky. " The powerful group." The school
of Tschaikowsky and the " group."
XII. Two fronts in contemporary music. The music of the declining
bourgeoisie. Musical culture in the U.S.S.R.[55]

Just before this theory of the economic determinism of music
history appeared in Russia, it had been stated briefly in this country.
According to Ruddyar D. Chennevière,[56]

" art's development ceaselessly and closely *moulds itself upon the evolution of human civilization.*" His aim is " to lay a new foundation-stone
for . . . a study of music from the social point of view."

The dual manner of manifestation is creation and execution. The
dual essence of musical art is psychic (spiritual) and social.

When the two phases of creation are realized in different individuals,
notation, the intermediate element, becomes necessary. Notation consists
at first of oral-gesture, explanation, and movement. But this is not precise, so the ideograph provides a written musical language. But symbols,
if incomplete, are misleading; so the phonographic (immediate, direct)
reproduction is the last precise, mechanical and accurate stage of notation.

The historical sequence is as follows: (1) the bard (creator and interpreter), who wandered as a " messenger of the gods," while religion
is centralized around the family hearth. (2) With the grouping of
families into villages and cities, ritual art and music become the pre-
rogative of a priestly cult. " The abyss between the creative and executive
phases not yet disclosed. . . . Music will *issue* forth from the temples
and be polluted by the contacts of the street. . . . The executant, formerly a *creator, then a religious celebrant, has become an artisan.* Soon
he will be a proletarian! " (3) " The nineteenth century begins, princely
and royal courts lose their prestige; and before long the tidal wave of
capitalism sweeps beauty — already much diminished — out of existence.
The machine (the pianola marks the extremist limit of the antimusical)
which destroyed music may yet revive it, through the phonograph and
electricity."

Today, the flyleaf of the *Workers' Song Book,* published by the
Workers' Music League (New York, 1934) carries this announce-
ment:

MUSIC PENETRATES EVERYWHERE
IT CARRIES WORDS WITH IT   IT FIXES
THEM IN THE HEART   MUSIC IS
A WEAPON IN THE CLASS STRUGGLE

[55] Pre-revolutionary music histories in Russia were few in number, conventional
in tone, and evidently designed for conservatory students [46, 134, 135, 141, 226].
[56] " The Rise of the Musical Proletariat," *Musical Quarterly,* Vol. VI, 1920, p. 500.

The Foreword goes on to demand a new revolutionary music, to replace the bourgeois art of old, employing the assumptions used by the histories just cited. So whether for evolution or for revolution, a philosophy of music history is necessary. But the question remains, Must a valid philosophy have to choose between one of two extreme ideologies?

VI. MUSIC HISTORIES IN OTHER COUNTRIES

The spread of music historiography to all parts of the Western world testifies to the growing interest in the subject. Two of the four Swedish works [69, 75, 221, 243] date from the productive 1860's, but all four in Holland's list [211, 218, 275, 276] date from 1928. They seem to follow conventional patterns and give comparatively little attention to their national arts. A Danish history of music, by Panum and Behrend, however, gives extensive information about Scandinavian music [138].

Spain has also produced four modern works [155, 194, 267, 289], but Portugal only one [213]. Latin-American schools are demanding their own texts, beginning with Barrenechea's work in Argentina [308], a capable work by Señorita Herrera y Ogazon in Mexico [272], and a novel work by the Brazilian de Andrade [309], which actually begins with the music of his own country!

Tagore's *Universal History of Music* [137] is interesting for the notes on Hindu music, and even Turkey [251] has a text for school use under the new régime.

Ever since Calvisius [1] got from Creation to his own day in sixty-five pages, the project of picturing "the general history of music" as a whole has appealed to many. To carry out this project, two great cosmologies have been used: first, Christian theology, then the doctrine of Progress.

Philosophies and theories of origins, development, and evolution have been formulated, and each of these has a history. It is the province of Part II of this book to explore these in relation to this body of literature which has engaged so many active minds.

PART II
PHILOSOPHIES OF MUSIC HISTORY

INTRODUCTION

I. CONTINUITY AND ANALOGY

ANY attempt to make a general history of music which will be a useful synthesis of data must have what we call continuity. When a presentation is criticized for lacking continuity, reference is usually made to the need for unity, coherence, and relevance of the details to the whole. But the word continuity, when applied to the subject itself, is capable of various interpretations. And it is in defense of these interpretations that philosophies of music history have been formulated, in order to see the subject, if not as a whole, at least in its broadest aspects. Hence the term has far more significance than that which is usually attached to it in ordinary usage.

Roughly speaking, there are two main interpretations of continuity, the static and the dynamic. The static notion is that of a continuous series in a system of classification. The continuous, in this case, is something to be observed and studied in a fixed hierarchical scale, the members of which are so disposed as to shade by imperceptible degrees into those "above" and "below." This concept, that of the great Chain of Being,[1] was at the basis of Père Mersenne's *Harmonie universelle* (see Chapter 1) and of all the early treatises which emphasized the medieval classifications, divisions, and genera of music. Music is the only one of the fine arts which has been tied up with the concept of the scale. The tonal scale, therefore, being demonstrable with mathematics, was considered as a worthy subject of university study throughout the Middle Ages. But as Mersenne stated in 1627, and many still believe today, music was always " a *part* of mathematics." Now as long as music was or is studied mathematically, no *history* of music is possible. And no history was possible as long as men like Bontempi [7], Brossard [8], Malcolm [10], Grassineau [14], and Martini [19] were primarily interested in the classification of *modes* and *genera* (see Chapters 2, 3).

[1] See A. O. Lovejoy, *The Great Chain of Being,* Harvard University Press, 1936.

Now this static notion of continuity has not been emphasized in these pages, except to show its unhistorical character. In reviewing the works discussed in Chapter 1, it may be noted that the Lutheran pioneers paid little or no attention to *modes* and *genera,* but that the Catholic scholars called attention to the "timeless," eternal verities involved in such divisions and in the unchanging "laws" of acoustics. It is hoped, however, that enough has been said to open up another vista of research, which is beyond the scope of this book, namely, investigation of the relationships between the concepts of the scale in musicology and in philosophy — the musical scale on one hand, and the scale of nature and being on the other. Now that Lovejoy has made a study of the latter as a "unit-idea" in the history of philosophy, one of many modern theorists interested in the history of ideas might find some interesting parallels. It might be found that the medieval and Renaissance interest in the finely-divided *enharmonic* scale, impossible in practice, but alluring in theory, was merely another manifestation of the age-old interest in "the infinite divisibility of the continuous." [2]

But when histories began to be written in chronological order it was with a dynamic concept of continuity; not with the extreme Heraclitean notion of continual flux, but with what Lovejoy very aptly calls a "temporalizing of the Great Chain of Being." In the case of music, the old classifications of "organical" or vocal and instrumental music began to be studied, not merely as forty-five different kinds of *musica* in a fixed order but in terms of men and events which brought about advancement from one "stage" to another in time. At first, with the use of such chronological tools as were available, the gaps were very wide, as in Calvisius [1], where the development of the art from Creation to 1600 was sketched in sixty-five pages. By 1763, John Brown [20] was able to envisage thirty-six well-defined "stages of development;" but, as will be shown in Chapter 11, on Evolution, the demand arose in the nineteenth century for history "without gaps." This concern was also noted in Chapter 6, in dealing with the organic hypothesis.

But in order to apply the static concepts of continuity, namely that of the unbroken *continuum* and that of "infinite divisibility" to a dynamic concept of history, it has been necessary to resort to

---

[2] See p. 17, n. 31 for reference to the fact that there has been no such parallel with the spectrum scale in art history.

analogy. Music, with mathematically demonstrable scales and with certain definite "forms" or "designs," has tended to be regarded as consisting of organisms which change in time. Thus the problem for the music historian of the nineteenth century was thought to be solved by regarding music as *a* mysterious entity that has developed, progressed, or evolved from certain definite origins.

The organization of Part II of this book therefore comprises four chapters respectively on the "Origins," "Development and Progress," and the "Evolution of Music," and a chapter summarizing the sequential patterns involved. This latter, Chapter 12, will carry the inquiry down into the field of music education, to show how important these patterns are in popular as well as in scholarly schemes of organization. All of the indicated philosophies of music history show attempts to find continuity in a dynamic sense in the history of music; but all employ analogy as extensively as did Father Mersenne in 1627, when he tried to show continuity in static contemplation. In short, both the static and the dynamic concepts of continuity have employed a mystic cosmology to see the subject as a whole: the cosmic theology-science of Mersenne was supplanted in the nineteenth century by the cosmic Law of Progress, Doctrine of Development, or Dogma of Evolution. The latter was based upon the belief that

"On account of the *infinite divisibility of the continuous,* there always remain in the abyss of things slumbering parts which have to be awakened, to grow . . . to advance to a more perfect state. And hence no end of progress is ever reached."

Leibnitz wrote that passage ("On the Radical Origin of Things") in 1690, during the period when the first "Histories of Music" began to appear in the vernacular. Until long after his day, continuous "stages of development" were defined in a genealogical chain of men and events. Then with the full realization of the possibilities of Leibnitz' analogy, and with the organic hypothesis, music was treated, in the nineteenth century, as a continuously evolving whole (see Chapters 6 and 11).

"After 1800 the (German) historians secured increased attention to the factor of continuity in human experience, and they gave to that concept a richer content. . . . It is a mark of objectivity in social science to treat each object of attention as *an incident in a causal series of human experiences reaching back into the impenetrable beginnings* of the human career. . . ."[3]

The next chapter will endeavor to show, however, that all attempts to find a "causal series of human experiences reaching back into the impenetrable beginnings" of music have been as mystic and futile as the old attempt to locate the first causes of music in the "music of the spheres." Not only that; they have even obscured the true recognition of another important concept of continuity.

II. CONTINUITY IN HUMAN EXPERIENCE

Encouraged by twentieth-century thinkers who have reminded us of other definitions of continuity, the last chapter, Chapter 13, will endeavor to point out certain interpretations of continuity in music which can recognize both the dynamic and the static elements in musical experience; to show that continuity may mean

"*Relative sameness through a series of changes.* . . . In so far as any of the determining conditions of an aspect of reality remain *unchanged*, in so far that aspect is said to be continuous."[4]

More recently, John Dewey has said, in reply to those who subscribe to the Heraclitean notion of continual flux:

"Nature and life manifest *not flux, but continuity,* and continuity involves forces and structures that endure through change; at least when they change, they do so more slowly than do surface incidents, and thus are, relatively, constant. But change is inevitable even though it be not for the better. It must be reckoned with. Moreover, changes are not all gradual; they culminate in sudden mutations, in transformations that at the time seem revolutionary."[5]

Roscoe Pound, in dealing with systems of law, has also made some acute observations on the subject of historical continuity. He rejects the static definition of continuity, but finds truth in it to the extent that "there is continuity in traditional modes of professional thought and in traditional rules of art." He believes that "these modes of thought and rules of art are a powerful restraining

[3] Albion W. Small, *Origins of Sociology*, N. Y., 1924, p. 40.

[4] J. M. Baldwin, *Dictionary of Philosophy and Psychology*, N. Y., 1901, article on "Continuity."

[5] *Art as Experience*, Minton, Balch and Co., N. Y., 1934, p. 323. Further discussion of Dewey's explanation will be found under "Periodization," pp. 267–268.

force," particularly in times when old materials are being re-adapted for new uses in the system to meet "new wants or new forms of old wants." [6] But what Pound calls the "fallacy of continuity" lies in the notion that the content of a system remains the same, "thinking that because there had been no tearing down of the whole at one time, and no definite replacing of the whole at one stroke, the present structure was to be identified with the one which first stood upon the site."

Instead of looking at the development of law systems from Roman origins, or, in the case of American law, from Norman-English common law, comparison is made with the history of an old Roman church:

"How much of what men use today is the Servian wall or the Roman basilica, or the church of the twelfth century or even the church of the Renaissance? Such a picture is much nearer the truth than the picture of the organic evolution and continuous identity with which the historical school made us familiar." [7]

To this the author might have added that, with all the changes in style, the fundamental idea-system which demanded a temple had been continuous.

III. CHANGE AGAINST CONTINUITY

The concepts of change thus advocated by Dewey and Pound have not yet been applied extensively to the writing of music histories. It may be noted that Chevailler advocated the use of Dewey's term "transformations" [245], as did Bekker [238, p. 22], in his "Changes in Musical Form," and Otto Kinkeldey, in his paper on "Changing Relations in Musicology." Kinkeldey [305] begins by pointing out the relations that have remained unchanged; from that point he is able to point out the changes in relations as different generations of men have looked at these unchanging factors, also the changing styles that have resulted. The emphasis in modern musicology is on style rather than form. The old concept of "evolving form" is being rejected for a clearer view of musical activity. "Style" is a word which immediately suggests

[6] In short, he agrees with Baldwin that "traditional modes of thought and rules of art" are "determining conditions that remain unchanged."

[7] *Interpretations of Legal History*, N. Y. The Macmillan Co., 1923, in the Cambridge Studies in English Legal History, ed. by Harold B. Hazeltine, pp. 39–41.

" use; " the latter word always connotes modification of existing materials as well as new invention. As Aristotle once said,

> " Clearly, then, all the processes that result in anything ' coming to exist ' . . . start with some subject that is already there to undergo the process."— *Physics,* 190b.

It is obvious that music historians have been obliged to use the " traditional modes of professional thought " that have colored man's views of art and culture. These inherited ways of looking at the record have been so generally accepted throughout the nineteenth century and even in this generation that to challenge them may seem to some a rash undertaking. But as pointed out in the Introduction to this book, such a challenge would not have been possible until this last decade; now that similar challenges are confronting the methods of the social sciences, it is time that the young discipline of musicology should put its house in order.

The plea in these pages is for abandonment of monistic philosophies of music history; for a return to the tolerant spirit of that great musician and scholar, Michael Praetorius, who could enjoy all kinds of music, ancient and modern (*veterum et recentiorum*), and music for all kinds of social use and communication. In an age that is showing less and less tolerance of differences, the word continuity itself needs pluralistic definition. Our musical heritage presents continuities that are not to be tossed aside; and other nations, other cultures have their continuities, which we may learn to understand and enjoy, with all their " differences." The latter should certainly never be dismissed as " inferior," at a " lower stage of development " in a " causal series " that illustrates our " summits of perfection."

On the other hand, static contemplation of the past and of continuities other than our own may go so far as to neglect the continuous necessity for the emergent new, for the encouragement of the artist who has something vital to say about the changes going on about us. Artists are the " antennae of civilization," but since the Baroque era few historians of music have given space to the musicians of their own day.

It has taken three centuries for the word *modern* to come to mean *contemporary;* and now that it does mean that, it is too often looked upon as a word of dangerous portent.

CHAPTER 9

THE QUEST FOR ORIGINS: "THE CLEAREST VIEW"?

"He who considers things in their first growth and origin (physis) will obtain the clearest view of them."— Aristotle: *Politics,* 1, 2.

"The quest for origins has been of absorbing interest. It would seem that we can never understand anything at all until we have discovered its origin in something which preceded it."— Woodbridge: *The Purpose of History,* p. 63.

It is a rare history of music that does not begin with "The Origins of Music." Therefore, the queries to be raised in this chapter include the following:

1. Is it necessary, or even possible, to get back to "first growth and origins"?

2. Why has it been deemed necessary?

3. What methods have been used?

4. What is the difference between historical origins, properly speaking, and speculative origins which lead back admittedly into "the gray dawn of history," where "the clearest view" is impossible?

5. Is the "thing which preceded" the *only* medium by which we can understand history?

6. Granting its value and necessity, is it sufficient? May there not be other important sources of historical evidence, such as correlations with contemporary events and living realities?

"All social laws, indeed all universal laws as well, have one characteristic in common: they explain the becoming, but never the beginning of things, the ultimate origin. This limitation must be insisted upon the more emphatically since the human mind is given to inquiry after the genesis of things. It desires knowledge of the first arising, the ultimate origin — a tendency fatal to science; whereas with all the laws cognizable it can apprehend only the perpetual becoming.

"Hence, none of the questions about the ultimate origin of human associations belong in sociology, if indeed they belong in any science whatever!"—Ludwig Gumplowicz, *Outline of Sociology*, tr. by F. V. Moore, Academy of Political Science, 1899, pp. 85, 86.

At the beginning of Chapter 5, it was pointed out that histories of music, during the eighteenth century, came to regard music as *an* art that had "developed" in the course of time. This was a radical departure from the spirit and methods of Praetorius, who set out, in 1615, to study musical arts from a polyhistorical point of view. And although all the Lutheran historians—Calvisius, Praetorius and Printz—could reconcile the divine origins of music with the facts of music in Nature, and with the obvious powers of man's invention, these concepts came to be separated and pitted against each other during the Enlightenment. A summary of the numerous origin theories found acceptable by Printz was given on p. 24, and it was remarked that if he were alive today, he might be instructed if not amused by the zeal with which "The Origins of the Art of Music" have been pursued by specialists interested in only one phase of the subject. Few historians since 1690 have been content with pluralistic explanation. If the subject of origins is taken seriously, it means that the "most likely" one has to be approved, for the sake of some argument.

It was also remarked that at the beginning of the Enlightenment, that critical turning point in the history of ideas, men rejected the notion of celestial music to devote themselves to measurable, comparable, and knowable matters. But it was found that at the beginning of the Romantic period, with the revival of Christianity for its beauty as well as for its truth, that historians began once more to be fascinated by the mysterious and the unknown. Hence this chapter begins with "The Fascination of the Inexplicable." But this has come to mean, not the inexplicable in the music of the spheres or the First Cause, or Divine Creation, but the inexplicable as the *undated*—the unknown in man's history here on earth, in the dim, unrecorded past.

It is undoubtedly true that "man has, throughout a great part of his historic march, walked with face turned backward." Even when seeking to explain something in his present daily experience, man has, since the early Greek thinkers, posed the question, "What is the origin of this phenomenon?" But it has been pointed out that the thing to be explained does not of itself demand a return to the past; it remains in the present.[1] Only the above question asked by man himself directs his thought backward.

I. THE FASCINATION OF THE INEXPLICABLE

"In the beginning" stands not only at the opening of the Mosaic account of world history, but also on page 1 of most histories since.

But the Greeks were not entirely satisfied with the belief in Divine Creation as a complete explanation of the beginning. They believed in the divine origin of many of the good things of life that were "gifts of the gods" to mortal men, and music was one of these.[2] And to these polytheistic searchers after truth, Nature as a whole offered challenging problems. These problems were not settled, as they were for a fairly unified monotheistic Hebrew nation, by the authority of ancient law and common belief. "The Greeks," as we so loosely designate them, consisted of various groups, too often bitter rivals, living on islands and peninsulas of varying size. They evidently looked at Nature in all her various moods and aspects and formed as many different hypotheses concerning the origins of matter and of life. H. F. Osborn, among others, suggests [3] that the marine life about the shores of Greece must have led Thales of Miletus to decide that water had provided the original source of everything. Observation of barren hills and the growth of land vegetation when stimulated by water was undoubtedly another factor of "proof." At any rate, the observed fact of change has ever since been closely associated with the other observed fact of growth under favorable conditions and of decay after certain limits of time or after favorable conditions have been removed or interfered with.

Speculative minds meanwhile found other answers to the quest for the original source. Wind, breath, and clouds suggested that air must have been the original *physis* [4] in nature. Anaximander's concept of "terrestrial slime" was not merely a transient theory: Oken takes it up in 1805 in *Die Zeugung,* referring to this original sub-

---

[1] See Teggart, *Theory of History,* Ch. 8.

[2] "Venerable is therefore music altogether, as being the invention of the gods." Plutarch: *Concerning Music.*

[3] *From the Greeks to Darwin,* N. Y., 1894.

[4] J. L. Myres shows that Roman translation of Greek terms has confused their meaning, that *physis* really meant "how things actually grow," rather than origin or fundamental substance. *The Political Ideas of the Greeks,* N. Y., 1927, p. 384.

stance as *Ur-Schleim*. Then, too, the phenomena of rapid change were as suggestive as the processes of slow growth and decay; consequently fire and the eternal flux also became focal centers of naturalistic inquiry. Observation of visible motion, flame, flowing river, falling bodies, etc., evidently led men to envisage the course of events as being describable in terms of movement; and this movement came to be regarded as necessary and continuous, until checked by some interference from the outside. Here we find the framework for the Idea of Progress which emerged two thousand years later, although the Greeks had no conception of that belief, as such.

The prescription for "the clearest view" is therefore older than the philosopher to whom it is ascribed. At any rate, ever since the days of Aristotle it has been accepted as a fundamental necessity, in spite of occasional warnings, as, for example,

Allzuvieles Fragen nach den Ursachen sei gefährlich; man solle lieber an die Erscheinungen als gegebene Tatsache halten.

This admonition, from Goethe, is quoted by H. J. Moser in an important but little-known article on method in music history, published in 1920 [208]. Moser even goes so far as to condemn the evolutionary theory as applied to the study of "primitive" music or Oriental music as an early stage in the development of harmonic consciousness in the human race as a whole. But he then turns to the evolutionary treatment after all, in order, as he confesses, to simplify the picture of history in general, to envisage two different racial lines of development. One is supposed to have had a horizontal, and the other a vertical, concept of music "from the beginning." Carrying that to a logical conclusion, in the biological analogy, the harmonic "seed" grew like a beanstalk, the melodic "germ" like a pumpkin vine. This growth of two differing organisms is "evolution" just the same.

Such assumptions belong to a philosophy of history, and not to a scientific discipline that can be called history proper. The latter calls for the discovery of historical origins, in the first known emergence of a particular form or style of musical activity. Therefore the title of this chapter does not refer to the quest for original sources of information, or for the origins of certain forms, opinions and practices in known, discoverable, or decipherable records of the activities of man. Such quests are the legitimate and necessary tasks of the historian. But the "quest for origins" becomes futile for the purposes of history when it searches in the dim, undated, undecipherable past, behind and beyond events. Such quests will yield nothing but unproved assumptions upon which to erect speculative structures of pure theory into which facts are fitted by way of illustration.

Even in an objective text, prepared by a careful scholar who has no theories to prove, one may find an occasional backward glance, a wistful yearning for knowledge that cannot be had. For example, Karl Nef [210] begins thus:

"It would be instructive to know the beginnings of music, inasmuch as we could infer from these its actual nature. For this reason numerous philosophers have evolved hypotheses.

"In still more recent times, the quest for the origin of music has been pursued by a more reliable path through the investigation of the musical practices of primitive, savage, and half-savage peoples."

Then the author shows how this "reliable path" has led to the conflicting theories of Stumpf, Wallaschek, and Bücher. Cognizant of the excellent practical results obtained by Jacques Dalcroze in rhythm education, the author finds Bücher's view of "the beginnings of dramatic art, in the rhythmical movements accompanying work, the incitement to all music and poetry . . . more plausible," while also admitting the Wallaschek theory that primitive instruments condition the music.

But Combarieu, at the beginning of his great *Histoire de la musique* [189], says, with much greater confidence,

"I am anxious to unravel the question of origins. I believe I have succeeded in doing so, thanks to an idea which, bringing together the most primitive conceptions of musical art and those of great philosophers and modern composers, . . . brings a little order and unity into a subject which appears extremely confused. This idea is no *a priori* assumption, an hypothesis developed first and sustained afterward with the help of texts: it is the unexpected reward of a long task of observation which makes me confident of its validity."

The actual theory presented by Combarieu is discussed below; the point to be noted here is that he found it necessary to promulgate it, while it seems to bear no essential relation to the remainder of his work. And yet, careful examination indicates that the theory is of great importance. First, let Combarieu continue with the statement of his theory:

" Music began by being a magic performance which was asked by the first men to perform the most improbable miracles; and for thinkers, even for the dilettante who no longer believes in miracles . . . it has preserved, more or less noticeably, the mysterious character of this great moral force. The Greek of the Homeric epoch made use of an incantation to stop the blood of a wound; the American Indian has a special song to conjure up a storm; Schopenhauer says that music expresses a truth superior to all material reality (*Universalia ante rem*), and Wagner, in his *Beethoven*, develops this theory at length: that the composer of the Ninth Symphony, thanks to the possibilities of his art, had direct intuition of the eternal verities. . . . The primitive, the savage, the metaphysician, the composer agree in their conception of music. In the light of origins, all history is illuminated and put in order: First, magic with its incantations; then, religion with its lyricism in various forms (hymns, odes, and dramas); finally, emergence of an art which separates itself gradually from dogma to become organized parallel to sacred song and to pass through these three phases: (1) secular diversion, (2) individualistic expression, and (3) naturalism (Beethoven). Such are the great periods of history."

In spite of the author's disclaimer in the first paragraph cited above, this theory was advocated by him in his first book, *La musique, ses lois et son évolution*,[5] first published in 1907. German music, particularly that of Wagner, was casting its spell over neighboring countries. Combarieu had studied in Germany, and had become familiar not only with research techniques in musicology but also with German metaphysics. The net result was his conclusion that "the musical metaphysics of the Germans and primitive magic were one and the same thing."

" ' The power of the composer,' says Richard Wagner, ' is nought else than that of the magician. It is really in a state of enchantment that we listen to one of Beethoven's symphonies.' Is this the brilliant epigram of a writer, such as we often find in musical criticism? No; rather it is the phrase of an artist, a philosopher, and an historian all in one." [158], pp. 105, 106.

What Combarieu termed musical thought " is found particularly in the great modern symphonists (p. 9). . . . The Germans may be considered as the kings of music, since they have produced a

---

[5] " The belief in the efficacy of musical magic is one of the most important facts in the history of all civilizations, and there are perhaps none on which we have such ample information. The first weapon — offensive and defensive — of magic was the chant." [158].

Bach, a Handel, a Beethoven, a Weber, a Schumann." (p. 161).
According to the Germans, real music is the symphony,

" the opera is only a sorry alliance of music with a false poetry and rude
sketches of the plastic art; it is an invention for the use of non-musical
minds which are unable to enjoy music without that ' thin broth,' the
erotic poetry of a libretto (according to Schopenhauer)." [158], p. 93.

But for Combarieu himself, "our operas and the whole of our
religious music may be considered as a survival of magic."

Combarieu, therefore, began his historical writing in the belief
that modern symphonic musical thought, untranslatable into other
terms, has a magic effect; that since music has in it something
mysterious and inexplicable, the modern mind, though freed from
many superstitions, is often obliged to speak the same language
as that of primitive folk.

It is herewith maintained that this theory, even with the aid of
modern techniques and a wealth of factual illustrations, is merely
a rationalization of the old, persistent doctrine of the divine origins
of music. Combarieu's history is a worth-while contribution to
music history from the sociological point of view. This fact makes
the use of such a theory particularly impressive. But it is difficult
to see how a theory advanced because of the " inexplicable " nature
of music can provide " the clearest view."

The foregoing paragraphs serve as an introduction to the study
of this concern with origins. Moser, Nef, and Combarieu have been
cited in order to show how irresistible is the temptation to philosophize on the subject, even among some of the most objective
scholars named in Chapter 8.

It now remains to classify the various types of theories and the
arguments for which they provide basic premises. For the sake of
convenience, three general classifications are made, under the general heading of " law," for if a theory can be made to conform to
what is commonly termed a " law of Nature," a " law " of human
association, or a " law " of embryonic genesis, it carries more weight
than a basic assumption concerning origins stated as such. Only
the first two types of theory are discussed in this chapter; the third
is discussed later, with the doctrines of Progress and Evolution.

II. ORIGINS IN "LAWS OF NATURE"

Most of the historians cited in Chapter 3 were devoted to an ideal concept, that of Divine Law. The notion that music was "of an essence wholly divine" has continued to figure, more or less, in all general histories of the art, when presented by men who were primarily interested in vocal music. The voice of man, the natural instrument of God's creature, was originally and ideally suited to divine worship, therefore it was held to be superior to the artificial instruments of man's invention. But with the secularization of musical arts, and the perfection of instruments, the modern historian faces the general view that "real music is the symphony." So with this reversal of popular opinion comes the rationalization of the divine-origin theory noted above, in Combarieu; vocal and religious music is a "survival of magic;" the symphonic art of Beethoven is a culmination, in which a composer glimpses eternal verities in writing wordless music for instruments.

The other historians mentioned in Chapter 3, opposed by the divine-origin theorists, were those who found validity in pagan theories of naturalistic origins. Extensive use of these theories does not appear in modern music histories, perhaps for the reason that they are not useful for the support of religious or social theory. But where they do appear, they indicate concern with the "laws of Nature." It is obvious that a trained musician must be familiar with the way things work in the phenomena of sound. Origin theories of this sort are, therefore, on firmer ground than romantic explanations of the inexplicable. The first of these theories point to the laws of Nature explainable by means of mathematics; another set of theories deals with the origins of our media of expression (instruments). The origins of the latter are explained by the theory that man's first efforts were the result of his attempts to imitate the sounds of Nature — the singing of the birds, the wind in the rushes, and the sounds of reverberating hollow bodies. According to the first theory, music's essence is in numbers; according to the second, it began in imitative artifacts.

1. MUSIC AND NUMBERS

The fundamental facts commonly called the laws of sound vibration have been known for so many centuries that the discoverer of them cannot be named with certainty. Scientific accuracy does not permit us to perpetuate the name of Pythagoras as that of the first musical theorist, for none of his writings have come down to us. But from the earliest literature discussed in this volume, down to the present day, he has been hailed as the discoverer of the mathematical bases of music.[6] The laws of the vibrating string, however, were known by the Chinese independently and contemporaneously with, if not before, Pythagoras. At any rate, natural philosophers, ever since, have been interested in the so-called Pythagorean conception of music, because of its close association with numbers. Roger Bacon describes the medieval study of this relationship in the *Quadrivium,* when he says, speaking of education, that

"children begin by learning the things which are better known to us and to be acquired first. But mathematics is of this sort since children are taught to sing, and in that same manner they can grasp the method of figuring and counting, and it would be far easier, and it would even be necessary, for them to know about numbers before singing, because in the proportions of numbers the whole rationality of number is explained in examples, as authors of music teach, as well in ecclesiastical music as in philosophical." [7]

Leibnitz, four centuries later, says, "Music is an unconscious counting, or a felt relation of numbers" (*Arithmetica nescientis se numerare animi*), and in our own day a calculating musician of the highest intellectual gifts waxes romantic over the mystic Greek notion of the music of the spheres:

"Music is a part of the vibrating universe. . . . It may be that we must leave earth to find that music. But only to the pilgrim who has

[6] One modern writer has a chapter on "The Researches of Pythagoras." One typical statement of the Pythagorean legend is given by Addison: "Who would have thought that the clangorous sound of a blacksmith's hammers should have given *the first rise to music?* Yet Macrobius, in his second book, relates that Pythagoras, in passing by a smith's shop, found that the sounds proceeding from the hammers were either more grave, or acute, according to the weight of the hammers. The philosopher, to improve this hint, suspended different weights by strings of the same bigness, and found in like manner that the sounds answered to the weights. This being discovered, he finds out those numbers which produced sounds that were consonants; first, that two strings of the same substance and tension, the one being double the length of the other, gave that interval which is called *diapason* or eighth; the same was also effected from two strings of the same length and size, the one having four times the weight and tension of the other." From "Pythagoras, Music, and Mathematics," in the *Spectator,* No. 334.

[7] *The Opus Majus,* tr. by Bridges, as quoted in McKeon's *Selections from Medieval Philosophers,* Scribner, 1930, Vol. II, p. 49.

succeeded on the way in freeing himself from earthly shackles, shall the bars open." [188], p. 13.

In 1711, Addison again refers to Pythagoras thus:

"This man reduced what was only before noise, to one of the most delightful of sciences, by *marrying* it to mathematics; and by that means caused it to be one of the most abstract and demonstrative of sciences." [8]

Aided by the progress in laboratory equipment and research techniques the "marriage" between music and mathematics is resumed at the present day. Modern psychologists interested in the mathematical definition of sound and rhythm relations, are devoted to criticism of the "laws of Nature" laid down by academicians of the eighteenth century and accepted as such ever since. They are engaged in the same field of research in which the psycho-theologians of the Middle Ages were active, but with none of the fetters of medieval scholasticism, or of academic theory. Now the question is whether the theorists of this school are not fettered by a new deity, the modern God of Science.

There has been little agitation of this problem of the physical bases of music for the last two centuries. During the sixteenth century the most bitter disputes were waged over the scales and intervals that were proper, and in Chapter 2 the correlations between these quarrels and the famous Ancient-Modern controversy were noted. Bold experimenters like Ramis de Pareja, Nicola Vicentino, and Zarlino were "moderns" who dared to investigate even the forbidden territory of quarter-tones. But with the final rejection of the modal system, with its melodic freedom, one major and one minor scale were chosen, and the major came to be looked upon as *the* scale. This new system worked, showing good practical results with new instruments and instrumental combinations, so after the days of Rameau, who published the first "modern" treatise on harmony, [9] the scale was regarded as a matter fixed, once and for all, like the names of the months and the days of the week. Rameau's theories were contemporaneous with Rousseau's Nature philosophy. The major triad and the major scale came to be known as the chord and scale of Nature; the melodic line of the Italian aria, so highly regarded in the eighteenth century, came to

[8] *Spectator*, No. 334.
[9] J. P. Rameau, *Traité de l'harmonie*, Paris, Bellard, 1722, 432 pp.

be looked upon as "natural melody," and the four-measure phrase the "normal" and "natural" metrical pattern.

Then in the early nineteenth century Villoteau, on Bonaparte's expedition to Egypt, made the epochal discovery that quite different, "outlandish" scales seem to natives of other lands to be as natural as our major seems to us. Ever since that time, the psychologist has played an active part in comparative musicology, the name now given to musical ethnology. But no scientific results developed until the invention of the phonograph. Accurate measurement of all scale differences were made possible by A. J. Ellis' system which divided each half step into 100 equal "cents." [10] Among the benefits brought by such researches are: (1) accurate methods of understanding the infinite and subtle possibilities of music and the ways in which other musical systems have been developed along lines entirely different from our own; (2) demonstration of the absurdity of the old notion, current since Rameau, that "all music is either major or minor;" (3) falsity of old dogmas concerning consonance and dissonance; and (4) proof of the possibilities for new musical instruments, new styles and methods [11] of composition, and new fields of enjoyment. Mathematical and psychological research in the laboratory has given valuable confirmation of all this. The electrical reproduction and production of tone is the most familiar achievement. "Synthetic" tone-color is as common and as feasible as synthetic dyes and flavors.

But some mathematical theorists, elated with the practical success of their demonstrations, are going too far. For example, Max Meyer [12] not only believes that musicians "ought to rejoice at the discovery that theirs is an art whose products are capable of far more exact description than the products of the painter or the dancer," but also that the sources or "origins" of musical understanding itself are to be found in numbers. His modern restatement of the Pythagorean theory is that "the numbers of vibration rates are of significance for musical theory not for physical, but for

[10] See Helmholtz, *Sensations of Tone,* ed. by Ellis, London, 1875.

[11] Joseph Shillinger, at the 1937 Convention of the M.T.N.A. and A.M.S. in Pittsburgh, demonstrated actual melodic invention, composed with mathematical techniques, by a student with no "musical knowledge."

[12] *The Musician's Arithmetic: Drill Problems for an Introduction to the Scientific Study of Musical Composition,* University of Missouri Scientific Studies, Vol. IV, No. 1, 1929.

physiological-chemical reasons. Our nervous functions depend on those ratios when we hear music. The musician who abhors numbers therefore abhors the way leading toward an understanding of musicianship, an understanding of the psychology of music." (pp. 8, 9). Meyer also asserts later (pp. 135, 136) that "Rhythm is no essential element of music . . .

. . . it is probable even that every kind of distinct grouping by accentuation could be absent and still leave a specious group of tones (being a group only because there are no further tones, i.e., because they are all and no more) nevertheless deserving to be classed as music."

This merely means that the author would regard such an isolated "group" of tones as worthy of the name music because it would still contain the elements of music in which he is exclusively interested.

Meyer is supported in this claim for "essential" harmony, exclusive of rhythm and melody, by the composer-theorist Alfredo Casella. In a preface entitled "The Nature and Origins of Music," Casella says:

"Rhythm, although indispensable . . . , is an extra-musical and, so to speak, 'inorganic concept.' It is only the propelling element." . . . The science of tone-colour — a science closely resembling chemistry — is at present the most powerful and progressive mainspring in music. . . . Of all mediums of sound, harmony — that is to say the simultaneous combination of three different notes — is alone essentially and fundamentally musical. . . . The only "specifically musical" element of music is *harmony,* because it *finds its origin in a physical phenomenon.* . . . Melody, on the other hand, stands in no direct relation with natural physical phenomena and represents the grossest and most primitive form of music . . . since it was "the only music of ancient civilizations." [230], pp. xix, xx.

Casella's attempt to find the origins of music in the laws of Nature thus rejects completely any effort to make the study of origins a matter of historical importance to human beings.

It is a curious argument, to say the least, to say that there is nothing "specifically musical" about rhythm and melody because they were the only media available to primitive man. Casella thus pits himself against both principal origin theories, the divine and the human.

The case for melody is presented by James L. Mursell, who finds melody "the primary musical phenomenon." [13] But this statement belongs in Section III of this chapter, under origins in "Laws of Human Nature."

2. ORIGINS IN IMITATIVE ARTIFACTS

The naturalistic theories cited in Chapter 3 merely referred to the experimental ways in which man stumbles upon the "laws of Nature" when he hits a resonant, hollow trunk, or twangs a taut string. The origins of instruments are easily discoverable in primitive examples, and there need be no argument about them when examples and pictures are available. But argument begins as soon as there is disagreement as to priority. First there have been the endless arguments concerning the priority of vocal or instrumental music. When the latter theory gained the ascendancy, there then arose the arguments as to which instrument was the original result of man's inventive powers.

Influenced by Rowbotham, and Von Bülow's famous dictum, "In the beginning was rhythm," most histories, in recent years, have pictured primitive man striking a hollow log, or gourd, thus discovering the first instrument to be the drum. But although Richard Wallaschek supports the theory that rhythm was the original element in music, he does not agree that the drum came first. Survivals of pre-historic flutes and pipes made from animal bones convince him that these are older. Wallaschek [127] therefore lists this historical order — (1) pipe, (2) song, (3) drum, the reverse of Rowbotham's series. But Willy Pastor, in his "Music of Primitive Peoples" [180], finds that the drum family came first:

"All stringed instruments are later than the percussion instruments. All melodically used instruments . . . are secular, which indicates their late origin. . . . The most interesting melodic instruments have not resulted from development, but are retrogressions from more perfect borrowed examples."

All these considerations bring up the old question as to whether music is originally and essentially an art or a science. This problem bothered Bonnet, the first French historian, who wrote on the subject as follows, in his Preface to the *Histoire* [9],

[13] *The Psychology of Music*, N. Y., Norton, 1937, pp. 99, 137, 300.

" We presume that Moses must have known whence came the origins of music, from the word of God himself, to whom he spoke face to face, as to one who was accustomed to speak as his friend."

Moses does say that " Jubal invented music about the year 230 after Creation . . . but he does not say how he invented it, or whether he made it an art or a science."

After dwelling on the miraculous effects of music described in the Scriptures and in Greek myth, and as shown in the effects upon animals, the return to the problem brings this conclusion:

" This art being part of mathematics, we may well believe that Adam, having had the perfection of knowledges from God, could pass the principles on to Jubal and Enos."

III. ORIGINS IN " LAWS OF HUMAN NATURE "

1. ORIGINS IN HUMAN INSTINCT

The quotation in the last paragraph above indicates the importance of the theory of music's origins in the inventive ability of rational men. But before discussing this, the less important theories of origins in man's unconscious or unpremeditated actions deserve attention. These theories, advocated by Plato, Darwin, Spencer, and others, are very well known, but figure very seldom as bases for historical presentation.

The Platonic theory of music's origins in the festival dances in honor of the gods is familiar:

" The young of all creatures cannot be quiet in their bodies or in their voices; they are always wanting to move, and cry out. . . . But, whereas other animals have no perception of order or disorder in their movements, that is, of rhythm or harmony, as they are called, to us, the Gods, who, as we say, have been appointed to be our partners in the dance, have given the pleasurable sense of harmony and rhythm; and so they stir us into life, and we follow them and join hands with one another in dances and songs." . . .[14]

This, however, only represents part of Plato's theory concerning music, and need not be stressed. Plato's concern was not so much with the origin of music as we conceive of the term, but of the effects of all the arts known as *music* upon the individual and society.

[14] *Laws*, Book II, 654, Jowett, 2nd ed., Oxford, 1875, Vol. V, p. 223.

The Spencerian version of Plato's theory, which found the origin of music in excess nervous energy and in impassioned speech, appears throughout the literature, sometimes as a mere comment, sometimes in connection with the theories concerning origins of music, dance, and poetry. But when Spencer says, "The lowest form of language is the exclamation," in his "Essay on Progress, its Law and Cause," he is interested in that statement of origins as a basis for his important "Law of Universal Progress" from homogeneity to heterogeneity.

Darwin's theory of the origin of music is purely biological; he rejects Spencer's theory, because it does not go back far enough! Mere human origins give inadequate proof of "evolution:"

"As we have every reason to suppose that articulate speech is one of the latest, as it certainly is the highest, of the arts acquired by man, and as the instinctive power of producing musical notes and rhythms is developed low down in the animal series, it would be altogether opposed to the principle of Evolution, if we were to admit that man's musical capacity has been developed from the tones used in impassioned speech. We must suppose that the rhythms and cadences of oratory are derived from previously developed musical powers.

"I conclude that musical notes and rhythms were first acquired by the male or female progenitors of mankind for the sake of charming the opposite sex." [15]

As far as can be ascertained, the only use of the Darwinian theory in history of music (except for the chapter on "Music and Love" in Combarieu's *Music, Its Laws and Evolution*) is in a modern German textbook (Mayer-Vollerthum [291]). In the latter, the author recalls an experience in the hills of Tuscany, where he overheard a loving couple improvising love duets. He could scarcely control his emotions, for he realized that he was in the presence of a natural revelation of the origins of music.

Wallaschek argues against the Darwinian and Spencerian theories in favor of the theory of rhythmical origins.

"The origin of music must be sought in the rhythmical impulse in man. . . . If it be asked whence the sense of rhythm arises, I answer, from the general appetite for exercise. That this desire occurs in rhythmical form is due to sociological as well as psychological conditions." [127], p. 231.

[15] Darwin, *The Descent of Man*, from the 2nd ed., New York, pp. 652, 653.

So far the most exhaustive treatise on *The Influence of Music on Behavior* is by Charles M. Diserens (Princeton, 1926). Origin theories of biological evolution are treated as " background for studies of specific musical effects," and as a general hypothesis to support inductive argument. Darwin's sexual-selection theory is approved with reservations that reconcile arguments against it, reminding the reader that, after all, what Darwin meant by music was merely " ordered noise."

2. ORIGINS IN INDIVIDUAL GENIUS

Chapter 6 has reviewed certain histories based upon the great-man theory, in which " epochs " were named after the individuals who seemed to dominate the musical life and thought of the period in which they lived. It was pointed out that the most popular figures at a given time and place in history are frequently forgotten by later generations; that historians often find supreme genius in composers who were comparatively obscure in their own day.

We are concerned here, however, with the basic assumptions involved in the great-man theory in music histories. These assumptions have also been stated in terms of " law; " once again we find concepts of divine law pitted against human-nature theories concerning man as an independent, self-sufficient creature. A hint of this controversy was indicated in the section in Chapter 3 entitled " Was music revealed, imitated, or invented? " Theories concerning the origins of music in innate genius tended, as shown in Chapter 6, toward a modification of the divine-origin theory. But as music histories began to be written in the days when scientific discovery, invention, and exploration were broadening the horizon, the " founders " of music were looked upon as " inventors." The frequent use of this term by Burney and others gives evidence of a preference for rational explanation; only with the Romantic revival of Christianity did historians return to the explanation that great composers were those to whom eternal verities were " revealed." It has already been pointed out that Jubal, Pythagoras, Guido d'Arezzo,[16] and later Dunstable and others were singled out

16 " After many centuries of darkness, Guido arose: and with a Force of Genius surpassing that of all his Predecessors *invented* the art of Counterpoint . . . yet this very circumstance which seems to promise so noble an Improvement in Music was a strong concurrent Cause of compleating its Divorce from Poetry." [20].

as the inventors of instruments, musical theory, notation, polyphony, composition, and so on.

During the Renaissance, with the awakening of men to the worth of the individual, the old tendency to lodge all wisdom, or its source, in one supreme figure had become very common. Aristotle was not the only one chosen; sometimes it was Homer, Virgil, or Cicero. In 1555, Loys le Caron, in *La Philosophie,* went farther back, to find the source of Greek wisdom in Moses. It then became necessary with the aid of Biblical chronology to list the individuals by whom accumulated wisdom had been passed on.

" Through Noah and his sons, a great portion of the experience and inventions of the old world was providentially saved. . . . The branches of the human family, separated forever from the parent stock . . . brought with them the old traditions to the different quarters of the world in which they settled. The nations that grew out of these primitive tribes, forgetting, in process of time, the history of their real origin, generally believed the leader of their colony to have been himself *the first man and the inventor of music.* . . . Hence it was that China, Hindostan, Chaldea, Phoenicia, Egypt, and even Greece, though but a colony from a colony, warmly contended for this imaginary honour, and in their zeal for priority, many of them corrupted their traditional chronology, and degraded history into fable. . . .

"No nation boasts a higher antiquity than China; and could the opinion of the learned Allix, Miston, Shuckford, Bedford, and others be maintained, that Noah left his children and settled in China immediately after the deluge, there would be little reason to dispute its pretensions." [45], pp. 1, 10.

Now to return to some theories of genius that were in vogue during the eighteenth century. They may throw some light upon the methods of histories that stress biography after the manner of Kiesewetter, who named his epochs after great men.

Criticizing the types of theory to be discussed in Chapter 11, and already reviewed in Chapter 7, Cecil Gray says that the

"evolution of musical forms does not constitute the history of an expressive art such as music any more than a philological study of language could pass for a history of literature, or a description of a man's physiological development for a biography. . . . Talent is the only thing that matters — the idioms of one generation are forgotten by the next. *Genius alone is absolute;* everything else is relative, impermanent, unessential." [246], pp. 2, 3.

This notion has an interesting history. In 1774 the Rev. Alexander Gerard, in *An Essay on Genius,* defined it as "the leading faculty of the mind, the grand instrument of all investigation . . . without the knowledge of which a regular method of invention cannot be employed." (p. 3).

As for the origins of genius, Gerard opines that "genius of every kind derives its immediate origin from the imagination" with the correcting functions of judgment and reason. To go back to a theory for the origin of imagination, one can turn again to Joseph Addison, who said, in his "Essay on the Pleasures of the Imagination" in the *Spectator,* No. 417, June 28, 1711:[17]

"It would be vain to enquire, whether the power of imagining things strongly proceeds from any greater perfection in the soul, or from any nicer texture in the brain, of one man than another. But this is certain, that a noble writer should be born with this faculty in its full strength and vigor so as to be able to receive lively ideas from outward objects, to retain them long, and to range them together, on occasion, in such figures and representations as are most likely to hit the fancy. . . ."

Returning to Gerard:

"If a man shows invention, no intellectual defects which his performance may betray can forfeit his claim to Genius . . . and the degree of this faculty, that we ascribe to him, is always in proportion to an estimate of the novelty, the difficulty, or the dignity of his inventions."[18]

It therefore became the chief task of the historians of the arts to determine, by various criteria, the "degree" of greatness of the artists, regardless of conditions imposed by time, space, or society.

Today, modern psychology denies the existence of "faculties," but carries on the eighteenth-century tradition by claiming the power to measure the "degree" of genius possessed by the individual.

[17] No. 413, the "Essay on Imagination," provided an ontological argument for the divine origin of esthetic pleasure: "One of the *final causes* of our delight in anything that is great may be this. The Supreme Author of our being has so formed the soul of man that nothing but himself can be its last, adequate and proper happiness. Because, therefore, a great part of our happiness must arise from the contemplation of his Being, that he might give our souls a just relish of such a contemplation, he has made them naturally delight in the apprehension of what is great or unlimited."

[18] For a theory concerning the origins of genius, as propounded in the Industrial era, see Edwin Paxton Hood's *Genius and Industry: the Achievements of Mind among the Cottages,* London, 1851. The four great teachers are *Poverty, Labour, Home,* and *Nature.*

Acting on the belief, then, that "genius is absolute," the wizards of the measuring stick have made extravagant claims that are now being modified. The nonacademic world still continues to judge genius by results. So although tests have succeeded in grading certain abilities, it remains questionable as to whether that mysterious "vitamin" called musicality has been successfully isolated and measured.

Determination of the intelligence quotient has been attempted, not merely with living subjects, but with some of the great personages of history [19]— Bach, Luther, Napoleon, Beethoven, and many others. The variability and scarcity of biographical materials must have made such a study very difficult, but the tabulated conclusions look very formidable and convincing.

One verdict among critics of the various tests indicates that the chief value of the latter is negative; that persons showing a *lack* of aptitudes and abilities have been properly discouraged from going to college, studying music, or managing a business. The question then arises: "To what extent has failure been due to discouragement resulting from failure to pass such tests?" The next question is whether the ability to pass such tests (except tests for knowledge and achievement) indicate true creative ability. Finally, the most searching query is to what extent and under what conditions the so-called "gifted" individual has made good.[20]

Modern musicology, at any rate, is not concerned with theories of genius. The conviction has been growing for several decades that individual "original" talent is non-existent or unfruitful in an unfavorable environment. Students of history have therefore turned their attention to the social scene; but here again, "laws," this time of group activity, figure in theories of origins.

3. THEORIES OF SOCIAL ORIGINS

There are four general types of origin theories which are concerned with the musical activities and the musical communications of social groups, large and small. These are found in (a) the quest for "original" groups, with "uncontaminated" or "undeveloped" music, (b) the nationalistic theories of folk origins, (c) the eco-

---

[19] Catherine Cox Miles: *Genetic Studies of Genius,* Stanford University Press, 1925.
[20] See Mursell, *The Psychology of Music,* pp. 299, 300.

nomic theories of work origins (or, after work, in the play-impulse), and (d) the theories of origins in magic and ritual.

A. The Quest for "Original" Groups

During the eighteenth century, when certain philosophers were advocating the return to Nature, it was maintained by Sir William Temple and Vossius that the original virtues of the ancients were to be found among the Chinese, who had been unspoiled by contact with Western civilization. The affectation of the pigtail and the general craze for *chinoiserie* seem to have been in deference to this theory; at any rate, the contemptuous term *Zopf* has been given by nineteenth-century Germans to the Rococo period. There was a general tendency, during the Enlightenment,[21] to urge standards of good taste which called for naturalness and simplicity, and although little was known about the music of China, it was held up as a romantic ideal. But, as already noted, when Burney, for example, dealt with actual folk music that was "different," he was apt to find it "barbarous, uncouth, and inferior to real music, which rises from a complete scale."

Sir John Hawkins dealt summarily with Temple and Vossius and their romantic notions that Chinese music must be excellent because it was ancient, thus offering another sidelight on the old quarrel:

"As to the general prejudices in behalf of antiquity, it has been hinted above that a reason for them is to be found in that implicit belief which the course of modern education disposes us to entertain of the superior wisdom and ingenuity of those who in all these instances we are taught to look upon as patterns the most worthy of imitation; *but it can never be deemed an excuse for some writers for complimenting nations less enlightened than ourselves with the possession or enjoyment of arts which it is pretended they have lost.* These men (like Temple and Vossius), upon little better evidence than the reports of travellers, and the relations of missionaries, who might have purposes of their own to serve, have celebrated the policy, the morality, and the learning of the Chinese, and done little less than proposed them as examples of all that is excellent in human nature." [27], p. xxiii.

But Hawkins dismisses "the nations and tribes among whom the simple dictates of *nature* seemed to be the only action; but the subjects here treated are of the *science* and the *scientific practice* of music; how

[21] See Chapter 5.

the best music of the barbarians is said to be hideous and astonishing sounds. Of what importance can it be to enquire into a practice that has not its foundation in science or system, or to know what are the sounds that most delight a Hottentot, a wild American, or even a more refined Chinese? "

Hawkins' German contemporary, Herder, averred:

" There is such a marked difference between the music of the East and that of the West, that even if we knew more, we should find little to suit our ear."

In other words, these men were intolerant of differences.[22] They were contributing to the belief that gained ground in the nineteenth century, namely, that extra-European arts and culture were at lower stages of development than those known in Europe. Thus the quest for the " original " group turned, in evolutionary anthropology and music history, back to the " lowest " groups in the scale, where primitive " origins " were to be found.

In recent years, European music has spread to all parts of the world. This may be due to the comparative simplicity of our Western patterns. The comparative musicologist, now fully alive to the value of differences, is hastening to preserve, by means of phonograph records, the treasures of interesting folk music which are in danger of extinction.

John Brown, in 1763, in his *Dissertation,* pointed out that

" the Irish, Welsh, and Scots are strictly *Natives,* and have a Music of their own: the English on the contrary are a foreign Mixture of late-established Colonies; and as a consequence of this, have no Native Music. He who would find the *original Music* of England must seek it in *Wales.*

" Before the Roman Empire fell to Ruin, its Rulers took Care to the utmost of their Power to extirpate the Native Music of the barbarous Countries which they conquered. . . . This was a high stroke of Policy; for their Native Songs being (as in ancient Greece) the Repository of their Religious and Political System, nothing could so effectually subdue the minds of these Barbarians as the Banishment or Destruction of their Bards and Druids."

And Combarieu shows how the same levelling process once took place under the auspices of the church:

[22] Sir Hubert Parry is just as intolerant with reference to Oriental music as late as 1911. (*Style in Musical Art,* reprinted in London in 1924.)

"In the Middle Ages, the geographic map of the spoken language had numerous and distinct colors. On one hand, Provençal, on the other French. In the French, four principal dialects: the Burgundian in the East; the Norman in the West, etc. . . . There was just such a map of music in all countries. Political centers created musical centers. Melodies were organized around the spoken tongue and followed its peculiar genius.[23] The fundamental scale, modes, rhythms, were determined by local custom. . . . The church ignored, obstructed, effaced all this. Upon local practices, she superposed a common usage." [189], I, p. 355.

Objective histories of music must recognize the splendid work that comparative musicology has accomplished in preserving the music of isolated groups. This work of preservation is carried on not only in other lands, but in our own country. And it is not merely a matter of museum-collecting; it is a matter of preservation through encouragement. Polish songs in Cleveland and Texas; Finnish songs in Minnesota; Kentucky "Lonesome Tunes," some of which, brought long ago from England, are now forgotten in the mother country; cowboy songs; Appalachian, Mexican, and Indian songs are all part of our national heritage. American music can never be more or less than the sum of the musical arts cultivated in these Varied though United States. (See Chapter 13 for further discussion.)

The old custom of beginning music histories with a condescending chapter on "primitive" music is thoroughly reprehensible, in the light of modern knowledge. Oriental music and other exotic systems are anything but "primitive." The findings in extra-European systems should be treated as contemporary, living phases of art, having a long and worthy tradition of their own, not as dead relics of an early stage of development.

Today the highly civilized music of the East is being studied seriously and new materials are being made available.[24] On the other hand, Chinese and Japanese students have taken readily to European music, which to their countrymen has always been as incomprehensible as theirs is to us. Tokyo now maintains a conservatory of a Western type, while Japanese prima donnas sing

---

[23] It may be noted here that Combarieu refutes his own earlier theory that music "is formed by a thought without concepts." [158], p. 107.

[24] See John H. Levis, *Foundations of Chinese Musical Art*, Peiping, 1936; also Sir Francis T. Piggott, *The Music and Musical Instruments of Japan*, 2nd ed., Yokohama, 1909; Hisao Tanabe, *Japanese Music*, tr. by Shigeyoshi Sakabe, Kokusai Bunka Shinkokai, Tokyo, 1936.

"Madame Butterfly." Meanwhile Oriental music is being adapted to Western symphony orchestras.

Simultaneously with the beginnings of this new scientific interest, Debussy discovered great artistic possibilities in the music of a Javanese orchestra at the Paris Exhibition of 1900; and Western Europe became conscious of a new and great musical art in Russia from Mussorgsky to Stravinsky, an art strongly tinged with Oriental influence. Comparative musicology can and does show that our musical system is not the only one; that our kind of musical enjoyment is not the only esthetic pleasure possible. These modern comparisons, with the aid of actual recordings of the fascinating and complex art of the Balinese, Siamese, Africans, Hindus, and others bring the music of distant lands to our firesides, and open to the modern composer new vistas, particularly in the field of rhythm. In the latter the European proves to be a mere tyro in comparison with the East Indian or African.

But the old method of treating exotic music at the beginning of the histories, as if it were all to be studied as exhibiting phases of primitive music, still persists. Scientific observers and recorders still assume that they are dealing not merely with systems of great antiquity, quite different from our own, but with "stages of development."

Comparative musicology, besides performing the praiseworthy and prodigious task of recording, comparing, and analyzing folk music in all parts of the world, is endeavoring, in spite of authoritative warnings, to connect its findings with monistic history. (See Chapter 10, 1.)

In 1904, Hugo Riemann sounded the following warning:

"Musical ethnology, one of the youngest branches of musicology, with the research technique made possible by phonograph records of primitive folk songs, and with precise study of the construction of instruments, is arriving at conclusions which slap old traditions of tone-relations in the face (with the discovery of intervals of ¾ of a whole step, the 'neutral' third, etc.).

"But this is in no case a matter of historical research, to permit our presentation of conditions in the past to be deduced from such observations in the present. Here a serious note of warning to the music historians is in order, not to allow their sight to be dulled by the exact investigators who employ the methods of the natural sciences." [150], Vol. I, Preface.

Unfortunately, Riemann himself was not aware of the strength of the tradition which dictated the search for origins, for he had an opportunity at that point to show how absurd it is to assume that our European system has grown out of these extremely different systems, or from a parent stem for whose roots no shred of real historical evidence exists. Instead, the classic theorist in him takes the floor, and he weakens his case by continuing thus:

" The striking agreement as to the division of the octave into twelve half-tones, which was arrived at independently by the Chinese, Greek and peoples of the European West, is *an historical fact. This was the last stage* of a seven-tone-scale whose two tetrachords each consisted of a half-step *inserted* alternately among two or three whole-tones; and this historical fact is not to be thrown overboard by a few miserably bored flutes from Polynesia or some questionable vocal performances by colored women." [150], Vol. I, Preface.

It is a pity that this great scholar should have weakened his first paragraph with the obvious assumptions implicit in the second. At any rate, we find that his sensible " note of serious warning " has been disregarded.

Twenty years later, a new *Handbuch* appeared, under the distinguished guidance of Guido Adler (1924). So far is Riemann's advice disregarded that the article chosen for the first pages of Volume I is the following by Robert Lach, a Vienna musician who has become interested in comparative musicology:

Die Musik der Natur — und Orientalischen Kulturvölker

[Note the confusion in putting together primitive cultures and Oriental civilizations]

" The question which is found at the beginning of every history of music, that concerning the *origins* of music, leads from the realm of music history, first, into that of her sister discipline, comparative musicology, then beyond into that of the natural sciences. The quest for the primitive origins of music was first undertaken, in fact, by the natural scientists, not the music historian. As is well-known, Charles Darwin was the *first* [sic] to raise the question of the origin of music, first with reference to the music of animals and especially the songs of the birds. His solution of the question was to regard the songs of birds as a means of natural selection, the consequence of which was that only the best singers among the females received preference. Hence the present perfection of bird song is a result of progressive sexual selection from generation to generation.

" Connected with this theory and analogous to it was his attempt to explain the earliest attempts at music among men. He assumed that primitive man demanded outlet for his excitement in tone, just as do animals — especially the aforementioned bird species. In support of this assumption he indicated that even today the speech of excited Negroes passes over into song; and that even under civilized conditions the excited speaker instinctively turns to musical cadences and rhythms, so that in the rhythms and cadences of oratory we may detect an atavistic relapse to a capacity for tone-production developed in pre-human epochs, a tendency called forth by intense emotional excitation." [224], I, p. 3.

Then follows an account of numerous other theories which agree and disagree with Darwin: Spencer's theory of overflow of nervous energy; Wallace and his theory emphasizing the desire for pleasurable satisfaction; Karl Groos' modifications of the sexual-selection theory; theories concerning the play impulse, the imitation impulse, the beautification instinct, imagination, to say nothing of the rhythmical impulse emphasized by Bücher and Wallaschek. Lach then describes the origin theory most popular in Germany today:

" Carl Stumpf,[25] again, in his *Anfänge der Musik* [182] has traced the origin of music to the lingering on one musical tone, which happens in the very nature of things, when you try to make your voice heard at some distance; this resulting greater or greatest tightening of the vocal cords produces a longer vibrating high tone, in which Stumpf sees the first step toward singing, that is the border line over against mere speaking. As the second step, in fact the real creative act of music, Stumpf further sees the resulting multiple sounds (harmony) caused by assembling several voices, for example, of different sex or vocal range, which then in the further course of development led to the use of definite transposable intervals. As last and latest theory of the origin of music, we mention, among others, that represented by Fausto Torrefranca, according to which its rise is to be derived from the primitive cry uttered by the first man in the condition of highest passion, which according to the increase or decrease of emotion during the act of producing sound suffers modifications of the initial pitch, in the sense of rising to a higher and sinking to a lower tone (level) so that inflections and modulations result, which in the course of further development lead to the origin of groups of tones and melismas, and so to music. . . .

" If we attempt to list comprehensively the characteristic traits which make up the picture of primitive music, we can give the following as

[25] Dr. Stumpf, modern psychological pioneer in this field, while professor at the University of Berlin, instituted a collection of folk records at that institution which is second to none.

the outstanding attributes: as concerns the tone material, the use of one or a few tones, in constant repetition, with tiring monotony. . . . *It is the observation of this typical phenomenon that caused the English musicologist, John Frederick Rowbotham* (in his *History of Music,* London, 1885–1887) *to assume various stages of development of primitive and archaic music."* [224], pp. 4, 5.

B. Nationalistic Group Theories

All group theories recognize that art is a means of communication between human beings. Music, according to these theories, is a social art, and its origins are to be found in the gregarious instinct, not alone in impersonal physical phenomena or the responses thereto by individuals, as important as all these matters may be.

It was a healthy reaction when a few historians began to hint that the character of the folk group had much to do with the development of the artist, as well as innate genius.[26] In 1885, the French historian Clément [111] mentioned the obvious fact that " one could. not imagine a Raphael from the Malay peninsula, or a Mozart from among the Zulus." But instead of going on to examine and compare musical life in different societies, with the interactions of individuals, groups, and cultures, this hint was too often lost. The demand for nationalistic history and the powerful influence of the Evolution theory perpetuated the old genealogical method, with each national art having its " roots " in its own folk song, developing independently from, but sometimes by dint of a " struggle " with, other cultures. Those that had an international point of view followed up the evolution of forms, ignoring men, events, and general cultural modifications as much as possible.

In the " struggle " between cultures, certain national groups gain supremacy, as, for instance, the Netherlands composers in the fifteenth-eighteenth centuries, the Italians from the late sixteenth to the eighteenth, and the Germans in the eighteenth and nineteenth.[27]

Thus, when " great " music is produced largely in one area, importation and imitation is resorted to in other countries, to the unfortunate neglect of national resources.[28] But attempts to remedy

---

[26] And that " men of genius appear mostly in groups." (Friedrich Hertz, *Race and Civilization,* N. Y., 1928, p. 55.)

[27] The internationalism of sixteenth-century music has not yet been fully investigated as a study in culture exchange and modification under various social conditions.

[28] See Cecil Forsyth's illuminating study of *Music and Nationalism,* in which an inquiry is made into the reasons for England's failure to develop a national school of opera.

this neglect sometimes result in sterile chauvinism, in unproductive attempts to be completely independent.

National histories such as Ernest Walker's *History of Music in England* (1907, 1924) do no more than chronicle men and events in music within the country, with little reference to external influences that were so important. On the other hand, a nationalistic work like Moser's *Geschichte der deutschen Musik* sets forth with the avowed object of exalting not only the recorded achievements of German music, but also the supremacy of his " race " in influencing the evolution of Occidental music long before the records begin. So unfortunately the most valuable of these origin theories, the recognition of the influence of indigenous folk music, is carried to an extreme that is tragic in its consequences.

Considerable space was given to the German and Italian nationalists in Chapter 8. This section is concerned entirely with the theoretical bases employed. It has been pointed out (p. 164 ff.) that one theory upon which German nationalistic histories of music are being based is the theory advocated by Carl Stumpf, in his *Beginnings of Music* [182]. Now Stumpf was a psychologist, not a historian; his theory is mere observation of the psychological processes that take place when a strong-lunged male shouts to another who is beyond the reach of the ordinary voice.[29] H. J. Moser, during his nationalistic period, picked up that theory and made it a hypothesis for the origins of a virile, manly Germanic art of music. As a musicologist, as already pointed out, Moser now modifies the extreme position that he once took, but the theory stays in Germany today, because it is very useful to a State bent on developing a war psychology. Such a theory, coupled with belief in a " pure " German music, will not be downed until Germany returns to humanistic internationalism.[30]

---

[29] It is in this same spirit that Mursell cites Stumpf's theory, in his chapter on " Tonal Foundations of Music," in *The Psychology of Music*, p. 99.

[30] One of the most recent and amazing applications of the Nordic, Germanic theory is by Arnold Schering, one of the foremost musical scholars in Germany today. In his *Beethoven in Neuer Deutung* (Leipzig, 1934), he maintains that Shakespeare furnished literal inspiration for Beethoven's thematic material and this offers proof of the " German, masculine art " common to both. In this art, man stands as the center of reflective thought, not as a detached ego in repose, but as a being that must constantly defend himself against daemonic powers." (p. 115). Schiller is included, as having inspired the sonata, op. 106, with his *Jungfrau von Orleans.* Kinship of various sonatas and quartets with Shakespearean plays is proved

It is as difficult to find any " pure " folk music that can be labeled exclusively by one name, as it is to isolate a pure racial strain. If such a pure race with its own unadulterated folk song could be found, it is doubtful whether such isolated folk music would prove to be the source of any of our art music. The latter has developed as an international, interracial product, as Moser himself was obliged to admit, when he said, back in 1914, that the very " struggle " between cultures that he envisaged had resulted in " a mutual enrichment (*Befruchtigung*) of both inimical principles " and that that very enrichment " has brought Occidental music to the wonderful heights it now occupies." [195].

The tragedy of the situation lies in the fact that the history of music might have been presented not as a struggle, but as a friendly interchange of ideas in spite of hostilities in other realms of society. A strongly nationalistic historian will do little or nothing to foster the belief so fondly entertained, a generation ago, in " Music as an International Language." [31] And unfortunately nationalistic historians are not confined to the Continent.

Recently some English musicians have been endeavoring to combat the domination of foreign music by calling attention to their own riches of national folk art. Among them is Ralph Vaughan-Williams, himself a composer of distinction, whose works show the influence of this " back-to-folk-song movement." He has taken to literary defense of his position, and the assumptions back of nationalistic history are clearly apparent in some lectures delivered in this country [310]. He has found it necessary to include a chapter entitled " Some Tentative Ideas on the Origins of Music." The disputed question of " communal authorship " is distinguished from the theory of " communal origins." Granting, " for the sake of argument," that " one man invents a tune," he argues for both theories because of the modifications resulting in oral transference. " The

---

by fitting themes to quotations. Thus, e.g., the quartet, op. 130, is inspired by *Midsummer Night's Dream*, the Appassionata, op. 57, by *Macbeth*, and so on. Ernest Newman indulges in plain speaking concerning what he calls the " wild nonsense " of racial theories concerning differences in music. ("Music and Race," in *Studies in Music*, reprinted articles from *The Musician*, edited by Robin Grey, Scribner's, 1901.) " The plain truth evidently is that German music became deeper in content than the Italian, because the social circumstances of the two nations were different." (p. 305).

[31] See the essay, so entitled, by Daniel Gregory Mason, in *Music as a Humanity*, also published by American Assn. for Internat'l Conciliation, N. Y., 1913.

case for communal origins cannot be proved, yet I do not see how it can be disproved."

Observation of Negro groups in our own South has led to interesting inferences concerning communal theories. Some one might conceivably develop a theory of origins based upon spontaneous generation of harmony and counterpoint as by-products of religious emotion. Sober research might reveal, however, that such observable phenomena do not explain everything. It would be interesting, for instance, to examine the available books of American hymn tunes together with all the Negro Spirituals accessible. One might find that the latter are frequently disguised versions of the former.

Darius Milhaud, in writing his *Création du monde,* was called upon to provide music for a ballet suggesting the Gold Coast of Africa. He used American jazz rhythms, under the mistaken impression that the origins of the latter in Negro folk music proved a homogeneity with African music. He forgot that the Southern Negro sings as well as speaks a dialect of the English language unknown in Africa.

Mechanical theories of "diffusion" will not explain such phenomena, for the thing we know as folk song is susceptible to the same complex modifications that other phases of culture undergo as a result of intrusions and migrations. Where no intrusions have taken place, the old songs persist, with slight modifications, but without evolving into other forms, even though persons of natural talent pass them on.[32] There are examples of such persistence and stability in the folk songs of remote districts in Ireland, Wales, Scotland, Brittany, and Spain. But in Italy, for the most part, the desire for novelty in music has precluded the preservation of old songs, although the Italians have preserved remains of other arts with the utmost fidelity. And in Germany the dividing line between *Lied, Volkstümliches Lied,* and *Volkslied* is often very difficult to find. Who can say which came first, as a matter of general law: "communal" group music or individual, conscious art, such as that developed by the first actual characters in our historical records, the bards, minstrels, and troubadours?

[32] For examples of old English folk tunes preserved in this country and forgotten in England, see Howard Brockway, *Lonesome Tunes from the Kentucky Mountains,* Ditson, Musicians' Library, and new arrangements by Annabel Buchanan of *White Spirituals* from the Virginia Mountains, N. Y., J. Fischer & Bro. The most comprehensive studies of White Spirituals are by George P. Jackson, *White Spirituals in the Southern Uplands,* and *Spiritual Folk Songs of Early America.*

At any rate, the whole fascinating study of folk song is so complex that many pitfalls lie in wait for the investigator who overworks the very appealing theory of the origins of musical art in folk music, with all its elements of truth. It is obviously true that unless folk music is developed somewhere, no sophisticated art can flourish, and that "you can hardly expect a gardener to be able to cultivate beautiful flowers in a soil which is so barren that no wild flowers will grow there." But need we "presuppose that there *must* be wild flowers of music *before* we occupy ourselves with our hydrangeas and Gloire de Dijon roses"? [310], p. 28. Possibly the wild flowers of music were cultivated with the same proud care that was given to the hydrangeas. It is merely repeating old assumptions already discussed to say that musical "art is something inborn in man" or that "in early days the music of the people was of necessity national." [310], p. 96. If "Music in Bach's time [33] and in Bach's community was looked on not as an international art but as a local craft," then why did Bach copy with avidity the works of French and Italian composers, making their forms his own, fusing them with German thoroughness into something new and vital?

So long as the search for origins is confined to actual songs, whether preserved by tradition or in writing, the quest is really historical, and one's ideas need not be tentative. But it is a different matter when tentative ideas are based upon assumptions concerning origins in general, in order to bolster nationalistic doctrines.

Nationalistic theories fail to recognize that all the evidence of history points to the importance of small rather than large groups. The earliest characters in the actual history of music· are little groups of bards, minstrels, strolling players, troubadours and trouvères. One can find very little evidence to support a theory for the emergence of music, whether "wild" or "cultivated," among large crowds. Musical skills are learned, practiced, and perfected in very intimate circles.[34]

Obvious reasons have impelled writers to dwell proudly on the

[33] Admitting that Bach, with all of his absorption of foreign music, remained essentially German, one may point to Handel, "in Bach's time." By living in other countries, he became thoroughly Italian, or English, or international.

[34] To realize the truth of this in history, cf. Charles W. Hughes, *Chamber Music in American Schools*, Mt. Vernon, N. Y., 1933. Under this unassuming title is a very valuable history of music in small groups, from the days of the troubadours to the present.

.

periods during which achievements in the favored area were particularly impressive. But comparisons of all music histories show that England, Italy, France, Spain, Germany, Belgium, Holland, Russia, Finland, and our own country have had or are having their periods of intense musical activity, with other periods when creative work was at a standstill, except for neighborly importation and imitation. The best general histories recognize these facts and deal with them objectively. A great service can be rendered to the cause of education when the conditions under which creative activity takes place are analyzed and better understood.

C. Economic Theories of Group Origins

It has been shown that theories concerning the origins of music in group psychology are being used in attempts to demonstrate the absolute superiority of national cultures. At the same time, another origin theory, with the same method, is being employed by those who are interested in establishing a new economic order that shall cut down and across national barriers. Reference has already been made in Chapter 8 to Karl Bücher's *Arbeit und Rhythmus,* the work which supplied the basic theory of origins for Chemodanoff's Marxian history of music. This theory refers to a well-known fact that much folk music is closely associated with the rhythms of work. Barge songs, sea chanties, ditties, and hosts of other examples offer contemporaneous and wholly convincing evidence of the fact that these particular songs arise from labor and are used to lighten it. But Bücher was not satisfied with such simple observations, for he had an economic theory of history. So this obvious fact and the evidence supporting it had to be used as illustrations to support the theory that *all* music arises from the rhythms of work. Hence the title of the last chapter of this influential book: *Der Rhythmus als ökonomisches Entwicklungsprinzip.* The economic principle is manifested "instinctively" during the "childhood of the human race" by means of rhythm. This principle is that man shall get the best out of life with the minimum of effort and strain, and with no waste of energy. The author concludes that work rhythms and work songs were the means used "from the beginning" not only to lighten labor but to speed up production, and that music had its origin in this principle. Before the invention of improved tools and labor-saving machinery, rhythm was the only means available for achieving these ends.[85] It was the bond that united all the arts — the "arts of movement" (music, dancing, and poetry) and the "arts of rest" (sculpture and painting). These arts, in turn, were undifferentiated from work and play, the arts of movement growing out of the execution of work, and the arts of rest growing out of contemplation of the results of work. Bücher felt that his research had uncovered

"a series of threads, the ends of which are widely separated in this modern world; but the beginnings of these threads come nearer together the farther back we follow them, and finally come together in one point.[86] This point lies close to the boundary of the region where pathless darkness enshrouds the earliest history of mankind. And if we follow with the eye of the spirit the ways traversed through the centuries, we then recognize that we are dealing with a process of social evolution, a process which may be looked upon on the material side as integration to differentiation, on the personal side as going from unity to division of labor." [136], p. 397.

Shortly after the appearance of Bücher's *Arbeit und Rhythmus,* Karl Groos published *Die Spiele der Tiere* (Jena, 1896). After Darwin's sexual-selection hypothesis, it had become fashionable to invoke the comparative method in order to determine the origins of human impulses in the animal kingdom. Westermarck had done this in his *Origins of Marriage* (1889), so Groos followed suit with an application of his theories to *Die Spiele der Menschen* (1898).[87] In the meantime Bücher was influenced by Groos' first book to reverse his first theory.[88] He was led to conclude that

"labor among primitive peoples is something very ill-defined. The further we follow it back, the more closely it approaches in form and substance to play. All regularly sustained activity finally takes on a rhythmic form and becomes fused with music and song in an indivisible whole. It is accordingly in play that technical skill is developed, and it turns to the useful only gradually. *The order of progression must therefore be reversed; play is older than work, art older than production for use.* Even when among the higher primitive peoples the two elements begin to separate from each other, the dance still precedes or follows every

[85] Bücher quotes an undocumented report dated 1835 which asserts that "with clever and attentive utilization of rhythmical energy" in public works, mining, refining, and factory labor, production could be increased 25 per cent. [136], p. 419.
[86] For Combarieu's diagram illustrating this method, see p. 232.
[87] Cf. *The Play of Man,* tr. by E. L. Baldwin, N. Y., 1901.
[88] In *Die Entstehung der Volkswirtschaft,* 3rd ed., Leipzig, 1900; 1st ed., 1895.

more important work (war, hunting, harvest) and song accompanies work." [89]

This at least shows an open-mindedness not displayed by the doctrinaires who make such eager application of Bücher's original and discarded theory.

Bücher's theories are those of a materialist who was not interested in man as a religious animal. It is not surprising that his theory should be taken up so seriously by Marxian theorists, who find no place for religion in the State, and that Chemodanoff should carry it perhaps farther than Bücher intended by going on to "prove" that *all* music arose in the "struggle for existence." But work songs are not the only music encountered in folkways. It was convenient for Bücher to ignore other types that would not illustrate his explanation.

On the other hand, it has been possible for other theorists to develop their hypotheses by completely ignoring the evidence used by Bücher. This is evidently the case with Combarieu [40] and others who find the origins of music in magic rites and in the instinct of vocal utterance as a means of worship. These theories have been discussed at the beginning of this chapter.

Summarizing these various psychological theories, we find the origins of music located as follows:

(1) *In divine creation,* coeval with the first attempts at vocal expression or language by the first human beings, endowed, as Adam was, with necessary knowledge.

(2) *In numbers,* as illustrated by the music of the spheres, made by the planets in their orderly movements, and as demonstrated in the laws of sound-relations in Nature.

(3) In the *imitation of Nature,* as illustrated by childish and primitive practices, and in the empirical invention of instruments.

(4) In the *moods* (emotions) of the individual, in the "soul." As music could directly imitate these moods, the *ethos of music,* in its various modes, was an important problem in education. The laws for "good" music, then, are not of "Nature," but of the cult, church, academy, or tribunal that decides what music is good for its adherents. This function was performed by the church in the

[89] From the translation entitled *Industrial Evolution,* by S. M. Wickett, N. Y., Holt, 1901, pp. 28, 29.

[40] Bücher's book is not available in English, but Combarieu gives a detailed summary of the work-origin theory in his *Music, Its Laws and Evolution.* [158], Ch. II, I.

Middle Ages, and today is performed for Germany by the *Kultus-ministerium*.

(5) In the *genius* or *talent* of the individual. This theory is always popular in an age that glorifies the virtuoso.

(6) In *national consciousness,* group solidarity, in folk music "instinctively" expressive of the characteristics and aspirations of one nation in one area. These theories are especially popular in countries where the militaristic ideal is fostered.

(7) In *class consciousness,* in the group solidarity engendered by common enterprise, work, and play. Rhythm is the prime factor in this theory.

(8) In the *religious* impulse, in the communal feeling of awe leading to rites of worship, beginning with music in *magic.*

(9) In the *dramatic* instinct — impassioned speech, sexual selection, the emotion of fear, heroic narration, desire for social approval.

(10) In the *dance* instinct — the desire for exercise, the play impulse.

In summarizing the position taken toward these theories, then, it is essential to note that all of them recognize certain truths. Together they illustrate the many-sided nature of music. Music is important in simple cultures, whether in magic, in work, or in religion. It exerts its magic upon us, also, and we see its value in education. Genius and talent are important; students with ability should be encouraged and given opportunities; intelligent guidance should, at the same time, encourage individuals to enter those vocations for which they are best fitted. Music is a science and also an art; folk music can and should be treasured and perpetuated; nationalism can be as worthy a concept as personality (and equally revealing). Some of our greatest music was inspired by work rhythms and dance rhythms, and our musical heritage would be very poor without religious music — from carol, chant, and chorale to oratorio. And it would be equally poor without secular music for entertainment.

But we are discussing the history of *all* these manifestations of creative activity. When any account of these activities is narrowed to the particular interests of an investigator with a theory and this investigator attempts to explain the history of the whole from assumptions based upon a fragment of abstracted truth, the fallacy should be obvious.

IV. ORIGINS IN MUSICAL STRUCTURE

For want of a better term, this heading refers to the theories concerning the origins of our forms of musical expression. Greek theories of this type were entirely bound up with poetry, but even then speculation concerning the theoretical bases of music itself was most active. As a matter of fact, although very few examples of Greek music have come down to us, there is considerable information at hand concerning the structure of their scales. " A little knowledge is a dangerous thing," for on the slender bases available, volumes have been dedicated to the task of proving that the plainsong of the Christian church had its origins in ancient music. Some are written to prove specific origins in Hebrew, Syrian, Greek, Coptic, or Byzantine forms. Without pausing to examine the merits of any of these theories, it only needs to be observed that the quest for origins is just as active in this field as in the physical and psychological avenues, but with no more conclusive results and no unanimous consent.

Many a baffled investigator asks, " Since we have so much information regarding the other arts, why can we not fill the lacunae in music history? " The common-sense answer is that at least some appreciable remnants of early Greek art can be seen, touched, and studied; but very few records exist by means of which we can have any idea of Greek music as it was sung or played. About the eleventh century A.D., fourteen hundred years after Aristoxenus, the great Greek theorist, men began to record music which can now be put into modern notation.[41]

1. ORIGINS IN SCALES

Burney has been quoted as saying that "real music arises from a complete scale." The early preoccupation with scales in many histories and systems of music teaching sometimes indicates that the belief is still widespread. This is undoubtedly due to the emphasis on scale drill in instrumental study, but, as indicated in Chapter 2, great concern over scales is not evident in the history of music until keyboard instruments began to call for decisions with reference to

[41] Even when medieval and Renaissance music has been deciphered, one of the greatest problems of music history remains — how it sounded in actual performance. See Schering, *Aufführungspraxis der alten Musik*, Leipzig, 1931; Haas [260].

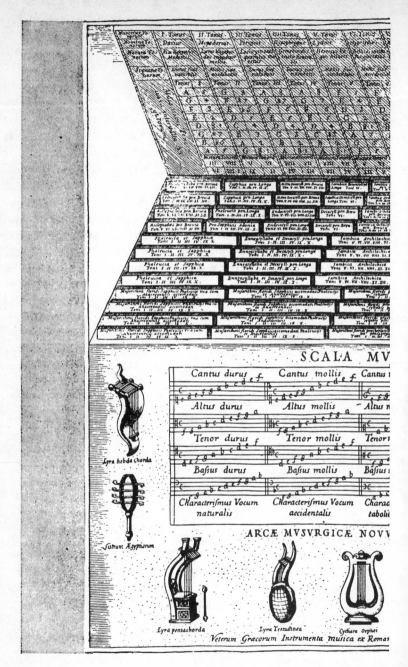

SCALA MV...

ARCÆ MVSVRGICÆ NOV...

Veterum Græcorum Instrumenta Musica ex Roma...

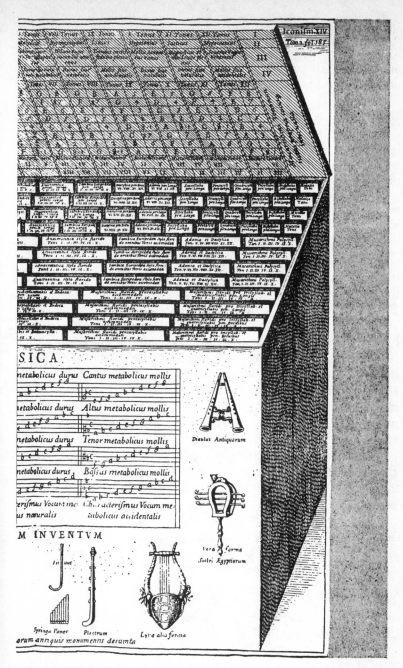

the exact tuning of intervals.[42] No scales are necessary for vocal music alone. The modes of ancient music were evidently regarded more as functional melodic patterns than as scales in the modern sense.

"Historically speaking, the scale is primarily what we call today a product of the laboratory or of the study, the creation of a Pythagoras or of a Ptolemy; according to these scholars it remains a . . . handy means of exposition for purposes of tuition. Mozart, in the scene with the Commander in *Don Juan,* Beethoven, at the commencement of his first piano concerto, wrote, no doubt, melodious sequences for instruments which may be called scales; but such works belong to a period when the theories of the schools had their influence on the genius of the masters." [158], pp. 121, 122.

The theories of the schools also had their influence on the writing of music histories. It was for this reason that controversy over the scales, modes, genera, and divisions was made the subject of Chapter 2 of this volume. Many composers, during the seventeenth and eighteenth centuries, succeeded in settling many controversies by simplifying the problems. In the *Well-tempered Clavichord,* by Bach (1721), and about the same time in the treatises of Rameau, the twelve *modes* of the Middle Ages were reduced to only two, one major and one minor. The system of equal temperament permitted transposition of music to any one of twelve keys, but no matter how many keys or pitches are used, there remain but two scales. To make matters still simpler, the major scale, after its triumphant acceptance in the eighteenth century as the *scale of Nature,* came to be considered as *the scale,* with the minor dependent upon it as a relative. This concept, still dominant in music teaching, is an eighteenth-century notion, and a serious obstacle to the understanding of minor as a fundamental tonality. Because of it, all older music which did not fit neatly into major-minor categories was considered " Gothic barbarity," in keeping with the prejudices of the day. And this notion accounts for the fact that until recently this music, even most of the music of Bach, was unknown and incomprehensible to most of Christendom. Even today, for the average layman, all simple, obvious, happy music is major; all sad, chromatic, "different" music is minor.[43]

---

[42] See pp. 218–219, from Kircher, in which scales are neatly classified, boxed, as it were, for selection.

[43] Combarieu [158], pp. 126–130, has a section on "The Minor Mode" in which this matter is considered in detail. After quoting Zarlino, Masson, Rameau,

If the historian believes that the origins of music are in the scale, and with Fétis that music "bears all its consequences within itself," then he will agree with Joseph Yasser that

"We should not lose sight of the fact that a genuine musical scale is, in a way, an organic phenomenon, which, like everything else live and organic, is bound to grow, to expand, to evolve continuously. It is essentially an evolving not a static phenomenon." [288].

Yasser is supported by Casella, who believes that

"Our music has sprung from the patient, incessant and progressive penetration into the law of resonance [44] . . . from the successive exploitation of the octave, fifth and fourth (ninth to twelfth century), the third (thirteenth to sixteenth century), the seventh (seventeenth and eighteenth century) and major ninth, the augmented fifth, and the perfect eleventh (nineteenth and twentieth century). . . . This evolution became the vertebral system of our progress, and it contributes, at the same time, the only true justification of musical art." [230], p. xxi.

The most astonishing theory of origins in the scale, with the biological analogy, is provided by Winthrop Parkhurst, in *The Anatomy of Music* (Knopf, New York, 1936). (Polyphony is the "Physiology of Music.")

"The first great step in the evolution of music was the development of a scale, or spinal column. Music did not begin to walk on its hind feet, or even to crawl about on all fours, until it had acquired the equivalent of that bony structure (p. 11) — four limbs (called voices) spring out from that scale and are joined by it. . . . These segments are unified by tonality . . . just as the spinal cord gives inner unity. . . . (p. 40). Inversions are the flesh, discords are the muscles (p. 55).

2. ORIGINS IN SYMMETRICAL PATTERNS

According to Moser [209] the Germans were the first to make music in duple measure, analogous to the heartbeat. As a matter of fact, however, this popular form of metrical symmetry became

---

and the other eighteenth-century theorists who upheld the major scale as "a direct shoot from Nature," Combarieu gives an impressive list of older compositions in minor keys which express gaiety as successfully as cheerful music in major keys; then he goes to the other extreme, and argues for the "original" nature of the minor, that it "has its origin in instinctive social life."

[44] In support of this statement, Casella cites Jean Marnold, Bulletin of the *Institut général psychologique*, Paris, 1908, No. 2.

so favored in the eighteenth century as being "natural" that it has come to be the accepted classical, normal pattern ever since. Even when triple measure is used, the musical phrase appears in two-measure or four-measure groups. There is no evidence, however, to support any claim for its origin in one particular country. (See p. 164).

This "natural" four-measure pattern has an easily discoverable origin in many folk dances of western European countries, but that does not mean that all folk dances employed this "natural" phrase. Composers of the Enlightenment favored this pattern, evidently because of its *symmetry,* a doctrine important in those days, because of the desire to revive the Greek concepts of balanced form. Classic architecture, classic poetry, and classic drama reflect this. The cast for eighteenth-century Italian opera called for three couples, no more and no less, to whom arias (in four-measure phrases) had to be assigned with the same meticulous symmetry with which the peristyle was erected backstage.

It has been suggested that early Italian opera was a synthetic compromise. The *recitative* was the concession to the desire for the revival of Greek declamation, and the orchestral accompaniment was an achievement of modern progress. But the *recitative,* adapted to the rhythms of speech, came to be eclipsed in popular favor by the *aria* with its graceful, symmetrical patterns.

The eighteenth-century quarrels over opera were, therefore, as indicated in Chapter 5, quarrels over the relative merits of musical declamation in speech rhythm and of lovely airs in symmetrical, sensuous body rhythms. The Ancients favored *recitative,* and the Moderns favored *aria* as originating in "Nature." [45]

Symmetry, then, since the eighteenth century, has been a sort of "original principle." Even the major scale, with its two identical

[45] " The servitude to music makes necessary the most ridiculous faults, where *arias* are sung while a city is sacked," says Voltaire. In his *Dissertation sur la tragédie Ancienne et Moderne,* he goes on to say: " The Italian *recitative* is precisely the *melopoeia* of the ancients . . . and the choruses in some of them . . . resemble the ancient chorus so much the more, in being set to a different kind of music from the *recitative,* as the strophe, epode, and antistrophe were sung by the Greeks quite differently from the *melopoeia* of the rest of the play." But — " what can be more absurd than to terminate every scene with one of those detached airs, which interrupt the business, and destroy the interest of the drama, in order to afford an opportunity to an effeminate throat to shine in trills and divisions, at the expense of the poetry and good sense?" For Addison's famous ridicule of Italian opera in England, see the *Spectator,* Mar. 21, 1711, in Everyman's Library, Vol. I, p. 68.

tetrachords, 1 2 34, 5 6 78, with a half step at the end of each, meets the test demanded.

3. ORIGINS IN "TONE-SPEECH"

Obviously music (*Tonkunst*) without tone is a contradiction in terms, but what is referred to here is the theory that music has its origin, in the esthetic sense, in tone for its own sake. It is a theory as old as the tales of Orpheus,[46] but in its modern form can be credited to Richard Wagner. Contrary to the usual opinion, Wagner's aims were not identical with those of Monteverde and Gluck, who wanted to reform the opera in such a way that music would enhance the meaning of the text. *Tristan* and the *Ring* cycle would consume far less time if that were the case, and excerpts therefrom would not be so effective in symphony concerts without singers. Ever since Wagner, the merits of an artist, for many, often hinge upon the question as to the ability to "produce beautiful tone." There is a tendency, also, to emphasize the love of tone for tone's sake in music education.[47]

Wagner did not put his theory as simply and bluntly as that. He chose rather to clothe his thought in the terminology of contemporary science. Wagner will be quoted again, in Chapter 11 on Evolution, but the quotations below will serve to show his theory of origins. This theory was that language began in tone, and that to have the transcendent effect desired in the art of the future, it must end there; ordinary drama, with the language of the street and the newspaper, can reach no great heights of emotion, and tone must be clothed with the consonants of speech to be more effective. Hence the rise of the biological analogy in somewhat the same manner employed by his contemporary Herbert Spencer. Spencer described in detail the alimentary and circulatory functions of the body politic, and Wagner the physiological relationship of musical tone, vowels, and consonants.

[46] See also p. 18, for a discussion of Mersenne's basic theory, that tone is the *objet matériel* of music.

[47] Wagner could not have been uninfluenced by Schopenhauer, who said, " If music is too closely fitted to the words, and tries to form itself according to externals, it is striving to speak a language which is not its own." *The World as Will and Idea*, Bk. III, 52, in *Selections from Schopenhauer*, N. Y., Scribner, 1928, p. 182.

"Tone-speech is the beginning and end of word-speech. The march of this evolution is such, however, that it is no retrogression (and not a cycle) but a progress to the winning of the highest human faculty; and it is travelled not merely by mankind in general, but substantially by every social individual. . . .

"A mode of expression similar to that still proper to the beasts was, in any case, like the first employed by man and this we can call before us at any moment — as far as its substance goes, by removing from our word-speech its dumb articulations and leaving nothing but the open sounds. In these vowels, if we think of them as stripped of their consonants . . . we shall obtain an image (a clearer view) of man's first emotional language." [61], pp. 224, 225.

"We have called the enclosing consonants the garment of the vowel, *more precisely,* its *physiogonomic exterior* . . . let us call them *still more accurately* the fleshy covering of the human body, organically ingrown with the interior; we thus shall gain a faithful image of the essence both of consonant and vowel, as well as of their organic relations to each other." [61], pp. 272, 273.

Elsewhere Wagner maintained that "tone is the heart of man; also that Beethoven's "Harmonic melody . . . divorced from speech, was capable, *though merely borne by instruments,* of limitless expression." (pp. 110, 121).

It is not surprising to find theories of music's origin in tone, *per se,* in the nineteenth century, when such great progress was made in the technical perfection of instruments. Sonorous, sustained, organlike harmonies with the sensuous vibrato of string masses were possible to a degree never known before. Richer harmonies, with the enlargement of orchestral choirs, chromatic music for keyed brass, all helped weave a spell of magic enchantment for the moderns. The ancients, such as Fétis, remained loyal to the agile, sparkling clarity of eighteenth-century music. So, as in the seventeenth century, the moderns had to develop philosophies of value to show progress. Fétis found progress "only in material elements . . . all the rest is decadence;" so Wagner had to defend his theories with a doctrine of origins for the art of the future.

Romantic mysticism replaced medieval mysticism. The churchmen had argued for the origins of music in an ineffable mystery at Creation, man's first vocal utterance. For Wagner the ineffable mystery was in Nature; the Word was no longer so important; the mysteries of the cosmos could be revealed in tone.[48]

[48] See Paul Bekker, *The Story of the Orchestra,* N. Y., Norton, 1936, especially the chapter on "The Cosmic Orchestra" of Wagner.

This all leads back to Combarieu's mystic theories of origins discussed at the beginning of this chapter. These show how powerful German metaphysics was on French thought at the beginning of this century. Schelling, Schopenhauer, and others had established the German position that music written to words is " a low and commonplace task." Combarieu, under this influence, was led to define music as " thinking in sounds," even as " thinking without concepts. . . . Real music is the symphony."[49] [158], pp. 9, 10, 93, 94.

But this is all contrary to French and Italian tradition. Combarieu was heir to centuries of interest in language and literature, poetry and drama, and belief that the language itself was musical. So when Combarieu came to write his history, his interest in tonal " magic " dwindled after the first few pages. He wrote his splendid chapters on the Latin achievements in plainsong, polyphony, opera, and lyric tragedy without any reference whatever to tonal " magic."

The Germans, however, had only succeeded in getting their language into serious opera at the close of the eighteenth century. Wagner was therefore, in still another sense, a modern on the defensive, so he was obliged to elaborate another theory for his art of the future, a theory of primal origins in language as well as in tone. He therefore found virtue in the qualities of the language that had made it despised by Frederick the Great and other influential persons a century earlier. Its frank, open vowels and forceful consonants make it an ideal language, the only " primal " language that can have a fruitful union with tone, in Wagner's opinion.

Wagner admits that the Italians and French did as well as could be expected, in evolving a successful alliance with music and poetry. But he does not point out, as Paul Bekker has recently, in *The Changing Opera,* that each composer must find the creative possibilities for dramatic music in his own language. Instead, the bio-

[49] In this connection it is interesting to note that even when origins are found in rhythm, the writer may mean *tone*. Thus Combarieu is supported by Willy Pastor, who has been quoted as arguing for the priority of rhythm. But Pastor makes two classifications of rhythm, " The stimulating rhythm . . . also a soporific one." The former " may be derived from any regular sound," or " meaningless noises . . . an art of tones. . . . For the hypnotic rhythm, on the contrary, the quality of the tone and its mode of expression are of the utmost importance . . . an art of *tone*." Convinced that these two kinds of rhythm represent entirely different stages of development, Pastor decides that the hypnotic rhythm is the older and links it up with magic and witchcraft, " the oldest known philosophy of the world." [180], pp. 682, 683.

logical analogy above becomes the basis for his chauvinistic theory of musical " growth." So in the spirit with which Fichte addressed the German nation [50] less than fifty years earlier, Wagner says:

" The German alone possesses a language whose early usage still hangs directly and conspicuously together with its roots; Italians and Frenchmen speak a tongue whose radical meaning can only be brought home to them by a study of older, so-called dead language."

From the above, and from a study of Wagner's scores, it is evident that Wagner was not interested in rhythm *per se*. In this respect his theory differs from that of his contemporary Rowbotham. The latter gave primacy to the drum by maintaining that percussion is the primeval sound in Nature. Rowbotham admits that " the origin of vocal music must be sought in impassioned speech," [113, one-vol. ed., p. 32] but — and here is where Wagner and Rowbotham agree —

" the savage who for the first time knocked two pieces of wood together . . . was patiently examining a mighty mystery; he was peering with his simple eyes into one of Nature's greatest secrets. The something he was examining was rhythmic sound, on which roots the whole art of music.

" Now what is this mysterious differentia of *rhythmic sound,* as we find it in nature, which separates it so widely from non-rhythmic sound of every description? In one word the *innuendo of design.*" [113], one-vol. ed., pp. 7, 8.

Theories that regard *instrumental tone, per se,* as an original source of musical structure or musical pleasure are apt to employ similar assumptions; the elements of musical structure are inherent in sustained *tone,* or in *rhythmic sound.* The origin theories swing full circle, to find instruments prior to speech and song. The voice itself comes to be regarded as an instrument which was perfected only after " external " instruments were first used. But yet

" The oldest, truest, most beautiful organ of music the origin to which alone our music owes its being, is the *human voice.*

" The musical instrument is an echo of the human voice, so constituted that we can only detect in it the vowel resolved into the musical

[50] " Only a ' primitive ' folk who have kept their native independence, resisted conquest, and defied absorption, can call themselves a nation. Only the Germans are such a primal people."— *Addresses to the German Nation,* 1807–1808.

tone — but the instruments themselves have a *consonant-like* character."
[61], p. 307.

These structural theories, therefore, like the physical and psychological theories described above, have been presented in terms of laws of Nature. They themselves are concerned with both physical and psychological elements. All have been propounded by men seeking, not to improve the art of music and ways of teaching, but to prove a theory for its own sake. All have elements of plausibility and truth, but no one theory can be accepted as a point of departure for the history of all kinds of music among all men.

The two chapters which follow attempt to show how the writing of music history got from origins to modern times, and vice versa. With a theory of origins to begin with, other theories, borrowed from methods used in the social studies, enabled historians to show " development " of the art from its earliest or lowest stage (1) through a genealogical chain of gifted men (2) in a line of continuous " progress " (3) by means of an " evolutionary " process common to all organic life.

CHAPTER 10

THE "DEVELOPMENT" AND "PROGRESS" OF MUSIC

REFERENCE has already been made to the tendency, since the eighteenth century, to deal not with the history of musical arts, but of *The Art of Music* as some one thing or entity which has gradually developed its potentialities, thanks to the progress of knowledge.

Turning again to Parry's very influential *Evolution of the Art of Music*, the quotations cited in Chapter 7 show his interest in the "unconscious and spontaneous," though embryonic music of "the primitive savage." Throughout this work constant reference is made to the "stages of development" through which the art has passed.

"At the very bottom of the process of development are those savage howls which have hardly any distinct notes in them at all. . . ." [126], 1st ed., p. 53.

Folk music represents a higher stage:

"The savage stage indicates a taste for design, but an incapacity for making the designs consistent and logical; in the lowest intelligent stage the capacity for disposing short contrasting figures in an orderly way is shown; in the highest phase of the pattern-type of folk-tune the instinct for knitting things closely together is shown to be very remarkable. . . . A higher phase still is that in which the skill in distributing the figures in symmetrical patterns is applied to the ends of emotional expression." [126], p. 82.

Medieval music was also very "primitive":

"In the early middle ages . . . all the music employed was vocal or choral, and almost totally devoid of any rhythmic quality [1] or anything

---

[1] The confusion here is due to Parry's failure (a) to distinguish between rhythm and measure; (b) to recognize that vocal music can be adapted to the speech rhythms of prose (as in plainsong and *recitative*) or to the measured rhythms of

which represented gesticulatory expression. . . . Dance music demands very little in the way of harmony. . . . But vague melodic music, and vocal music which is sung by voices of different pitch, seem to call imperatively for the help of harmony; [2] and unless the instinctive craving for choral harmony had led men to overcome its initial difficulties, the art could never have developed that particular kind of regularity in time which is independent of dance rhythm." (p. 89).

All through the Middle Ages and early Renaissance,

" human creatures had to go through a long probationary period, and to get accustomed to the sounds of chords in themselves, before they could begin instinctively to classify them in the manner in which they ultimately came to serve as the basis of modern harmonic art." (p. 95).

Parry shows condescension toward " the primitive melodic music of the church," when " there were no bars," and when singers " did things very much by ear." (p. 98).[3]

" Almost every rule of art which a modern musician holds inviolable is broken incessantly, and there are hardly any pieces of music, by the most learned or the most intelligent musicians up to the fourteenth century, which are not too rough or uncouth to be listened to by even the most liberal-minded and intelligent musician without such bewilderment as often ends in irrepressible laughter." (p. 103).

Thus we find Parry echoing the sentiments of his compatriot Burney, who, a century earlier, had censured Monteverde for breaking the " inviolable rules " laid down by eighteenth-century theory. Both Burney and Parry regard the standards of their own day as infallible criteria. " The art of music " for them was something that had developed its potentialities through " stages," each of which was " superior " in some way to the stage previous. With the aid of nineteenth-century scientific doctrines, however, Parry was able to state his belief in terms of " natural law."

The development of musical art was, for Parry, akin to the development of man himself; his reference to the seventeenth cen-

---

dance music (body rhythms). This is one of the fundamental difficulties in the teaching of rhythm in our schools today.

[2] An assumption that would be denied by Orientalists and modern students of plainsong.

[3] In 1893, musical students who played " by ear " were discouraged by most teachers. There probably has never been a time in the history of music, before or since, when so much dependence has been placed on the printed page in music education. Even in recent years, the writer has been criticized by a conservative colleague for teaching Ear Training in a Harmony class!

tury as an "immature period" has already been cited, and similar statements are to be found throughout. Music was only "spontaneous" with primitive savages in their "unconscious" expressions, and at the modern stage of perfection when spontaneity had been "recovered." Between primitive and modern times there were stages of slow progress, during which men did not make music spontaneously(!); their efforts were directed toward the great difficulties that had to be surmounted before the full potentialities of the art could be developed:

"The excessive difficulty which such things (the problems of counterpoint) presented to them is sufficiently indicated by the productions of the most celebrated composers, which present the same sort of aspect to a mind capable of unravelling them, that the artistic efforts of a baby just out of its cradle do, when it tries to represent mankind or its favorite animals." [126], p. 99.

This makes interesting reading only one generation later, now that modern musicologists, "with minds capable of unravelling" the secrets of medieval notation, have revealed the riches of Gothic music,[4] and the beauties of the *ars nova* (14th c.)

In short, the doctrine of development found favor with scholars who believed that nineteenth-century European culture represented the highest stage of development in time and space.

Historically, modern music, for Parry, was the highest development of art through the ages, and all other periods were stages of struggle, unfolding, and preparation. He believed that culturally European music was the apex of historical development. All extra-European music was representative of an earlier, immature stage through which our ancestors had to pass in previous centuries. Parry showed just as little knowledge of and respect for other music systems as for early stages of Western music. Resorting to prediction on the basis of current "laws" of cultural development, he asserted that Japanese music

"will probably go through the same phases as early medieval music, and the Japanese sense of harmony will develop in the same manner as that of Europeans did long ago." [5] [126], p. 95.

[4] Long before Parry's death in 1918, Friedrich Ludwig had begun (1902) to publish his researches on medieval polyphony. For a summary of this research, see Adler's *Handbuch* [224], Vol. I, pp. 159–295.

[5] For further discussion of this statement, see the references to the actual processes of music history now observable in modern Japan, in Chapter 13.

The falsity of this prediction will be discussed later, but the assumptions involved in this use of the comparative method come up for analysis in the next section. Parry was merely adopting the generally accepted premises of evolutionary anthropology. The chief spokesman for this branch of scientific inquiry in England, throughout the Victorian era, stated the case thus:

" The Educated World of Europe and America practically settles a standard by simply placing its own nations at one end of the social series and savage tribes at the other. . . . The principal criteria are the absence or presence, high or low development, of the industrial arts . . . the extent of scientific knowledge, the definiteness of moral principles, the condition of religious belief and ceremony, the degree of social and political organization, and so forth. Thus on the definite basis of compared facts, ethnologists are able to set up at least a rough scale of civilization. Few would dispute that the following races are arranged rightly in order of culture: — Australian-Tahitian-Aztec-Chinese-Italian." [6]

I. THE COMPARATIVE METHOD

" To impress men's minds with a doctrine of development will lead them . . . to continue the progressive work of past ages, to continue it the more vigorously because *light has increased* in the world, and where *barbaric hordes groped blindly, cultured men can move forward with clearer view.*"

The chapter previous began with Aristotle's prescription for " the clearest view," the quest for origins. Again, another path toward " the clearer view " is offered in the quotation above, from the last page of Edward Burnett Tylor's *Primitive Culture* (1871). This calls for a doctrine of development in order that " the progressive work of past ages " may be continued.

At the beginning of this pioneer treatise in modern anthropology, Tylor explains his doctrine of development thus, and links it up to the quest for origins:

" As experience shows us that arts of civilized life are developed through successive stages of improvement, *we may assume* that the early development of even savage arts came to pass in a similar way, and thus, finding various stages of an art among the lower races, we may arrange these stages in a series *probably* representing their actual sequence in history. If any art can be traced back among savage tribes

[6] Edward Burnett Tylor, *Primitive Culture*, London, 1871, Vol. I, Ch. 2, p. 27.

to a rudimentary state in which its invention does not seem beyond their intellectual condition, and especially if it may be produced by imitating nature or following nature's direct suggestions, *there is fair reason to suppose* the very origin of the art to have been reached." [7]

The last quotation seems to indicate a sort of circular type of research, namely, that the origins of an art had to be located in order to prove the doctrine of development which was employed to locate them. But this was also the method used by Combarieu, whose origin theories, discussed in Chapter 8, were further elaborated in *La musique et la magie* [175]. In Chapter IV, "Method and Sources," a diagram shows how history affords knowledge of pre-history:

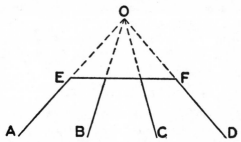

"The method is that habitually followed in archaeology. The phenomena A, B, C, D are clearly observable, but only to a certain limit, EF; from there, a thick mist hides them from view, so that we cannot follow them to the source. I know, however, that these series come from a point higher than EF; does not my knowledge of them authorize me to prolong them in thought, and to say that they have in O their common departure? The region above EF (dotted) is pre-history; the region below is history accessible to direct analysis. O is the principle from which *everything* has set out. If I admit that there is continuity in the development of things, I am obliged to place magic incantation at O. Here the series A B C D represent all categories of proof which are at our disposal: documents . . . texts . . . monuments, traditions . . . to which we add the information gathered among the savages and semi-civilized peoples which are still static in the practice of very old usages.

"It is a matter of mounting as high (far) as possible into the past, and, having arrived at a limit, to get an idea of what is beyond according to the agreement and convergence of all that is on this side.

"One of the simplest means of practicing this method . . . is to analyze the meaning of certain words which we still use today. . . .

[7] Tylor, *Primitive Culture*, Vol. I, pp. 63, 64.

"The philological historian finds weakened, but certain evidence of old superstitions. . . . The faith has disappeared; the word, witness to it, has *survived*, but the word helps us to trace the faith." (Words such as enchant, charm, ode are analyzed.)

In short, "the doctrine of development" urged by Tylor presupposes (a) that the lowest, "original" stage of development can be found somewhere on the planet, among a static group, (b) that other more advanced groups are in varying, but higher stages of development, (c) that the highest stage of development is to be found in the European arts of the present, but that the only evidence for these beliefs is "weakened" evidence, namely "survivals"[8] of old practices from an earlier stage.

It has already been pointed out, in Chapter 7, that the belief in Western civilization as the highest stage in a line of cultural development was basic in late nineteenth-century music histories. Tylor's statement concerning the sequential order of certain cultures was quoted in connection with the theories of development in Parry's *Art of Music*. It has also been pointed out that nineteenth-century social theory completely reversed the eighteenth-century concept of the noble savage, to place him at the lowest stage of the developmental series.[9]

The doctrine of development assumed, furthermore, that culture always evolved uniformly, that the stages of development were always in the same order. Thus it was believed, with Comte, that "the different stages of evolution may all be observed at once."[10]

The belief was accepted, therefore, that cultural change in historical time could be mapped chronologically, by comparing backward people with groups that had progressed. This method, a logical instrument for deducing a chronology, was called the Comparative Method and hailed by many as "the historical method."

[8] See Margaret Hodgen, *The Doctrine of Survivals*, London, 1936.

[9] Of course, this was done before the nineteenth century; John Brown, in 1763, remarked that "By examining savage life where untaught Nature rules, we find that the agreeable Passions . . . no less than their Contraries, . . . are thrown out by the three Powers of *Action, Voice,* and the *articulate Sounds*. . . .

"Among the Savages in the lowest scale . . . their Gestures are horrid and uncouth: their *Voice* is . . . *howls* and *roarings:* their Language is like the Gabbling of Sheep. . . .

"But a step or two higher, we shall find this Chaos . . . rising into an agreeable Order and Proportion." [20], p. 27.

[10] *The Positive Philosophy of Auguste Comte,* tr. by Harriet Martineau, London, 1856, Book VI, Ch. III, on "Comparison of Co-Existing States of Society."

Edward A. Freeman, for example, began his work on *Comparative Politics* as follows, in 1873:

"The establishment of the Comparative Method of Study has been the greatest intellectual achievement of our time. It has carried light and order into whole branches of human knowledge which before were shrouded in darkness and confusion. . . . Into matters which are for the most part incapable of strictly external proof it has brought a form of strictly internal proof which is more convincing, more unerring."[11]

Perhaps the most thoroughgoing exponent of the Comparative Method in the history of music histories is the Rev. Rowbotham, whose *History of Music to the Time of the Troubadours* is cited in Chapter 7. Much of the author's evidence concerning "ancient" music is derived from observation of or information about "primitive" music being made in the present. The assumption is, furthermore, that this music of present-day savages is exactly the same sort of music that every culture makes, at a correspondingly low stage of development.

Rowbotham also tried to compare his stages of One-, Two-, and Three-Note Scales with William D. Whitney's classification of language stages:

1. The Monosyllabic Stage is equivalent to the pentatonic scale, with the "great" scale (G A B) "isolated" from the "little" scale (D E).

---

[11] As there is great difference between the Comparative Method and simple "methods of comparison," great care must be taken in using this term. As Oliver Strunk points out (in "Sources and Problems for Graduate Study in Musicology" in M.T.N.A. *Proceedings*, 1933, pp. 105–116), "the ideal material for comparative study is obviously that in which the influence of the extraneous factors remains constant . . . in accordance with this general principle we compare similar, analogous, commensurable works." Strunk was making reference to *technical comparisons of musical styles*. Ernest Newman also applies the term Comparative Method to his plea for comparisons of music with other arts in historical studies. (See *Gluck and the Opera*, London, 1895, Introduction.) Newman goes on to condemn the "metaphysical . . . Hegelian method that Wagner and his disciples have followed." The difficulty lies in the fact that this "Hegelian metaphysical method" is identical with the Comparative Method (so named by Comte). It was an unfortunate name, but the name has stuck, and still refers, in sociology and anthropology, to a logical, not an inductive, method, "by which the different stages of Evolution may all be observed at once." Such a method is one of analogy; *the Comparative Method and simple comparisons are two different things*.

For a graphic illustration of the Comparative Method, and the way in which it works, see Alexander Goldenweiser, *Early Civilization*, N. Y., Knopf, 1926, p. 22. On that same page, Goldenweiser gives the verdict of the modern anthropologist: "this method, if used uncritically, could be used to yield proof of any theory of social development whatsoever."

2. The Agglutinative Stage: the two scales agglutinated by means of the "insertion" of the fourth (C).

3. The Inflectional Stage: "When, by the *insertion* of the seventh, the scale is enabled to pass *naturally* to the octave, and to modulate to a new scale on the keynote of its fifth." [113], 2nd ed., p. 45.

But Whitney used these terms with no such reference to ideal "stages of development." They are classificatory in terms of structure, but the conclusions reached concerning "stages" in language development are always with reference to the evidences furnished by specific languages and social groups, with cognizance of actual historical changes that are known to have occurred within these groups. No broad generalizations are laid down to be proved, into which facts are fitted by way of argument. Whitney says, for instance:

"The Chinese language is, in one most important and fundamental respect, of the very lowest grade of structure and poverty of resource. *But it is also the most remarkable example in the world of a weak instrumentality which is made the means of accomplishing great things;* it illustrates, in a manner which the student of language cannot too carefully heed, the truth that language is only an instrumentality, and the mind the force that uses it; that the mind, which in all its employment of speech implies a great deal more than it expresses, is able to do a high quality of work with only the scantiest hints of expression, catching from the connection and from position the shades of meaning and the modes of relation which it needs. It is but a difference of degree between Chinese inexpressiveness and the frequent overloading of distinctions which in our view characterizes some of the agglutinative idioms: for example, the American Indian; and, with a right view of language, one is as explainable as the other. A few scratches on a board with a bit of charcoal by a skilled artist may be more full of meaning, may speak more strongly to the imagination and feeling, than a picture elaborated by an inferior hand with all the resources of a modern art-school." [12]

But of course Rowbotham's principal scheme is bound up with

"the order of the three stages in the development of pre-historic music, the drum stage, the pipe stage, and the lyre stage, which, it seems to me, are to the musician what the theological, metaphysical, and positive

[12] William D. Whitney, *Life and Growth of Language* (1875), p. 238. See also Lin Yutang, *My Country and My People*, N. Y., 1935, pp. 290–297.

stages are to the Comtist, or the Stone, Bronze, and Iron Ages to the archaeologist." [113], 2nd ed., p. 6.

Today the questions of origins and development are still bothering some comparative musicologists who have not yet abandoned the Comparative Method. Lach, for instance, in the passage cited from Adler's *Handbuch,* goes on to remark that Rowbotham had a rational scheme of historical development, namely, that epochs of music history showed development from a one-tone stage to stages in which two, three, then five tones were used. But, as Lach admits,

"even though this difference, by and large, obtains in a formal sense . . . we must, on the other hand, not overlook the fact that in numerous chants of primitive peoples, often a series of quite widely separated tonal steps are used, which cannot be adapted to the scheme just mentioned." [224], I, p. 5.

Curt Sachs encounters this same difficulty, and remarks with regret, *Die Brücken zwischen beiden Stilarten sehen wir noch nicht* [266], p. 13. That shows faith in an old belief, but it is very doubtful whether the "bridges" will ever be seen. Tylor's prescription for a "clearer view" does not work.

Lach is also concerned over another problem that is "not yet solved." Just as the bridges between Rowbotham's early stages and the complicated music sung by primitive peoples in actual reality have not yet been found, so it is also with

"the question of the historical priority of vocal or instrumental music. The example of the North-American Indians seems to argue in favor of a purely vocal development up to a certain point, also the fact that the development of European art music went on for a millennium and a half (into the fifteenth century) in a purely vocal field. . . .[18] In answering one (other) question which stands at the beginning of all music history, instrumental music seems to have a big say. That is the question of the origin of the scale, that is, of the tonal system in general. . . . How does a scale originate? How did the human mind suc-

---

[18] This is part assumption and part inaccuracy. Instruments *were* used in the thirteenth-century Parisian school, and the Florentine *ars nova* (fourteenth century). Some even maintain that *a cappella* music did not appear until the sixteenth century. As a matter of fact, Edward J. Dent even says that "Those who perform sixteenth-century music nowadays are apt to imagine that all sixteenth-century music was sung without instruments; but the Sistine Chapel was possibly the only place where vocal music was sung unaccompanied." "Music of the Renaissance in Italy," reprinted from the *Proceedings of the British Academy,* London, 1933, Vol. XIX.

ceed in building up its musical forms in different lands, at different times, among different peoples and races . . . ? The solution of this most complicated problem, perhaps the *main and fundamental problem of comparative musical science,* is all the more complicated and difficult, inasmuch as it is as much of a problem for psychology, ethnology, and sociology as it is of musical science." [224], I, pp. 10, 11.

This appeal finds no aid coming from these three sciences, because they too have been seeking in vain for answers to the same problem of origins in their own fields, and the dim, gray "dawn of history" yields nothing but arguments — a new argument for every archaeological discovery. These sciences got comparative musicology tangled up in the question of origins from the start.[14] Now that the benefits of the study are being apparent in music of the present, why not give up this quest for a series that can never be historically dependable?

The histories of these extra-European systems are as different from our Western histories of music as their languages and music systems are different from ours. *Comparisons of histories* are and will continue to be fruitful fields of investigation; but all attempts to make different histories fall into one linear scheme of development involve great, if not insuperable, difficulties, the same that are faced when all origins are sought in one explanation. It is time, therefore, to examine these notions of development and progress.

II. THE ANALOGY OF DEVELOPMENT

I. MUSIC AS AN ORGANISM

When Calvisius, our first historian, used the term *progress,* he evidently used it with somewhat the same meaning that has been given the word throughout the history of the church, to mean *development* of inborn, inherent potentialities. This latter fact has been pointed out by Robert Flint,[15] who quotes Vincent of Lerins as follows:

[14] Stumpf says in his *Anfänge der Musik* that "Virchow, in 1886, complained to the Berlin Anthropological Society of their lack of interest in the primitive history of music, as the only gap in their researches to date. This indifference was due to the scarcity of reliable materials. But Waldeyer, in 1903, before the same group, was able, with the aid of the phonograph and the mensuration of old instruments, to show that the findings made possible were of the greatest extent and significance." [182], p. 7.

[15] *History of the Philosophy of History,* N. Y., 1894, p. 100.

"The entire Church and each believer, arise, grow, and develop, as the human body does. But progress (*profectus*) is not change of nature (*permutatio*); development is not compatible with loss of identity. Man only reaches the perfection and maturity of his being by the growth of powers which were all contained in germ in the child. Wheat should not produce tares, the rose-tree of the Church should not bear thistles." From the *Commonitorum adversus profanas omnium novitates hereticorum.*

Calvisius was a Lutheran heretic, but heir, nevertheless, to centuries of thought that could look upon music as an entity that had started, under divine auspices, with certain potentialities. A long line of devoted artists had succeeded in developing these God-given, germinal possibilities. Vincent of Lerins had even said, "To deny or oppose progress would show malevolence towards men and impiety towards God." Calvisius, as already shown in Chapter 1, was willing to imply such a charge against Pope John XXII, who had opposed the progress or development of polyphonic music in the fourteenth century.

There was nothing incongruous in the belief that music was somehow an organism, capable of development. Medieval thought "proceeded from the idea of a single Whole " . . .

"An organic construction of Human Society was as familiar to it as a mechanical and atomistic construction was originally alien. . . . Mankind constituted a Mystical Body, whereof the head was Christ . . . the one and only Head, for were the Emperor an additional Head, we should have before us a two-headed monster." [16]

Music, then, for early historians, was an organism, the "handmaid of religion." Devout musicians and writers on the subject believed, therefore, not only in the divine origins of music, but also in churchly control. "The rose-tree of the Church should not bear thistles." Consequently, the divine art of music should bear worthy fruit. The church and State were to complete each other, so also sacred music and secular music were to do the same. But devotion to the church came first; in the eighteenth century, J. S. Bach would write *Soli Deo Gloria* above the keyboard music written for his children, and in the twentieth century one of England's foremost secular composers knelt in prayer, so it is said, before con-

[16] Otto Gierke, *Political Theories of the Middle Ages,* tr. by F. W. Maitland, Cambridge, 1900, p. 23.

ducting an orchestra concert. Until the days of Schubert, at least, the education of composers began, usually, in a church choir school.

2. "STAGES OF DEVELOPMENT"

The other phase of the development analogy is the nature of the process. Flint, in his paragraphs on the history of the Idea of Progress, quotes Tertullian:

"In the works of grace, as in the works of nature, which proceed from the same Creator, everything unfolds itself by certain successive steps. From the seed-corn sprouts first the shoot, which by-and-by grows into the tree; this then puts forth the blossom, to be followed in its turn by the fruit, which itself arrives at maturity only by degrees." From *De Virginibus Velandis*, Ch. I.

The development of the church is then sketched through childhood and manhood to maturity. Similarly the Roman historian Florus had envisaged childhood (origin), youth (early action), manhood (conquest), and old age (inactivity) in the successive life stages of the Roman people as a whole.

The frequent use of this analogy has been noted, especially in Chapter 6, where the periodization according to the three or four ages of man was so frequently found in Romantic histories of music. The implication, in these cases, is usually, however, that development had risen to perfection or near-perfection. The old tie-up with the organic theories of the church no longer exists, however; the biological analogy stands on its own. Sometimes music is likened to botanical organisms:

"In the countless centuries before Palestrina music grew slowly and uniformly, like a plant; in the short three hundred years between Palestrina's and Beethoven's death it had its inconceivably rich and various blossoming." [17]

That calls to mind the Pascal analogy already quoted in these pages.[18] But Pascal added important reservations which should be kept in mind:

"We see that geometry, arithmetic, music, natural philosophy, medicine, architecture, and all sciences which are amenable to experiment

[17] D. G. Mason, "The Periods of Music-History." [286], p. 28.
[18] See p. 91.

and reasoning *must be developed* if they are to reach perfection. The ancients found them barely outlined by those who had preceded them; and we shall leave them to those who come after us in a more finished state than we received them. . . . Their *perfection is dependent on time and labor."*

3. DEVELOPMENT IN A GENEALOGICAL CHAIN

Pascal recognized, therefore, that the picturesque biological analogy was not an explanation; such a figure of speech could not explain history. When he wrote that passage, Father Kircher, as shown in Chapter 1, was collecting his musical miscellany, Mersenne and Praetorius were assembling their data and discussing theory, the Venetians were developing their new styles of music drama, and experiments were being conducted in instrumental music, with chamber concerts of all sorts. There had to be some orderly presentation of all this data, so when eighteenth-century historiography began in the field of music, the old genealogical frame of historical writing was the natural basis for the orderly narration of biographies. During the Middle Ages the musician, like the artist, had worked in devoted, unselfish anonymity " for the glory of God." The individualism of the Renaissance stopped all this, and one of the two searchlights of historical investigation ever since has been focussed upon the composer. Biographies are one *sine qua non* of music history; musical documents are the other. The only trouble with these materials of history is that they are too scanty, but research is bringing more and more to light. Gratitude is due for the materials available and to the scholars who have unearthed them. The point to be noted here is that the genealogical chain of biographies not only makes readable narratives but also allows the retention of the development analogy.

The aim has always been to present these biographies in a chronological series, a genealogical chain, to show how the work of one generation was transmitted to the next. If a composer dies without leaving any " school," as did Henry Purcell in 1695, the historical lament is as great as when the king dies without issue. The only recourse left is to skip to another country and start another genealogy, usually without reference to the different conditions, or the entirely different place that music occupied in another society. It is still something of a new departure to compare contemporaneous music in various countries. For example, Mussorgsky is seldom mentioned except in chapters on Russian music, very rarely as a mid-century contemporary of Liszt and Wagner. To do the latter would upset the genealogical scheme of development.

As pointed out in Chapter 6, the great-man theory received authoritative sanction during the Romantic period, but later in the nineteenth century there arose widespread dissatisfaction with the purely biographical method. In 1784, Kant in his *Idea of a Universal History* had said that "each individual man would necessarily have to live an enormous length of time in order to learn by himself how to make a complete use of all his natural endowments." There must be, it was felt, some focal point of investigation which would enable history to envisage the development of music beyond the life-span of individuals. The current concepts of progress and evolution and the biological analogy gave the cue, and music history, like the histories of other arts, began the study of the "evolution of form." The biographical *method,* however, was not abandoned: long-lived forms, rather than mortal men, became the objects of investigation. "Sound, rhythm, and timbre are the principal characters in this history, in the form of melody, harmony, measure, and instrumentation," as already quoted, from Lavoix, who adds, "This is a history of music, not of musicians." This method is justified by the obvious truth that music is, in one of its phases, an art of design, and that musical understanding may be developed by learning to recognize the forms and styles of musical composition. Music is not only an art of design, but has its own literature. In this literature we can and do seek for the origins of various forms, and that is and should be the legitimate task of the research student. Such a quest for actual, historical, original documents has nothing to do with the speculative "quest for origins" that was discussed in Chapter 9. There can be no possible quarrel with the searchers for the origins of the sonata, the symphonic poem, the sonnet, the ode, the Doric column, the nave, or the use of the clarinet in symphonic structure. The "evolution" of these forms, however, was treated as if they were organisms that had a life history.

4. THE HIERARCHICAL CONCEPT

It is hardly possible to organize the genealogical chain of developers without being influenced by the old notion of hierarchical order. Value judgments creep in, in order to show that a "culmination " is reached after a " transition period " during which time a few minor links in the chain, known as " forerunners," pave the way for somebody else. The need of a series and the old dependence upon the genealogical method are felt in the following passage from Burney:

" *In order to preserve a kind of historical chain, and to connect distant times together,* it is as necessary to give a chapter to Roman music, as, in visiting distant regions, it is, sometimes, to pass through large tracts of desert country, in order to arrive at places better worth examining." [26], I, 473.

Some histories still treat the middle of the eighteenth century as Burney treated Roman music history. The Mannheim School is a sort of No-Great-Man's-Land lying between the fertile areas of Bach and Handel on one hand, and of Haydn and Mozart on the other.

But the hierarchical concept of " higher " and " lower " are not only found in the genealogical chain of composers. The Aristotelian concepts of classical values are even yet apparent in music histories. As a matter of fact, the whole concept of development itself goes back to Aristotle. As he said in the *Physics:*

" *Those things are natural which,* by a continuous movement originated by an internal principle, *arrive at some completion."*

As for the development of the highest form of drama, as explained in the *Poetics:*

" It was in fact only after a long series of changes that *the movement of Tragedy stopped on its attaining to its natural form."*

These statements are the basis in Aristotle for the conservative, classical view of development, the view that for centuries kept tragedy in leading-strings; the view that gave comedy a lower place in the hierarchy than that accorded to tragedy; the view that tragedy must never include any of the lower orders of society, except by way of comic relief, and the view that comedy must never show the noble-born in anything but a favorable light (until the revolutionary activities of Beaumarchais and Mozart).[19]

---

[19] This aristocratic attitude still survives among opera-goers. The pompous splendor of *grand* opera, and its character as tragedy, commend it to some as a " higher " form than light opera, even higher than such polished works of art as Mozart's *Marriage of Figaro,* or Rossini's *Barber of Seville.*

According to Aristotle,

" Poetry soon broke up into two kinds according to the differences in character in the individual poets; for the graver among them would represent noble actions, and those of noble personages; and the meaner sort the actions of the ignoble — Tragedy originating with the authors of the Dithyramb, the other with those phallic songs which still survive as institutions in many of our cities.— Advance after that was little by little, through their improving on whatever they had before them at each stage."

The last sentence shows how careful one should be in saying that " the Greeks had no notion of progress." Three fundamentals of the modern notion of progress to be discussed below are found in the quotations just cited, those of continuous, gradual, and necessary advancement. But progress could never go beyond the final end predicated in the beginning.

Belief that the history of tragedy has traversed gradual stages of development up to the completion of its end is essentially the same concept that is employed by Tylor, the anthropologist, in tracing the history of culture. For developmentalism these stages were more or less fixed in character, and " the sequence is invariable, if there is no impediment." (Physics, 199b).

For a modern combination of several of these developmental concepts, one can turn to the Preface of Vincent d'Indy's Cours de composition musicale. The analogy is reversed, in order to show the possibility for the student to develop, just as the art, as an entity, has developed through the ages:

" L'homme est un microcosme.
La vie humaine, en ses états successifs, peut représenter chacune des grands périodes de l'humanité. . . .
Le but du présent ouvrage est de faciliter à l'élève . . . la connaissance logique de son art, au moyen de l'étude théorique des formes musicales, et de l'application de cette théorie aux principales œuvres des maîtres musiciens, examinés dans leur ordre chronologique. . . .
. . . La base naturelle (du Cours) est la division de l'histoire de musique en trois grandes époques:
1. Epoque rhythmo-monodique (3me au 13me siècle)
2. Epoque polyphonique (13me au 17me siècle)
3. Epoque métrique (17me siècle)." [20]

[20] Vincent d'Indy, Cours de composition musicale, Paris, Durand, 1907, Preface.

Furthermore, when the student is asked, at an early stage in his development, to write *monodies* in medieval plainsong style, it is explained that this is necessary because the plainsong melodies of the church were *génératrices* of all our modern music, with the possible exception of the fugue, which developed from early polyphony.

This belief, then, that the development of the student should parallel the development of music rests, in turn, upon an analogy elaborated in medieval thought. The *Schola Cantorum,* of which d'Indy was the director, was primarily founded, as the name implies, for the preservation of the highest ideals in church music. These ideals also govern, to a large degree, the secular music written by students in this conservative institution. There is, in this case, a possible *raison d'être* for this type of educational theory, for the support of an old and highly esteemed tradition. It is difficult to see, however, how the medieval analogy of development of a hypothetical organism known as music can be of value to secular educational theory. The latter is no longer under ecclesiastical dictation; we study church music as an important and vital means of human communication, but we are just as much interested in other phases and arts of music.

The term development is found in encyclopedias and dictionaries as a technical term with definite meaning in photography, biology, and in mathematics; it is not to be found, however, in the *Encyclopedia of Social Sciences.* Modern anthropologists no longer accept the beliefs of Tylor; there is no reason why musicologists and music educators should not abandon them also. In the first place, acceptance of the theory of development is bound to continue the old, smug theory that because of our material progress, our civilization is the highest stage of perfection. For example, even the latest edition of Pratt's thoroughly objective *History of Music* has a chapter including Oriental music, entitled " Semi-Civilized Music."

In short, some of the facts not yet fully recognized may be summarized as follows:

1. " Primitive " music from many of the cultures very low in Tylor's scale of development is apt to be too subtle and complex even for the Western musician with conventional training, to say nothing of the uncultivated layman.
2. It is impossible to find any agreement as to historical sequence

in any musical system without dated materials, and even with an accurate chronology, no uniform scheme of "development" can be found.

3. The notion, previously challenged, that art music grew out of folk music has entailed a kindred fallacy, namely that art (classical) music is a higher, because a more complex, development than popular music. The reverse may sometimes be the case, if such classifications are to be permitted at all.

4. Great misunderstanding exists with reference to the history of American music. The history of our musical life has yet to be written. When it does appear, it will expose errors in pronunciamenti about "the slow development of American music." New England had a tradition that was stamped out by "Progress" and the importation of foreign musicians who came as missionaries to the heathen. Early American church music had a real folk-vitality, now being preserved and revived in certain leisurely regions of our southern states, but forgotten in our proudest edifices.

From the foregoing it is evident that our notions of development involve the modern Idea of Progress. The next section studies the use of the word *progress* in histories of music, with its analogies of motion upward in the scale of development, or forward in time.

III. THE IDEA OF PROGRESS

I. THE IMPROVEMENT OF MUSICAL ARTS

"We have even some new varieties (of dramatic art), such as the tales, the courtly epistles, the *operas,* each of which has given us an excellent author, to whom antiquity has no one to oppose, and whom posterity will probably never surpass. Were there only the *songs,* a type which may possibly perish, and to which no great attention is paid, we have a prodigious quantity of them, all full of fire and spirit; and I maintain that if Anacreon had been acquainted with them, he would have ranked them high above most of his own."

The lines above are from a *Digression sur les Anciens et les Modernes,* in 1688, three years after the birth of Bach and Handel, by Fontenelle, one of the first writers in the history of social theory to use the word *progress* in the modern sense. When the average person says " we have made progress," a value-judgment is involved, meaning that some particular achievement is a better solution of a problem, a better satisfaction of a need. He also means, probably, that still better solutions and satisfactions will be found in the future. The word *progress* today expresses confidence and optimism, belief in human intelligence, and in the possibility of its continual improvement. But this meaning did not dawn upon human minds until the seventeenth century, during the Baroque era with which this history of music histories began.

The initial chapters sought to show the importance of the Quarrel of the Ancients and Moderns in early music historiography. As Comte himself said:

"The idea of continuous progress had no scientific consistency, or public regard, till after the memorable controversy . . . about a general comparison of the ancients and moderns." [21]

The arguments of the Ancients sought for origins in a remote past which should be emulated; the arguments of the Moderns sought for origins in individual genius which was profiting by the slow, continuous, and necessary advancement of knowledge which was taking place, and which had been taking place "from the beginning." [22] Another concept that contributed to the Idea of Progress, elaborated by Galileo and Descartes, proved very helpful to the moderns, namely, the axiom of the stability, regularity, permanence, and immutability of the "laws of Nature."

The encyclopedic activities of certain tireless savants were matched only by the general improvement and dissemination of scientific knowledge. Research and invention were as beneficial to the arts of music as to others. A new national consciousness developed in Germany after the Thirty Years' War, and the first general history of music in the German language appeared while French was still the official language of the Berlin Academy of Sciences.

So it is frequently remarked that the seventeenth century, like the twentieth, was a revolutionary age of experiment. Old shibboleths were being abandoned, and new discoveries were revolutionizing the lives of men. In music, instrumental forms became more completely emancipated from vocal styles. Keyboard instruments, secular monody, the violin family, all came into their own. Studied merely as a manifestation of a daring, experimental age, seven-

21 *Positive Philosophy*, Book VI, Ch. II.
22 Teggart, *Theory of History*, pp. 80–82.

THE "DEVELOPMENT" AND "PROGRESS" OF MUSIC   247

teenth-century music is fascinating, but it is much more than that, hence another general characteristic of the century must be kept in mind, namely what may be called the *Baroque zest for living*.

The lusty, courageous spirit of the Baroque era imparted to the experiments of that day a spirit transcending the atmosphere of a mere laboratory. The painted domes of northern Italian and south German churches, giving the illusion, from below, of the open sky, are much more than evidence of a new scientific technique. Frescobaldi, singing a part in his organ music before rapt audiences at St. Peter's, in Rome, illustrates something more than a "stage in the evolution of instrumental forms from vocal music." The thrilling music of Gabrieli, sung by double and triple choirs, with brass accompaniment, in the colorful Church of St. Mark, Venice, means something more than a "stage in the evolution of the harmonic concept." Men were very busy in those days *making* music history. We need to blow the dust from the histories that have been written about it — it was an experimental age, but the experiments left permanent results.

A third characteristic which must be kept in mind is *the increasing secularization of musical art*. The Roman Church modified the puritanical tendencies of the Counter-Reformation in response to pressure from a theater-loving public. The Puritan régime in England stopped this process for a while, but with the French infiltration under Charles II, Restoration anthems also showed secular tendencies, with a note of frank joyfulness. It is no wonder that during the Baroque era the *Idea of Progress* should have emerged with clarity, not merely because of the framework provided for it since the days of the Greeks, but because of the buoyant, optimistic character of a society that could produce Elizabethan culture, Baroque art, modern mathematics, opulent opera, lusty tavern songs, vital drama with and without music, stunning ballet, stage machinery, while, at the same time, men were beginning to colonize new worlds.

But philosophers have not allowed mankind to be content with a mere "belief in the *possibility* of progress." Since the days of Fontenelle, it has been necessary to foster "belief *in* progress" as a law of the universe. At first, the law was, as pointed out in the first half of this chapter, that of development, the gradual unfolding of inherent potentialities in an "invariable sequence." Aristotle had taught that this *normal* development would take place always, of necessity, except for accidental interference, and then stated that "a science of the accidental is not even possible." (*Metaphysics,* XI). Finally, Herbert Spencer, in 1850, in his *Social Statics* (Part I, Chapter 2) built upon that in stating his Law of Progress:

> "Progress is not an accident, but a necessity. Instead of civilization being artificial, it is a part of nature; all of a piece with the development of the embryo or the unfolding of a flower."

"Laws of Nature," however, should not have to depend upon analogy.

2. THE ANALOGY OF MOTION

"The first characteristic of the environing world that makes possible the existence of artistic form is rhythm."

"The participation of man in nature's rhythms, a partnership much more intimate than is any observation of them for purposes of knowledge, induced him to impose rhythm on changes where they did not appear." [23]

Perhaps historiography, itself a form of art, has tended "to impose rhythm on changes where they did not appear." Music histories are especially susceptible to this tendency, since music itself is an art of organizing sound in time, an art of movement.

Again we can turn to Aristotle's *Physics* for influential statements concerning the problem of change, movement, and time. "Time is not movement," but for Aristotle and many a thinker since, it is possible to treat "movement and change as equivalent." But "time is neither movement nor independent of movement. For we perceive movement and time together . . . further, when we think some time has elapsed, we think that simultaneously there has been some movement." (*Physics,* 218).

Man's sense of direction and concern over "Whither Mankind?" have led him, therefore, to a seemingly inevitable interpretation of history in terms of movement and direction. Three great uses of the analogy of motion have been and still are in use in the writing of music histories, as in other fields. These are, of course, motion in a circle, motion up and down, and motion forward or backward in a straight line. Hence the terms cycle, generation and degeneration, rise and decline, uplift and depression or degradation, progress and regress, progression and recession, and so on.

[23] John Dewey, *Art as Experience,* pp. 147, 148.

A. The Cycle

"It follows that the coming-to-be of anything, if it is absolutely necessary, must be cyclical — i.e., must return upon itself. . . .

"It is in circular movement, therefore, and in cyclical coming-to-be that 'the absolutely necessary' is to be found." [24]

The Greeks made the realistic observation that everything in nature which grows and develops must also decay and die. Consequently the concept of necessary movement in all things made them apply the processes of natural growth and decay to social change, also. Aristotle, for example, maintained not merely that men show tenacity in clinging to opinions, but that "the same opinions appear in cycles among men not once or twice, but infinitely often." (*Meteorologica*, I, 3).

Christian doctrine, after St. Augustine,[25] abandoned the cycle theory, consequently early historians of music do not mention it. John Brown used the mechanical concepts of the eighteenth century in his "Rise, Union, Power, Progressions, Separations and Corruptions of Poetry and Music" and expressed belief in their eventual reunion again. But secular historians of music have seldom employed the cycle interpretation; since the seventeenth century historical motion has gone forward "in a right line."

The cycle appears, however, in an interesting book on method by Alfred Lorenz [248], son of Ottokar Lorenz, the famous historian. It is at the opposite pole from Moser's theory of a struggle between races endowed with harmonic and melodic principles. Lorenz feels, with Ranke, that the Germanic and Romanic peoples possess a certain unity since the migrations, and swing from one tendency to another with a certain unanimity.

The revolutions in music history which bring about drastic changes, according to Lorenz, are found around 400, 1000, 1300, 1600, and 1900 A.D. The last three hundred years are divisible into three centuries, with three generations in each, all divisions showing wave-tendencies toward either the harmonic or the melodic principle. Lorenz at least shows a healthy reaction against the vague

---

[24] Aristotle, *De Generatione et Corruptione*, II, 11.

[25] "Christ died for our sins, and rising from the dead, He dieth no more. 'Death hath no more dominion over Him' . . . 'The wicked walk in a circle' not because their life is to recur by means of these circles, which these philosophers imagine, but because the path in which their false doctrine now runs is circuitous." (*The City of God*, tr. by Marcus Dods, Edinburgh, 1881, Vol. II, XII, 13, 14).

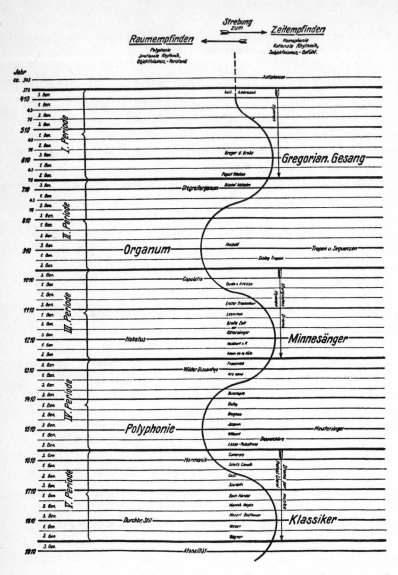

DIAGRAM FROM LORENZ'S "MUSIKGESCHICHTE IM RHYTHMUS DER GENERATIONEN"

250

periodization of evolutionary history, which usually speaks of an enormous Monodic Period, extending over centuries, followed by a Polyphonic, then by a Harmonic Period. Furthermore, the basic idea recognizes vital changes that can take place in one generation, as a sort of pendular swing away from the tendencies of the older generation. Lorenz' diagram is reproduced herewith as the best summary of his thesis; it shows an over-simplified picture, as any explanation based upon analogy is apt to do. Composers, as in the case of C. P. E. Bach, do often feel that the techniques and styles of the older generation no longer offer solutions of their problems, but Stravinsky, part of a revolutionary movement a few years ago, is now a neo-classic revivalist. To explain these changes in terms of a mechanical diagram based upon the old cycle theory is to over-look many causal factors in the social environment.

The cyclical rhythms of Lorenz would have been too petty for the Greeks; theirs worked in periods of thousands of years. More nearly approaching the pessimistic grandeur of the Greek concept is that of Oswald Spengler, in *Der Untergang des Abendlandes*.[26] A mystic use of the Comparative Method is to be found in Spengler's theory of the history of music. The music of Wagner is held up as a culmination, and at the same time as marking a beginning of decadence. The Apollinian culture reached the same "stage" in its downward course at the period of Pergamene sculpture. Cultures, treated as organisms that have their birth, growth, decay, and death, bearing in the latter the seeds of the new, are for Spengler not merely metaphorical analogies. They are presented, as in Hugo's Preface to *Cromwell*, as matters of historical fact. The Apollinian, Magian, and Faustian cultures are as definite as the historical figures of Dante and Napoleon. The fact that the beginnings and ends of the former cannot be dated without a *circa* at least one hundred years in width is of small consequence. When one is painting history on a cosmic canvas, such minutiae and hair-splitting formulae as (1265–1321) and (1769–1821) are the mere trees that keep the artist from seeing the forest.

But this reaction against dry dates and mere biography is going too far when history attempts to do without them. Spengler's mistakes in matters of fact cannot be excused, and he fully deserves

[26] *The Decline of the West,* tr. by Charles F. Atkinson, Knopf, 2 v. One-vol. ed., 1932, 1934.

the criticisms that have resulted.[27] But there are those who may say that in spite of these slips and errors, the great analogies pointed out by Spengler are too impressive to be disregarded; that in general the picture in its great, broad aspects is trustworthy. If the reader of Spengler is able to sift out these analogies and treat them merely as interesting esthetic sidelights, he may gain legitimate pleasure out of them. The danger is, however, that the reader may be led to regard these analogies as matters of fact and as adequate historical syntheses. As with Hegel's philosophy of history, impressive profundity makes the picture attractive to some readers.

Culture-histories, since the World War, have, of course, abandoned the old belief in progress held so confidently before 1914. Hence there is some tendency to revive certain phases of the cycle theory, in explaining the "decay and death" of old ideas and of old cultures and the "birth" of new ones. It is not so obvious in Friedell, whose popular work, less profound than Spengler's, gives more attention to significant parallels in music, art, and all phases of culture.[28] The cycle is more explicit in Sorokin's *Social and Cultural Dynamics,* in which music, like all other arts, passes through cyclical phases which he designates the sensate, the ideational, and a combination of the two.

As for the concern over degeneration from a Golden Age, it is at least as old as Hesiod; historians are very apt to look upon the music of their present as inferior or decadent. Even Andreas Werckmeister, who made the progressive suggestion for equal temperament in 1690 which was put into effect by Bach (see Chapter 2, above), proposed an inquiry "into the causes of the decay of sound-music." [29]

Gerbert and others found decay in church music after Palestrina (see Chapter 5) and Fétis, in 1873, found decadent tendencies in the music of his day, due to the excessive use of modulation, which had been one of the "elegant riches of tonal art in Mozart, that model of perfection." [86], I, p. x.

But today, a believer in the worth and dignity of modern music explains:

[27] See Gustav Becking, *Die Musikgeschichte in Spengler, Logos,* IX, 284, also Alfred Einstein, *Oswald Spengler und die Musikgeschichte, Zeitschr. für MW,* Oct. 1920, Jahrg. 3, Heft 1, pp. 30–32.
[28] Egon Friedell, *Kulturgeschichte der Neuzeit.* Munich, 3 vols., 1927, 1928, 1931. Tr. by C. F. Atkinson, *A Cultural History of the Modern Age,* 3 vols., N. Y., 1933.
[29] *Musikalische Paradoxal-Discourse,* 1707.

"No matter how beautiful, how satisfactory or how scientific the art of a period may be, we know that it encloses seeds of its fruition, and at the same time, of its destruction. At the height of perfection, decay begins. The spirit of beauty caught in a net, subjected to a microscope, and preserved in alcohol, becomes a museum specimen. Nor can art flourish in the strait-jacket of standardization. And so we see, throughout the centuries, *three inevitable stages* in every art epoch: *Youth, maturity* and *decay*. The fact that the epochs overlap creates friction. The new is seldom welcome; it breeds alarm and distrust. In time, it proves its right to a place in the sun, becomes over-confident and arrogant, and finally, after a life and death struggle, is supplanted by an upstart, a usurper. And the cycle begins again!" [285], p. 5.

Max Nordau, however, did not believe that it is always necessary for the new to grow out of the "rotting, decaying ruins" of the old. He maintained, with considerable insight, that progress is not measured by "growth and development" of "new forms," but only by the growth of knowledge; and that this is the task of consciousness and judgment, not a matter of instinct.[30]

B. Progress Upward

"The progress of art through the ages may be represented by an ascending spiral which at each turn passes the same points of a vertical plane, but at different heights, forever drawing nearer to a point situated in the infinite, which is the ideal."— Lavignac, *Music and Musicians* [131], p. 379.

"The Rise of Music" is a term found in at least two English histories of music (John Brown [20] and Joseph Goddard [167]), and Busoni has already been quoted as saying, "It may be we must leave earth to find that music . . . of the vibrating universe." It is worthy of note that our Western arts of music began in the Middle Ages, when men's thoughts and aspirations were turned heavenward. Consequently all idealistic interpretations of music history stress the concept of upward progress.

There is a certain inspiring quality in the Busoni quotation above, and no rhapsodical description could be too fervent from a listener who had just experienced a feeling of uplift on hearing the "Sanctus" from Bach's B minor Mass. But the fact that a

[30] Max Nordau, *Degeneration,* tr. from 2nd German ed., 4th ed., N. Y., 1895, pp. 554–555.

person has a feeling of being taken "up," out of the daily rut on hearing inspiring music is no justification for a belief that the art of music progresses upward like that, through the ages.

The same elements of mystic obscurity are involved in the evolutionary assumptions that music grew up from certain roots, and that certain kinds of music are great by reason of a higher stage of development. Alfred Einstein, in reply to certain criticisms of evolutionary analogies in his short history [204], explained, in the second edition, that he did not mean to argue that music has always developed upwards in a straight line, nor did he mean to underestimate or deny the factors of individuality and personality. It is very easy in this second edition to see how this criticism may have arisen. One can find such expressions as these at random:

"opera began to *take root* in England in the court masques " . . . "it was out of these many elements that the early classical sonata *built itself up*." . . . "In *Euryanthe* the seed was planted from which, at Wagner's hands, the whole form of music drama was to grow," etc. [204], pp. 101, 206.

Detailed analysis of the analogy of growth belongs in the next chapter, on the "Evolution" of music. We are only concerned here with the notion of direction. The phenomenon of plant growth involves spreading roots (horizontally) and upward shoots. One of the Romantic texts discussed in Chapter 6 ([66], p. 64) explains the spiral progress described by Lavignac. Fischer showed that biological motion is spiral, due to the horizontal and vertical tendencies of the growing organism. He therefore concluded that music history proceeds in the same way. In other words the downward tendency that plants show to some extent is overlooked; progress must continue toward "higher" things.

The systems of harmony instruction in vogue in the nineteenth century placed great emphasis on the study of figured bass. The figures six-four, e.g., above a bass note meant that the other notes of the chord were a sixth and a fourth, respectively, *above* that tone. The fundamental tone of a chord is known as the *root*. Our intervals are reckoned upwards, and it has become a commonplace to believe that "Harmony grows from below upwards, as a perpendicular pillar." [61], Vol. I, p. 115. Modern theory, however, is giving far more attention now to rhythm and melody. The old concept of harmony as a study of "progressions" from one "perpendicular column" to another has been tried and found wanting, and so has the old scheme of teaching harmony and counterpoint as separate subjects. Possibly our habits of thinking in linear terms affected our teaching; at any rate the two studies are not separate "Divisions of Music" but merely two different ways of looking at musical structure. Thus our "sense of direction" seems to have had its effect on theories of history, composition, and value-judgment.

Today, however, for some, music is on the "downgrade" [296]. In music itself, our terms "high" and "low" are conventional attributes. The Greeks used the terms in reverse, as for them the high notes were those playable on the long strings of the lyre, those which compelled the player to reach higher up on the instrument. And within a single century great changes in our psychological reactions to what we call high and low notes can take place. The cult of the high note has always had its adherents, possibly, but in the seventeenth century, fashion was such that Riemann could call it the "General-Bass Period." (See Chap. 8, 1). In the Baroque era, students learned to play from a figured bass, thinking upward; later developments brought surface melody to the fore, so that students now are called upon to "harmonize melody," meaning usually a soprano part. Before the eighteenth century, the tenor was the leading part; today the alto, originally a high part sung by a tenor, is the low female voice.

Schopenhauer, without taking into account the changing fashions in part music, could say:

"Bass is, for us, in harmony what unorganised nature, the crudest mass . . . from which everything originates and develops, is in the world. Now, further, in the whole of the complemental parts which make up the harmony between the bass and the leading voice singing the melody, I recognise the whole gradation of the ideas in which the will objectifies itself. Those nearer to the bass are the lower of these grades, the still unorganized but yet manifold phenomenal things; the higher represent to me the world of plants and beasts. . . . Lastly, in the *melody*, in the high, singing, principal voice leading the whole, and progressing with unrestrained freedom, I recognise the highest grade of the objectification of will, the intellectual life and effort of man." [31]

[31] Schopenhauer, *The World as Will and Idea*, III, 52, pp. 178–179.

Of course, what we call "high" tones are heard in "low" tones as "partials" in a series, but Schopenhauer is not referring to that, as that physical fact might weaken his theory.

But it is not even a theory; it is pure analogy, and a profound way of saying that Schopenhauer's favorite singer was a soprano, probably a coloratura, as Rossini is mentioned a few paragraphs later as the master of pure music. It is merely a statement of esthetic preference, but to make it impressive it is couched in the developmental terms of hierarchical value discussed in the section previous.

The passage is also pertinent to this inquiry as an example of two-dimensional analogy; that is, in addition to the hierarchical series upward, there is the analogy of the progress forward of the human will. Bass parts, as Schopenhauer points out, move most slowly:

"A quick run or shake in the low notes cannot even be imagined. The higher complemental parts — move more quickly, but yet without melodious connection and significant progress." But —"in the *melody* . . . in the unbroken significant connection of *one* thought from beginning to end representing a whole, I recognise the highest grade of the objectification of will." . . .

In other words, Schopenhauer takes exactly the opposite point of view from that of Pope John XXII, who forbade singers to "deprave the melody with descants . . . running to and fro." [32]

C. Time and Musical Progress

One of the most oft-repeated statements in histories of music is that music "is the youngest of the arts" or the last one to develop. The basis for these statements is due to the observation that great sculpture, for instance, developed in antiquity, but that symphonies were not perfected until modern times. Here again, one finds the confusion in thinking which results from attempts to explain history in terms of linear development.

For example, Henry Tipper's essay on *The Growth and Influence of Music in Relation to Civilization* [143] in attempting "to consider the growth and development of music chiefly in relation to the moral influence it has exerted" and "the ideal forces of which

[32] See Chapter 2. Also note the contrary opinions held by Aristotle and Parry regarding coloratura and ornamentation as "inferior" types of art.

it is the exponent," said that *"Music, of slower growth than any other art, assembled all her forces,* and with the remote and near, with *Nature's song* and the far-off vibration of *heavenly harmony* in the soul, feeling as no other art had done the impulse of Christianity, she burst into immortal epic and sweetest song of hope and love."

But in another case it is the gradual development of the human brain itself that has retarded music, according to Dr. Wallace, whose study of psychological evolution was cited in Chapter 8:

" Characteristics there were in the work of each composer from Monteverde to Bach, but while their value may be esteemed from an archaeological standpoint, they offer us little help in elucidating our special study of cerebral development . . . these were merely the first steps that had to be taken before the brain was in a condition to sustain the concentration imperative for the composition of a work in which a theme was handled with breadth and freedom." [172].

Edward MacDowell had an historical explanation:

" If Aristoxenus had had followers able to combat the crushing influence of Euclid and his school, music might have grown up with the other arts. As it is, music is still in its infancy, and has hardly left the experimental stage." [186], p. 79.

Nietzsche also believed that

" Music of all the arts that know how to grow up on the soil of a certain civilization, makes its appearance last of the plants, perhaps because it is the most intrinsic, and consequently arrives latest — in the autumn and withering of each civilization." *Nietzsche contra Wagner,* pp. 69–70.[33]

These debates over the tempo of changes in our musical arts raise interesting questions regarding the history of rhythm. Man has " imposed rhythm " on his interpretations of history, and he has also made great changes in his rhythmical habits and his ways of measuring time. The bar-line, for example, was not used until the seventeenth century. Even then it did not have the significance it had later. Baroque music had great freedom of rhythms, a melodic flow that was continually expanding; later, the eighteenth-

[33] Edward J. Dent's answer to these arguments is quoted at the close of Chapter 2.

century *galant* style is in neatly spaced patterns that can only be analyzed in terms of measures.[34]

Exact and regular metrical patterns in eighteenth-century classical music are curiously contemporaneous with the neatness of stages in historiography (see p. 22). The larger forms and broad outlines of musical style in the seventeenth and nineteenth centuries are, in a broad sense, contemporaneous with looser and broader periodization in histories of the art, respectively.

Until the Renaissance, time was rarely measured by mechanical means. A correlation is significant here between the history of clocks and the history of music; the history of our written music and of our mechanical clocks is almost exactly parallel.[35] In other words, from the eleventh to the thirteenth centuries, man commenced to do two things that he had never done before. First, he began to measure time with purely mechanical movements which had to be started with an initial movement (winding) by man himself; second, he began to record music in written symbols which would indicate not merely the approximate pitch, but also the relative time duration of musical tones. Where men had hitherto been dependent on the sun for time measurement, or on the natural ebb of sand or water (silent means of information), the clock now began to remind men, with audible ticks, of the "flight of time." And in music, the element of measure, if not new, was at least novel in the great possibilities it opened up for group music, and the recording of secular dance forms formerly known only by tradition.

D. Motion in a Straight Line

After both these devices came to be perfected more fully, man, fascinated with movement and mechanism, sought new worlds to conquer. So in this lusty Baroque era, the demand for a perpetual-motion machine was contemporaneous with the "perpetual canons" of musical savants. By the beginning of the eighteenth century, and about the time when the first histories of music began to appear, Newtonian physics was beginning to contradict the old Greek notion that primary motion was in a circle. According to Newton,

---

[34] Compare, for example, an Elizabethan madrigal or a Bach fugue with an Italian *aria* or classical minuet of the mid-eighteenth century.

[35] Lewis Mumford, in *Technics and Civilization*, sets the invention and use of clocks down as a significant beginning of what we call our era of technology and industry, noting its sociological importance in accurately estimating hours of work and hours of rest.

motion, once started, tends to continue in a *straight* line, until and unless deflected. So although perpetual motion was manifestly impossible in man's mechanics or music, it was evidently a fact in the universe, and although individuals still had to face death and decay, the race was immortal and capable, eventually, of unlimited perfectibility. Pascal's analogy of the life of the race and of the individual became so firmly fixed in social thinking that until recently it has never been questioned as a valid basis for sociological theory. And although perpetual motion proved to be merely a hope in physical science, it seemed to be perfectly feasible as "law" in social science, by means of analogy.

With "laws of progress" to fortify optimism, the answer to degenerationists and skeptics can always be that given by Tylor, that progress forward is the primary motion.[36] Thus the investigator is only limited to deciding whether the movement in a given area or period is forward, in the dominant direction, or temporarily backward, because of certain conditions that hinder progress. Hence few have seen any conflict in the analogies thus presented by Tylor, at the beginning of his *Primitive Culture:*

"We may fancy ourselves looking on at Civilization as in personal figure she traverses the world; we see her lingering or resting by the way and often deviating into paths that bring her toiling back to where she had passed by long ago, but, direct or devious, her path lies *forward,* and if now and then she tries a few backward steps, her walk soon falls into a helpless stumbling. It is not according to her nature, her feet were not made to plant uncertain steps behind her, for within her forward view and in her onward gait she is of truly human type."[37]

Just a few pages earlier, however, the author has pictured culture not as self-moved but as something which is carried:

"In striking the balance between the effects of forward and backward movement in civilization, it must be borne in mind how powerfully the diffusion of culture acts in preserving the results of progress from the acts of degeneration. A progressive movement in culture spreads, and becomes independent of the fate of its originators. What

[36] "History, taken as our guide in explaining the different stages of civilization, offers a theory based on actual experience. This is a development-theory, in which both advance and relapse have their acknowledged places. But so far as history is to be our criterion, progression is primary and degradation secondary; culture must be gained before it can be lost." *Primitive Culture,* Vol. I, p. 38.

[37] *Ibid.,* I, 69.

,is produced in some limited district is diffused over a wider area, where the process of 'stamping out' becomes more and more difficult. Thus it is even possible for the habits and inventions of races long extinct to remain as the common property of surviving nations; and the destructive actions which make such havoc with the civilizations of particular districts fail to destroy the civilization of the world." [38]

This optimistic statement still leaves unanswered the questions as to how culture, music, art, and other phases of civilization come to be, change, suffer neglect, and disappear, and what the forces are that cause men to tear down what they have built up.[39]

Historians of music have not, as a rule, been enthusiastic about perpetual progress. A few encomiums will be found in occasional works, as in those by Bonaventura and Hull; [40] but usually the developmental, genealogical, and hierarchical patterns have been most in evidence.

It now remains to discuss the evolutionary analogy of " growth " in music histories.

BIBLIOGRAPHY
(In addition to references in the notes)

Condorcet, *Esquisse d'un Tableau historique des Progrès de l'Esprit humain,* Paris. 1795. One of the most inspiring documents in the History of the Idea of Progress, contemporaneous with Beethoven's setting of Gellert's *Die Ehre Gottes in der Natur.*

Delvaille, *Essai sur l'histoire de l'idée du progrès jusqu'a la fin du* 18me siècle, Paris, 1910.

Teggart, " The Idea of Progress and the Comparative Method " in *Theory of History,* as cited.

Encyclopedia of Social Sciences, N. Y., 1933, Articles on " Music " by Charles L. Seeger, Helen H. Roberts, and Henry Cowell, under the subheadings " Music and Musicology," " Primitive," " Oriental," and " Occidental Music," Vol. 11, pp. 143–165.

[38] *Ibid.,* I, 39.

[39] The gospel of progress in the nineteenth century was quite indifferent to destruction; " the art of War is the highest, most exalted art," says Oken in *Elements of Physiophilosophy* (1810, Eng. Ed., 1847). Musical rhythm forward in a straight line is the characteristic of the military march, a form known only to Western, " progressive " civilizations. The national military march is a patriotic product of the modern era since the Thirty Years' War, hence a history of this form would be very instructive. The march rhythm also pervades the hymns of the church militant in this century, particularly those of Protestant and non-conformist creeds.

[40] Hull [244] is sure that music " sweeps on, scornfully, as it were, to greater conquests;" Bonaventura [192] that music is constantly progressing, even though it is " led astray " at certain periods.

CHAPTER II

THE "EVOLUTION" OF MUSIC

I. HISTORY WITHOUT GAPS

AN EARLY, if not the first, use of evolution as a biological term appears in Charles Bonnet's *Contemplation de la nature,* in 1764. For this scholar the word was synonymous with development.[1] Bonnet believed in Divine Creation and in the Chain of Being, in which each species is independent but fixed, each with its own potentialities, each possessing characteristics which merge by very slight or even imperceptible degrees into other species "above" and "below." But by 1800 the idea of continued progress was so widely accepted that it began to be applied to the science of biology. Erasmus Darwin, grandfather of Charles, could then say, still keeping the Creation concept, that

"God created all things which exist, and *these have been from the beginning* in a perpetual state of improvement." *Poetical Works,* London, 1806, III, p. 191.

In the meantime the concept of gradual, orderly, progressive, continuous change was being introduced into other scientific fields.[2]

In 1859 Charles Darwin took the final step: in the *Origin of Species,* as already cited, new species are constantly displacing the old, as a result of natural selection. Thus, while denying the fixity of species, he also denies the doctrine of Special Creation. That denial was the occasion of great opposition from the theologians, but the application of the idea of continuous progress of the species was accepted by others with more assurance than by Darwin him-

---

[1] 2nd ed., Amsterdam, 1769, Vol. I., p. 165. The term was also used by Bonnet to describe the force, or *impulsion,* which caused the yolk to develop into the embryo. Upon this evolution or impulsion, *la liqueur fécondante* acted as a stimulant. (p. 169).

[2] Immanuel Kant, *General History of Nature and Theory of the Heavens,* 1755; Laplace, *Système du monde,* 1796; James Hutton, *A Theory of the Earth,* 1795.

self. Always the careful scholar, he expressed his doubts as follows, in the *Origin of Species:*

"The main cause . . . of innumerable intermediate links not now occurring everywhere throughout nature, depends on the process of natural selection, through which new varieties continually take the places of and supplant their parent-forms. But just in proportion as this process of extermination has acted on an enormous scale, so must the number of intermediate varieties, which have formerly existed, be truly enormous. Why then is not every geological formation and every stratum full of such intermediate links? Geology assuredly does not reveal any such graduated chain; and this, perhaps, is the most obvious and serious objection which can be urged against the theory." (pp. 292–293, Everyman's Ed.).

But even before Darwin wrote the above, the organic hypothesis had been seized upon by Romantic historians as an explanation of musical changes over long periods, as a result of slow, gradual processes that showed "no gaps." In discussing "The Organic Hypothesis and Triune Theories" (in Chapter 6, II of this book), the works of Krause and Fischer were cited as parallels to Victor Hugo's interpretation of history in his *Preface to Cromwell.* It was noted that all of these postulated not merely the organic unity of all phases of culture, but gradual growth over three great periods of time analogous to the ages of man. Opposing this mystic point of view was Kiesewetter, who spoke, in the title of his history, of *stufenweise Entwickelung.* The latter term meant *evolution* in the sense employed by Bonnet, a synonym for *development;* Kiesewetter's great men were the fixed stages of development in a genealogical line.

But genealogies are finite, especially when it comes to selecting them for a history; so the new scientific term was borrowed from biology. With the concept of continuous, progressive growths of innumerable kinds of music, an all-inclusive picture was possible, one that was much more comprehensive than Kiesewetter's epochs named after single men.

This kind of interpretation had been essayed even before 1800, by Forkel, whose incomplete *Allgemeine Geschichte* was cited in Chapter 5 under "Progress and Poetry." Although the history itself did not get through the sixteenth century, Forkel managed to state his philosophy of music history in the *Einleitung* [30], Vol. I. As far as can be ascertained it is the first history of music to suggest this theory of progress without " gaps." Elisabeth Hegar [290] found " evolution " in Gerbert, Burney, and Hawkins, but these men were more interested in genealogical " development." Forkel was interested, like John Brown, in both music and poetry. But, for Forkel, there never was any separation. Both arts grew up together; both arts have the same " divisions " — grammar and rhetoric. The notion of development is present, but with broader implications:

Musical grammar consists of the following three divisions: melody (scales), harmony, and rhythm, with the auxiliaries of acoustics, musical mathematics (timbre), and notation.

Musical rhetoric is divisible into musical periodology, ways of writing musical forms, the organization of musical ideas with reference to the piece as a whole, and finally performance of musical compositions. The auxiliary to music rhetoric is musical criticism, deemed very necessary for the historian. Criticism must concern itself with (1) the necessity and basis of rules, (2) the beautiful, whether absolute or relative, and (3) musical taste.

Just as harmony is the highest development of musical grammar and expression, so the fugue is the highest of musical forms developed by rhetoric.

II. THE PROBLEM OF PERIODIZATION

Forkel begins by making a statement which defines progress in terms of development:

" Arts and sciences grow, like all creations of Nature, little by little, *until they reach perfection.*" (*Einleitung,* Vol. I).

But the stages of development are not narrowly fixed, because of the organic unity of what Hegel later calls the most romantic of the arts, Poetry and Music: " Every age has certain characteristics and tendencies impressed upon it by its spirit, customs and ways of thinking, and these can all be observed, not only in the living language, but also in the arts which are bound up with language and constitute a living language of their own." (II, p. 696).

Music, therefore, the " language of the emotions," has a history that is exactly parallel to that of language, and the origins of both are identical. " Music is inborn in man, and is as necessary a part of his system as speech."

Forkel's scheme of periodization, therefore, is oriented with reference to the above theory. Just as each " division " of music is divided into three, so also there are three periods, but very indefinite in character.

I. A very long period, in which many people are still living at present, where the only media of tonal communication are by means of rhythm. Tone and speech are rude, simple, unorganized sounds.

II. There comes to be a similarity between the expressions of sensations and of ideas. Simple scales develop with simple inflections of speech.

III. Ideas and sensations spring from a common potentiality (*Grundkraft*) in the soul, and, as the expressions of both become perfected, it is proved that both powers obey the same laws. Artistic expressions must, therefore, be as manifold as our manifold sensations. Harmony, the highest development to which music has attained, makes possible the greatest variety of expressions. It has been invented and perfected as the result of the invention of our instruments.

Not until the nineteenth century proper do these three great periods of evolution come to be named Monodic, Polyphonic, and Harmonic. Forkel anticipated them, however, and Auguste Comte, later on, in the *Positive Philosophy,* helped to fix this triad pattern for a century to come. Rowbotham's drum-pipe-lyre periods, Wallaschek's pipe-voice-drum sequence, have been cited as parallels to Comte's law; and in 1907 Combarieu could reiterate that " Music has known a theological age, with plainsong; a metaphysical age, with the great symphonists, Bach, Haydn, Mozart, Beethoven; and the present, with composers so occupied with realism, we might term the positive age." [158], p. 201.

In Chapter 6 some comment was added on the age and persistence of the number *three* in social theory, but the full significance of these triadic and triune theories was not apparent until a survey was made of all the schemes of periodization in use at the present day. There is a great show of disagreement as to detail, e.g., as to when the " late polyphonic period " ends, but as a rule these disagreements fade out in the larger pattern. The triple scheme of periodization is so common, in fact, that departures from it, until recently, have been very rare. Hugo Riemann [150] proposed triple division of each large period (nine in all), and that is followed, for instance, by Stanford-Forsyth [203] and Arnold Schering, in his *Tabellen zur Musikgeschichte* [197]. Maurice Emmanuel [183] finds three periods in each of two large divisions, ancient and modern. Alfred Casella finds three periods in harmonic evolution to the twentieth century:

I. *Absolute diatonism* (to first half of the seventeenth century). Complete absence of modulation. Culmination in Josquin des Près.
II. Development of *modulation* and modern scales (1650–1750). Culmination in Bach.
III. Introduction of *chromaticism*. Summit in Wagner. The twentieth century is extending chromatic possibilities to atonality [230, p. xxii].

C. H. Kitson, in a theoretical treatise,[3] postulates three divisions in the Polyphonic Period. Bertrand [193], d'Acosta [132] and Johannes Wolf [261] are among others cited in Chapter 8 who accept triple division as natural. Popular texts frequently adopt this periodization, and then turn back to biography, genealogy, and " stages of development." The large periods make an excellent frame into which to fit the material. In 1862, Hullah, in his *History of Modern Music* [70], claimed to have four periods, but the first did not really count. As he explained,

" The history of modern music may be divided into *periods*. During the first there was little produced of any interest, other than historical, to the musician." This period, to the year 1400, corresponds to the period of world history " commonly assigned to its formation out of chaos." The second period was 1400 to 1600; the third and Transition Period, 1600 to 1750, and the fourth and Modern Period, 1750 to the present.

As already indicated, in Chapter 6, at least one nineteenth-century historian got away from the prevailing triad pattern. Gustav Schilling [53] found five periods in his *Vorgeschichte* and five in his *Eigentliche Geschichte der modernen Musik,* from 1600 to 1840, making ten in all. But his periods, although just as symmetrical in number, vary greatly in length;[4] furthermore, they are oriented partly with reference to men, partly to events, and partly to the

---

[3] *Evolution of Harmony*, Oxford, 2nd ed., 1924, p. 1.
[4] I. *Vorgeschichte*: 1, From the early Christian era to experiments in *organum* (1–900). 2, To the invention of notation and mensural music (tenth to twelfth century). 3, To a regulated system of contrapuntal music (thirteenth to fifteenth century). 4, To the emergence of classical concepts of form (1500–1560). 5, From the beginning of Italian supremacy to the invention of opera (1560–1600).
II. *Modern Period:* 1, Monteverde to Scarlatti (1600–1700). 2, From development of instrumental music as independent art to the victory of lyric over dramatic elements — a *geistig* tendency towards form (1700–1750). 3, From Gluck's reforms to the Viennese School, Mozart and Haydn (1750–1800). 4, Recent history, with Beethoven and Rossini (1800–1830). 5, From the last French revolution to the present (1830–1840).

history of musical thought. Schilling's opinions and statements may no longer be authoritative, but his method and interests are worthy of more attention than they have received.

But with all these sequences, or successions of periods, the historian has had to choose between the *Nebeneinander* method (successive dates, events, and lives) or the *Nacheinander* (the evolution or unfolding from one stage, one style, one form, one generation to another). Schilling and Ambros, in effect, raised the question as to whether we may not stop occasionally to examine the *Zusammen* (the forces and people that work together at one given time, to get things done).

As for the evolutionary periods that unfold *Nacheinander,* without gaps, serious scholars have worked faithfully to show how musical styles change in time, and they are right in realizing that something which undergoes change has to be kept in view — otherwise the chain of events and men does not explain anything coherently. One difficulty is, however, that the evolution concept, a mystic, poetic one, tends to give the impression that the unfolding process is automatic. " Art tends to modify itself " is a phrase found in Fétis and Parry, and repeated in substance by many others. And when it comes to debates over periodization, some interpreters feel sure that the periods "arrange themselves." The Introduction to the Oxford History [146] and even Adler's introduction on the subject [224] use this phrase. Note also that Adler seeks the " clear " view:

" In order to form a *clear picture* of the musical materials developed in the West during the Christian era, they must be arranged in order. This is most certainly the case in the very close relation existing between the organic progress of music as an independent art with the spiritual currents within the various divisions of history, with due consideration for the ties that the tonal art has entered into with other arts, especially the art of poetry, in the successive stages through which it has passed. In the foreground stands the independent development of music, for never before has musical art arrived at such perfection and self-sufficiency as it has in Western Christendom. *With this point of view the periods of style arrange themselves,* as it were (*gliedern sich von selbst*)."

Period I. To c. 1000 — supremacy of the church —" Monodic-Choral " in the service of a gradually perfected liturgy.

Period II. c. ninth century — fifteenth and sixteenth — Polyphonic Period, beginning with " Heterophony," churchly use and secular practice enrich each other. Many are the stages, all constantly changing. In the midst of this period, a movement is noted, particularly in the fourteenth century, to make solo forms heard against an increasing polyphonic complexity. This tendency gets the upper hand and finally dictates the style of the late sixteenth and early seventeenth.

Period III. 1600–1900 — Homophonic Period. Monody in early opera (music-drama). Church and music-room also affected by monody and the harmonic style.

Persistence of polyphony — further developments for voices and instruments. New forms grow out of the relationship of homophony and polyphony.

"With these purely musical groupings of the great highlights of our historic music are associated *other periodizations* which are borrowed either from general history or the history of the fine arts, particularly of architecture."

The last paragraph indicates Adler's position, already mentioned, concerning music's relation to the other arts. He is cautious concerning relationships at any given time, as he feels that each art follows its own evolution. Adler's belief, in short, is that each art has its own periodization. For him the task of music history is the research into and presentation of the products of musical thought in their processes of evolution; that scientific research must bring forth everything that can throw light on "the evolutionary processes of musical art." [207]. Adler's approval of a linear genetic method [5] is not shared, however, by John Dewey, who says:

"In order to justify continuity, historians have often resorted to a falsely named 'genetic' method, wherein there is no genuine genesis, because everything is resolved into what went before. But Egyptian civilization and art were not just a preparation for Greek nor were Greek thought and art mere re-edited versions of the civilizations from which they so freely borrowed. *Each culture has its own individuality and has a pattern that binds its parts together.*

[5] In his *Methode* (p. 44), Adler criticizes some origin theories, but finds the "genetic method" acceptable. Even when he condemns the biological analogy, when carried to its naive extremes, he nevertheless admits that it is *geistvoll* and "enticing." Adler was strongly influenced by Hans Tietze, who, in his turn, was greatly impressed by the theories presented in Bernheim's *Lehrbuch der historischen Methode,* Leipzig, 1903. Bernheim gives first place to the genetic method. The pragmatic or *lehrhafte* method is second, one step above the old Greek and Roman narrative method. For a defence of the modern concept of what a pragmatic method should be, see Sidney Hook, "A Pragmatic Critique of the Historico-Genetic Method" in *Essays in Honor of John Dewey,* New York, Holt, 1929.

"Nevertheless, when the art of another culture enters into attitudes that determine our experience genuine continuity is effected. Our own experience does not thereby lose its individuality but it takes unto itself and weds elements that expand its significance. A community and continuity that do not exist physically are created. The attempt to establish continuity by methods which resolve one set of events and one of institutions into those which preceded it is doomed to defeat." [6]

The problem of periodization, therefore, goes much deeper than superficial arguments over date-boundaries, style-periods, and so on. As long as the concept of large evolutionary periods are deemed necessary, in order to envisage history without gaps, these difficulties have to be faced:

(1) the sudden breaks with the past, which cannot be explained on the basis of slow, continuous, progressive evolution of new forms.

(2) the confusion noted above, in which there is agreement as to the large periods, but radical disagreements as to *how* music evolves, whether

(a) the arts are united, and evolve together, or whether

(b) each art follows its own course of evolution.

As in summarizing origin theories, truth can be found in all these evolutionary arguments, and a naive realist might be permitted to state the matter thus:

(1) Musical habits *do* change slowly, over long periods of time, and it takes an important event or series of events in cultural history to jolt the average person out of complacent content with nothing but old music. Innovation, therefore, means modification of the old, or new uses for old materials to meet new needs. But, on this basis, the periods will not " arrange themselves."

(2) As for music's relationships with other phases of culture, it is true

(a) that it is just one way of artistic living, that it is closely tied to all other phases of the cultural pattern, among a given people, in a given area, at a certain time;

(b) but it is also true that music is more closely allied to certain arts than others, and that these relationships change, in kind and in degree, with other changes in the social structure. Music does have its own techniques which call for special study, but even these change, not because the art " bears its consequences within itself "

[6] *Art as Experience*, pp. 335–336.

but because these techniques have to be revised to meet new conditions.

These considerations will form the subject-matter of the last chapter. The remainder of this chapter is devoted to the analogies employed in evolutionary explanation. These involved not only the older concept of development from one definite stage to another, up to perfection, but also the modern concept of progressive growth of one species *into* another.

Two concepts tended to qualify this doctrine: first the Darwinian theory of natural selection [7] and the Spencerian theory of progress from the homogeneous to the heterogeneous. The first has not been so important an element in music historiography as the second, and Spencer's influence was discussed at length in Chapter 7. A few comments should be added, however, on this concept of musical " growth," the notion that the art form bears within it the seeds of change and progress.[8]

III. THE ANALOGY OF GROWTH

I. DOES HARMONY GROW?

There is, perhaps, no phase of music that has appealed more strongly to the lovers of biological analogy than that of harmony. As a poetic concept it has inspired some of Wagner's music, as in the Prelude to *Das Rheingold*. The single bass note in the opening measure not only suggests that heavy gold lying at the bottom of the river, but also a germinal tone [9] over which the partial tones generated by the fundamental are gradually added. Then an ascend-

[7] " In music, as in all else, the strongest triumph, only to recommence the struggle, and to be overcome in their turn. Thus is evolution produced." Combarieu, [158], p. 308.

[8] Occasionally this concept refers to the growth of music by accumulation. This is a fact, not an analogy, if reference is made to the progressive accumulation of data, resources, literature, and instruments. But when " the stream of music " or the " ocean of harmony " or the " well-springs of folk-song " are used, they are often used synonymously with " seed " or " roots " to explain how one kind of music comes from another.

[9] " From the fundamental note of harmony, music had spread itself into a huge expanse of waters, in which the absolute-musician swam aimlessly and restlessly to and fro, until at last he lost his nerve. . . . What moved him to return (to shore, in quiet waters) was . . . the admission that he possessed a faculty which he was unable to use, the yearning for the poet." [61], p. 288.

In another paragraph, Wagner says, " Our modern music, in a sense, has evolved from naked harmony."

ing melodic figure is heard, first in fragments, then in acceleration as a whole, then in diminution, until finally the hearer is engulfed in a flood of harmony.

One of the fallacies of the romantic nineteenth century, however, was the notion that music was *better* as it became grander in proportions. Harmony " grew " to luxuriant heights; the seventh chord grew to a ninth, and then to the eleventh and the thirteenth. Unable to grow beyond that, chromatic twigs embellished the branches with passing notes and luscious suspensions. At the same time, the orchestra grew from an average of forty, say, to one hundred and twenty-five for the *Sacre du printemps* by Stravinsky or Schönberg's *Five Pieces for Orchestra.* Organs grew to Brobdingnagian proportions, and so did festival choruses. The close of our Civil War was celebrated in Boston with an orchestra of 1,000 and a chorus of 10,000. In 1873, " World Peace " was celebrated appropriately with forces that had grown for the occasion to double that number.

Such matters only belong in this context to illustrate the fact that belief in progress, during the Victorian era, the " Gilded Age," was colored by pride in ostentatious expansion, and this has been reflected even in such matters as the history of harmony. If the bigger is better, then " growth " will explain " development."

Even Donald F. Tovey, usually very objective, comes perilously near this error, in his article " Harmony " in the *Encyclopaedia Britannica* (14th ed.). The reader is asked to note the " evolution " of the opening measures of Wagner's *Tristan and Isolde.* Unable to show early sketches, such as Beethoven would have made in polishing and refining his material, Tovey begins with a simple cadence such as *might have been* made in the sixteenth century, then follows with other variations in the style of various composers, such as they *might* have written *if* they had all chosen to develop the same germinal theme! Each is more complicated than the one previous, until the theme as it appears in the prelude reaches even more luxuriant growth in a passage from the second act. The deceptive character of all this is apparent when one realizes that only the originals at the end of the series have ever existed in the past. Professor Tovey's " early stages," composed by himself, have nothing but a theoretical existence in history.

If one were to examine different harmonizations of an old melody, in chronological order, one could often find the opposite of luxuriant growth, namely, progressive simplification. Lutheran chorales were frequently harmonized for double chorus in the seventeenth century, by such men as Praetorius. J. S. Bach, with all his richness of harmonization, was usually content with four voices. The simplest harmonizations are to be found in the *Choralbücher* of the late eighteenth and early nineteenth centuries.

2. DOES MUSIC "GROW" FROM "ROOTS"?

The nationalistic hypotheses of music history for which Wagner was so largely responsible [10] are definitely committed to this analogy of growth. The same arguments used by R. Vaughan-Williams [11] are used by Richard Eichenauer.[12] Eichenauer, a Nazi extremist on the subject, closes his book with this plea:

"Will the future bring us masters who will be of our spiritual type? Race research regards that as a biological, not as an artistic, problem. Art is not root, but blossom. Care for the roots; the blossoms will take care of themselves." [13]

C. W. Gluck, to name one famous composer, was born or "rooted" in Germany, so of course he is named by the Germans as a German composer. But in the Lavignac *Encyclopédie* he is listed among French musicians, and not without reason, although there are delicious Italian fruits from the Gluck tree, also. Now Gluck certainly was an organism — no analogy is involved in that statement; he had his "roots" in Germany, but if the roots were all that mattered, there would have been no *Orfeo* and no *Iphigénie en Aulide* in operatic literature.

International "grafting" has often been followed by productive results, by new music that would never have appeared otherwise. This suggests another hypothesis, one that is concerned with the

10 See Ch. 9, p. 226.

11 *National Music*, [310], discussed in Ch. 9.

12 *Musik und Rasse*, [281], discussed in Ch. 9.

13 It is a curious fact that those who use this analogy have never noticed the excellent results obtained in horticulture by *grafting*. Luther Burbank became known as a wizard not merely by cultivating *roots* but by grafting and cross-pollination. Burbank was a creative artist, who composed new horticultural products with old materials, old species. His first order was for 20,000 prune trees to be ready in nine months; ordinarily nearly three years would be necessary if roots alone were cared for. He achieved the "impossible" after planting almond seeds because they would grow more quickly at that time of year. (W. S. Harwood, *New Creations in Plant Life*, New York, 1912, p. 15.) From that point Burbank went on to create new and useful species, with untried but now common experiments.

varied functions music serves in society. The most successful church musicians in history, for example, seem to have been those who have written secular music also. And composers for theater, dance, and concert hall have done well to write for church, home, and school. The "evolution" of church music has not been due to organists rooted to the choir gallery, but also to men of the world like Byrd, Monteverde, Purcell, Handel, Hasse, Fux, Mozart, Gounod, Mendelssohn, Arthur Sullivan, and many others. Genius is never found in a deep hole, rooted to any one function for music making.[14]

Similarly, the history of European music must take into consideration the "class" concept. The Marxist interpretation reviewed in Chapter 8 goes to an extreme, as any monistic interpretation may, but the fact remains that few composers show the vitality necessary for great art, if they and their music have been rooted to one class in society. The literature of music abounds in aristocratic forms and popular styles which range from music racy of the soil to the favorites of the bourgeoisie. Again, application of this test to individual masters is bound to reveal versatility and ability to communicate, which is a great essential. Even Chopin, by nature, culture, and environment an aristocrat in the best sense, was inspired by the folk dances of his native Poland, as well as the valse of the salon and the dreamy nocturne. Mussorgsky, however, hailed as the "Prophet of the Revolution," and as a musical representative of the proletariat, was of aristocratic birth and a song-writer of exquisite finesse.

IV. THE WAGNERIAN INFLUENCE

Wagner's theory of the radical superiority of the German language has already been cited, also his theory of origins in tone-speech. But altogether there are three phases of evolutionary thought in Wagner's philosophy, and all are of great importance because

---

[14] So far, this hypothesis seems to hold except for Victoria and a few other contemporaries in the sixteenth century who wrote nothing but church music, and that of an amazing vitality to this day. But in Spain at that era, there was no separation of sacred and secular. The life and thought of all classes seem to have been bound up in fanatical devotion to religion. Before the expulsion of the Moors, however, monks like Juan del Encina were successful in dramatic as well as in liturgical music.

of their influence ever since on our systems of composition, historiography, and music education. These three phases are:

a. The revival of the triune theories discussed in Chapter 6.
b. The evolutionary process by which a new art is to be born of a mystic union between poetry and music; that the new is born from the old.
c. The "root" or germinal theory of folk art just mentioned.

These theories all involve what a modern psychologist calls "pseudo-mysticism," [15] and lend support to those who regard music as one of the esoteric mysteries of the cosmos.[16]

I. THE UNITY OF THE ARTS

Wagner's project for unity in the opera house was a greater success than other schemes for unity that appeared in his day. Auguste Comte had dreamed in his *Positive Polity* of a united Europe, after Napoleon had tried in vain to bring it about by force;[17] and German humanists had dreamed of a Europe united culturally under the leadership of a united Germany. But with all the compelling vitality of Wagner's music, one may question whether he really effected the union of the arts postulated in his theory. Even more may we question his quasi-mystic theories as to how this union was to be effected.

In a world torn by commercial rivalries, with practical politicians intent on personal and national advantage, there was a vast gap between dreams and reality. Wagner, for example, believed with Marx that with certain changes the State would gradually be dispensed with (*vernichtet*), that it would wither away.[18] Both these men still wield great influence in musical and economic thinking; both, as already indicated, were revolutionists, and both looked for eventual unity, as a result of a universal belief or "social religion,"

[15] Knight Dunlap, *Mysticism, Freudianism and Scientific Psychology*, St. Louis, 1920.

[16] As, e.g., in C. H. A. Bjerregaard, *Lectures on Mysticism and Nature-Worship*, M. R. Kent, Chicago, 1897, p. 37, an essay on "Music and Numbers" or "how you can enter the plane of the Fourth Dimension . . . one of the secrets of Wagner's influence . . . he was a mystic. Through Schopenhauer he was connected with the East and there he learned about vibrations."

[17] And in Comte's *Positive Polity*, the artist was to help bring about this unity. See *Système de Politique Positive ou Traité de Sociologie, instituant la Réligion de l'Humanité*, Paris, 1851, Vol. I, *Discours préliminaire*, Part IV.

[18] *Opera and Drama* [61], pp. 195–205.

as Wagner called it. And this unity was to emerge with the interaction of two elements, as a new, third condition. But, for Marx, final synthesis was to come as a result of struggle (antithesis); for Wagner it was to come through the power of love. Thus, in explaining how union of the three humanistic arts (dance, tone, poetry) is to be brought about, he says,

"Man by love sinks his whole nature in that of woman, in order to pass over through her into a third being, the child, and yet finds but himself again in all this loving trinity, though in this self a widened, filled, and finished whole, so may each of these individual arts find itself again in the perfect, thoroughly liberated art work." [19]

In the context from which this excerpt is taken, "Art and Revolution," it becomes apparent that Wagner's wishful thinking about the *Vernichtung des Staates* is because of State interference with the individual artist who is to bring this unity of the arts to pass. Marx was vitally concerned over the welfare of great masses of people, but that concern, with Wagner, is secondary. He wanted freedom for himself, the artist, but argued homogeneity for the mass merely as a philosophy for his *Nibelungen Ring*. The irony of it all is that Wagner's argument for unity in pagan roots has been taken seriously and put into effect in Germany today, so successfully that the totalitarian State has grown in power. It is the freedom of the individual artist that has now been *vernichtet*.

Wagner's argument concerning the "loving trinity" brings into relief the triune theories discussed in Chapter 6. He was in his impressionable 'teens when Hugo, Krause, Hegel, and Comte were propounding the Law of Progress and the concepts of unity concerning which men were so optimistic. The rehabilitation of Christianity after the restoration of the Bourbons and the esthetic interests in religion at this time have also been alluded to, so it is not unlikely that the doctrine of the Trinity had more influence on men's minds than it had had during the Enlightenment.

At any rate, as the triunity of ancient, medieval, and modern came to provide music history "without gaps," the music of the Middle Ages and Renaissance, held in such contempt during the Enlightenment, began to occupy the center of the historical picture. But the mystic aura of romance surrounded the use of this ma-

[19] *Prose Works*, 2nd ed., 1895, Vol. I, p. 149.

terial.[20] The Middle Ages and Renaissance came to be turning points or transition periods in the growth and development of culture from ancient to modern times. Old music and old styles were therefore performed with nineteenth-century harmony rather than in the medieval styles and modes which were not yet understood. It is safe to say that certain phases of the Gothic revival in the nineteenth century appear to the careful musicologist as misleading as some phases of the Classic revival had been in the century previous.

We have also seen how the perfect major triad, the unifying " chord of nature," came to be accepted as basic, and the seven-tone major scale came to be *the* scale. Seven and three have always been numbers to conjure with, and Wagner uses the latter as an important concept in his theory. But modern research has demonstrated the great diversity of scales in old music, to the enrichment of modern art. And Wagner proves that, in practice, diversity is more important than fixity in symbolic numbers. He found possibilities in the chromatic 12-tone scale [21] that had been explored by Gesualdo. This was the scale which was to inspire Arnold Schönberg to make even more radical experiments a generation later. And when Wagner tried to reach the apotheosis of trinitarian symbolism in a trilogy, a prelude (*Das Rheingold*) had to be added. But when men are concerned with pure theory, it is easy to stick to the number-magic and the word-magic out of which theories are often made.

The disparities between theory and practice, between romantic dreams and nineteenth-century reality, between the new quest for beauty for its own sake and the growing ugliness of ordinary life seem, in a sense, the results of mystic ways of thinking. In ecstasy (a state of " standing away from " or " out beyond "), a pseudo-mystic can envisage unity on a higher plane. Thus he can forget that here below it can only be achieved by intelligent co-operation. How else can one explain the following statement from Lorenz Oken, one of the pioneers in evolutionary theory, in 1810?

[20] Besseler's admirable study of *Die Musik des Mittelalters und Renaissance*, Vol. 10 of Bücken's *Handbuch*, begins with the nineteenth-century revival of plainsong and polyphonic music. He shows how the style of this music was not understood by musicians who attempted to present it with nineteenth-century notions of measure and " expressive " harmony which disregarded modal idioms.

[21] In *Tristan and Isolde*, the chromatic idioms of which caused great difficulties for contemporary musicians.

" As in the art of poetry all arts (music and dance) have been blended, so in the art of war have all sciences and all arts.

" The art of war is the highest, most exalted art; the art of freedom and of right, of the blessed condition of man and of humanity . . . the principle of peace." [22]

2. BIRTH OF THE NEW FROM THE OLD

In the quotation from " Art and Revolution," Wagner stated that man is born again and finds a larger self by sinking his nature in woman and identifying himself with her and the child. This might appear to be a secular version of the Scriptural injunction for man's spiritual rebirth through God and the church. But it will be seen from the next section that Wagner favored the pagan mythos, not the Christian tradition, although he borrowed from the latter when he pleased, for poetic inspiration. Therefore Wagner's " loving trinity " is not to be traced to Christian mysticism, but rather to the older ethnic trinities of pagan mythology.

It has just been remarked that in a state of ecstasy, the mystic achieved unity with a higher power, by sublimating or getting beyond unity in a mortal sense. At least the great mystics, Plotinus the Neo-Platonist and the Christian saints such as Teresa, Catherine of Siena, and John of the Cross, did so, to the enrichment of religious and poetic literature. But the question has been raised as to whether the Romantic theorists of the nineteenth century were really mystics, because they merely made application of mystic phraseology to " prove " that the new emerges from a biological union of two older elements.

Wagner, after reading metaphysics, apparently felt bound to show that his new art of the future, something that had never been created before, must be thoroughly justified from a philosophical standpoint. So to meet his critics he used a common tool of contemporary thought — the biological analogy.[23]

He made use of the love concept in some such sense as is found in Plotinus, who distinguished between divine love and mortal love,

---

[22] *Physio-Philosophy*, pp. 664–665. The same pseudo-mystic, ecstatic praise of war is to be found in Ruskin's *Crown of Wild Olive* (1866).

[23] Wagner's *Opera and Drama* was written about seven years before Darwin's *Origin of Species*, and nearly twenty years before *The Descent of Man with Relation to Sex*. The sources of Wagner's theories are in very old uses of biological analogy. See also Levi L. Paine, *The Ethnic Trinities, and Their Relation to the Christian Trinity*, Cambridge, Mass., 1901.

between the worship of Venus on a higher "Platonic" pla... the gratification of desire on the carnal level.[24]

The Biblical personification of the body of the church as the bride and of Christ as the bridegroom [25] may have been familiar to Wagner, but his symbolism lacks the spiritual subtlety of that tradition. As already noted, Wagner was more interested in Norse gods who united with Mother Earth to produce heroic broods of mortals. At any rate Wagner asserted that

"Every musical organism is by its nature womanly; it is merely a bearing, and not a begetting factor; the begetting-force lies clean outside it and without fecundation by this force it positively cannot bear. Here lies the whole secret of the barrenness of modern music." [26]

"Music is a woman. . . . She must be loved by the poet (the man), must surrender herself to him, in order that the new art-work of the future may be born . . . the begetter must be the artist." (p. 376).

The origin theories in tone-speech quoted at the end of Chapter 9 connect with this description of the "instinctive" origins of folk melody:

"When the folk invented melodies, it proceeded like the bodily man, who by the instinctive exercise of sexual functions, begets, and brings forth man . . .

"Harmony and rhythm are the shaping organs . . . the blood, flesh, nerves, and bones, with all the entrails" but "melody is this finished man himself." (p. 104).[27]

Somewhere "upon the path of progress from word-speech to tone-speech," Wagner feels that he

"reached the horizontal surface of harmony, . . . that aboriginal womb of all the kin of tones. . . . We are to plunge the poetic aim, as a begetting moment, into the full profundity of this Ur-Mother element, in suchwise that we may prompt each atom of its vast emotional chaos to conscious individual manifestment in a compass ever stretching wider." . . . (p. 284).

[24] *Ennead* VI, Bk. IX, 9.
[25] See Mark II: 19; John III: 29; Ephesians V: 25; 2nd Cor. XI: 2; or Rev. XXI: 2, 9; XXII: 17.
[26] *Opera and Drama* [61], p. 109. This is Wagner's way of demonstrating his belief that the artist could do nothing new within the framework of the dry *recitative* and the metrical regularity of the *aria*. Within the circumscribed aria he can only vary, not invent (p. 108).
[27] For a recent use of this analogy, see Winthrop Parkhurst, *The Anatomy of Music*, as cited in Ch. 9.

Beethoven's notebooks, which show
re-wrote his melodic themes, Wagner

y no means posits melody as something ready in
measure lets it be born before our eyes." (p. 106).

ch brings to mind the debates which are still heard
y as to whether melody comes out of harmony, or vice
ve.

For Wagner, everything new had to be explained in terms of generation, hence the necessity for all these analogies involving unity, love, the trinity, birth and rebirth, and so on.

It now remains to indicate Wagner's contribution to the theory of Eichenauer quoted above, that national musical art must grow out of native folk music, that the great necessity is to care for the " roots."

3. GERMAN MYTHOS VS. CHRISTIANITY

In the essay " Opera and Drama," Wagner, like Aristotle and Tylor, has a prescription for a clear view, namely, that in the saga of Siegfried " we may look with tolerable clearness into the primordial germ " [61], pp. 161–163. It is claimed that " Christianity tried to drag up the root of the Germanic folk tree, so that the Mythos became incapable of procreation." This, as noted before in Chapter 8 and in Chapter 9, on " Origins," is a summary of the thesis advanced by Chamberlain and Gobineau, and is well covered by Friedrich Hertz, in *Race and Civilization*. The fallacies involved have been exposed, not only in argument, but also in demonstration by such men as Luther Burbank. If the tree analogy must stand, so must the verse, " By their fruits shall ye know them." Such masterpieces as *Messiah, Don Giovanni, Elijah, Le Prophète, Creation, Orfeo* and *Orpheus aux Enfers* were written by composers with Germanic roots, but what a wealth of variety is there, as a result of cross-breeding and intermingling of cultural elements!

Several of the works mentioned above are by Jewish writers against whom Wagner and Eichenauer directed their shafts. But there is nothing in the scores of Mendelssohn, Meyerbeer, or Offenbach which can be termed " Jewish music " any more than it can be called " German music." Mendelssohn became a Victorian Protestant, Meyerbeer an international figure, and Offenbach a typical

Parisian. But when forced into isolation, "the Jewish people has created a special type of music, an interpretation of the spiritual and social life, of its ideals and emotions," into which "foreign elements were incorporated until they became organic parts of the musical body."[28] Such statements allow the Jew no answer to the Nazi anthropologist; theories of "roots" keep groups apart. The Jew could call attention, if he so desired, to the fact that there is no "Jewish music" outside of the synagogue. The Jew can point with pride to his contributions to Western musical culture, side by side with Catholics and Protestants. The latter have their own hymnologies, but their musical histories are of cults and institutions, not of Catholic and Protestant peoples.

To return to Wagner's contention, Christianity did not uproot German culture, although it changed it. We are told now that the blond heroes who left their native forests to invade Italy became "softened"[29] upon learning Christian music. But German Catholic music is far from being "soft," even the Baroque arts of the South. Much less can that appellation be given to Lutheran musical culture. In the music of J. S. Bach we find a mingling of both religious traditions. As a matter of fact, although the biological "roots" of German civilization are in the North, its rich and varied "fruits" are also the results of pollination with Mediterranean, Anglican, Gallic, and Slavic cultures.

Wagner's work is a living refutation of his own theory. It is generally agreed that his most genuine folk opera, that is, the one which interprets the life of historically authentic Germans, is *Die Meistersinger*. And that begins and ends with the *chorale,* the religious folk song in which the sturdy Christian faith of the German people is rooted.

Furthermore, Wagner's own varied life, travels, and accomplishments are at variance with his complaint that the mythos "dispersed itself into individual fractions . . . the kernel of its action into a mass of many actions." In other words, the heterogeneity which for Spencer is a sign of progress, is for Wagner an evil. But the musical world is nevertheless thankful for the heterogeneity of Wagner's operas, for the fact that Venice, Switzerland, and Paris could inspire such totally different scores as the second

---

[28] A. Z. Idelson, *Jewish Music in its Historical Development,* N. Y., Holt, 1929, Preface and Conclusion.

[29] See Mersmann, *Eine Deutsche Musikgeschichte* [297].

act of *Tristan,* the "Forest Murmurs" in *Siegfried,* and the "Bacchanale" for *Tannhäuser;* also for the actual developments in Wagner's own art that found inspiration in the Bible for *Jesus of Nazareth,* in Italian history and Spontini for *Rienzi,* in medieval romance and Von Weber for *Lohengrin* and *Tannhäuser,* in Marschner and folk legend for *The Flying Dutchman,* and in the Christian sacrament for the Eucharist scene in *Parsifal.*

It is difficult to see how all these elements can be traced back to the "primordial germ" in *Siegfried.*

These views of Wagner's go to extremes, but so did those of his opponents. The controversy between the Wagnerites and the adoring worshippers of the absolute musician, Brahms (who himself remained aloof), still goes on.

Hanslick, in his reviews and in *The Beautiful in Music,*[30] was one of Wagner's chief critics. He assailed the mysticism inherent in Wagnerian esthetics and denied any causal *nexus* between music and feeling. He anticipated modern scholarship by maintaining that *style* in a composer is like *character* in a man (p. 104). Hanslick confined himself to moderate statements and had no philosophy of history. But in Victorian England the matter went beyond esthetic debate into this field of morals. In the next chapter, the Rev. H. A. Haweis [85] is quoted to show how Wagner's plea for unity was completely reversed, to show that progress to the highest emotional plane should be in pure music (music without words). Since that time, there have been two extreme schools of thought in the teaching of music appreciation. One argued, in line with Wagnerian theory and Romantic thought in general, that music is romance,[31] that the beauty and meaning of music is bound up with literary values. The other school has maintained that the appreciation of music must concern itself with the enjoyment of music for its own sake, as an art of design. The success of this school and its dependence upon history in sequential patterns will be pointed out later.

But before leaving Wagner, it is necessary to return to his use of analogy and some of the confusions which it still involves in evolutionary explanation.

[30] Tr. by Gustave Cohen, 7th ed., London, 1891.
[31] As, for example, in Edward Baxter Perry, *Descriptive Analyses of Piano Works,* and *Stories of Standard Teaching Pieces,* Phila., 1910.

V. THE CONFUSION OF ANALOGIES

Wagner was not consistent in the use of analogy. In one quotation above, the absolute musician was swimming in the sea of harmony, helpless without the aid of the poet. Then just as the poet is to plunge the poetic aim into the surface of harmony, he is placed on a ship: " this trusty ship is the conqueror of the endless floods of harmony — *the orchestra.*" (p. 301). But it develops that " the orchestra is not merely the conqueror of the waves, but itself those conquered waves." (p. 306).

But this confusion is no momentary lapse into mixed metaphors on the part of one writer. Similar confusion is found in practically all explanations of the history of music " inspired by that great doctrine of the nineteenth century, the doctrine of evolution." Ever since Wagner's day, the belief has been widely accepted that music has

(1) developed as an art-organism (a very old belief, as shown in Chapter 10);

(2) progressed from stage to stage in some direction or with reference to some value (since the seventeenth century);

(3) differentiated itself, from homogeneous tone and primitive forms, according to Spencer's formula (as shown in Chapter 7);

(4) and finally, that new musical forms and styles have gradually and continuously " evolved," " grown " and been " generated " from and out of those which went before (a doctrine which dates from the end of the eighteenth or the beginning of the nineteenth century).

These concepts have provided a wealth of analogy with which music history was to be explained to the student and layman in simple terms. It is not surprising, therefore, that confusion of these theories should result.

I. THE CONFUSION OF GROWTH ANALOGIES

Growth can be explained, as already noted, in biological or in cumulative terms. And if the growth or progress or development of music is a natural process, certain undesirable factors may retard it. The Rev. H. R. Haweis in *Music and Morals* [85] believed that

"the old tonality (before 1600) was the great obstacle to all progress. A scale of notes arranged on the uniform system was the
remedy." (p. 119). Others felt that growth was endangered by
"such men as Euclid (who) apply mathematics to musical sounds,
and a system of cold calculation to an art that had needed all the
warmth of emotional enthusiasm to keep it alive." [186], p. 79.
Centuries later, folk music saved the art "from the frightful mechanical ingenuities of Josquin and his fellow workers." [203],
p. 155.

According to MacDowell,

"Had it not been for the little weeds of folk song which managed
with difficulty to survive at the foot of this arid dust heap, and which
were destined to . . . bloom into such lovely flowers in our times, we
might yet have been using the art to illustrate mathematical calcula-
tions." [186, p. 79].

And according to Forsyth, the art was saved from extinction in
the sixteenth century by the successors of Josquin who "cleared
away the choking masses of blind-weed that lay on the foot-hills
leading upwards to the heights of Palestrina." [203], p. 155. These
men, as they toiled up the slopes, found

"the ever-changing but never-ending stream of folk-song. And it was
at this spring that the musicians of the early sixteenth century took
their first draught . . . of humanity. It toned up their constitutions
marvellously." (p. 160).

In another passage "the heights of Palestrina" are compared to
the heights of the Elizabethan madrigal school:

"When two towering mountains exist in two widely separated lands,
it is folly to attempt their measurement with the yard-stick. Their geological formations differ. At the foot of one are olives and vines; at the
foot of the other elms and oaks." (p. 169).

But the mixture of metaphors is confusing: Palestrina is now a
mountain, and then a ship:

"It must not be imagined that the muddy stream of misplaced ingenuity dried up suddenly with Josquin's death. On the contrary, it
continued to flow for many years. But it was not on the main stream.
And its impurities were only a fleck on the surface when it met the
big tidal wave that brought Palestrina's galleon up to her anchorage."
(p. 157).

Another explanation is that art music, as Vaughan-Williams says, is a "cultivated crop" and that folk songs are "wildflowers":

"It is well to fix this fact firmly in one's mind; that there always have been, are still, and possibly always will be two co-existent types of music — the wild and the cultivated. . . . But both of these types derive directly from their common ancestor (prehistoric) *song*." [203], p. 201.

But growth is not merely biological, the stream analogy returns in the same phraseology used by Surette and Mason still earlier, who asserted that "the stream of pure native melody was independent of the art-song and followed its own natural channel." [164], Vol. 1, p. 30.

Forsyth goes on to say that

"This simple type of chant or charm (primitive folk song) is the head-water from which all music flows. But . . . it branches off into two main river-systems, the (ecclesiastical) art-music and the folk-music. Of the two the former has by far the most varied course. The boat starts smoothly enough in charge of the medicine-man. He is succeeded by the pagan holy-boly, and the holy-boly by the Christian priest. . . . At various points . . . this stream intersects with the other. And this occasional intersection produces, as we have seen, somewhat violent changes in its current.

"Meanwhile, the broad stream of folk-music flows placidly on." [203], pp. 204–205.

But whereas ecclesiastical music in this analogy is a stream, it was also represented as a metallic basis for the blindweed that had to be cleared away on the slopes of Palestrina:

"Plainsong itself never underwent any process of evolution. The music expanded under the heat of new energies, but the core inside remained cold and rigid. Meanwhile, men were trying every possible expedient to keep the two in contact while giving an appearance of novelty to the resulting art-work."

Thus the amazing contrapuntal arts of the Flemish masters of the fifteenth century resulted in "frightful mechanical ingenuities" because they carried on "endless (and perhaps necessary) experiments in the art of lengthening and shortening the notes of the various parts so that they would fit together." (pp. 155–156).

From the above it is apparent that one analogy leads to another.

Popular presentations of music history and appreciation often assume that to describe music as music (with musical terminology) makes for technicalities. So to make music "interesting" it must be described in terms of something else — assuming that the latter will be more easily understood. In the above, recourse was had to biology, geology, metal working, navigation, suffocation, and trailblazing. In other textbooks for school use, analogies have been found from many other fields, even "home-brew."

But this tendency toward negative explanation is common in all analogies of the growth of music. The analogies reviewed above are only corollaries of the general belief that music cannot be understood in its "present state;" that it must be described as coming out of something else. Let us examine one of the statements only. The analogy of Palestrina as a "height" leaves the impression

(1) that he was alone in a rarefied atmosphere, whereas modern research shows him to have been a worthy member of a group of gifted men, but no greater than several other men, e.g., Lassus, Victoria, Morales, Philip de Monte, or even Gesualdo;

(2) that the "strata" supporting Palestrina were "remote" from those supporting the Elizabethan madrigalists; the madrigal was an Italian genre of part-singing brought to England by an enthusiastic amateur, Nicholas Yonge. The imitation of the Italian madrigal and adaptation of it to English needs and tasks was not merely a result of the work done by previous generations of Englishmen; it was the result of a new "intrusion." As for Palestrina, he was in contact with and profiting by the work of Spanish and Flemish artists;

(3) that after Palestrina no further height was reached, that new formations had to be built from the ground up, forgetting the continuance of the Baroque traditions into the seventeenth century, with the modifications demanded by contemporary taste;

(4) that Palestrina "improved upon" the work of his predecessors. The facts are simply that Palestrina's work is better known to us than that of Josquin des Près. Josquin's music offers great difficulty, a fact which may indicate that our standards of vocal performance of polyphonic music are not up to those of the fifteenth century. But it should not make fifteenth-century music a subject for contempt because it is "different;"

(5) that fifteenth-century Flemish music was far removed from

folk elements. Facts indicate widespread participation in a culture that was highly humanized and in many ways worthy of emulation.[32]

2. WHAT DOES EVOLUTION MEAN?

At the beginning of this chapter, Bonnet the biologist was cited, for his synonymous use of "evolution" and "development." In modern histories of music the word evolution seems to mean any one of the four concepts named above — development, progress, differentiation, or new growth. So when it is stated that "plainsong never underwent any process of evolution," it is hard to understand what is meant. Possibly it means that plainsong has never undergone any change. If so, the statement needs qualification; but if true it refutes the evolution doctrine, namely, that everything is constantly changing; that new forms are constantly evolving from the old. The *persistence* of plainsong, since its fixation in the Catholic Church, is an item for Chapter 13.

BIBLIOGRAPHY
(In addition to works cited in the notes)

Benedetto Croce, *History, its Theory and Practice,* as cited, Part I, Chapters VI–IX, and Chap. VI in Part II, on "The Historiography of Romanticism."

Frederick J. Teggart, "A Prolegomena to History," *University of California Publications in History,* Vol. 4, 1916, especially the sections dealing with history and philosophy, history and evolution.

[32] See Van der Straeten's *Histoire de la musique dans les Pays-bas.*

CHAPTER 12

SEQUENTIAL PATTERNS SUMMARIZED

THEIR INFLUENCE ON MUSIC EDUCATION

I. A FEW QUOTATIONS

THE TWO previous chapters have attempted a difficult task, one that may yet need further clarification and qualification, in future studies or by abler hands. That task is to get at the historical meaning of certain terms, words which have been used in philosophies of music history. If the attempt has been fairly successful, then the assumptions involved in the quotations which follow may be more clearly isolated and defined. These quotations have been located since the preceding chapters were written. Like many others which might have been chosen, they each epitomize some phase of the philosophy of music history in terms of development, progress, or evolution. Objections will be summarized in pp. 292-302 of this chapter.

1. PROGRESS, *meaning* DEVELOPMENT

" The perusal of Chronological Tables illustrating the history of music . . . enables the lover of music to obtain in a short time a comprehensive and clear view of the *gradual development of the art* from the earliest period of its cultivation recorded in history to the present day. . . . *There is no disconnection in the progress of an art.* . . .

" He (Czerny) gives an account of the music of the nations before the Christian era, of the music of our forefathers during the Middle Ages, and of the rise of our modern tone-art. This Section is arranged in eighteen Periods." [91], pp. 171-172.

2. PROGRESS, *meaning* IMPROVEMENT

" Just as the compositions of Pergolesi, of Handel, of Leo, etc., are infinitely above Carissimi's and Corelli's, so our good French masters are very superior to those admired at the end of the last century." [1]

[1] Quoted from Cahuzac by Wanda Landowska in *Music of the Past,* N. Y., Knopf, 1924; a lively rejoinder to doctrines of Progress.

3. PROGRESS, *meaning* MOVEMENT FORWARD IN TIME

" In Music, almost more than any subject which is at all controlled by the mind of man, there is a *ceaseless and inevitable progress.* Sometimes it may appear to be in a wrong direction, to be rushing headlong towards the abyss of cacophony, or meandering along devious and objectless ways of insipidity. Also *the rate of Progress must vary* considerably from time to time. Yet however slow such progress is, it can never for an instant be said that the stream part is stationary, and however rapid it may be there is always a sufficient modicum which moves with a steady flow, and keeps the *regular continuity of the stream, from its source in the beginnings* of human expression to its close, the day when it shall lose itself in the ocean of Infinity. And when that which has been carried in a wrong direction is eliminated by the passage of time, it is always found that an advance upon right lines has been made by the main body which still remains." [2]

4. PROGRESS, *meaning* A RISING CRESCENDO

" An historian of music said to me one day:

" ' In every age, we encounter the reproach addressed to innovators that they make excessive use of heavy sonorities (as did Fétis). The panegyrists of the past do not suspect that, in the *gradual upward movement of force* resides one of the greatest elements, if not the essential element, of musical progress.' " [3]

5. PROGRESS DOWNWARD, TO THE LOWER CLASSES

" If we now enter for a moment the music-halls of the metropolis, we shall notice that *the happy change is extending downward.* The members of our cathedral choirs do not disdain to produce before these once despised, and, it must be confessed, equivocal audiences, the partsongs of Mendelssohn and the ballads of Schubert." [4]

6. THE CESSATION OF PROGRESS, *meaning* DISINTEGRATION

This statement shows the dismay of the conservative, in a revolutionary period when new musical compositions cannot be fitted into the old time and value patterns:

" To-day, the division of music into distinct kinds, hierarchized according to their nobility, a division which resembled, in former times,

---

[2] Herbert Antcliffe, *Living Music,* Boston Music Co., 1912, p. 1.

[3] Landowska, as cited, Chap. VIII, which goes on to give a telling refutation of this enticing theory.

[4] Haweis, *Music and Morals* [85], p. 429. See also [296].

that of society with its graduated stages, becomes more and more ef-faced. This confusion of genera, a result of the confusion of classes and of the throwing over of all conventionality, is above all visible in the theater; grand opera and opéra-comique continually encroach on one another, and have become almost indistinguishable. This transformation is equally visible in the Symphony. In what category can we place a work like the *Prélude à l'après-midi d'un faune,* of M. Debussy? . . .

"In politics 'anarchy' signifies *the absence of a ruler;* in the matter of art it means the absence of all law of any kind forced on a composer." [158], pp. 202–203.

7. THE RECOVERY OF PROGRESS, *through* EDUCATION

A. Through Science, as Member of a Trinity

"*Music is a Language* . . . it possesses an intensity of expression and power of communicating emotion to which no spoken language can attain. . . .

"*Music is an Art.* The most subtle, the most ethereal and the most evanescent of all the arts. . . .

"*Music is a Science* . . . It is even a science of mathematics in the highest degree, for, after all is said and done, all the elements and all the processes that go to make up a musical work find their explanation and their *raison d'être in numbers* and in combinations of numbers. Unfruitful of herself and by herself, by strengthening Art and augmenting its productive power, 'Science is a dial that marks the hour of the progress accomplished.'" [5]

In England and America, however, educators have rebelled at dry, mechanistic ways of teaching music. But there has been a similar rebellion against the extreme, mystic and, to some, repellent theories of Richard Wagner. First, the moralist's theory, from Victorian England; this argues for the restoration of *progress through education* by a second method, the *antithesis of Wagner's plea for unity:*

[5] [147, p. 1]. Note the similarity of the argument to that in Wagner's theory of the "loving trinity." Later in this same book, Lavignac urges "the trinity of the *do,*" showing that three acts are involved in the first step with the young student: (1) *write do* on a staff; (2) *play do* on the keyboard, and (3) *sing do.* (pp. 89–90).

B. Through Separation of the Good from the Evil

" The opera is a mixture of two things which ought always to be kept distinct — the sphere of musical emotion and the sphere of dramatic action. . . .

" I say nothing against music being associated with situations, as in the *Midsummer Night's Dream*, or as in an oratorio. It is only when music is made part of the situation that it is misapplied. Let the event be in all cases left to the imagination. . . .

" We regard it (opera), musically, philosophically, and ethically, as an almost unmixed evil. . . .

" As opera is the most irrational and unintellectual form of music, so that class of cabinet music called string quartets is the most intellectual.

" The growing popularity of the orchestra is a sure sign of the popular progress in music . . . orchestral playing, in dealing with harmony, brings us directly into the abstract region of musical ideas." [6]

It is possible therefore, by taking the true pathway of " Pure Music " to progress

C. Through Development of Taste: Appreciation of the Higher Good

" In every drama there is a progressive history of emotion. This and not the outward event, is what music is fitted to express, and this truth has been seized upon by *Germany*." [85], p. 431.

Thus it has been assumed (1) that, as Combarieu said, " Real music is the symphony," (2) that the greatest " heights " of emotional expression have been reached by the German symphonists, and that therefore the goal of musical appreciation should be the symphony. But as in the development of art and the race,

" this particular study of the appreciation of music necessarily gets its results gradually and slowly, and requires . . . patience in the student. . . . We may thus figure the study of music appreciation as a sort of climb, laborious but exhilarating, up the mountain of art from the simplest and most primitive types like folk song to the most complex and elaborate, such as symphonies. Each individual, in developing his taste, thus passes naturally ' From Song to Symphony.' " [227].

[6] [85], pp. 423, 425–426, 431.

The student begins with folk songs, because they are "spontaneous."[7] Then,

"As men's lives have become better ordered, as higher standards of living have appeared, the sense of beauty has grown until, finally, this steady progress has resulted in the creation of certain *permanent types*. It must be kept in mind, however, that these primitive types are largely the result of instinctive effort, and not of conscious musical knowledge. The science of music, as we know it, did not exist when these songs were written."[8]

Then "Franz Schubert, justly called the 'father of the song,' began that extraordinary adventure which led music from the folk-song to the art-songs of Schumann, Franz, Brahms, Grieg, Wolf and Strauss." [227], p. 29.

The climb then leads through "Opera and Oratorio: the Earliest Artistic Music" to the much more important art of independent instrumental music.

"Before this point could be reached music had to go through a long phase of development, a sort of infancy, in which it was confined to the church." (pp. 57–58).

Finally, when Beethoven is reached,

"The reader . . . cannot but have been impressed by the character of preparation for some supreme achievement of which this development seems to partake throughout. All the laborious steps lead on to a goal which even in the splendid work of Haydn and Mozart is not quite reached." [164], p. 161.

After such a course of development, by listening actively, with ears, heart, and mind, by discriminating and analyzing, one comes to "appreciate" a Beethoven march, although the one by Sousa seemed more "catchy" and easier to grasp at first. The author does not say that Beethoven is "superior," and he is genuinely sincere

[7] See the quotation from Parry given in Ch. 7, III, in which "unconscious spontaneity" is found in the first stage, analysis in the second, and "recovery of spontaneity" with "right principles of action" in the third. According to that, medieval and Renaissance music belongs in the second stage, and is consequently a "transition" from the "spontaneous" to recovery of the spontaneous. Perhaps this is the reason for the great skips in music-appreciation texts which consider all "art music" previous to the eighteenth century as a mere period of apprenticeship or preparation.

[8] Surette and Mason [164], p. 17. Note here the similarity between this postulate of "permanent types" and Combarieu's plea for fixed and hierarchized divisions or categories.

here, as always, when he says that only a snob would reject the Sousa march because of its popular appeal. But in a note the author remarks that history is only adduced when composers, schools, and periods will contribute to the development of taste. It is apparent, therefore, that the developmental theory of history elaborated by Sir Hubert Parry (see Chapters 7 and 10 in this book) is the basis for Mason's system for developing taste. Beethoven's march is " superior " because of its place not in time, or in nationality, but in the developmental scale, " from simple to complex." Progress is therefore recovered through the evolution of taste.

So at this point, several passages are needed to show the misleading use of evolution patterns in music appreciation.

8. EVOLUTION, *meaning* PROGRESS FROM SIMPLE TO COMPLEX

" In the opening years of the eighteenth century, D. Scarlatti and J. S. Bach . . . were writing mostly brief dances in simple . . . forms. . . . Only a hundred years later Beethoven . . . was entering upon . . . (the second ' Period '),[9] in which he wrote Sonatas . . . that have never been excelled for breadth, solidity, and subtlety of architecture and for intense and various expression.

" This wonderful growth, like all evolutionary processes, was the gradual working out of a few simple principles. . . . Like other evolutions it was marked by a constantly increasing *differentiation,* so that elements that in its early stages were simple, as animals low in the zoölogical scale — for instance, molluscs — are simple, became in the end highly complex. . . . The first movement of Beethoven's *Hammerclavier* Sonata, op. 106, is to Scarlatti's Pastorale as a dog or a horse is to an oyster." [10]

For a description of the biological development of the orchestra itself, Combarieu says:

" For the study of musical evolution a more definite object than the musical mind might be taken: the orchestra, for instance, is comparable at the present day to some gigantic and powerful animal. . . .

" The orchestra experienced, at first, the indeterminate stage. . . . In the seventeenth and eighteenth centuries a specialization of the functions begins to appear . . . (Gluck's orchestra) may well be compared to a new-born child whose frame and organs are not fully formed. At

---

[9] Beethoven's life, like other histories, has been divided into three stages.

[10] [227], pp. 125-126. There are three stages in this evolution from Bach and Scarlatti to Beethoven. In a later chapter, the orchestra and its music goes through three stages of evolution in the Classical period.

the present day . . . the orchestra has reached the adult age, in possession of all its organs, which are clearly differentiated." [158], pp. 305–306.

But all these evolutionary patterns are in terms of development. It remains to show how the student of composition is supposed to learn from a dead art, because from that deceased ancestor a modern art evolved.

9. EVOLUTION, *meaning* GENERATION OF THE NEW FROM THE OLD

" The robust and ingenious art of the early masters is dead, just as the contrapuntal style is; but both have given birth to other artistic manifestations, which could not have existed without them and their fertile gropings. . . .

" That is Counterpoint." Therefore,

" Counterpoint becomes a precious and incomparable auxiliary for the completion of the higher studies of Harmony. . . .

" Counterpoint is a dead musical language which has given birth to the living musical language of the present day." [147], pp. 266, 264.

" Even a perfect work of art should be regarded as the seed deposited in the soul of posterity for it to continue to produce greater and more perfect things." [11]

The Critical Summary, which follows, reviews each of the foregoing statements. The numbers 1–9 in the summary refer back to the numbers in the above section.

II. CRITICAL SUMMARY

I. SOME OBJECTIONS TO PROGRESS THEORIES

1. The chronology of history is an indispensable tool, and the pattern presented by Czerny and Engel [91] is a useful, orderly presentation of the data furnished by biography, musical scores, and events in *general* history. Another great advantage of Czerny's scheme is the opportunity given for *comparative histories,* for without comparisons [12] historical facts remain isolated.

---

[11] Richard Strauss, " Is there a Progressive Party in Music? " (The Fontainebleau Manifesto), quoted by Landowska, as cited, p. 6.

[12] *Comparative history,* dealing thus with facts, is something quite different from the *Comparative Method* (see Ch. 10, 1), which compared, not facts, but hypothetical " stages." The stages are merely outlined, in Czerny and Engel, not compared in a developmental series.

2. The assumption that "our" music of the present is, must be or should be "better" than that of the past is a flattering one for the *amour-propre* of the "modern" composer. This volume has attempted to show that this bold premise has been the basis for comparison ever since the Quarrel of the Ancients and Moderns. Since that time, in other words, ever since general histories of music have been written, there have been two camps who have warred bitterly over this premise. The composer who wants to "break with the past" is pitted against the "old fossil" who believes that music "died" with some old master. Both are imposing a scale of value on the data presented by Czerny and Engel.

A few years ago, a very young and eager composer said, in a gathering of musicians: "I don't want to write music like Beethoven's; I want to write music that is *better* than his!" The answer to his first statement is that no twentieth-century composer need be expected to imitate the music of the century previous; he is free to write for the age in which he lives: Beethoven did. But Beethoven did it so well that the "moderns" are still learning something from him; the second statement made by the young man merely indicates the hold that the Idea of Progress has had on our minds.

The young man who made that statement has developed since that time. He himself has made progress; he is now one of the leaders in American music education, but he no longer talks that way; he is now convinced, with Wanda Landowska, that

"In every epoch one believes to serve us by ridding us of the burden of our treasures. The right of inheritance is suppressed in music. We are reduced to living on our daily resources. The domain being thus reduced and limited, there is a rush on the fashionable author to discover in him all the horrors and all the beauties. . . .

"But we want no more of these liberators, these false Messiahs. . . . Masterpieces are not wolves and do not devour each other, as Gounod said."[18]

3. But this Idea of Progress has been so powerful that it was regarded as a law of Nature (see Chap. 10, III). The statement by Antcliffe sums up admirably the assumptions discussed under "The Analogy of Motion" in Chapter 10, and in "The Confusion of Analogies" in Chapter 11 of this book.

[18] *Music of the Past,* as cited, p. 176.

Cahuzac's assumption finds progress in a hierarchical scale of value, in which composers represent fixed stages in a developmental scheme. Antcliffe goes farther and imposes the analogy of the flowing stream on the chronological data. As already noted, this analogy of the stream is a very familiar one, and Engel himself made a place for it, hypothetically. Engel did not actually use the analogy as a basis of interpretation, but he did say:

"A musical 'Stream of Time' might exhibit in various colours the natural connection between the several branches of the art of music, and their modifications conspicuous in its history." [91], p. 171.

One difficulty with the stream analogy is that it leaves no room for the enjoyment of quiet "pools of loveliness" or even exquisite lakes among the towering mountains of Great-Man's-Land.

4. The notion of progress upward has been illustrated in the theories of Fischer and Lavignac, who saw the history of music in terms of spiral ascent; in Schopenhauer's mystic scale of Will-Development from the bass upward; in Wagner's assertion that harmony grows upward like a pillar, and in the theories of upward growth of harmony and folk music from roots. Many others could be cited, and all can be met with the same objection — that everything that continues upward must, sooner or later, come down. There surely must be a law of gravitation in music history as in physics. As Landowska points out, the theory of the upward movement of sonority would make things very easy for the interpreter: the older the music, the more delicate the sound. That is all very well in going from the modern pianoforte and orchestra back to the harpsichord and chamber orchestra of the eighteenth century, but in the Baroque seventeenth century the theory breaks down. From Baroque magnificence and the use of *every available means for sound* to the Rococo delicacy, refinement, and economy of the *galant* style, seems like a *de*crescendo. But a cycle of history in terms of dynamics is out of the question; who would be so rash as to predict that our own Era of Amplification will be succeeded by a return to earphones (as desirable as that might seem to some)?

5–6. Interpretations of the opposite of musical progress, in terms of degradation or disintegration are apt, as in these examples, to show some correlation with similar interpretations of society. The moralist, since Plato, has argued that the "lower" grades of music should not be allowed to contaminate the "higher" classes of society.[14] The hierarchy of value is therefore tied to the hierarchical notion of class structure. The fixity of musical styles and human beings in rigid categories is very convenient for those who would keep both musical and human organisms "in their proper place."

There is a certain condescension in Haweis' remark. His cathedral singers are going "down," just as Plato's graduate students were to go below into the "cave," to bring the joys of Schubert and Mendelssohn to the "lower classes." Occasionally one still hears remarks to the effect that "Music is an aristocratic art" and "Thank God, the vulgar never *will* like him!" [217], p. 137.[15]

Combarieu wrote his lament over disintegration at the turn of the century, when Debussy, Schönberg, and Stravinsky were composing "transformations or mutations which at the time seem(ed) revolutionary." At the same time, movements for social reform were under way, and the stability of fixed classifications in society was threatened. The proletarian appeared in serious opera and ballet;[16] not as mere buffoon, or in the safe refuge of distant romanticism, as in romantic opera; but in his everyday working clothes. And in spite of Haweis' note of alarm, it was found that "the lower classes" were just as capable of appreciating music as those "in the higher brackets" (often more so).

So Combarieu viewed with anxiety "this confusion of *genera,* a result of the confusion of classes," and he shrank in terror from that "great animal" the modern orchestra, with its "unbridled flow of instrumental force in which one seems to hear growling the formidable voices of the crowd." [158], p. 204.

But Combarieu was not discouraged, for "this state of dissolution is at the same time one of fruitful regeneration." (*Ibid.*)

2. CONFUSED EVOLUTION PATTERNS IN THREE COUNTRIES

A. Unity and Generation Theories in France

As noted above, Combarieu accepted the Wagnerian theory echoed by Richard Strauss. (9). Both accept the theory that new music grows out of the old, and Lavignac uses that theory (9) to show the need for studying counterpoint. This involves the theory of natural selection; as Combarieu says,

[14] See the last paragraph of the Athenian's speech, in Book III, 701, Plato's *Laws.*
[15] Quoted with reference to Scriabin.
[16] As in *I Pagliacci, La Bohème, Petroushka.*

"Species once extinct never reappear (Darwin). In music also, in which there is continuous evolution, we may speak of 'extinct species.' At the present day many kinds once held in honour have disappeared from use." [158], p. 314.

These questions therefore are important, "What species *do* survive?" And what species are *capable* of new generation? It is assumed that "masterpieces" survive, in answer to the first question. But in answer to the second question, Combarieu claims that at the same time, it is only the masterpieces that can generate new progeny!

"Living beings are distinguished from material bodies by the faculty they have, after having been engendered, to generate in their turn. The belief in spontaneous generation is now classed among errors championed by nobody. A musical work is a spontaneous creation, but this spontaneity could not exist had it not proceeded from and, as it were, been called forth by a more or less distant heredity. A masterpiece, symphonical or lyrical, is never an isolated fact. If preceded by a line of ancestors, to it succeeds a line of descendants. Hence we see that compositions cannot be likened to living beings, except in the case of compositions of a superior order." [158], pp. 308–309.

Now the confusion in these statements is apparent: How could a great masterpiece survive for posterity if it is to be considered only as a parent form for new (and "better") works?

In England, these generation theories have not been well received. Haweis' statement (7B) offers evidence of the Victorian attitude toward opera as "a defective form," and the Victorian was not to be convinced of its worth by Wagner's arguments for "the loving trinity." French writers had no such scruples; as pointed out in Chapter 8, the union of the arts was no anomaly to them; worship, dance, ballet, pageantry have all been dramatic elements of French culture. But the Puritan influence on opera and drama has already been remarked; in Haweis we merely find Victorian conformation of the "decree of separation." So a philosophy of music history based on unity and generation was impossible in England. Furthermore, since the modification of evolution theories in biology, the analogy of musical generation only appears occasionally as a picturesque metaphor. Two phrases in Combarieu's statement, however, have been and continue to be influential in Anglo-American systems of teaching which link history to appreciation. These phrases are those which refer to *spontaneity* and to "*compositions of a superior order.*"

B. Spencerian Theory in England and America

Combarieu and Lavignac in France, Sir Hubert Parry in England, and Daniel Gregory Mason in this country were or are all historians, all leaders in music education, and all desirous of extending the scope of music appreciation. The achievements of these men are not for one moment to be under-estimated; they have stood for progress in the field of education and one should give due recognition of their achievements. That their efforts have not been in vain is evidenced by the increasing attention now being given to the study of music in English and American schools.

These remarks are therefore not made in any attempt to belittle the work of these men — far from it. The only aim is to continue to trace the assumptions followed up in these pages. In doing so, it is found that Parry and Mason have used evolutionary theory, not in the Darwinian-Wagnerian sense accepted by the French, but in the developmental sense employed by Spencer and Victorian anthropology. The methods and assumptions in Parry's *Art of Music* were analyzed in Chapter 7. The use of the same methods was discussed in Chapter 10, under the Comparative Method. In both chapters an attempt was made to show that these theories of development assumed that Western European culture is at the apex of cultural development; that all Oriental, African, Indian and other forms of music are "inferior."

In spite of the grave responsibility faced by modern education for inculcating better international understanding, no textbooks on music history and music appreciation in general use in our schools stress the value of *each* musical system *in its own culture;* the tendency still exists, to compare "semi-civilized" or "primitive" systems with our own highly "advanced" and "superior" forms of art. Progressive music teachers who wish to demonstrate the exquisite beauties of Balinese, Javanese, Hindu, East African, and Indian music can easily find volumes of record materials for demonstration, but no support for such demonstrations in our textbooks on *appreciation*. The condescension of Haweis in referring to the "lower classes" can be paralleled with "The First Steps as Revealed by History" with quotations from exotic music to illustrate "The First Stage," then "a step or two higher," before going on

to the "superior" achievements of music in Western civilization.
[164], I, pp. 10–11.

The same concern is manifested with *differences* in our own
Western music. Chapter 13 will try to show that these differences
offer new possibilities for comparison, enjoyment, and learning.
But on the basis of developmental theory, it seems impossible to
enjoy, analyze, and appreciate a work of musical art in terms of
its own period, as a vital interpretation of the culture in which the
composer lived, moved, and had his being. According to current
instruction, every work must be compared with some other in a
sequential pattern, either in time or in value. Everything has "developed" from something else, and must find its place in the
categories. But Combarieu complained that the categories were all
confused; progress was at a standstill. For him the remedy was
to wait for "new generation," in the hope that it might be better.
Mason finds a better remedy, however, and that is to *elevate taste*
by means of a course of "development." Thus, in the present,
students may learn to appreciate the *highest* and *best* in music, by
climbing upward, thus following the upward evolution of the art.

The climb "upward" is through certain fixed stages, at each of
which the student is to contemplate the advance made over the
stage previous, from the lowest stage of primitive music to "real
folk song," then to art song and the small forms of instrumental
music to the larger work for chamber music and symphony. These
successive stages of contemplative study will insure the student's
progress and restoration of the "division of music into distinct
kinds, hierarchized according to their nobility." Certain difficulties
are apparent, however. First, the impression is given that folk song
worthy of the name must be very old. This is misleading, because
new folk songs are being composed and passed around orally,
every day, in many parts of the world. Where it is not done, it
could be done, with encouragement — even in a schoolroom. Second, the assumption concerning the origins of "communal" folk
songs in instinct reappears. This was discussed in Chapter 9.

Third, the sequential pattern assumes that the art song is the
aftermath of folk song. As already pointed out, the reverse may
be the case.

Fourth, to call Schubert the "father" of the art song is to revive
the great-man theory in a naive sense, to the neglect of the Englishmen, at least from John Dowland onward; the song literature of

the Romance countries, from the troubadours to the Italian melo-
dists of the seventeenth century; the German singspiel writers down
to Mozart; and song writers in our own country. Francis Hopkin-
son was writing songs before Schubert was born.

Finally, the neglect of music with words is the most glaring
defect of modern textbooks on musical appreciation. The *Lied* is
studied not so much for the union of words and music as for the
" principles of design " which make the art song a mere " preparation " for the enjoyment of " real music "— the symphony.

Opera is not condemned, as in Haweis, but neglected just as
carefully as if it were for moral reasons.[17] References to early church
music as a stage of " infancy " and to the " absence of rhythm " in
sixteenth-century music must be rather confusing to the thousands
of students in this country who are singing old music in our *a
cappella* choirs. Teachers of theory are awakening to the fact that
sixteenth-century counterpoint was a matter of counter-*rhythms*
conditioned by the rhythms of speech. The revival of interest in
Gilbert and Sullivan, novel speech rhythms in our popular music
(the quaint folk music of Manhattan cliff-dwellers), the increasing
use of *recitative* all give hope that the separation of " pure music "
from speech and drama may not continue indefinitely.

Finally, the comparison between the marches of Beethoven and
of Sousa offers a very interesting exercise for any student. But any
value-comparison between the two in a sequential pattern will inevitably involve analogy (unless we are content to note that Sousa
comes a century later in the chronological chart).

According to the Progress theory, the Sousa march must be better, because we have moved forward to bigger and better marches
— or else it is worthless, because music has slid backward since
Beethoven.

According to the generation theory, one march is a direct de-
scendant of the other. The German nationalist will claim both,
because of original " roots; " the 100-per-cent American will argue
differently.

But according to the theory of Development, a scale of value is
involved, in a sequential pattern, " from folk song to symphony."
Beethoven the symphonist stands at the peak of the mountain to

---

[17] Twenty pages out of 238 are given to opera in Mason [227], but not one in
Surette and Mason's *Appreciation* [164].

be climbed by the student; Sousa is at a lower level, more easily "appreciated" because his march is more "catchy" at first.

There are difficulties here, however, because Professor Mason does not say *which* march by Beethoven:

1. If he means the Finale of the Fifth Symphony, there will be no argument concerning the greater complexity and subtlety of that magnificent paean of joy and confidence in human perfectibility. But why compare that work with Sousa's interpretation of the cocky, carefree, impertinent, crisp, devil-may-care confidence of our Spanish War era? Each served and can still serve a different function; neither can take the place of the other.

2. If reference is made to Beethoven's funeral marches, either from the Sonata op. 26, the Eroica Symphony, or the Allegretto from the Seventh Symphony (although the latter is not so labelled), then comparisons of any kind are doubly difficult. Questions of functional significance and emotional appropriateness would seem to rule out comparisons altogether.

3. But if Beethoven's "Turkish March" from *The Ruins of Athens* be compared with "The Stars and Stripes Forever," there might be some very intelligent arguments in favor of Sousa's as the "better" military march. The simple repetitions in the former would seem to place it low in the developmental scale, compared with the more complex rhythms of Sousa's thematic material, his ingenious descants for the piccolos, and counterpoint for the trombones.

It is difficult to see why students should not appreciate both men, each for his own worth. Adequate appreciation and comparison of these respective composers' contributions might involve a comparison of *all* of Beethoven's marches, compared with *all* of Sousa's. That study would reveal the variety of Beethoven's works in that style, for the various functions called for in religious, dramatic, festival, concert, and intimate performance. Sousa's limitations would appear when all of his marches, on the same pattern, are found to have been written either for the opera stage or the parade ground.

Similarly, the same difficulties arise with the developmental analogy when the attempt is made to find the inevitable "three stages" in the development of form from Bach and Scarlatti (early eighteenth century) to Beethoven (early nineteenth). The sonata form, in citation 8, appears in Scarlatti's *Pastorale* as an organism low in the scale, as homogeneous and undifferentiated as an oyster; within less than a century "it" has become as fully differentiated and "developed" as a quadruped. A Beethoven minuet illustrates the "second stage." But Bach, Scarlatti, and Beethoven wrote great quantities of music for all sorts of functions; they did not work on the development of a "form." There is no sonata or symphony in the history of music which has been passed on for completion or modification to successive generations; *each composer writes his own.*

Students of architecture do not study the "evolution of cathedral form," although successive generations of men do work on the same structure. They study *styles,* because each generation endeavors to perpetuate its peculiar ways of doing things in the changes and additions made. But in music, *style changes even more rapidly* than in architecture, because each artist builds his own structure and can change form and style at will. *In his own development* different styles come to expression, due to his interests, his patronage (a very important matter), the functions his music has to serve, and the prevailing modes of thought in his environment. Thus the scale of "development" can only be made to work when a few isolated works are used for illustration to prove the theory. The expanding melodic line of Bach's dance music is, as already pointed out, far more complex than Beethoven's Minuet in G; no two fugues of Bach have the same form, and all are so different from Beethoven's that there is no comparison. Comparison of Beethoven's Moonlight Sonata with Bach's Chaconne or Passacaglia might reverse the "three stages." The scale of "development," like all the other Progress patterns, is a *reversible pattern* imposed upon the chronological tables of Czerny.

C. The Social Significance of Sequential Patterns

The organic hypothesis of the Romantic era held that culture, in all its phases, evolves as a whole; that the new is generated from the old. These generation theories lead, as has been noted, into mystic belief, either that the new will continually improve, or that it will eventually ruin civilization. Such hypotheses can ignore the separations and divisions that exist in modern society, and have not yet made any objective conclusions possible. But hypotheses based upon separation are as inadequate as those based on unity.

Art, as Tolstoi said, should be communication. Of all the arts,

the musical arts of harmony, rhythm of speech, rhythm of movement, and inflection of tone might conceivably be not only the
"international language" postulated by Mason (as cited), but also
an interracial, intercultural, intercommunity, and interclass means
of communication. But, probably more than in any other art, the
philosophies concerning music history tend either toward the mystic
organic hypothesis just noted, or else to theories of *separate* evolution and the belief in *divisions* of music which are often as rigid
in music education as they were in the days of Ornithoparcus and
Grassineau (see Chapter 2.)

The sequential pattern (1) of Czerny and Engel had two
parallel columns, one listing musical events and the other events
in general history. In 1886, William S. Rockstro interpreted those
parallels thus:

"Side by side with the political history of a nation . . . runs a col-
lateral narrative, dealing with its advancement in Science, Literature,
Commerce, and the thousand units that make up the sum of its general
civilization.

"Side by side with the exoteric history of Art, as set forth in the
achievements of the men of Genius . . . runs the esoteric record of its
technical development." [117], Preface, 1918 ed.

But the author, while offering a very suggestive tool for the use
of the student, gives no suggestions for its use. Current philosophies
of music history only allowed one interpretation, namely, that the
two "streams" of culture were flowing "side by side," that art
and technique themselves evolved separately. Today, Bücken, Bekker, Dyson and others have called attention to some of the functional relationships of music to the culture in which it appears.
The old concept of parallel streams postulates a separation which
does not exist.

The citations from Haweis, Combarieu, Mason and Surette,
above, reveal another picture of separate series of development.
Haweis demanded that music and drama should go their ways
separately; Combarieu, although recognizing drama in his *Histoire*
[189], had defined music in his earlier work [158] as "thinking
in tone — without concepts." Parry contributed to this with his
strictures on early opera, and his emphasis upon "the rise of music
as an *independent art.*" Surette and Mason, strongly influenced by
Parry, have practically omitted opera and church music, as already
noted, from "music appreciation."

Music and drama, as if in obedience to Haweis' doctrine of separation, have therefore gone their respective ways in American music education. There is no general history of opera published in this country; no general history of religious music; both could very well be combined in a history of dramatic music. Do we fear that music will say something that we do not want to hear? Combarieu heard the "growling . . . formidable voices of the crowd" in modern orchestral music; his *Histoire* stopped with Wagner; others had to bring it down to the present from which he shrank in dismay. Will we not be suspected of wanting to remove music from the ordinary concerns of life if we continue to follow Haweis' advice, and keep "pure music" in a realm undefiled by dramatic utterance, in a separate scale of development?

In any case, this method of separation is exactly the same one employed in nationalistic theories of separate evolution and in the communistic theories of music history in class separation. The nationalistic theories have been discussed at length in Chapters 8 and 10, but an additional word of explanation should be added here on the communistic theory.

The ideological platform of the Russian Association of Proletarian Musicians stated this philosophy of music history, in substance: There are two streams of evolution; one from folk music, the music of the toilers, the exploited and the oppressed, and the other of art music, the older music of the ruling class, followed by that of the bourgeoisie. At first bourgeois music was revolutionary, resulting in the art of Beethoven. But with the decay of capitalism it has become decadent. The trained artists must therefore devote themselves to the service of the folk — the toilers.[18]

This pattern is very interesting when compared with the music-appreciation pattern, which also begins with folk music. In this pattern, according to Forsyth, the artists of the sixteenth century drank at the spring of folk music to bring life to a mechanical art. According to that theory, music educators could praise George Gershwin for living in Catfish Alley to get atmosphere for *Porgy and Bess,* to revitalize an art steeped in European romanticism. That would be impossible, however, in the scale of value provided, in which folk song must be old, and very remote from our own. Folk music for this scale must be the selected, "permanent types" from which pure music for instruments has evolved. The "Evo-

---

[18] See Nicolas Slonimsky, *Music since 1900,* Norton, N. Y., 1937, pp. 549 ff.

lution of Folk Music" as such is usually dropped in "Chapter II."

Another romantic evasion of folk music and of social realities is found in the anthropological approach fostered in educational circles since the days of Edward MacDowell. Attention was called to this sequential pattern in the comments on the *Creative Music* movement [19] initiated by Satis Coleman. Influenced also by Parry's theory of development, and Rowbotham's doctrines, a course of development from "little savages" on upward was to follow the development of the art. Now this system did not and could not possibly begin with primitive music; it could only begin with surmises as to what primitive music might be like. Edward Mac-Dowell used Indian themes very successfully in his music, possibly on the assumption that American music should recognize the aboriginal idiom. But it is difficult to follow a line of evolution from early Indian music down to MacDowell, because there has been none of the cultural interaction between Indians comparable to that which the whites have had with the Negroes. The extermination and isolation of the Indian have allowed very few Indian musicians to acquire any of our musical techniques, but they are extremely musical and their music is anything but primitive. On the other hand, MacDowell's own development was conditioned by his eleven years in Germany, not among Indians. So the sequential patterns involve social confusion: in one course of study, the child is uprooted from his urban environment to follow a sequence which only exists in theory, to begin with "savagery" in order to progress to European ways of making music; in the other, the American child begins with folk song remote from his own, not to continue in channels of song and vocal communication, but to leave these lowlands in order to climb the heights of sonata form.

Why not begin with the student where he is?

Why not find a point of departure in the student's own environment, in his own experience, and from that build up a learning sequence which will gradually give him a wider and truer appreciation of his musical heritage?

These questions have become very insistent, with the inauguration of projects of that character in other fields of work. The result is that some imaginative teachers of music are turning away from the artificial sequential patterns imposed by conventional texts to find the *learning sequence* appropriate for a given situation. When that

[19] In Chapter 8, III, 1.

is once found, teachers can turn back to available texts, to pick and choose from the content to suit their purposes.

Some teachers, not only of appreciation and history, but also of theory and composition, are also beginning to recognize the possibilities for spontaneous creative activity in one's own environment. Some have gone so far in that direction that the term "creative" has almost become a magic catchword, with as many different interpretations as were formerly applied to "Nature."

The questions raised above therefore demand further inquiry into the history of our ideas; why has "the simplest and easiest to know" been sought in a remote, even hypothetical past?

3. THE PROBLEMS OF "SIMPLICITY" AND "NATURE," "SPONTANEITY" AND "CREATION"

The exploration of the philosophical and educational implications involved in these terms is far beyond the scope of this inquiry. All that can be done is to point out a few historical uses of these terms in the literature of music history and music education, in the hope that others may be induced to explore them more carefully.

A. Man and Nature; Music and Simplicity

Descartes said, in his *Discourse on Method,* that we should begin "with objects the simplest and easiest to know" and proceed by "assigning in thought a certain order (even if a fictitious one)" [20] in order to arrive at "knowledge of the more complex." The dualism of mind and matter was another concept which Descartes helped to fix in modern thinking. Much later, just as modern histories of music began to appear, Jean-Jacques Rousseau found nothing in his overcivilized environment which was "simple and easy to know," so he contributed to the eighteenth-century belief in the naturalness and simplicity of the "noble savage." Modern thought may have misinterpreted or exaggerated Descartes' emphasis on the necessary sequence; but at any rate, ever since Rousseau, Nature and simplicity have been something we must "get back to;" civilized man should "get away from it all" to recover simplicity and "spontaneity." The Back-to-Folk-Song movement of Parry and the Back-to-Savagery methods of Mrs. Coleman are closely related to Rousseau's theories. Now Rousseau himself said

[20] These words were added by the translators in the *Works,* Cambridge Ed., Vol. I, p. 92.

that facts were to be laid aside " as they do not affect the question." He confessed no interest in "historical truths" but in

"conditional and hypothetical reasonings, calculated to explain the nature of things rather than to explain their actual origin." [21]

The quest for origins, as shown in Chapter 9, is no search for "historical truths" nor for *actual* origins; it is merely an attempt to explain "the nature of things." The "actual origin" of traditional folk songs is unknown; they are therefore well fitted as educational material for those who believe, with Rousseau, that we must get *back* to a hypothetical State of Nature.

From this State of Nature Rousseau used a sequential pattern, beginning with "the first instincts." This makes it possible to say that "primitive folk songs" are "instinctive," not the result of "conscious art; " the latter is only found at "a higher stage of development." For Rousseau these first instincts were self-preservation, the search for nourishment, and the urge to reproduce. Wagner, as noted above, found analogy in the latter for his theory of folk song, but MacDowell found it in "the first law of Nature"—self-preservation. In Chapter 8 of this book, MacDowell is quoted on origins. In the context he quotes Theophrastus, but does not cite the source of his information. He says that Theophrastus found the origins of music in the whole range of human emotion, a sufficiently broad theory to admit of no argument. [22] But as if impelled by Rousseau, MacDowell, like Rowbotham, insists on finding the *simplest, strongest* emotion of all, in *fear.*

And in the following passage the assumptions of several centuries are summed up in the notion that man and Nature are not only separate, but pitted against each other:

"Man is not part of Nature . . . Mankind lives in isolation, and Nature is a thing for him to conquer. Nature exists, while Man *thinks.* . . . The strain of Nature in man gave him the dance, and it is his godlike fight against Nature that gave him impassioned speech." [186], "Song vs. Instrumental Music," p. 28.

[21] Jean-Jacques Rousseau, *A Discourse on the Origin of Inequality,* N. Y., Everyman's Library, 1927, pp. 175–176.

[22] Theophrastus' word for "origins" was the equivalent of the Latin *principia,* according to G. M. Stratton, in *Theophrastus and the Greek Physiological Psychology before Aristotle,* N. Y., Macmillan, 1917. Stratton lists the *principia* as "pain, pleasure, and inspiration; *any one of these* may change the character of the voice so that it loses its customary form and becomes musical." (The italics are mine. W. D. A.)

From that MacDowell, like Rowbotham, concludes that man commenced his "control of Nature" by using simple natural objects, such as hollow logs, for the production of rhythmical sounds. This spontaneous, instinctive process therefore marked the origins of music. Of all the numerous origin theories, this is one of the few known and accepted in American education.

Now Edwin A. Burtt has made a brilliant analysis of the assumptions involved in MacDowell's statement that "Man is not a part of Nature." In *The Metaphysical Foundations of Modern Physical Science* (London, 1925), Burtt traces the steps taken in modern science to remove man from his own universe in order that he could come to some scientific conclusions about it. But he concludes that in so doing man paid a stiff price for his mathematical and scientific achievements. He finds that the revolution in man's ways of thinking about the universe began between 1500–1700. This was the period when the controversies over musical instruments and their problems were so heated (as noted in Chapter 2). Burtt also finds that

"teleological explanations, accounts in terms of Use and the Good, become definitely abandoned in favor of the notion that true explanations, of man and his mind as well as of other things, must be in terms of their simplest parts." (As cited, pp. 15–16).

We have found in this inquiry that since that same period, during the "rise of instrumental music as an independent art," the debates as to whether music is an art or a science are as insistent as the debates over the conflict between science and religion.

At any rate, our musical instruments are among the great achievements of science and invention; they have therefore been hailed as symbolic of man's "control over Nature," from the savage in the State of Nature, beating on a hollow log to frighten away evil spirits, to the drummer in Beethoven's symphonies.

The Nature-philosophy of Rousseau then meets the Nature-philosophy of his contemporary Rameau, who, as shown before, managed to fix eighteenth-century concepts of natural harmony and natural form in theory teaching for a century and a half.[23] The

---

[23] A leader in American theory of music puts it this way: "Of all the possible scales, there is *only one fundamental or natural scale, namely our major*. . . . The *source and genesis of all music are the chords*. . . . *The minor mode is artificial,* a modification of the major mode in which *Nature* acquiesces." Percy Goetschius, *The Structure of Music*, Phila., Presser, 1934, pp. 14, 53, 54. Cf. Chap. 9 of this book

Italians of the eighteenth century with their concepts of melody were accepted by Burney and other influential writers as the arbiters of simplicity, grace, and "natural" art. The frequency of the four-measure, four-phrase formula in the simpler music of that classical period has perpetuated the tendency to regard four as "natural."

So deeply ingrained is this reverence for the "normal" four-measure phrase that a recent textbook finds it necessary to explain a five-measure phrase by Schubert as containing "an extra measure!"[24] In the same text a French folk song containing thirty-one measures, instead of the normal thirty-two, is analyzed as showing an "elision" of one measure (p. 29).

Parry and other nineteenth-century theorists (but not Combarieu) then were able to find that the spontaneity of "primitive folk song" was "recovered" in the eighteenth century, after "principles of design" had been laboriously groped for by the poor, benighted forerunners who worked in the darkness of the centuries before the Enlightenment.

This all sounds very convincing until one studies the Bach family, to name only one.[25] The Bach methods of music education, typical of the eighteenth century, did *not* involve going "back to" anything. Bach learned music by avidly hearing and *copying the music of his older contemporaries.* His many children did the same; they found simple, natural, spontaneous elements *in the music about them;* all of them wrote dance music in the popular forms of the day, then they turned around and wrote, sang, and played variations on pious hymn tunes. The *Inventions* were very difficult for a student of the Victorian era, brought up on Kohler's *Piano*

---

on "Origins in Numbers" and "Origins in Scales;" also Chap. 5 on the Enlightenment.

It might also be noted in this connection that such authoritative pronouncements concerning "Nature" have been possible, again, because of Cartesian theory. Descartes postulated the "invariability of the 'laws of Nature;'" consequently a theory, if put forward in the sacred name of Nature, can and must be applicable to any music, any students, at any time or place!

[24] Spalding, *Music as an Art and a Language,* Boston, 1920. "When an extra measure is systematically introduced into each phrase of four measures we have what is known as 'five-bar rhythm.'" (p. 63).

[25] "Music appreciation" includes the study of the music of J. S. Bach, not as a continuer of the great Baroque traditions and of medieval polyphony, but as a "founder." Surette and Mason's text [164] jumps from folk song directly to the polyphonic music of this composer.

Method, which began with *simple* whole notes in the "simple, natural" key of C, in the "simple, natural" G clef. But these *Inventions* were elementary exercises for Bach's children (who read in all clefs and all keys) and are getting to be that today, once more, in modern methods of piano teaching.

The Bach family were so proficient in improvisation that a *quodlibet* was a favorite pastime.[26] But the nineteenth-century teacher, as already noted, was very much concerned with Parry's "principles of right action," so that ear training and spontaneity tended to be suppressed. The improvisations and antics of a modern jazz band are shocking to many, but they are regarded by some thinking observers, like Panassié, as healthy signs, comparable to the extemporaneous freedom of eighteenth-century artists, of which we have accounts, but no records in notation.[27]

At any rate, none of the masters praised in laudatory texts on appreciation went *back* in the beginnings of their education; the backward tendency in our sequential patterns was unknown to them. They began as *apprentices* in choir schools, theater orchestras, chamber orchestras and learned music as a *craft* which had functional value in a society which demanded *new* music without rejecting the old. They cared nothing about primitive savages; the eighteenth-century romancing on that subject did not affect music-education methods, although composers like Mozart, Haydn, and others introduced some amusing *Chinoiserie* and "Turkish" trifles to yawning courtiers. Young people knew folk songs, to be sure, but they did things with them; they also knew Italian opera and French dance music, and they learned to vary them. Today, the Variation is again being introduced in orchestral arrangements of the song hits of the day. The study of that form could very well begin with the modern devices of this sort, then work backward through Romantic forms to the eighteenth-century variety.

If Mozart and Haydn were to come to life today, they might conceivably gasp with admiration at the mechanical but "simple" and

[26] *Quodlibet* is Latin for "jam session."

[27] Teachers worried over youthful absorption in "jazz" and "swing" will never win converts by exhortation and edicts concerning "good" music. To profess, better yet, to show sincere interest in jazz, then to ask students to describe it, to seek its *actual* origins, the uses for which it is designed, and the reasons for its appeal has been known to get interesting results. The "jazz fiend" is sometimes inebriated and inarticulate about the subject; but those who can talk intelligently about it, as, e.g., Mr. Benjamin Goodman, can also discuss and perform other kinds of music as well.

" natural " music of Harline, Churchill, and others in Disney's pictures.[28]

If Palestrina and Orlandus Lassus were to come to life and hear the beautiful work being done in our school choirs and then the comparatively lifeless music of many adult church groups, they might be astonished at various things, among them the separation of music from the function for which it was intended.

If Wagner were to come back, it is hard to resist the surmise that he might find opportunity for unity of the arts without having to philosophize about it at all.

As pointed out in Chapter 8, in discussing Chavez and his *Toward a New Music,* there are exciting elements of interest in the music of the present in relation to new developments in technology, economic conditions, and social relationships. Keen young people are alive to them. Perhaps we, as teachers, do not begin with the child where he is, because we have not sought for the simple, natural phases of life that can be found in our complex society. Perhaps the reverse of Spencer's formula may be true, for is it not true that education begins with heterogeneity?

B. From the Complex to the Simple

Perhaps we have talked too much about the possibility of " an American music." Our America is only part of North America; Canadians can very rightly claim the right to be called Americans, although their musical heritage is largely British (and French in Quebec). But Central and South America contain heterogeneous groups, each of which is " recovering spontaneity " by finding natural elements in the music of its own environment.[29]

So *in certain localities* Indian music can be studied in its interaction with European styles introduced by colonists and missionaries. This is not the case in MacDowell's New England or New York, but it is possible in parts of Texas,[30] New Mexico, Arizona,

---

[28] Mozart's only organ music was for mechanical organs. Note also Haydn's interest in music which " clicks," as in the " Clock " symphony.

[29] See William Berrien, " Latin-American Composers and Their Problems," in the *Modern Language Forum,* Vol. XXII, Feb., 1937; also the *Boletin Latino-Americano de Música,* pub. in various South American cities in turn, under the direction of Francisco Curt Lange, Institudo de estudios superiores del Uruguay, Seccion de Investigaciones Musicales, Montevideo, Uruguay. (Ano II, Tomo II, e.g., Publ. in Lima, has 479 pp.) See also Mario de Andrade, [309]; the first chapter begins with Brazilian folk music.

[30] See Lota May Spell, *Music in Texas,* Austin, Texas, 1936.

California, and some other areas. In Louisiana the French-Creole element is important; in Maine and Vermont, the French-Canadian; in Cleveland, San Francisco, New York, and Chicago, the polyglot elements that make up our urban populations. In Santa Barbara, California, successful festival programs were put on recently by the various nationalities represented in the city, each vying with the other to display the musical, choreographic, and poetic beauties of a cultural heritage. This was done under the wise encouragement of a public-school system which has gone far beyond the old fallacy of " 100-per-cent Americanism." We are beginning to see that the glory of these United States is not merely in its unity, but in its differences. If the music history of the United States be studied as the combined music histories of each state, with tolerant enjoyment of the contribution each has to offer, we may begin to see new possibilities in the study of folk song.

So just as America is a heterogeneous term for different countries in two continents, it is by no means simple when it means " the United States." And as it is with states and provinces, so it is with individuals. Every student possesses a heterogeneous heritage, a heterogeneous bundle of dreams, likes and dislikes, and a musical vocabulary that is richer than any known to previous student generations in history. Many a young student, thanks to the wide dissemination of music by radio and record, has absorbed the rudiments of the musical system about him before entering the schoolroom. Sometimes these rudiments involve rhythms, melodies, and harmonies that would have seemed " advanced " or complicated to an older generation. For that reason, there are communities where students are now studying courses in music appreciation which begin with Stravinsky and Richard Strauss, Gershwin and the complicated musical arts of Bali, then work backward in time to " simpler " styles of music which are not in fashionable vogue at the moment. There is no set formula for a learning sequence, but it need never lose sight of that which is significant in the student's present experience, in the history being made in his own day.

If in answer to the paragraphs above, the reply is that we are not in a position to evaluate the present, that might be granted; but this warning against setting up absolute values in art is worth noting:

" Since all values are dispositional values, and dispositions are subject to the empirical laws of mutation, it follows that neither in the individual nor in the social consciousness can a value be in any sense absolute." [81]

As Goethe said, we may as well accept *Erscheinungen* as *gegebene Tatsachen,* as, in the words of Turgot, we must eventually deal with *la nature, telle qu'elle est.*
Why then have we continued to look backward for spontaneity and worth-while creation?

C. The Problem of "Spontaneous Generation"

One more phrase in that mine of information on evolutionary method, Combarieu's *Music, Its Laws and Evolution,* gives the cue to a possible answer. As already cited, on p. 296, he remarks that "the belief in spontaneous generation is now classed among errors championed by nobody."

That remark leads one to reflect upon what may be only a curious coincidence. The rejection of the great-man theory by leading music historians in favor of evolutionary histories of musical form is contemporary with scientific rejection of the theological doctrine of Special Creation and the theory of spontaneous generation which lingered on until the days of Pasteur.

In Chapters 3 and 6, it was remarked that the great-man theory in music histories was, in a sense, a rationalization of the theory of music's divine origin. Music of the highest order could only come from divinely endowed, "original" genius. On that basis a history could be organized into epochs, each of which was dominated by one leading figure. But when evolutionary biological concepts came to modify music histories, the composer had to be studied in terms of his inheritance and his "antecedents," then in terms of a "link" or progenitor through whom music was passed on to "successors." All the Before and After concepts are essential, to be sure, but the great man no longer stood on his own as he had under the great-man theory.

Now "great men" are facts to be recognized, and theories about them can never be completely superseded, nor will the divine-origin theory ever be completely discarded. Millions of people still believe in Creation, as ultimate origins are as inexplicable as ever.

So Combarieu, who also rationalized the divine-origin theory in

[81] Baldwin, *Dict. of Philos. and Psych.,* as cited; article on "Worth," Vol. II, p. 825.

his belief that music began with magic and ritual, contradicts himself thus, just a few pages earlier than his denial of spontaneous generation:

"Genius is musical intelligence at its highest point, but it wholly escapes physiology. It is often served by moderate or defective organs. It is unconscious and spontaneous.

"It is a power which resembles the primary principles of Nature." [158], p. 249.

But for the student who is not a genius, education *is* possible, and that is also to proceed from the simple to the complex. Combarieu does not advocate going from savagery to civilization, or from folk song to art, but from one note to more notes, still a very popular theory in music teaching:

"The formation of a musician's talent [32] . . . brings clearly to mind the formation of a living being. In lieu of studying it in history, it can be viewed in the individual, who repeats and often exemplifies the evolution of the species. The musical mind of the child who has just learnt his notes, their places on the keyboard, and the elements of the grammar, only knows the parasitical life. When he has reached exercises in harmony, he resembles, listening to his master's word, the embryo which in the maternal womb assimilates nutritive matter. He develops, as the biologists say, by the addition of new to pre-existing parts.

"After having placed notes one atop the other, in order to construct chords, he passes on to the study of counterpoint; and it is for him a new life, a kind of metamorphosis, like that of a tadpole which, first adapted for the aquatic life of ponds, afterwards fits him for life on land. He eliminates from his mind certain now useless ideas; henceforth left to himself, his evolution continues unceasingly, either continuing the line of heredity — or the mysterious impulsion of nature, or adapting himself (*necessarily,* but as far as in him lies) to outside conditions." [158], p. 303.

The last phrase in the above, among all the medley of theories he presented in one volume, was the one that enabled Combarieu to write his three-volume history of music in relation to society. It was a saving phrase, not sufficiently stressed in English and American histories until the last few years of the present decade.

[32] "Talent" is a sliding scale of value in the hierarchy of pupil-value, beginning at the bottom with the tone-deaf, and culminating in genius. A person, thus, may not be a genius, a spontaneous creator, but may nevertheless have talent to some degree.

Montaigne once uttered a profound truth which could have suggested a way out of confusion. In his "Essay on the Education of Children" he says:

"Truth and reason are common to all, and are no more proper unto him that spake them heretofore, than unto him that shall speake them hereafter. The Bees do here and there sucke this and cull that flower, but afterward they produce the hony, which is peculiarly their owne, then it is no more Thyme or Majoram. So of peeces borrowed of others, he may lawfully alter, transforme, and confound them, to shape out of them a perfect peece of work, altogether his owne; alwaies provided his judgement, his travail, studie and institution tend to nothing, but to frame the same perfect." [33]

Although this sounds somewhat like a defense of plagiarism it does show how things work in the transmission of ideas. It has always been thus in the history of music. Lully, though born an Italian, succeeded in writing music that was truly expressive of the France of his day, as "clear and distinct" as Descartes' ideas, and as formally precise as the gardens of Versailles. The Gallophile Charles II brought French music to England at the Restoration, and sent young Englishmen to Paris to study. What they brought back was not French music, but new ways of making English music. Henry Purcell, England's "greatest composer" was the one to profit by these "contacts" and "intrusions;" Handel, a few years later, came from Germany and profited by these men's achievements, to "shape out of them a perfect peece of work, altogether his owne." Bach stayed at home, copied all the foreign music he could get, mingled with the Italian and French musicians at the German courts of his day, thus enriching his fundamentally German art. In recent years Dvořák lived for a time in this country. Then he returned to his own land, not with music "From the New World" but with *new ways* of writing *Bohemian* music.

These are what have been called the "processes" of history. To understand these processes and their importance in education we do need more "comparison of histories," and the assemblage of great masses of historical data. [34]

But to *utilize* this data and make it meaningful may well be the joint task of the popularizer and the musicologist. There need be

---

[33] From the contemporary translation by John Florio, in the *Harvard Classics*, v. 32, p. 38.

[34] Teggart, *Theory of History*, p. 189.

no conflict between popular education and research, but there seems to be at the present time.

4. ENTWICKELUNG VS. MUSIKWISSENSCHAFT

The first music historian to survey the subject as a whole "from a single lofty point of view" was a German. Ever since Calvisius, his countrymen have been leaders in scholarly research, sometimes carried away by emotional speculation, but always busy collecting *knowledge*. The recovery of old music, the deciphering of old notation by Germans, has spurred similar activities in neighboring countries. Never content with enjoying a few selected masterpieces as representing "the past," the historical frontiers have been pushed back several centuries in as many decades. The old belief that medieval and Renaissance music was labored and mere preparation for real art is overthrown with the increased knowledge of the spirit as well as the letter of old music. The recovery of these arts can never be complete, or wholly authentic, to be sure, but enough is already known to reveal the artistry, the spontaneity, and human qualities of music that is beginning to come into its own.

In the modern university scholarly research is now made more feasible by the use of micro-photography of rare works, and inexpensive photostat editions of neglected music are being made available. The scholar is no longer concerned with documents alone; he is seeing to it that this old music is performed as a means of enriching our present-day musical life. In other words the opportunity is now open for the scholar to become a popularizer of old music, and for the popularizer to enlarge his sympathies and widen his knowledge.[35]

As shown in Chapter 1, music history in popular form was at first combined with studies in theory. Today, in American schools, history is too often divorced from both theory and practice, to be combined with this curious, ill-defined study known as appreciation.

Baldwin's *Dictionary of Philosophy and Psychology* (2nd ed. 1920) gives the following definition of appreciation: "A way of formulating the distinction between judgments of value and those of science, which latter pertain to fact."

The study of the appreciation of music, however, has not always been designed to help students get that distinction. The only kind

[35] See the Introduction.

of history that is brought into "appreciation" is the developmental simplification based upon analogy with biography and scales of value. Judgments of value are given more importance than judgments of science, which pertain to fact. *Appreciation* is reserved for symphonic music; the fate of older music is *depreciation*.

Now that the research scholar has brought old music to life, how mystified our high-school students would be, after singing Lassus, Byrd, Morley, Weelkes, Costeley, Jannequin, Victoria, to have M. Lavignac arise and tell them that "counterpoint is a dead art"! If he were alive today, he would probably repudiate that youthful remark, as the great *Encyclopédie* which he started refutes it over and over. French scholars now are grateful to men like Ludwig, who, as already noted, was responsible for bringing the thirteenth-century glories of French Gothic music to light. Musical archaeology proves to be an exciting adventure.

It is the research scholar who finds the spontaneity in old music that was denied to it by Parry; it is the research scholar who finds music in the human life of medieval society and in the life of the present day. On one hand, Edward J. Dent finds "Music in the Social Life of the Middle Ages" in the Introductory Volume, or apologetic after-thought for the *Oxford History of Music* [257]; and on the other hand, Hugues Panassié finds material for scientific research in *Hot Jazz* (English ed., Witmark, 1936).

It is the popularizer, however, who is apt to find spontaneity and value only in certain approved types. In American and English popular music education certain esthetic and formal standards are held up in a scale of developmental value; in Russia the music of the workers was held up as the permanent type from which great art must evolve; in chauvinistic education the supreme fount and source of all musical art is the folk and art music of "our" area. (The latter is to be recommended as a point of departure but not necessarily as the highest good.)

It is for this and kindred reasons that appreciation and general history of music are not recognized as worthy subjects of study by some universities. But the remedy does not lie in continued separation and division. The popularizer need not fear the contempt of the seminar group, and the latter will not be stigmatized as "purely academic" if both are united in teaching *music*.[36]

---

[36] One of the healthiest signs of the times, in this respect, is the Joint Convention. The Music Teachers' National Association, The National Association of Schools of

5. IS MUSIC AN ORGANISM OR AN ACTIVITY?

Chapter 11 attempted to show the confusion of analogies in evolutionary explanation. This Summary has aimed to expose the confusion existing in these sequential patterns. We have inherited these tools of presentation, and we have come to use them automatically. The writer had used them for years until chance and research led him to investigate them. Educators may say in all sincerity that they do not want to impose standards of value on students as if by authority, but the scale of value and the "invariable" sequence are the bases for our attempts to settle problems and get "continuity."

The source of this sequential-pattern craze is of course the notion that music is somehow an entity; some thing or organism that develops in time, with "forms" that evolve in progression. So a re-definition of our terms is called for. What *is* music after all? The cue is given by an historian of language who has had to face the same difficulty (although this notion of a mystic organism has not affected language and the other arts as much as it has the history of music):

"Language is frequently spoken of as a 'living organism'; we hear of the 'life' of languages, of the 'birth' of new languages, and of the 'death' of old languages, and the implication, though not always realized, is that a language is a living thing, something analogous to an animal or a plant. Yet a language evidently (obviously) has no separate existence in the same way as a dog or a beech has, but is nothing but a function of certain living human beings. Language is activity, purposeful activity, and we should never lose sight of the speaking individuals, and of their purpose in acting in this particular way." [87]

Music, and the American Musicological Society were formerly poles apart in their thinking. They now meet jointly every year to learn from each other. Separation still exists, however, between teachers in "public school music" and other teacher-organizations.

[87] Otto Jespersen, *Language, Its Nature, Development, and Origin*, Geo. Allen and Unwin, London, 1922, p. 7.

Note that the word "origin" is at the end of the title, contrary to traditional (continuous) practice. In a few paragraphs at the close of the book, Jespersen says of this unimportant matter that the origin of language was probably in inarticulate, half-musical utterances in attempts to communicate.

6. THE REALITIES THAT LIE CLEARLY BEFORE US

Chapter 9 began with Aristotle's prescription for "the clearest view;" Chapter 10, with Tylor's doctrine which was to give "clearer view," and hovering over all is Flint's statement that the Idea of Progress makes possible "a single lofty point of view." But these views have seemed to involve confusion and obscurity. Finally Jesperson reminds us that we can see human beings and be clearly aware of their activities. To corroborate this, with relation to the confused debates as to spontaneity, one can turn to a wise psychiatrist, accustomed to dealing with human problems, who says that

"we should occupy ourselves with the emergent person," and that the frequently-raised questions as to "nature and nurture" are not so essential as "the far more accessible and important question of what the person does with it all." "Somehow the world likes extremes where at least some of us like to keep to a perspective for what can have common acceptance, a vision that need not blind us to *realities that lie clearly before us.*" [38]

The constructive possibilities of that statement are apparent in contradistinction to the following item from the Psychoanalytic credo: "Psychoanalysis never describes phenomena as they 'are,' does not describe them in the light of their momentary peculiarities. A phenomenon is not comprehensible to a psychoanalyst unless he can describe how it has come about." [39]

If the reader will now juxtapose these last quotations with those that appear at the beginning of Chapter 9, the issue will be clearly defined. Meyer throws down the gauntlet to those who, from Aristotle to Bernfeld, have insisted that we can only understand a thing by seeking for past origins in preceding events and situations. He implies with good reason that this insistence has blinded us to "realities that lie clearly before us." He maintains that "a science of life without full respect for life where it lives and when it lives is not true science" [40] and raises some questions that are highly constructive.

[38] Adolf Meyer, M.D., Address on "Spontaneity" in *A Contribution to Mental Hygiene Education,* Program of the Mental Hygiene Division of the Illinois Conference on Public Welfare, Chicago, Oct. 1933, p. 22.

[39] Siegfried Bernfeld, "Psychoanalytic Psychology of the Young Child" in the *Psychoanalytic Quarterly,* Vol. IV, No. 1, 1935.

[40] Meyer, as cited, p. 31.

"Whether we study the units or the group or the part, the questions are always the same simple questions of critical inquiring common-sense:

What is the fact?

The conditions under which it occurs and shows?

What are the factors entering and at work?

How do they work?

With what results?

With what modifiability?" (p. 28).

These questions are as valuable to the student of music history as they are to the student of individuals. The history of music should serve, as stated in the Introduction, to explain certain interesting activities in modern life; if we concern ourselves unduly with origins, we deal with

"activities taken out of their present setting and given a meaning in terms of a hypothetical and theoretical historical self." [41]

The arts of music are fascinating because of their endless manifestations in different ways. There is no one art of music, with a "hypothetical and historical self" that had its origin in one principle, one people, one situation, or one area.

"To discover and verify truth, it is no longer a question of establishing a small number of simple principles from which the mind needs only let itself be carried along on the tide of consequences; *one must begin with nature as she exists.*" [42]

[41] Frederick H. Allen, M.D., "Some Therapeutical Principles," *American Journal of Psychiatry,* Vol. 94, No. 3, Nov. 1937, p. 673.

[42] From Turgot's discourse at the Sorbonne, "On the Successive Advances of the Human Mind" (1750). See *Œuvres de Turgot,* ed. by G. Schelle, Paris, 1913, v. I.

CHAPTER 13

CONCLUSIONS

COMPARISON, CONTINUITY, AND CHANGE

IN THE Introduction, the problem of method was posed for the young science of musicology, and in conclusion it is raised once more as the central question for this study. Having pointed out the confusion of analogies in both scholarly and popular presentations, the question is, How can they be avoided?

In the first place, there are certain fundamental words and terms that can be used which need not suggest analogy at all: simple words such as *change, comparison, contrasts, competition, revival, modification, combination, expansion, contraction,* and *embellishment.* In the conclusion of the chapter previous, the inclusive word *activity* was suggested as a possible definition for language and music, in social terms. All of the words above describe activities.

In the second place, there are expressions and terms which suggest the lack of activity and opposition to the words above: the *unchanging,* or the *stable,* the *similar,* the *static,* the *serene,* the *satisfied,* the *symmetrical,* and the *regular.* These are some of the characteristics and preferences of people who do not like *change,* who find *comparisons* odious, *contrasts* offensive, odd or peculiar, *competition* distressing, and *modification* in bad taste, particularly if the *familiar* is made to appear to be *different.* These considerations are related to the matters discussed in Part II, where it is pointed out that the very important term *continuity* can be used, without any suggestion of analogy, to suggest habit, persistence, systematic procedure, custom, tradition, authority, and so on. Finally, there are ways in which the terms *growth, development,* and *progress* can be used without resorting to analogy at all. *Evolution* is not included, because its meaning is too confused.

In short, it is suggested that one way out of confusion is to be as straightforward as possible about one's terminology, and to use terms concerning the meaning of which there can be no ambiguity — or at least as little as possible. Thus the accurate methods of musicology could be applied even to elementary instruction in the art, science, and history of musical communication.

In these concluding pages, therefore, an attempt is made to define historical musicology in these words, and to propose certain hypotheses and suggestions for future study, again using the same terms.

I. MUSICOLOGY AND COMPARISON

All scientific procedure involves comparison. Without the latter, no valid inferences can be made. Cabanis once said, in a " Letter on First Causes," in 1806, that we could not find out anything about our universe because we could not compare it with any other. Now in Chapters 1 and 2, it is to be noted that the Catholic musicologists of the seventeenth century, especially Mersenne and Cerone, and some of their successors, were just as interested in music of the universe, or " music of the spheres," as in the " worldly " music of human beings. The Lutherans could not be bothered with celestial music and finally everyone came to agree with Cabanis, since no one could hear this celestial music, much less compare it with something.

Now that celestial music is left in the realm of the inexplicable (an abode that is also prepared for ultimate " origins "), musicologists are content to study musical arts and styles in mundane systems that are comparable with each other. If, therefore, the business of musicology is to come to scientific conclusions concerning these matters, is not *all musicology comparative musicology?* And yet, a separate discipline exists (as pointed out in Chapter 10, 1), known as " Comparative Musicology," for the study of extra-European music. Here again is a separation that suggests division, which seems, as already pointed out, to continue the old patterns of cultural history. Parry was consistent in his use of " stages of development," because he believed that European music is " superior." Since " comparative musicologists " do not believe that, the use of the sequential pattern, as Chapter 10 indicates, is *not* consistent.

This will probably persist so long as scholars keep their faces turned entirely toward the past. So a few suggestions will be made later on the possibilities of comparisons of Oriental and Occidental music in the light of present-day change.

Before doing this, however, an attempt is made to show how musicology may compare styles within our own systems, then different systems within different world-areas, always with reference to that which has persisted, as a background against which changes and modifications bring forth new music different from the old.

1. WHAT ARE THE SIMPLEST AND EASIEST COMPARISONS?

Descartes was using no analogy when he advised us to begin with that which is simplest and easiest to know. So if the business of the musicologist is to compare one style with another style in order to come to conclusions about it, that ought to be a simple matter, if the comparisons to be made at first are not too difficult. What comparisons are the simplest? That is a question not yet raised in any treatise on musicology that the author has seen. But it is the first question that any science has to settle. Ancient chemistry dealt with only four elements — earth, fire, air, and water — because they are so different that comparison is simple. No student of physics ever started the subject until he could distinguish the four " humors " of old: hot and cold, wet and dry. There are many people in the world today who have not yet got beyond the elementary stage in music appreciation wherein they can distinguish fast and slow, high and low, or even loud and soft. It is said that General Grant knew only two tunes: one was " Yankee Doodle " and the other wasn't.

So it is suggested — and this is the hypothesis that may seem revolutionary in the field of musicology as well as that of popular music education:

The simplest and easiest comparisons are obvious, striking contrasts; the most difficult are of those which at first seem similar.

Application of that principle, which sounds so simple as to seem banal, makes possible two indictments: one of the musicologist and the other of the popularizer. The writer feels competent to render them, having tried to be both:

First, American musicology is beginning at the top, in its efforts to gain recognition as a learned science. This young discipline does not yet seem to have announced its " first principles," because it has not yet mapped out a program for any but graduate students whose task it is to make *difficult* comparisons; e.g., of a motet of disputed authorship which has to be compared with some *similar* works of the same general style. This does take skill, knowledge, learning, and all the cultural background demanded by Láng's statement quoted in the Introduction. But no one has as yet indicated how the student should start, down in Junior High School, to get the proper background. That same student, if he is to end up as a teacher of political science or of American history, begins by comparing striking events and changes in American life with simple comparisons of our history with that of other peoples.

Second, the popularizer *must* begin from the bottom, and is *obliged* to find the " simplest and easiest to know." But although that simple, sensible phrase of Descartes' has been overlooked by our musicologists, it is the popularizer who has been the victim of Descartes' second phrase. Chapter 12, in discussing the philosophical concepts of Nature and simplicity, showed how the " order of thought — even a fictitious one " has been imposed upon music education. Elementary approaches therefore do not involve simple comparisons of the " realities that are clearly before us; " the " simple " is identified with the " primitive," something to which the student must go back, in order to ascend the scale of development (and of value).

Now what are some of the simpler contrasts in style to which allusion is made? The following, in common use, are just a few that come to mind; the contrasts in style are as vivid and startling as in the comparative functions for which they are intended:

1. Military music and Gregorian plainsong.

2. *Recitative* (speech-rhythm) and lyric *aria* (metrical rhythm), for the functions of narration and contemplation in dramatic music.

3. A Lutheran chorale and a *coloratura aria*.

4. A fox-trot and a minuet.

5. A *barcarolle* (boat song) and a *tarantelle* (a rapid Italian dance). These are rhythmically similar, but very different in tempo (rate of speed).

Now all of these styles have a history: some a much longer history than others; some of them have persisted, without change, for centuries; and yet at the same time, some are the results of modification of some of the others. Some are regular and symmetrical, others are irregular and free.

The regular, symmetrical forms have persisted because of popular taste, particularly the Classical, four-measure pattern. (The dance forms, *aria,* and military music are apt to be regular: the chant, *recitative,* and chorale irregular.)

But even when two minuets have the same " form," that is, the same number of sections, each will have not only a different content but different style, if one was written by Mozart and one by Haydn. Both may have been written in the same year; at any rate that exercise in comparison is for a fairly advanced student, much more difficult than the easy comparison of *a* minuet with *a* foxtrot. But we are only intelligent about the things we are interested in; a comparison of two fox-trots might be very simple for the modern student and difficult for the teacher. All the music we are not interested in " sounds the same." The apocryphal story about General Grant is not plausible: he must have been able to distinguish the bugle calls. If so, with a little practice, he could have distinguished " Brünnhilde's War Cry " from " Taps."

But the simplest and most striking comparison that can be made, and one of the most revealing in the history of Western music, is the contrast between a military march (a) and a Gregorian chant (b), as for example: [1]

This is a simple comparison, but impossible under a sequential pattern scheme. The march is " a later development," historically. And to put them together throws the scale of value into confusion.

[1] Even an untrained person not able to read notation can see (1) the rhythmical contrast — the tramp, tramp of the metrical feet with Left! on every accent ($>$), indicated also by the bar-line divisions | | | | in the march, then the absence of these bar lines in the chant, with its free, flowing rhythm on the elongated vowel sounds, with an evenness and equality of note values; (2) the melodic comparison — the bold, commanding skips in the distances (intervals) between tones in the march, the gentle contour of the melodic line in the chant with its stepwise intervals.

In the matter of rhythm, this comparison illustrates the common confusion between rhythm and measure. According to Welch, *Appreciation of Music* (p. 15), this chant would have no rhythm, which is defined as being dependent on " strong and weak beats." It is not even music because " Music is written with vertical divisions; " that is, bars or measures. D. G. Mason has a freer concept than that in his " Tyranny of the Bar Line " and " A Note on English Rhythms," in his *Dilemma of American Music,* Macmillan, N. Y., 1929.

The fact that each is "good" for its own function makes the contrast even more striking and the communication more significant. But in music education it is impossible under present conditions, because few public-school songbooks contain Gregorian melodies and parochial schools do not go in for march tunes.

For this study, however, the implications for history are particularly important. The comparison for musicology is of the continuous with its modifications.

2. CONTINUITY AND MODIFICATION

Most general histories, in employing the usual sequential pattern, only treat the history of the chant just quoted under an early chapter on medieval music. To put it at the beginning of the book is logical enough, not only because it is old, but because it is the oldest of the musical arts we use today. But its present-day uses are seldom mentioned, as it has been considered the business of history to present it as an old form, "derived from still older ones, out of which grew" or "developed" other more complex forms. But plainsong is still a vital, living art. It has been carefully preserved, in spite of all the treatment it has received in its uses in all sorts of ways. Its history is a history of previous modification of older styles and of bitter competition, in which the Gregorian won over the Ambrosian, the Mozarabic, and the other local versions in different areas, thanks to the authority of Rome. Its history is one of neglect during the Enlightenment and spasmodic revival in the nineteenth century; finally of restoration in its pristine purity in 1903 by the papal *Motu proprio*. Chapter 2 described the distress of Pope John XXII in 1324–1325 over the hilarious modification of the sacred melodies. But it is not likely that our literature of polyphonic music would have been possible, without these processes of willful modification.

The continuity of plainsong is due, therefore, not only to papal authority but also to the labors of musicologists and priests who have devoted their lives to its preservation because they loved it for its serenity and its contrast to the militant music of the outside world. But these men would not part with the polyphonic music that was the result of tampering — so who is to say whether change or continuity is the wise course? Evidently both are necessary.

The continuity of military music, the opposite style in every respect, is also due in part to authority and in part to popular favor. Authority loved pomp and ceremony, and the march is a great regimenting device for stimulating patriotism. But the continuity of the symmetrical "tune" pattern of the four-measure phrase is not an imposition of authority; it is merely the continuity due to the love of the familiar, the satisfaction which is annoyed at innovation.

The Classical pattern has worked well, and many of our most cherished musical treasures are in this form. But woe be to the innovator who dares to emulate the masters and occasionally stray from the four-measure pattern (if he would be "popular"). Some young people today may think that modern popular music is revolutionary and far superior to old-fashioned ways. But the writer has a "Song Construction Chart" from "Tin Pan Alley" which is designed to guide budding composers into the paths of success.[2] It warns aspirants that he who would succeed *must* follow the outline laid down; this outline then sketches the Classical pattern regarded as the norm in the eighteenth century because of its long acceptance as "natural" since the Renaissance. It is far more dogmatic as an arbiter of taste than the papal *Motu proprio* in 1903.

In other words, as Pound says, the element of continuity (when defined as persistence) is to be found in traditional "modes of thought and rules of art." The content of these persisting forms does change, but the forms themselves only change at the hands of daring individuals who choose to break the bonds of tradition and overstep the bounds set by authority.

So when a writer on appreciation writes a chapter on "The Fundamental Form" and devotes a page to *Ach, du lieber Augustin* as illustration, explanation should be forthcoming as to *why* it is so regarded.

It is fundamental in militaristic countries today, but is no more fundamental in human nature than the urge of "genius" to get away from it occasionally, as Mozart, Haydn, Beethoven and Brahms did even before some of our moderns got away from it altogether, to get back to the freedom of Gregorian chant.

Very few people since Printz have dared to call the great Plato an "enemy of music." But the latter's famous statement in the *Laws,* holding up the arts of Egypt as ideal, went so far as to say that

[2] Published by Harold Potter, N. Y., 1936.

"their young citizens must be habituated to forms and strains of vir-tue. . . . No alteration is allowed in music at all. A lawgiver may in-stitute melodies which have a natural truth and correctness without any fear of failure. To do this, however, must be the work of God, or of a divine person. . . . The love of novelty which arises out of pleasure in the new and weariness of the old, has not strength enough to cor-rupt the consecrated song and dance. . . ." (Bk. II, 657).

Plato was right. When song and dance become "consecrated" by familiarity, authority, or tradition, it takes important crises and human daring to bring about any drastic changes in musical thought. The mere love of novelty itself never makes many pro-found changes in music. But with a loosening of religious, state, or academic authority, and with artists who are versatile enough to provide vital music for all kinds of functions, new kinds of musical communication enrich the art. And these new communications usually seem to come from composers who are not averse to writ-ing music for enjoyment, entertainment, and recreation, men who *vie with each other* to produce startling contrasts. This leads to a hypothesis concerning the factor of competition in historical proc-esses.

But before discussing that, there are other phases of modification and its processes. These are well treated, already, by theorists, from a technical standpoint; they are mentioned here as possible exer-cises in elementary comparison.[3]

II. THE PROCESSES OF MODIFICATION

1. COMBINATION OF STYLES

After a student has learned to recognize certain well-defined, con-trasting styles, another step might be the recognition of these in combination, as, for example, in such familiar items as the follow-ing:

1. Combination by alternation, as in the opening scene of Wag-ner's *Die Meistersinger,* where the romantic, nineteenth-century love theme is heard between the lines of the Lutheran chorale. (Really a parody of a prevailing practice in German churches in which the organist interpolated florid extemporization.)

2. Combination by addition, as in Chopin's *Berceuse,* where a

[3] They may also suggest exercises in musical composition.

highly developed modification of Italian *coloratura* style for the fingers is added to a simple modification of the old " Alberti bass " in a rocking rhythm. The same technical procedure was heard recently in some " swing " chamber music, where Goodman's clarinet and a facile pianist's right hand did most amazing pyrotechnics over the pianist's left hand and a drummer's imaginative rhythms.
3. Combination by harmonious intermingling, a much more subtle process than mere alternation or addition: Bach's chorale, " Jesu, Joy of Man's Desiring," with the combination of four styles: (1) The old medieval rhythm in the melody: ♩ ♩ ♩ ♩ ; (2) the harmonization for four voices; (3) the Rococo embellishment in triplet " divisions," over (4) a slow-moving ground bass.

But modification, as a rule, results not in mere mechanical combination; elements taken over from an older culture are made expressive in a new situation. These matters are suggested merely as elementary exercises in style-criticism. The incongruity of the examples, in juxtaposition, to which some might object, provides the very element of striking contrasts which are desired. There is no confusion possible, as in the old sequential patterns, except possibly in the mind of a modern composer who jumbles styles together with no historical knowledge, who, in other words, is not certain what it is he wishes to say or how to say it.

But the main point to keep in mind constantly, with these random examples, is that the original style (if a vital one) may retain its continuity, and it should, by all the means of preservation at our command. We still possess and enjoy plainsong, in spite of all that has been done to modify it; and we still continue to possess our classics, no matter what changes may happen to them. This is to be kept in mind in reading the next section.

2. CONTINUITY AND PARODY

Modifications in musical style also involve expansion and contraction of musical content or musical resources. It is not necessary here to go into all the possible ramifications of this statement, into the techniques of orchestration, and so on. But there is one phase of this process that is socially and historically important — the modification of old music and styles that are transplanted and adapted to new uses and functions. This may take place in at least three different ways for as many different purposes:

1. Secular, even frivolous, music can be and in creative periods has been slowed down, solemnized, and re-adapted for religious use. This was done by Luther and his associates, possibly also by the musicians of the early Christian era, in Rome and Syria.

2. The opposite procedure is perhaps even more common — the speeding-up, embellishment, and even parody of "consecrated" melodies for the sake of creative variety, to avoid monotony. The antics of medieval choristers were naturally distressing to pious authorities, but rather important nevertheless in the history of polyphony as a social art.

3. Transfer of vocal style to instrumental media (or *vice versa*), from one serious art function to another, is also a frequent occurrence. Witness the use of the Italian *bel canto aria* style in the piano music of Mozart and Chopin; the recent craze for "symphonic choirs," and the highly romantic transcriptions of Bach's organ music and Palestrina's motets for the modern orchestra, by Stokowski and others.

In short, the process of parody has been tremendously important in music history, as in other phases of cultural and political change. The modern "jazzing of the classics" is as shocking to the conservative musician as was the "measured dividing of the *tempora*" and the impious "running to and fro" condemned by Pope John XXII (see Chapter 2, 1). But it is difficult to see why this need be a matter of very serious concern. If a classic has real vitality, it will survive this ordeal just as great men survive the cartoons of journalism, especially when they are good-natured. It may be merely an exuberant symptom of healthy spontaneity; the serious question may be, How can the genius of modern musical playboys be diverted into other significant channels? What more serious functions can society provide for which new musical composition will be needed?

In the history of opera, parody has played its part. When the absurdities of *opera seria* became tiresome, *opera buffa* opened up new avenues of musical style and enjoyment. It was nearly a century before anyone had the courage to parody Gluck, but not until Offenbach dared to do so in his *Orpheus aux enfers* did the French operatic stage seem to take on new life.[4] And yet Gluck's music

---

[4] This is not a statement of cause and effect, but a reference to the fact that opéra-comique, not grand opera, gave the most vital impulse to French lyric drama. See Henri Prunières, "Defénse et illustration de l'opéra-comique," *La revue musicale*, No. 140, Nov., 1933.

has lost none of its luster and charm because of Offenbach's jest. The time may soon be ripe for a magnificent parody of Wagner's *Twilight of the Gods,* with all the opportunities it would offer for social and political satire. It could only be done in one of the few great democratic nations that remain, but with all the possibilities in modern orchestration and the cinema and stage techniques at our disposal, it might at long last inaugurate a new era in the history of opera as a potent social instrument. The eloquence and worth in Wagner would not disappear, but he would take his proper place in history as one of many great figures in music history, not as the apex of development through the ages.

And it must not be forgotten that parody may also serve a serious, even a religious, purpose, if we may broaden its definition. The Lutheran treatment of plainsong has already been mentioned. Today one may hear a Harlem choir and congregation sing the Twenty-third Psalm and Lord's Prayer to a quasi-Anglican chant, with the accompaniment of an orchestra comprising a jazz instrumentation, including the ubiquitous saxophone. But the vital emotion and deep piety with which it was invested would put to shame the average professional choir chanting in the usual perfunctory manner. The Negro Spiritual is, after all, a reverent, deeply emotional parody of Protestant gospel-hymn tunes, but a modification into which true creative elements have entered in, under the stress of genuine emotion.

The gospel-hymn tune itself, in its simplest and most banal form, is a style of music which might conceivably be called primitive. But it, again, is a modification of musical formulae borrowed from the classics of European music, notably from German sources, and simplified to meet primitive pioneer conditions. One need not turn to Negro genius, however, to find artistic improvements on this style. The "White Spirituals" of the South and the "Fuguing Choruses" of William Billings of New England [5] are evidence of the sort of creative ability which comes forth when religion shows real folk vitality.

Transcription is also a form of parody which has its good and bad features. This is not the place for recording esthetic objections,

[5] See John Tasker Howard, *Our American Music,* N. Y., 1931; also Isaac Goldberg, *Tin Pan Alley,* N. Y., 1930, Ch. 2, "Before the Flood;" and the *Original Sacred Harp* (Denson revision), Haleyville, Alabama, 1936. See also George Pullen Jackson's books, as cited.

but the implications for this study are important. One positive rule, if observed, could remove much of the objection on historical grounds. If Stokowski will frankly say "Passacaglia and Fugue," *Bach-Stokowski,* on every program, notice would thereby be served that the music performed is a modification by transference to a new medium, and to be judged accordingly. A musicological service would also be performed, if a Brandenburg Concerto were to be played twice on the same program; first with Bach's original instrumentation, and then by the modern aggregation, if so desired. Then listeners would have an education in style-criticism which is now denied them.[6]

III. COMPETITION IN MODIFICATION

This is a hypothesis which needs to be examined by the social psychologist; but since Printz mentioned it in the first history of music in German, there is justification for its mention here. In Chapter 1 he is quoted for his approval of numerous origin theories, all of which had bearing on the music of his own day. Among these he found that "the ambition to outdo others" is important. Now it is obvious that reference is made to the aim not merely to be "original," but *to please patrons.* And the history of Baroque and Classical music shows clearly that the patrons themselves were ambitious to keep up with the Joneses in acquiring fashionable composers and new music.

At the present day, competition in music education has come, unfortunately, to mean only one thing — competition in performance, and performance of old music at that. The concept of creative competition is much more important, but it is not a concept to be revived by artificial stimulants, such as prizes, boosters' committees, and pleas for recognition of national music.

Music histories of the future might find it interesting to recognize the importance of

[6] To ban transcription entirely would be a debatable procedure. Until the revival of the harpsichord becomes more widespread, pianists have to be transcribers of older keyboard music. But this revival is another refutation of the old sequential pattern. In the history of instruments, the harpsichord, although on an entirely different principle, came to be regarded as representing a "stage of development" in keyboard instruments. Now it is being revived, not merely to show the continuity of old music, but because it can be made to do things that are impossible on the pianoforte. New music for the old instrument is already appearing.

1. Competition between communities, each of which has a creative life of its own, expressive of its peculiar needs and peculiar capabilities.

2. Competition between groups and individuals within communities. Composers who get groups of people to perform or otherwise enjoy their music exercise an enviable power. Achievement seems to come as response to a challenge, in the creation of new music as in everything else.

Recognition of the first and wider phase of competition will reveal that the history of "Italian" music is the history of rival cities, each with its opera house, each with its own dialect, each with a different outlook. It is the history of music in Mantua, Florence, Rome, Naples, Venice, Milan, Venosa, Bergamo, Bologna, and the rest. The history of "German" music becomes the history of Dresden, Leipzig, Mannheim, Weimar, Cöthen, Hamburg, Halle, Braunschweig, Hanover, Berlin, and Munich. No wonder that Vienna, between those geographical areas called Italy and Germany, became a musical as well as a geographical center.

Wider areas than those of the cities themselves must be studied, to get the influences absorbed and radiated by each. Still broader domains must be compared in the histories of Spanish, French, British, and Netherland music. Whereas Italy and Germany only became nations in 1870, unity came to France much earlier. But until then her music history is that of North *vs.* South, troubadours and trouvères, Normans and French, Spanish to the south, Flemish to the north, Burgundy to the west, and England across the Channel. "French" music history is that of rival groups, all competing for power, until the centralization of authority in Paris under the Bourbons. When Spanish armies stopped marching through Burgundy to Flanders and gave up attempts to conquer England, the creative activities of Spanish musicians and artists ceased also. After England renounced all claims to French soil, and began to look for dominion in overseas trade, few musical achievements were recorded that were comparable to those known under the Tudors.[7]

Competition between individuals and groups is a well-recognized fact, concerning which much has been written, but it is a fact to be observed in connection with the other wide phases of competition just noticed. From the *jongleurs* of medieval society to Haydn

---

[7] See Cecil Forsyth, *Music and Nationalism,* a Study of English Opera, London, 1911.

and his *Capell* at the court of Esterhazy, music was sought as a means of stimulating loyalty and gracing festivity; in short, as a demonstration of cultural power. In the sixteenth century, choir boys had to be zealously guarded against kidnapping by rival princes; and composers, graduating from this competitive school, were assured of a competence under powerful patronage.[8]

When court life centered in Paris in the seventeenth century, and competition between other French centers ceased, sterility set in in the musical life of the provinces. In Paris, a similar sterility set in when Louis XIV suppressed competition in favor of Lully; but the resultant pantomiming of popular songs marked the beginnings of *opéra comique*.

Today competition for popular favor goes on under entirely different conditions. The commercialization of music, since Beethoven's day, has delivered the musician from one menial kind of economic servitude, but in other respects he is not so free as his liveried ancestor. The modern "Esterhazys" (at least in the United States) are the sponsors that buy "Time on the Air." (See "Music and Technology" in Ch. 8, II, 5.)

IV. DIFFERENT SYSTEMS IN DIFFERENT AREAS

All of the elementary comparisons mentioned above are concerned with our styles of Western music.

Comparative musicology, in the sense proposed at the beginning, can find still more startling contrasts and interesting similarities by comparing *systems*. This has already been suggested by Charles Louis Seeger, who has argued for a correlation of "Systematic and Historical Orientations in Musicology." [9]

Broadening the basis of Seeger's theory, a few simple, elementary comparisons will be mentioned in conclusion which might deal (1) with the striking contrasts observable now between different musical arts in different areas, and (2) the modifications that result from cultural mingling and imitation. (The value of particular arts in given areas was stressed in Chapter 12.)

The "subject that is already there" is always the musical system

[8] See the dedication to J. S. Bach's *Mass in B Minor*, for evidence of the stress under which the composer wrote this monumental music, of the anxiety with which he hoped his "humble skill" would merit greater preferment.

[9] In *Proceedings* of the National Meeting, American Musicological Society, Philadelphia, 1935.

of a people. Authority and tradition may conspire to keep the forms of expression within the system intact, but contacts bring change.

I. THE EURASIAN PICTURE

On this basis, one might begin the history of medieval music by comparing widely separated activities, events, and conditions. Study of music in medieval Eurasia (to mention only the Eastern and Western extremes) reveals two great borrowers steadily at work — Rome and Japan. While Buddhism and Chinese music were being introduced into Japan, Christianity and ancient modes were being spread and practiced throughout the Roman Empire to the west. In both areas, religion and music underwent profound changes. In music, in both cases, the mingling of "consecrated" forms of music with secular styles, dramatic entertainment, and the rest brought fascinating and varied results. In both cases, many arts from which the borrowing was done remained static. Chinese scholars have preserved their exquisite classical music as carefully as their literature [10] and as carefully as the Gregorian codex was kept from "contaminating" influences. In other words, the separation between "classical" and "popular" or dramatic music was complete in both areas. But in the East, for ten centuries, at least, the church tolerated the theater.[11] But with the fall of the Byzantine Empire conservatism became the rule in the Greek Orthodox Church, and freedom emerged in the West. Creative spirits, particularly in Britain, and what is now France and Belgium, had pure, unadulterated fun with the "consecrated" melodies, and thus the marvellous, complex arts of Western music began to emerge. After Peter the Great opened up Russia to Western influence, Italian musicians went to Muscovite courts, and in the nineteenth century Russian composers themselves began to develop the possibilities that had been latent and repressed so long.[12]

The Japanese developed interesting musical arts of their own quite different from the Chinese and Korean arts from which they had borrowed. But since the Westernization and industrialization of the country, imitation of our Western music has been as exten-

[10] See John Hazedel Levis, *Foundations of Chinese Musical Art,* Peiping, 1936.

[11] For the continuity of Greek drama in Byzantium and the combination of church and theater under the Iconoclasts, see Tunison, as cited, Ch. I.

[12] Note the use here of the verb "develop" as a human activity: the nineteenth century "doctrine of development" made music the subject of the sentence.

sive as Japanese imitation of our industrial techniques. The result is not merely Occidental plus Oriental music; new forms and styles never known before are emerging. And the process, with all its varied ramifications, is essentially the same process as the medieval process.[13] The early Buddhist missionaries from China did not succeed in displacing Shintoism, and our Christian envoys have not succeeded in displacing either one. But in each case it was a different Japanese culture that emerged as a result of the intrusion; and music, in each period, reflected the changes.

No one "general history" can ever cover the whole Eurasian picture, but it could open up vistas for further exploration.

After a world-wide view of musical systems, musical fixity, and musical change, one might turn to the developments in national areas within western Europe itself with more objectivity. Europocentric methods have heretofore obscured our view of historical processes, and certainly our "superior" notions concerning Oriental civilizations have done no good in promoting international understanding. A world-view should also include other systems, such as those of India, Africa, the Americas, and Arabia. But in these areas the problem is different, owing to the factors of European colonization.

Students in the western hemisphere and in the widespread British dominions have a potentially wider outlook on music history, at present, than that which is possible for some of the nations of continental Europe, with their tight national barriers.

2. MUSIC IN COLONIZED AREAS

The problems of music history in countries that began as Europeanized colonies during or since the modern era are particularly fascinating. In every case Europeans with their own styles of music settle down beside groups with totally different systems and practices. In some cases, constituted authority or tradition keeps the two systems rigidly apart, as in the British and Dutch dominions; in other cases a certain amount of fusion, conscious or unconscious, results, as in missionary enterprises and Latin cultures.

[13] But not as Parry predicted. For him the "evolution" of a Japanese sense of harmony would only be possible if their music was spared the "contamination" of our popular music. The "contamination" proves to be the necessary social factor in the process. (See Ch. 9, III.)

A. In the British Dominions

No finer example of the power of British authority and conservative tradition can be found than in the musical life of the British colonies. The schools are all staffed by teachers with British training; examiners in music education and adjudicators in annual festivals are brought, whenever possible, from London, Edinburgh, Oxford, Cambridge, or other British centers. Organists in Cape Town or Johannesburg use the same program materials as the municipal organists of Sydney, Melbourne, Wellington, Liverpool, or Bristol. The English histories of music used in dominion schools all teach that our musical arts have "grown" from primitive, embryonic forms still kept alive among the Bushmen, Fijians, and many other tribes under British rule. But the co-existence of these radically different art systems without appreciable change (until recent years), proves not that evolutionary progress is the rule, but that persistent fixity of "traditional modes of professional thought" is to be expected in both.[14]

This does not mean that native aborigines cannot learn to use European music. African tribes are said to be exceptionally quick in imitating everything they hear, and Maoris are contributing more and more to creative musical life in New Zealand. But in areas where social, economic, and caste separations are accentuated, as in India, music systems seem to remain as separate as they always have been.

Musicians of the Victorian era never seemed interested in possibilities of exotic systems, even in those of their own subjects. Our romantic "Songs of India," "Lakmés," and the rest came from imaginative Continentals.

Millions of Negroes under British rule, as in Africa, practice native musical arts of the greatest subtlety and complexity. But the Negroes in the United States, in contact with more numerous whites, have developed styles which are now affecting popular styles all over the world, music totally unlike any music in Africa.

---

[14] As for the persistence of custom in music for a functional purpose, the English-speaking countries are the only ones in which the "traditional" celebration of Christmas must include Handel's *Messiah*, and in which church wedding processions must (except in strict communions) be secular dramatic music by Mendelssohn and Wagner.

B. In the United States

The American Colonies made Calvinist psalm-tunes and British drinking songs part of our national heritage. There is much to be published concerning American music before the Revolution. With complete independence from Britain came more development of racy, virile music expressive of the pioneer spirit. The flood of immigration brought great numbers of foreign musicians, with Germans preponderant. European Romanticism affected our musical culture profoundly, and many thousands of young musicians studied on the Continent — comparatively few in England.

The only point to be emphasized here in connection with this vast subject is that with all the dependence the states have had on European music, there is a vast difference between that sort of dependence and the dependence found in British dominions. For better or for worse, there is not even a National Conservatory which sets up academic authority for the country, much less a Royal College to settle the " rules of art " across the seas.

The conditions under which the enslaved Negro population gradually came to influence our culture are unique, and so also are the circumstances under which the North American Indian was exploited. But with all the segregation of the musical arts of the Negro and Indian, folklorists until recently went to a curious extreme. Instead of studying the interaction of white with Negro music, and the definite separation of the music of the Indian, alone on his reservation, the music of these races was hailed erroneously and indiscriminately as the only folk music that the United States could claim. The romantic attempts to base art forms on these ignored the folk music of white Americans, and the results were Europeanized versions of quasi-Negro and quasi-Indian themes no more faithful to the originals than the attempts at musical *chinoiserie* in eighteenth-century France and Germany. (This matter has been discussed in Ch. 12.)

One interesting subject among many others for future study might be the comparison of the different kinds of music resulting from one borrowed influence in different areas. For example, there was French colonization in Canada and Louisiana, but French-Canadian and French-Creole music are two different things. That gay operatic center, New Orleans, has an entirely different history from the musical chronicles of conservative Quebec. Spanish missionaries were very active in Texas and in California; music schools for the Indians were in existence before those of the Pilgrims and Puritans in New England. Secularization of the missions cut short these activities in California, but it seems that in Texas some little-known musical activities have been going on under Catholic influence ever since, with curious fusions of church melodies, Indian dance tunes, and the music of Polish, Czech, and other immigrants.[15]

Mention has already been made of the persistence of old music in isolated communities, such as mountainous districts of Kentucky and Tennessee. In our centers with changing populations, however, all kinds of polyglot influences are discernible, in spite of the standardization imposed by the formulas of commercialized popular tunes, and "teaching pieces."

There is probably no country in the world that has access to more different kinds of music, both among its own people and in improved facilities for diffusing it. It would be a tragedy if it is levelled off into "classical" patterns in popular music, while symphonic or "good" music is composed by artists socially remote from their fellows.

C. In Latin America

Although the Latin influence has been important only for limited areas in North America, it predominates in Central and South America. But as in the case of the United States, all these colonized areas have broken away from their mother countries. The latter, Spain and Portugal, have, moreover, been static in musical developments since their days of wealth from, and power in, the New World. Wealthy Latin-Americans have looked more to Paris for education and culture. But in recent years, possibly due to commercial progress and the development of an intelligent middle class, more attempt has been made to develop the possibilities in native forms of music. Today, thanks to the energetic efforts of some gifted leaders, notably Villa-Lobos, Curt Lange, and others, progress in music is being made, comparable to the strides in public secular education.

No modification in native or imported European colonist music could possibly take place in Latin America so long as the old class divisions persisted in society; a wealthy, educated class importing

[15] *Catholic Music and Musicians in Texas,* by Sister Joan of Arc, C.D.P., San Antonio, 1936.

art from Europe for luxury's sake could never interact with a separate, poverty-stricken native class dependent upon old folk arts. The American Indians, from Alaska to Cape Horn, are extremely musical. It is too late to atone for the barbarous treatment of a "vanishing race," but civilized Americans are beginning to realize how subtle and exquisite are the arts of which they have been capable. We can only speculate upon the kinds of music that might have resulted if colonizing whites and aboriginal Indians could have come to live together in the intimacy known by whites and Negroes in the South. In Paraguay, in the seventeenth century, the Jesuit missionaries are said to have done wonders with musically responsive natives. In this unique and short-lived enterprise, the Jesuits founded a religious state within the Spanish empire, having come to the conclusion that the so-called "savages" of the primeval forests were much better fitted for the establishment of a religious state than were the white people.

"'For not only,' wrote the fathers in their reports, 'do the Spaniards makes slaves of the Indians, but they also destroy them.'"[16]

Finding that the natives would overcome their timidity and listen to the fathers when they sang, they made music a basic part of the project, until "almost every function of everyday life was performed to music."

Although this might be called one of the freaks of music history, it is interesting if for no other reason than its rarity. On one of the few occasions when Europeans have gone to work intimately with "primitive savages," peacefully, without exploitation, musical communication seems to have been possible in a very short time.

More often, unfortunately, Spanish conquerors destroyed culture to get gold. The music of Mayan and Aztec civilizations was probably of the same high quality as their other fine arts, but of the latter at least some ruins remain. Southern musicologists are recovering old music in Peru and other countries, and thus a more civilized generation hopes to atone for the sins of old.

The developments in Latin America are therefore to be watched with great interest. They may throw a great deal of light on the creative processes of cultural diffusion, after epochs of cultural destruction and social separation. (See Ch. 12.)

[16] René Fülöp-Miller, *The Power and Secret of the Jesuits*, tr. by F. S. Flint and D. F. Tait, N. Y., 1930, Viking Press, p. 283.

V. CONCLUSION

During the last two generations, music in Europe has come to be defined, more than ever before, in nationalistic terms — terms that exclude comparison in a scientific way. But one of the most obvious facts to which attention has been directed, throughout these pages, is that of the internationalistic diffusion and exchange of musical thought. And the importance of these processes becomes more apparent after attention has been given to the changes now taking place in musical systems throughout the world, for it does not seem unreasonable or unscientific to hazard this inference: that the changes in early European music came about by means of the same processes that are making changes today in the Orient, in South America, in the United States, and in the Soviet Union. Change, throughout the world, is taking place in the regions that are open to communication with others. In regions that are isolated, whether for geographical, religious, or political reasons, customary or " consecrated " music is handed down from generation to generation, and " new " music must not violate, satirize, or ridicule honored traditions. When the isolation is political, leaders can and do inculcate the belief that the national music of this area and the arts of this people are superior to those of any other group. When the isolation is tied up with religious factors, different groups within the same boundaries always have their own arts of musical communication. The music of one religious group is usually anathema to another, until each becomes interested in the music of the other for esthetic or other reasons. For example, militant Protestants, with their vigorous hymn tunes, are, as a rule, repelled by the contemplative serenity of plainsong, but the latter is more and more creeping into their hymn books. On the other hand, the guardians of " pure " sacred music have always had a fight to keep out militant, secular rhythms, music that seems to satirize the sacrosanct.

It seems apparent, at any rate, that these great processes of history have been important in the transformations of musical styles everywhere: cultural contact, competition, and willful modification, in spite of authority, tradition, and prejudice.

The history of music histories has been treated, in earlier chapters, with due respect for chronological order, but " continuity " has been found in the " persistence and fixity " of traditional beliefs

(1) in the theological insistence on the divine origins of vocal music; (2) in the support for this theory on esthetic and political grounds; (3) in the hierarchical ordering of arts and values; finally, (4) in the nineteenth-century notions of musical form as "organism," a modern pseudo-mystical concept which has done more than anything else to postpone the modern scientific approach to musicology as a study of *style*. It has now been proposed that future histories deal with this element of persistence of "traditional modes of thought" as the basic fact, explaining change as due to man's creative activities, not as a result of a cosmic law of progress.

Without analogy, the history of music as an art of communication can be tied more closely to the student's musical experiences here and now. It may even come to be recognized that folk music is still being made and always will be as long as people communicate with each other. If much modern folk music is trivial and worthless, it may be so merely because our other communications have the same value or lack of it.

Instead of putting up a fence around certain areas known as a Classical Period, or a Romantic Period, it proves possible, in modern works, to trace the history of both the Classical and Romantic phases of musical thought and to show the inevitable manifestations of both in all periods of creative activity. Without the concern for order, coherence, and design in the former, and the adventurous, imaginative spirit of the latter, it is difficult to conceive of any musical art. But the comparable emphases on one or the other and the reactions of one against the other are tendencies that make history in all phases of culture. Instead of referring to a "General-bass Period,"[17] the music of the seventeenth century is now treated by modern scholars as one of the most vital aspects of that lusty manifestation of the human spirit, known as the Baroque. This period is important, as we have seen, for the emergence of epochal discoveries, inventions, and ways of looking at the record.

As for value, it is difficult to see why the historian or the teacher should *impose* standards as to what constitutes "good" music. Standards are even more necessary than ever, but they will take care of themselves when music is regarded as a fundamental need *now,* with various styles which may all be "good" at the proper place and time.

---

[17] See Riemann, as cited in Ch. 8, 1.

As for time, the history of music can begin with any given present, now, or in the past, to enrich our own experience here and now. Modern musicology is concerning itself with all the forms and styles of musical communication man has employed *at any time and in any culture,* whether for the sake of religion, of loyalty to group or country, of pure esthetic enjoyment, or for sheer amusement. It may not be too much to hope that this young science may set a good example by defining its terms and dispensing with analogy. By so doing we may rid ourselves of a notion which always makes harmonious human relations impossible, namely, the belief that peoples and arts of different times and places are *ipso facto* inferior. Thus we may show that the person who can enjoy intelligently the largest variety of differences is the one that is best educated in the history of our manifold arts of music.

BIBLIOGRAPHY

Literature concerning the general history of music in chronological order

1. Calvisius, Sethus, *Exercitationes Musicae Duae. Quarum prior est, de modis musicis, quos vulgo tonos vocant, recté cognoscendis, et dijudicandis.* Apelij, Leipzig, 1600. LC. The historical part, *De origine et progressu musices*, comprises the last half of the book, pp. 74–139. A second edition appeared in 1611.
2. Cerone, Domenico Pietro, *El Melopeo y Maestro. Tractado de musica theorica y pratica: en que se pone por extenso, lo que uno para hazerse perfecto musico ha menester saber: y por mayor facilidad, comodidad y claridad del lector, esta repartido en XXII libros.* 2 vols. Gargano and Nucci, Naples, 1613. NY.
3. Praetorius, Michael, *Syntagma Musicum.* 3 vols. Kahnt, Leipzig, 1615. NY. For the title of Volume I see p. 12.
4. Mersenne, Marin, *Traité de l'harmonie universelle.* Par le Sieur de Sermes, pseud. Bandry, Paris, 1627. NY. For the full title see p. 15.
5. Kircher, Athanasius, *Musurgia universalis, sive Ars magna consoni et dissoni in X libros digesta.* 2 vols. Corbelletti, Rome, 1650. NY.
6. Printz, Wolfgang Caspar, *Historische Beschreibung der edlen Sing- und Klingkunst, in welcher derselben Ursprung und Erfindung, Fortgang und Verbesserung, unterschiedlicher Gebrauch, wunderbare Wirkungen, mancherlei Feinde und zugleich berühmteste Ausüber von Anfang der Welt bis auf unserer Zeit in möglichster Kürze erzählt und vorgestellt werden, aus den vornehmsten autoribus abgefasst und in Ordnung gebracht.* 240 pp. Niethens, Dresden, 1690. NY.
7. Bontempi, Giovanni Andrea Angelini, *Historia musica, nella quale si ha piena cognitione della teorica, e della practica antica della musica harmonica; secondo la dottrina de'Greci, i quali inventata prima da Iubal avanti il Diluvio, e poi dopo ritrousta da Mercurio, la restituirono nella sua pristina, antica dignitate come della teorica, e della practica antica sia poi nata la practica moderna, che contiene la scientia del contrapunto.* 280 pp. Costantini, Perugia, 1695. NY.
8. Brossard, Sebastian de, *Dictionnaire de musique, ce qu'il y a de plus curieux, et de plus nécessaire à scavoir; tant pour l'histoire et la théorie.* 112 pp. Ballard, Paris, 1703. Translated, with additions, by James Grassineau as *A Musical Dictionary* [14]. 347 pp. London, 1740.
9. Bourdelot-Bonnet, *Histoire de la musique, et de ses effets depuis son origine, les progrès successifs de cet art jusqu'à présent.* Cochart,

Paris, 1715. NY. The 1726 edition, published by C. le Cène, Amsterdam, was in four small volumes, volumes 2, 3, 4 containing a reprint of *Comparaison de la musique italienne et de la musique française* by J. L. le Cerf de la Viéville, 1704.

10. Malcolm, Alexander, *Treatise of Musick, Speculative, Practical, and Historical*. 608 pp. Edinburgh, 1721. NY.

11. North, Hon. Roger, *Memoires of Musick, 1728*. 139 pp. First published by E. F. Rimbault, ed., London, 1846.

12. Walther, Johann Gottfried, *Musikalisches Lexicon, oder Musikalisches Bibliothec*. W. Deer, Leipzig, 1738. NY.

13. Prelleur, Peter, *A Brief History of Music, wherein is related the several Changes, Additions, and Improvements, from its Origin to the Present Time*. Collected from Aristoxenus, Plutarch, Boethius, Bontempi, Zarlino, Th. Salmon, and many others. A 20-page supplement to Prelleur's *Modern Musick-Master, or the Universal Musician*, with practical methods for singing and instrumental music. Bow Church Yard Printing Office, London, 1738. LC.

14. Grassineau, James, *A Musical Dictionary*, a translation and augmentation of Brossard's *Dictionnaire* [8]. 347 pp. J. Wilcox, London, 1740.

15. Mattheson, Johann, *Grundlage einer Ehrenpforte, woran der tüchtigsten Capellmeister, Componisten, Musikgelehrten, Tonkünstler, etc., Leben, Werke, Verdienste, etc., erscheinen sollen*. 428 pp. Hamburg, 1740.

16. Marpurg, F. W., *Historisch-Kritische Beyträge zur Aufnahme der Musik*. 5 vols. G. A. Lange, Berlin, 1754–1778. NY.

17. Cassiaux, Dom Phil. Jos., *Essai d'une histoire de la musique* (1757). Unpublished manuscript in the Bibliothéque Nationale in Paris. The table of contents is published in Combarieu [189], 1925 edition, Vol. II, p. 315.

18. Marpurg, F. W., *Kritische Einleitung in die Geschichte und Lehrsätze der alten und neuen Musik*. 246 pp. G. A. Lange, Berlin, 1759. NY.

19. Martini, Padre G. B., *Storia della musica*. 3 vols. (incomplete). Lelio della Volpe, Bologna, 1757–1781.

20. Brown, John, *A Dissertation on the Rise, Union, and Power, the Progressions, Separations, and Corruptions of Poetry and Music, to which is prefixed the Cure of Saul, a Sacred Ode*. 244 pp. Davis and Reymers, London, 1763. A German translation appeared in 1769, an Italian version in 1772.

21. Blainville, Charles Henri de, *Histoire générale, critique et philologique de la musique*. 189 pp. Pissot, Paris, 1767.

22. Rousseau, Jean Jacques, *Dictionnaire de musique*. Veuve Duchesne, Paris, 1768.

23. Dard, *Nouveaux principes de musique, auxquels l'auteur a joint l'histoire de la musique et de ses progressions, depuis son origine jusqu'à présent*. Paris, 1769. LC.

24. Eximeno y Pujades, Antonio, *Del origen y reglas de la musica, con*

la historia de su progreso, decadencia, y restauracion. Obra escrita en italiano por el abate Don Antonio Eximeno, y traducida al castellano per D. Francisco Antonio Gutierrez, Madrid, Imprenta real, 1796. Original Italian edition, Rome, 1774.

25. Gerbert, Martin, *Di cantu et musica sacra a prima ecclesiae aetate usque ad praesens tempus.* 2 vols. St. Blaise, 1774. NY.

26. Burney, Charles, *A General History of music from the earliest ages to the present period.* 4 vols. Printed for the author, London, 1776–1789. 2nd edition in 2 vols., Harcourt, Brace and Company, N. Y., 1935. Citations are from the original edition.

27. Hawkins, Sir John, *A General History of the Science and Practice of Music.* 4 vols. T. Payne and Son, London, 1776. 2nd edition in 2 vols. (963 pp.). Novello & Co., London, 1875. Citations are from the 2nd edition.

28. Borde, J. B. de la, *Essai sur la musique ancienne et moderne.* 4 vols. Pierres, Paris, 1780. NY.

29. Leopold, G. A. J., *Gedanken und Konjecturen zur Geschichte der Musik.* Franzen and Grosse, Stendhal, 1780. NY.

30. Forkel, J. N., *Allgemeine Geschichte der Musik.* 2 vols. Schwickert, Leipzig, 1788, 1801.
    Vol. I. From the origins to the music of the Romans. 504 pp.
    Vol. II. From the early Christian Era to the sixteenth century. 776 pp., with a Preface on the relation of music to human nature, especially to religious feeling.

31. Gerber, Ernst Ludwig, *Historisch-biographisches Lexicon der Tonkünstler, welches Nachrichten von den Leben und Werken musikalischer Schriftsteller, berühmter Componisten, Sänger, Meister auf Instrumenten, Dilettanten, Orgel- und Instrumenten-Macher enthält.* 2 vols. Vol. I, 991 pp.; Vol. II, 860 pp. Breitkopf, Leipzig, 1790–1792. NY.

32. Kalkbrenner, Christian, *Kurzer Abriss der Geschichte der Tonkunst, zum Vergnügen der Liebhaber der Musik.* F. Maurer, Berlin, 1792.
    —— *Histoire de musique,* translation of the above into French. Strassburg, 1802. NY.

33. Eastcott, Richard, *Sketches of the Origin, Progress and Effects of Music, with an account of the ancient Bards and Minstrels, illus. with various historical Facts, interesting Anecdotes, and Poetical Quotations.* 277 pp. 2nd edition, S. H. Hazard, Bath, 1793. NY.

34. Choron et Fayolle, *Dictionnaire historique de musique, précédé d'un sommaire de l'histoire de la musique.* 91 pp. Paris, 1817. Merely an abridgement of [31].

35. Butler, Charles, *Reminiscences, With a Letter to a Lady on Ancient and Modern Music.* Pp. 311–351 of the 4th London edition, Bliss and White, New York, 1824. NY.

36. Jones, George, *History of the Rise and Progress of Music, Theoretical and Practical.* Pp. 285–398, extracted from the *Encyclopaedia Londinensis,* London, 1818. NY. The *Encyclopaedia Londinensis,*

or Universal Dictionary of Arts, Sciences and Literature was compiled and arranged by John Wilkes, London, 1810–1829, 24 vols.
—— *Geschichte der Tonkunst,* translation of the above into German by I. F. Edlen von Mosel. 277 pp. Steiner & Co., Vienna, 1821.

37. Busby, Thomas, *A General History of Music from the Earliest Times to the Present, Condensed from the Works of Hawkins and Burney.* 2 vols. Whittaker, Simpkin and Marshall, London, 1819.
—— *Allgemeine Geschichte der Musik,* translation of the above into German by Christian F. Michaelis. 2 vols. Leipzig, 1821.

38. Bawr, Mme. Alexandra Sofia, *Histoire de la musique (abrégée),* forming part of *l'Encyclopédie des Dames.* 338 pp. Audot, Paris, 1823. Only 279 pages are devoted to history. A translation into German was made by A. Lewald, Nuremberg, 1826.

39. Stoepel, Franz, *Grundzüge der Geschichte der modernen Musik.* 83 pp. Duncker & Humblot, Berlin, 1821.

40. Nathan, Isaac, *An Essay on the History and Theory of Music, and on the Qualities, Capabilities and Management of the Human Voice.* 226 pp. Whittaker, London, 1823. Historical comments are confined to pp. 1–18.

41. Krause, Karl Chr. Fr., *Darstellungen aus der Geschichte der Musik.* 224 pp. Dieterich, Göttingen, 1827.

42. Mees, J. H., *Abrégé historique sur la musique moderne, depuis le 4me siècle et spécialement relatif a l'école flamande.* 26 pp. Included with the *Dictionnaire de musique moderne* by Castil-Blaze. Brussels, 1828.

43. Müller, Wilhelm Christian, *Aesthetisch-historische Einleitungen in die Wissenschaft der Tonkunst.* 2 vols. Breitkopf & Härtel, Leipzig, 1830.
Vol. I. *Versuch einer Aesthetik der Tonkunst, im Zusammenhänge mit den übrigen schönen Künsten nach geschichtlicher Entwickelung.* 375 pp.
Vol. II. *Übersicht einer Chronologie mit Andeutungen allgemeiner Civilisation und Kultur-Entwickelung.* 440 pp.

44. Schilling, Gustav, *Musikalisches Handwörterbuch, nebst einigen vorangeschickten allgemeinen philosophisch-historischen Bemerkungen über die Tonkunst.* 185 pp. Neff, Stuttgart, 1830.

45. Stafford, William Cooke, *A History of Music.* 387 pp. Edinburgh, 1830. Printed for Constable and Company. Chapters I–XI were published in *The Musical Review,* N. Y., Vols. 2–15, May–Sept., 1838.

46. Kushenov-Dmitrevski, D. F., *Lyric Museum,* including an outline of the history of music, with an addition of several famous musical artists and virtuosi; different anecdotes and four portraits of distinguished composers. 295 pp. St. Petersburg, 1831. LC.

47. Kiesewetter, Raphael Georg, Edler von Wiesenbrunn, *Geschichte der europäisch-abendländischen oder unserer heutigen Musik: Darstellung ihres Ursprunges, ihres Wachstumes und ihrer stufenweise Entwickelung; von dem ersten Jahrhundert des Christenthumes bis auf unsere Zeit.* Breitkopf & Härtel, Leipzig, 1834.

—— *History of the Modern Music of Western Europe: from the first century of the Christian Era to the present*, translation of the above into English by Robert Müller. 300 pp., with Supplement, 30 pp. Newby, London, 1848.

48. Hogarth, George, *Musical History, Biography and Criticism: being a general survey of music, from the earliest period to the present time*. Parker, London, 1835. American edition, 181 pp., New York, 1845.

49. Schilling, Gustav, *Encyclopädie der gesammten musikalischen Wissenschaften oder Universal-Lexicon der Tonkunst*. 7 vols. Köhler, Stuttgart, 1835–1840.

50. Fischer, J. M., *Die Grundbegriffe der Tonkunst in ihrem Zusammenhange nebst einer geschichtlichen Entwickelung derselben*. Grau, Leipzig, 1836. NY.

51. Fétis, F. J., *Résumé philosophique de l'histoire de la musique*. (Introduction to *Biographie universelle des musiciens*. 8 vols.) Leroux, Brussels, 1835–1844.

52. Higgins, William M., *The Philosophy of Sound and History of Music*. 256 pp. Orr, London, 1838.

53. Schilling, Gustav, *Geschichte der heutigen oder modernen Musik*. 816 pp. C. T. Groos, Karlsruhe, 1841.

54. Celoni, Tertulliano, *Compendio storico della musica antica e moderna, estratto dai migliori autori e compilato da T. C.* 54 pp. Florence, 1842.

55. Von Winterfeld, Carl, *Der evangelische Kirchengesang und sein Verhältnis zur Kunst des Tonsatzes*. 3 vols. Breitkopf, Leipzig, 1843, 1845, 1847.

56. De la Fage, Adrien, *Histoire générale de la musique et de la danse*. 2 vols. Paris, 1844.

57. *A Manual of Music, containing a Sketch of its Progress in all Countries and a Comprehensive Vade Mecum of Musical Science*. 60 pp. London, 1846.

58. Blondeau, A. L., *Histoire de la musique moderne depuis le premier siècle de l'ère chrétienne jusqu'à nos jours*. 2 vols. Tantenstein and Cordel, Paris, 1847. Vol. I, 330 pp.; Vol. II, 336 pp.

59. Bird, Joseph, *Gleanings from the History of Music, from the earliest ages to the commencement of the eighteenth century*. 299 pp. Mussey & Co., Boston, 1850.

60. Czerny, Karl, *Umriss der ganzen Musik-Geschichte, dargestellt in einem Verzeichniss der bedeutenderen Tonkünstler aller Zeiten, nach ihrer Lebensjahren und mit Angabe ihrer Werke, chronologisch geordnet, nach den Nationen und Epochen abgeteilt, den gleichzeitigen historischen Ereignissen zur Seite gestellt, und mit einem alphabetischen Namenregister versehen*. 92 pp. B. Schott, Mainz, 1851. Czerny's chart was translated and improved by Carl Engel [91], pp. 171–227.

61. Wagner, Richard, *Opera and Drama* (1851), Vol. 2 in *The Prose*

Works of Richard Wagner, translated by W. A. Ellis. Kegan Paul, London, 1893.

62. Brendel, Karl Franz, *Geschichte der Musik in Italien, Deutschland und Frankreich.* Hinze, Leipzig, 1852. 8th edition, 634 pp., Matthes, Leipzig, 1893.

63. Debay, A., *Hygiène de la voix, et gymnastique vocaux. Histoire de la musique depuis son origine jusqu'à nos jours.* 336 pp. Moquet, Paris, 1852. History from p. 201.

64. Labat, Jean Baptiste, *Études philosophiques et morales sur l'histoire de la musique ou récherches analytiques sur les éléments constitutifs de cet art à toutes les époques, sur la signification de ses transformations.* 2 vols. J. Techener, Paris, 1852.

65. Renehan, The Very Rev. Laurence, *History of Music.* 235 pp. C. M. Warren, Dublin, 1858.

66. Fischer, J. M., *Musikalische Rundschau über die letzten drei Jahrhunderte.* 192 pp. Leipzig, 1859.

67. Ambros, August Wilhelm, *Geschichte der Musik.* 5 vols. F. E. C. Leuckart, Breslau, 1862–1878.

Vol. I. (1862) China, India, Arabia, and Greece. This was completely altered in the second edition (1887) by B. von Sokolowsky after the latest researches of Westphal and Gevaert. Ambros is even *quoted* as a stranger to his own book on page 142. The last 200 pages, on Oriental music, are all that remain of Ambros.

Vol. II. (1864) Early Christian music, plainsong, Hucbald, Guido, troubadours, trouvères, origins of harmony. 538 pp.

Vol. III. (1868) Netherlands school, England, Venice, Roman predecessors of Palestrina. 591 pp. The work of Ambros ended here, but a fourth volume was prepared from his notes.

Vol. IV. (1881) Roman school, sixteenth century; opera, theorists, organists. 487 pp. A new edition by Hugo Leichtentritt appeared in 1909. 913 pp.

Vol. V. (1911) Selected examples, fifteenth and sixteenth centuries, compiled from Ambros' manuscript by Otto Kade. 605 pp. Wilhelm Langhans, *Die Geschichte der Musik des 17, 18, und 19 Jahrhunderts.* 2 vols., Leipzig, 1884, is included in the 1884 edition of Ambros' "complete works."

68. Andries, Jean Jacques, *Précis de l'histoire de la musique, depuis les temps les plus reculés, suivi de notices sur un grand nombre d'écrivains didactiques et théoriciens de l'art musical.* 312 pp. Busscher, Ghent, 1862.

69. Bauch, Wilhelm, *Hanbok i Musikens Historia frau fornverlden intill nutiden for tonkoustens idkare sa val som for dess vauner i allmanhet utgifven.* Stockholm, 1862.

70. Hullah, John Pike, *The History of Modern Music.* A course of lectures delivered at the Institute of Great Britain. 210 pp., four chronological charts. Parker and Bourn, London, 1862. 2nd edition, 1875.

71. Merseburger, Carl Wilhelm (Paul Frank, pseud.), *Geschichte der Tonkunst, Ein Handbüchlein für Musiker und Musik-Freunde.* 300 pp. C. Merseburger, Leipzig, 1863. 2nd edition, 1870.
72. Reissmann, August, *Allgemeine Geschichte der Musik.* 3 vols., many examples. Bruckmann, Munich, 1863–1864.
    Vol. I. Pre-Christian Music: music under early Christian influence.
    Vol. II. Development of the Art through the Folk Spirit.
    Vol. III. Further Development through Individuality.
73. Schlüter, Joseph, *Allgemeine Geschichte der Musik in übersichtlicher Darstellung.* Engelmann, Leipzig, 1863.
    —— *A General History of Music,* translation of the above into English by Mrs. Robert Tubbs. 359 pp. R. Bentley, London, 1865.
74. Lindner, Ernst Otto Timotheus, *Abhandlungen zur Tonkunst.* I. Guttentag, Berlin, 1864.
75. Mankell, Carl Abraham, *Musikens Historia, i Korta berattalser lattfattligt framstalld.* 3 vols. Orebro, 1864. NY.
76. Basevi, A., *Compendio di Storia della musica.* 2 vols. Guidi, Florence, 1865–1866. Vol. I, 58 pp.; Vol. II, 53 pp. NY.
77. Trambusti, Giuseppe Romano, *Storia della musica, e specialmente dell'italiana.* 614 pp. Colonnesi, Velletri, 1867. NY.
78. Fröhlich, Dr. Joseph, *Beiträge zur Geschichte der Musik der älteren und neueren Zeit auf musikalische Documente gegründet.* Stahel, Würzburg, 1868–1874. In two parts, Part I containing the text and Part II the documents.
79. Von Dommer, Arrey, *Handbuch der Musik-Geschichte.* 607 pp. F. W. Grünow, Leipzig, 1868. 2nd edition, 1878. New revised edition by Arnold Schering, 1914 [196].
80. Booker, The Rev. Charles F., Inaugural Dissertation, University of Rostock, *On the History of Music down to the End of the Seventeenth Century.* 39 pp. Adler's Heirs, Rostock, 1869.
81. Fétis, F. J., *Histoire générale de la musique depuis les temps anciens à nos jours.* 5 vols. (unfinished). Didot, Paris, 1869–1876.
    Vol. I. Music of the Ancient Semitic Races.
    Vol. II. Music of the Arabs, Moors, Hindus, Persians, and Turks.
    Vol. III. Music of Asia Minor, Greece, Etruscans, and Romans.
    Vol. IV. Music of the Early Christian Era to the Eleventh Century.
    Vol. V. Music from the Twelfth to the Fifteenth Century.
    Three more volumes were planned.
82. Mendel, Hermann, *Musikalisches Conversations-Lexicon.* 11 vols. Heimann, Berlin, 1870. 2nd ed., 1880, Oppenheim, Berlin, with a 12th volume in 1883.
83. Ritter, Frédéric Louis, *History of Music,* in the form of lectures. 2 vols. Oliver Ditson Co., New York, 1870–1874. Vol. I, 311 pp.; Vol. II, 225 pp.
84. Galli, Amintore, *La musica ed i musicisti dal secolo X. sino ai nostri*

giorni, ovvero biografie cronologiche d'illustri maestri. 111 pp. G. Canti, Milan.

85. Haweis, The Rev. H. A., *Music and Morals.* Harper and Bros., London and New York, 1871–1872. 24th impression, Longmans, Green & Co., 1934.

86. Fétis, F. J., *Biographie universelle des musiciens.* 2nd edition, Didot, Paris, 1873. Two supplementary volumes by Arthur Pougin were added in 1878, 1880.

87. Frojo, Giovanni, *Saggio storico-critico intorno alla musica indiana-egiziana-greca e principalmente italiana.* 201 pp. Orfanotrofia, Cantanzero, 1873.

88. Chappell, William, *The History of Music.* Vol. I: *From the Earliest Records to the Fall of the Roman Empire.* 403 pp. Chappell and Co., London, 1874. Four volumes were projected. Fire destroyed materials for the second.

89. Köstlin, H. A., *Geschichte der Musik im Umriss.* 715 pp. Breitkopf. & Härtel, Leipzig, 1874. 6th edition. 1910.

90. Ricotti, Onestina, *La musica e i suoi coltori: Trattato elementare ad uso degli istituti educativi.* 306 pp. Paravia, Rome, 1874.

91. Engel, Carl, *Musical Myths and Facts.* Novello, London, 1876.

92. Von Ganting, Ludwig, *Die Grundzüge der musikalischen Richtungen in ihren geschichtlichen Entwickelung.* 39 pp. Breitkopf & Härtel, Leipzig, 1876.

93. Kraussold, Lorenz, *Die Musik in ihrer kulturhistorischen Entwickelung und Bedeutung, von den ältesten Zeiten bis auf Richard Wagner.* 106 pp. Grau, Bayreuth, 1876.

94. Marcillac, F., *Histoire de la musique moderne et des musiciens célèbres en Italie, en Allemagne et en France depuis l'ère chrétienne jusqu'à nos jours, avec un atlas de 22 planches.* 512 pp. Sandoz and Fischbacher, Paris, 1876.

95. Hunt, H. G. Bonavia, *A Concise History of Music.* 184 pp. London, 1877–1888. 2nd edition, Chas. Scribner's Sons, 1878. 16th edition, G. Bell, London, 1902.

96. Musiol, Robert, *Grundriss der Musikgeschichte.* Leipzig, 1877. 2nd edition, 1888, 279 pp.; 3rd edition, edited by Richard Hofmann, Leipzig, 412 pp.

97. Wangemann, Otto, *Grundriss der Musikgeschichte, von den ersten Anfängen bis zur neuesten Zeit.* 216 pp. Heinrichshofen, Magdeburg, 1878.

98. Langhans, Wilhelm, *Die Musikgeschichte in 12 Vorträgen.* 1879. Translated into English by J. H. Cornell, *The History of Music in 12 Lectures.* 184 pp. G. Schirmer, New York, 1886, 1896.

99. Grove, Sir George, *Dictionary of Music and Musicians.* 4 vols. The Macmillan Co., London and New York, 1879–1890. 2nd edition revised by Fuller Maitland, 1904–1909. 3rd edition revised by H. C. Colles, 1927–1928, 5 vols., plus an American Supplement edited by Waldo Selden Pratt.

100. Naumann, Emil, *Illustrierte Musikgeschichte: Die Entwickelung der Tonkunst aus frühesten Anfängen bis auf die Gegenwart.* 2 vols. Spemann, Stuttgart, 1880–1885.
——— *The History of Music,* translation of the above by F. Praeger, ed., with chapters on English music by the Rev. Sir F. A. Gore Ouseley. 2 vols., 1334 pp. Cassell, London and New York, 1886. After various German editions, the work is now completely rewritten (10th edition, Eugen Schmitz, ed., Stuttgart, 1934, [298]).

101. Challoner, Robert, *History of the Science and Art of Music. Its origin, development, and progress.* Designed as a textbook for the use of academies, seminaries, common schools, and private teachers. 305 pp. Newhall, Cincinnati, 1880.

102. *Musikens historia fra die aeldste tider til vore dage, populaert fremstillet.* 639 pp. Copenhagen, 1881–1887.

103. Bell, Nancy R. E., *Elementary History of Art.* An introduction to ancient and modern architecture, sculpture and music. By N. D'Anvers (pseud.). Chas. Scribner's Sons, London and New York, 1874–1876.
——— *Elementary History of Music.* 101 pp. Chas. Scribner's Sons, New York, 1882.

104. Bussler, Ludwig, *Geschichte der Musik. Sechs Vorträge über die fortschreitende Entwickelung der Musik in der Geschichte.* 176 pp. Habel, Berlin, 1882.

105. Collin, Mlle. Laure, *Histoire abrégée de la musique et des musiciens.* Delagrave, Paris, 1882. 4th edition, 1884, 364 pp.

106. Nohl, Ludwig, *Allgemeine Musikgeschichte populär dargestellt.* P. Reclam, Leipzig, 1882.

107. Riemann, Hugo, *Musiklexicon, Theorie und Geschichte der Musik.* Leipzig, 1882, 1900, 1905. 11th edition, Alfred Einstein, ed., Hesse, Leipzig, 1929, 2 vols., 2109 pp. A Nazi version is now appearing, in installments, ed. by Josef Müller-Blattau, Schott and Sons, Mainz.
——— *Dictionary of Music* (tr.). London, 1893, 1908. Translations have also appeared in French, Danish, and Russian.

108. Bisson, Alexandre Charles Auguste, *Petite encyclopédie musicale.* 2 vols. Hennuyer, Paris, 1881–1884. Vol. II, pp. 1–197, are devoted to *L'histoire générale de la musique;* pp. 109–395 to biographies.

109. Kothe, Bernhard, *Abriss der Musikgeschichte nebst einem Wegweiser für den Klavier und Orgel-Unterricht.* 244 pp. Leuckart, Leipzig. 11th edition, R. F. Procházka, ed., Leipzig and Prague, 1919, 496 pp. 12th edition, Leuckart, 1929, 563 pp.

110. Lavoix, Henri Marie François, *Histoire de la musique.* 368 pp. Quantin, Paris, 1884.

111. Clément, Félix, *Histoire de la musique depuis les temps anciens jusqu'à nos jours.* 800 pp., illus. Hachette, Paris, 1885.

112. Macfarren, Sir George Alexander, *Musical History,* with a roll of musicians and the times and places of their births and deaths. Harper & Bros., New York, 1885.

113. Rowbotham, John Frederick, *A History of Music to the Time of the Troubadours*. 3 vols. Trübner, London, 1885–1887. 2nd edition, Chas. Scribner's Sons, New York and London, 1893, in one volume.

114. Fiorentino, V., *La musica: lavoro storica filosofico sociale*. 328 pp. Marghieri, Naples, 1887.

115. Haberl, Franz Xaver, *Bausteine zur Musikgeschichte*. A series of musical biographies, beginning with Dufay. 3 vols. Breitkopf, Leipzig, 1885–1888.

116. Lillie, Lucy C., *The Story of Music and Musicians for Young Readers*. 245 pp. Harper & Bros., New York, 1886.

117. Rockstro, William Smyth, *A General History of Music from the Infancy of the Greek Drama to the Present Period*. Chas. Scribner's Sons, New York and London, 1886. 3rd edition, 1897. 4th edition, 1918, London, Low, Marston and Co.

118. Fillmore, John Comfort, *Lessons in Musical History*. Theo. Presser Co., Philadelphia, 1888.

119. Pohl, Richard, *Die Hohenzüge der musikalischen Entwickelung, in 6 Vorlesungen dargestellt*. 373 pp. Elischer, Leipzig, 1888.

120. Riemann, Hugo, *Katechismus der Musikgeschichte*. Hesse, Leipzig, 1888, 1897, 1901.
——— *Catechism of Musical History* (tr.). Augener, London, 1892.
——— *Abriss der Musikgeschichte*, a revision of the *Katechismus*, 7th edition, Hesse, Berlin, 1919 (?).

121. Henderson, William James, *The Story of Music*. Longmans, Green & Co., New York, 1889, 1890, 1892, 1897, 1898, 1901.

122. Prozniz, Adolf, *Compendium der Musikgeschichte*. 3 vols. A. Holder, Vienna, 1889, 1900, 1915.

123. Davey, Henry, *The Student's Musical History*. 148 pp. Curwen, London, 1889. 10th edition, 1927.

124. Matthews, W. S. B., *A Popular History of the Art of Music from the Earliest Times to the Present*. 536 pp. Theo. Presser Co., Philadelphia, 1891.

125. Svoboda, Adalbert, *Illustrierte Musik-Geschichte*. Grüninger, Stuttgart, 1892. Issued as a supplement to *Neue Musik-Zeitung*, 1892.

126. Parry, Sir Charles Hubert Hastings, *The Art of Music*. Kegan Paul, London, 1893. Later published as *The Evolution of the Art of Music* by D. Appleton-Century Co. The latest edition has additional chapters by H. C. Colles, D. Appleton-Century, 1930, 483 pp.

127. Wallaschek, Richard, *Primitive Music,* an inquiry into the origin and development of music, songs, instruments, dances and pantomimes of savage races. 326 pp. Longmans, Green & Co., London, 1893.

128. Untersteiner, Alfredo, *Storia della musica*. Hoepli, Milan. 3rd edition, 1910.
——— *A Short History of Music,* translation of the above into English by S. C. Very. 349 pp. Dodd, Mead and Co., New York, 1902.

129. Stolz, Jacob, *Allgemeine Geschichte der Musik*. H. Wagner. Graz, 1894.

130. Gebeschus, J., *Geschichte der Musik von den ältesten vorchrist-lichen Zeiten bis auf die Gegenwart*. 272 pp. Schultze, Berlin, 1895.

131. Lavignac, Albert, *La musique et les musiciens*. 592 pp. Delagrave, Paris, 1896.

—— *Music and Musicians,* translation of the above into English by William Marchant, with an appendix on "Music in America and the Present State of the Art of Music" by H. E. Krehbiel. 518 pp. Henry Holt and Co., New York, 1899, 1906.

132. Acosta, Paul d', *Essai de philologie musicale — Études d'histoire et d'esthétique comparées sur la musique à travers les âges*. 133 pp. Siffer, Ghent, 1896.

133. Lacombe, Louis, *Philosophie et musique*. 458 pp. Fischbacher, Paris, 1896 (posthumous).

134. Ragmadze, A. S., *Ocherski istorii muzykiet drevnieishikh vremen do polybiny XIX vieka chetyrekh chastiakh s dvienadtsat' iu notymi prilozheniiami Sostavil po lekteiiam, chittaym autorom v.* 705 pp. Moskow Conservatorium, 1896. LC.

135. Sacchetti, L. A., *Kratkaia istoriches kaia muzykal, naia khrest-omatiia s drevmeishikh vremen do XVII vreka*. 475 pp. St. Petersburg, 1896. LC.

136. Bücher, Karl, *Arbeit und Rhythmus*. Leipzig, 1896. 3rd edition, B. G. Teubner, Leipzig, 1902.

137. Tagore, Sir Raja S. M. (Saurindramohana Thakura), *Universal History of Music,* compiled from various sources, together with various original notes on Hindu music. 354 pp. Goswamy, Calcutta, 1896.

138. Panum, Hortense, and Behrend, William, *Illustreret Musikhis-torie en Fremstilling for Nordiske Laesere*. 2 vols. Nordisk, Copenhagen, 1897.

139. Henderson, William James, *How Music Developed: A Critical and Explanatory Account of the Growth of Modern Music*. 413 pp. F. A. Stokes Co., New York, 1898.

140. Matthew, James E., *A Handbook of Musical History and Bibliography from St. Gregory to the Present Time*. 486 pp. (Revised edition of author's *Manual of Musical History*, 1892.) G. P. Putnam's Sons, New York and London, 1898.

141. Prokin, N., *Kratkoe ruksvodste (konspekt) k izucheniiu istoria muzyki, sostavil svobodnyi khudozhnik*. 36 pp. St. Petersburg Conservatory, 1898. LC.

142. Smith, Hannah, *Music; How It Came to Be What It Is*. 254 pp. Chas. Scribner's Sons, New York, 1898.

143. Tipper, Henry, *The Growth and Influence of Music in Relation to Civilization*. E. Stock, London, 1898.

144. Soubies, Albert, *L'histoire de la musique*. 14 vols. Flammarion, Paris, 1898–1900. A classification entirely in terms of nationality:

Germany and Russia (2); Spain (3); Portugal; Hungary; Bohemia; Switzerland; Holland; Belgium (2); Scandinavia (3); British Isles (2 volumes).

145. Eitner, Robert, *Biographisch-bibliographisches Quellen-Lexicon der Musiker und Musikgelehrten der christlichen Zeitrechnung bis zur Mitte des 19ten Jahrhunderts.* 10 vols. Breitkopf, Leipzig, 1899–1904. Supplement, *Miscellanea Musicae Bio-Bibliographica* (1912–1914), edited by H. Springer, M. Schneider, and W. Wolffheim.

146. Hadow, H. W., editor, *Oxford History of Music.* 6 vols. Oxford, 1901–1905. 2nd edition, 1929–1932. Vol. VII, 1934. See also [257].

Vol. I. *The Polyphonic Period* (Part I), by H. E. Wooldridge. 2nd edition, edited by Percy V. Buck, "Method of Musical Art" (300–1400) omits the original chapters on Greek music, making the latter one of the subjects discussed (by Cecil Torr) in the Introductory Volume. In the 2nd edition the copious examples of old music occupy 150 pages out of 334.

Vol. II. *The Polyphonic Period* (Part II), by H. E. Wooldridge. 2nd edition, revised by Percy V. Buck, 1932, 500 pp. "Method of Musical Art" (1500–c. 1600). A little over half of the space is devoted to examples.

Vol. III. *The XVIIth Century,* by Sir C. H. H. Parry, 474 pp. New edition, with Preface by Edward J. Dent, 1937.

Vol. IV. *The Age of Bach and Handel,* by J. A. Fuller-Maitland. 2nd edition, 1931, 362 pp.

Vol. V. *The Viennese Period,* by W. H. Hadow. 2nd edition, 1931, 350 pp.

Vol. VI. *The Romantic Period,* by Edward Dannreuther. 2nd edition, 1931, 374 pp.

Vol. VII. *Symphony and Drama* (1840–1900), by H. C. Colles, 1934, 504 pp.

147. Lavignac, Albert, *L'éducation musicale.* 447 pp. Delagrave, Paris, 1902.

—— *Musical Education,* translation of the above into English by Esther Singleton. D. Appleton-Century Co., New York, 1903.

148. Crowest, F. J., *The Story of the Art of Music.* 190 pp. D. Appleton-Century Co., New York, 1902, 1915.

149. Keller, Otto, *Geschichte der Musik.* 440 pp. Friesenhahn, Leipzig, 1894. 2nd edition, *Illustrierte Geschichte der Musik.* 2 vols. Koch, Munich, 1903.

150. Riemann, Hugo, *Handbuch der Musikgeschichte.* 2 vols.; 5 parts. Breitkopf, Leipzig, 1904–1913.

Vol. I. (1904) 1. Greek Music.
(1905) 2. Middle Ages (to 1450).
Vol. II. (1907) 3. Renaissance (1300–1600).
(1912) 4. The Thorough-Bass Epoch (1600–1700).
(1913) 5. The Great German Masters.

A translation into English has been made by S. Harrison Lovewell; the unpublished manuscript, *A Manual of Music History,* is in the New York Public Library and in the Library of Congress. (See also Riemann's *Geschichte der Musik Theorie im IX–XIX Jahrhunderten,* Hesse, Leipzig, 1898, 1921, and *Grundriss der Musikwissenschaft,* Leipzig, 1908.)

151. Mason, D. G., "The Periods of Music History," in *Beethoven and His Forerunners,* Chapter I. The Macmillan Co., New York, 1904. Later editions: 1911, 1914, 1927.

152. Baltzell, Winton James, *A Complete History of Music.* 565 pp. Theo. Presser Co., Philadelphia, 1905. New and enlarged edition, 1931.

153. Kretzschmar, Hermann, editor, *Kleine Handbücher der Musikgeschichte nach Gattungen.* 10 vols. Breitkopf, Leipzig, 1905–1922. The first series of scientifically edited histories of this type. The editor himself contributed the volumes *Geschichte der neueren deutschen Lieder* and *Geschichte der Oper,* 1912 and 1919 respectively. Others in the series include: Johann Wolf, *Handbuch der Notationskunde,* 2 vols., 1913, 1919; Curt Sachs, *Handbuch der Instrumentenkunde,* 1920; A. Schering, *Geschichte des Instrumental-Konzerts,* 1905, *Geschichte des Oratoriums,* 1911; Karl Nef, *Geschichte der Sinfonie und Suite,* 1921; E. Schmitz, *Geschichte der weltlichen Solokantate,* 1914; P. Wagner, *Geschichte der Messe,* 2 vols., 1914, 1919; H. Bobstiber, *Geschichte der Ouverture,* 1913; G. Schünemann, *Geschichte des Dirigierens,* 1913; and Hugo Leichtentritt, *Geschichte der Motette,* 1908.

Kretzschmar also initiated the following series: *Führer durch den Konzert-Saal,* including *Sinfonie* and *Suite,* 1887 (6th edition, 1921); *Kirchliche Chorwerke,* 1888 (5th edition, 1921); *Oratorien und weltliche Chorwerke,* 1890 (4th edition, 1920). The series was augmented in 1932 by H. Engel, *Das Instrumental-Konzert,* and H. Mersmann, *Kammermusik.*

154. Leichtentritt, Hugo, *Geschichte der Musik.* 112 pp. Hillger, Berlin, 1905. (Hillger's *Illustrierte Volksbücher,* Vol. 36.)

155. De Roda Lopez, D. Cecilio, *La evolución de la música. Discursos leidos ante la Real Academia de Bellas Artes de San Fernando.* 66 pp. Madrid, 1906.

156. Canudo, Riciotto, *Le livre d'évolution de l'homme: Psychologie musicale des civilisations.* 326 pp. Sansot, Paris, 1907.

157. Dickinson, Edward, *The Study of the History of Music;* with an annotated guide to music literature. 409 pp. Chas. Scribner's Sons, New York, 1907.

158. Combarieu, Jules, *La musique, ses lois et son évolution.* Flammarion, Paris, 1907. Translated by F. Legge, International Scientific Series, as *Music, Its Laws and Evolution.* Kegan Paul, London, 1910.

159. Paine, John Knowles, *The History of Music to the Death of Schubert.* 314 pp. Ginn & Co., Boston and London, 1907.

160. Möhler, A., *Geschichte der alten und mittelalterlichen Musik.* 2

vols. Sammlung Göschen, Leipzig, 1907. Supplemented by the following, in the same format:

161. Grunsky, Karl, *Musikgeschichte (seit 1800)*. 2 vols. Vol. I, 121 pp.; Vol. II, 155 pp. Leipzig, 1908.

162. Pratt, Waldo Selden, *The History of Music, A Handbook and Guide for Students*. First edition, 1907; 1910 edition, 654 pp. Revised edition, 1927, 734 pp. G. Schirmer, New York. The 1935 edition has an added chapter on the early twentieth century by Arthur Mendel.

163. Spiro, Friedrich, *Geschichte der Musik*. 172 pp. Teubner, Leipzig, 1907.

164. Surette, T. W., and Mason, D. G., *The Appreciation of Music*. H. W. Gray, New York, 1907. 15th edition, 1924.

165. Torrefranca, Fausto, "Le origini della musica," *Rev. mus. it.*, pp. 555–594, *Anno XIV, Fasc. 30*. Turin, 1907.

166. Duncan, Edmundstoune, *A History of Music*. 191 pp. Vincent, London, 1908. A selected list of compact biographies.

167. Goddard, Joseph, *The Rise of Music, being a Careful Inquiry into the Development of the Art from its Primitive Puttings Forth in Egypt and Assyria to its Triumphant Consummation in Modern Effect*. 386 pp. Chas. Scribner's Sons, London and New York, 1908. See also *Rise and Development of Opera*, 1912.

168. Hubbard, A. L., editor-in-chief, *American History and Encyclopedia of Music*. 10 vols. Irving Squire, Toledo, Ohio, 1908. Biography, 2 vols.; Dictionary; American Music; Foreign Music; Opera, 2 vols.; Oratorio and Masses; Instruments; Theory.

169. Hamilton, Clarence G., *Outlines of Music History*. 307 pp. Oliver Ditson Co., Boston, 1908, 1919, 1924.

170. Riemann, Hugo, *Grundriss der Musikwissenschaft*. Quelle & Meyer, Leipzig, 1908.

171. Riemann, Hugo, *Kleines Handbuch der Musikgeschichte mit Periodisierung nach Stilprinzipien und Formen*. 292 pp. Leipzig, 1908.

172. Wallace, William, M.D., *The Threshold of Music*, with a chronological chart indicating contemporaries in art, science, and literature. The Macmillan Co., London and New York, 1908.

173. Batka, Richard, *Allgemeine Geschichte der Musik*. 2 vols. Vol. I, 300 pp.; Vol. II, 332 pp. Grüninger, Stuttgart, 1909.

174. Bellaigue, Camille, *Les époques de la musique*. 2 vols. Delagrave, Paris, 1909.

175. Combarieu, J., *Études de philologie III: La musique et la magie; études sur les origines populaires de l'art musical*. 374 pp. Picard, Paris, 1909.

176. Harris, Clement A., *Chronometrical Chart of Musical History, Presenting a Bird's-Eye View from the Pre-Christian Era to the Twentieth Century*. W. Reeves, London, 1909.

177. Woollett, Henri, *Histoire de la musique depuis l'antiquité jusqu'à*

nos jours. 4 vols. Fischbacher, Paris, 1909–1925. Prize essay, l'Académie.

178. Cooke, James Francis, *Standard History of Music, A First History for All Ages.* 260 pp. Theo. Presser Co., Philadelphia, 1910.

179. Landormy, Paul Charles René, *Histoire de la musique.* Paris, 1910. —— *A History of Music,* translation of the above into English, with a supplementary chapter on American music, by Frederick H. Martens. 397 pp. Chas. Scribner's Sons, New York, 1923.

180. Pastor, Willy, " Music of Primitive Peoples," translated for *The Annual Report, Smithsonian Institution,* 1912, pp. 679–700, from the *Zeitschrift für Ethnologie,* Vol. 42, 1910, pp. 654–675.

181. Storck, Karl, *Geschichte der Musik,* Muth, Stuttgart, 1904. 2nd edition, 1910; 4th edition, 1921; 5th edition, 1922. 2 vols. Vol. I, 488 pp.; Vol. II, 489 pp.

181A. —— *Musik und Musiker in Karikatur und Satire; eine Kulturge-schichte der Musik aus dem Zerrspiegel.* 447 pp. G. Stalling, Oldenburg, 1911.

182. Stumpf, Carl, *Die Anfänge der Musik.* Barth, Leipzig, 1911.

183. Emmanuel, Maurice, *Histoire de la langue musicale.* 2 vols. Laurens, Paris, 1911.

184. Hullah, Annette, *A Little History of Music.* 220 pp. Longmans, Green & Co., New York, 1911.

185. Colles, Henry Cope, *The Growth of Music: A Study in Musical History for Schools.* 3 vols. Oxford Press, 1912–1916. New edition, 1931, 3 vols. in one. Intended for popular reading and elementary instruction. Vol. I (1912), 159 pp., Troubadours to Bach; Vol. II (1913), 174 pp., Age of the Sonata; Vol. III (1916), 192 pp., Ideals of the Nineteenth Century.

186. MacDowell, Edward, *Critical and Historical Essays,* edited from lectures delivered at Columbia University. A. P. Schmidt, Boston, 1912.

187. Zschorlich, Paul, *Musikgeschichte.* 224 pp. Miniatur-Bibliotek, Leipzig, 1912.

188. Busoni, F., *A New Musical Aesthetic.* G. Schirmer, New York, 1913.

189. Combarieu, Jules, *Histoire de la musique des origines au début du XXme siècle.* 3 vols. Colin, Paris, 1913, 1920, 1924, 1930. Originally this work, in 2 vols., ended with the death of Beethoven; the third volume was added in 1920.

190. Lavignac, Alfred, *Encyclopédie de la musique et dictionnaire de la Conservatoire.* Directed by L. de la Laurencie, Delagrave, Paris, 1913–1931.
Partie Ière, Histoire de la musique, 6 vols. 3403 pp., 1920–1931; first 3 vols., 1913. The method of Soubies is adopted, with national divisions.
Vol. I. Antiquity: Egypt, Assyria, Syria, Hebrews, China, Korea, Japan, India, Greece; pp. 1–540. Middle Ages: Byzantine Music, Occidental Liturgic Music, Early Counterpoint; pp. 540–610.

Vol. II. Italy, pp. 611–911; Germany, pp. 911–971. (An appendix on Handel appears in Vol. V, pp. 3372–3395.)
Vol. III. France, pp. 1176–1814; Belgium, pp. 1815–1861; England, pp. 1862–1912.
Vol. IV. Spain, pp. 1913–2400; Portugal, pp. 2401–2470.
Vol. V. Russia and other countries. The United States, pp. 3245–3332, comes between the Canary Islands and the North American Indians.
Partie IIme, Technique — Esthétique — Pédagogie, 6 vols., 3920 pp., 1925–1931.

191. Gantvoort, Arnold Johann, *Familiar Talks on the History of Music.* 285 pp. G. Schirmer, New York, 1913.

192. Bonaventura, Arnaldo, *Manuele di storia della musica.* 254 pp. Giusti, Leghorn, 1914; 9th edition, 1926.

193. Bertrand, Paul, *Précis d'histoire de la musique.* 168 pp. Leduc, Paris, 1914, 1921.

194. Chavarri, Eduardo Lopez, *Historia de la música.* 2 vols. Cami, Barcelona, 1914–1916, 1929.

195. Moser, H. J., "Der Durgedanke als kulturgeschichtliches Problem," *Sb. der Int. Musikgesellschaft,* Vol. 15, Part 2, Jan.–March, 1914.

196. Schering, Arnold, *Handbuch der Musikgeschichte bis zum Ausgang des 18ten Jahrhunderts. Auf Grundlage des gleichnamigen Werks von Arrey von Dommer, 1868* [79]. *Als dessen 3. Auflage bearbeitet.* Breitkopf & Härtel, Leipzig, 1914.

197. Schering, Arnold, *Tabellen zur Musikgeschichte.* Breitkopf, Leipzig, 1914. 4th edition, 1934, 152 pp.

198. Sprüngli, Th. A., *Kurzer Abriss der Musikgeschichte.* 168 pp. Tonger, Cologne, 1914.

199. Tapper, Thomas (and Percy Goetschius), *Essentials in Music History.* 365 pp. Chas. Scribner's Sons, New York, 1914. There are also later editions.

200. Dandelot, A., *Résumé d'histoire de la musique.* Senart, Paris, 1915. 4th edition, 1929, 191 pp. with *Complément,* 79 pp.

201. Mason, Daniel Gregory, editor-in-chief, Hall, Leland, and Searchinger, C., *A Narrative History of Music,* the first 3 vols. of *The Art of Music* (14 vols.). The National Society of Music, New York, 1915. Historical introduction by C. H. H. Parry.

202. Joteyko, Tadeusz, *Historja muzyki polskiej, ponszechnej wxarysie.* 192 pp. Arcta, Warsaw, 1916. LC.

203. Stanford, Sir Charles Villiers, and Forsyth, Cecil, *A History of Music.* 384 pp. The Macmillan Co., New York, 1916.

204. Einstein, A., *Geschichte der Musik.* Teubner, Leipzig, 1917. 2nd edition, 132 pp. 4th edition, Sijthoff, Leyden, 1934, 167 pp.

204A.—— *A Short History of Music,* translation of the above into English. A. Knopf, New York, 1937. See also [316].

205. Baker, Theodore, *Biographical Dictionary of Musicians.* G. Schir-

mer, New York, 1918, 1919. Original 1905 edition now being revised by Paul Pisk.

206. Rau, Carl August, *Geschichte der Musik, vom Beginne der christlichen Zeitrechnung bis zum Ausgange des XIX. Jahrhunderts, in Tabellenform dargestellt.* 272 pp. Kösel, Munich, 1918.

207. Adler, Guido, *Methode der Musikgeschichte.* 222 pp. Breitkopf, Leipzig, 1919.

208. Moser, H. J., " Zur Methodik der musikalischen Geschichtsschreibung," *Zeitschrift zur Aesthetik,* Vol. XIV, 1920, pp. 130–145.

209. Moser, H. J., *Geschichte der deutschen Musik.* 3 vols. Cotta, Berlin and Stuttgart, 1921–1928.

210. Nef, Karl, *Einführung in die Musikgeschichte.* Kober, Basel, 1920. 2nd edition, 1930, 351 pp. This work by a Swiss scholar has been translated into French, Norwegian, and now into English for American students:
—— *An Outline of the History of Music,* tr. by Carl F. Pfatteicher. 386 pp. Columbia University Press, New York, 1935.

211. Hutschenruijter, Wouter, *De Geschiedenis der Toonkunst: Twaalf Voordrachten gehouden in de Volks-Universitait te Rotterdam.* 327 pp., without index. Amsterdam, 1920. A series of popular lectures. Pp. 316–320 are devoted to Netherlands music.

212. Reiss, Dr. Josef, *Historja Muzyki w Zarysie.* 424 pp. Warsaw, 1920.
—— *Encykclopja muzyki.* 325 pp. Arcta, Warsaw, 1924.

213. Moreira de Sá, B. V., *Historia da musica.* Oporto, 1920.

214. Sonneck, O. G., *Miscellaneous Studies in the History of Music,* with reprint of " The History of Music in America " (M.T.N.A., 1916), pp. 324–344. The Macmillan Co., New York, 1921.

215. Bourguès, Lucien, and Denéréaz, Alexandre, *La musique et la vie intérieure: essai d'une histoire psychologique de l'art musical; ouvrage illustré de 983 exemples, 18 figures, 19 tableaux de filiation musicale, et d'une planche hors texte representant les courbes dynamogénitiques.* 586 pp. Alcan, Paris and Lausanne, 1921.

216. Dreizin, U. T. N., *Muzyka i revoliutsiia.* 109 pp. Mogilev, 1921. LC.

217. Heyman, Katherine Ruth, *The Relation of Ultra-Modern to Archaic Music.* Boston, 1921.

218. Van Milligen, S., *Ontwikkelungsgang der Musiek van de Oudheid tot onzen Tijd: met Medewerking van Sem Dresden.* 624 pp. Wolters, Groningen, 1912: 3rd edition, Groningen, 1928, 744 pp. Very scant attention is paid to modern Dutch and Belgian music.

219. Chop, Max, *Führer durch die Musikgeschichte.* 304 pp. Globus, Berlin, 1922.

220. Coleman, Satis N., *Creative Music for Children: A Plan of Training Based on the Natural Evolution of Music, including the Making and Playing of Instruments.* G. P. Putnam's Sons, New York, 1922, 1928.

221. Norlind, Tobias, *Allman musikhistoria, frau aldre tider till nar-varande tid.* 845 pp. Wahlström and Widstrand, Stockholm, 1922. Issued in 9 parts, 1920–1922. LC.
222. Pannain, G., *Lineamenti di storia della musica.* 256 pp. Curci, Naples, 1922.
223. Rolland, Romain, *Un voyage musical au pays de la passé.* Hachette, Paris, 1920.
—— *A Musical Tour through the Land of the Past,* translation of the above into English by B. Miall, 235 pp., London, 1922.
224. Adler, Guido, *Handbuch der Musikgeschichte.* Frankfort-on-Main, 1924. 2nd edition, H. Keller, Berlin, 1930, 2 vols., 1245 pp. Contributions from 35 musicologists in various countries.
225. d'Hurigny, Franz, *Tout ce qu'il faut savoir de l'histoire de la musique des origines à nos jours.* 81 pp. Fauconnier, Paris, 1924.
226. Kochetov, N., *Outline of the History of Music.* 3rd edition of an older work. 198 pp. 1924. LC.
227. Mason, D. G., *From Song to Symphony.* Oliver Ditson Co., Boston, 1924.
228. Pratt, Waldo Selden, *The New Encyclopedia of Music and Musicians.* 967 pp. C. Fischer, New York, 1924.
229. White, Robert T., *Music and Its Story.* 184 pp. Cambridge University Press, 1924.
230. Casella, Alfredo, *The Evolution of Music throughout the History of the Perfect Cadence.* Chester, London, 1924. The text is in Italian, French, and English. There are 100 musical examples from the thirteenth century to Schönberg.
231. Bauer, Marion, and Peyser, Ethel, *How Music Grew, from Historic Times to the Present Day.* 602 pp. G. P. Putnam's Sons, New York, 1925.
232. Meyer, Kathi, *Das Konzert, ein Führer durch die Geschichte des Musizierens, in Bildern und Melodien.* 163 pp. Engelhorn, Stuttgart, 1925.
233. Respighi, O., and Luciani, S. A., *Orpheus: Initiazione musicale: Storia della musica.* 352 pp. Part II, pp. 137–352. Barbéra, Florence, 1925.
234. Scholes, Percy Alfred, *The Listener's History of Music.* 3 vols. Oxford University Press, 1925–1929.
235. Corte, Andrea della, *Antologia della storia della musica.* 2 vols. Paravia, Milan, 1929. Two editions. " Noteworthy pages in the historiography of musical art."
236. Hadow, Sir William Henry, *Music.* 256 pp. Home University Library, London, 1925, 1926.
237. Hamilton, Clarence G., *Epochs in Musical Progress.* 278 pp. Oliver Ditson Co., Boston, 1926.
238. Bekker, Paul, *Musikgeschichte als Geschichte der musikalischen Formwandlungen.* Deutsche Verlagsanstalt, Stuttgart, 1926.
—— *The Story of Music, an Historical Sketch of the Changes in Musical Form,* translation of the above into English by M. D. H.

Norton and Alice Kortschaak, W. W. Norton, New York, 1927, 277 pp. This book is also translated into French, *La musique*.

239. Bücken, Ernst, " Grundfragen der Musikgeschichte als Geisteswissenschaft," in *Jahrb. der Musikbibliothek Peters*, pp. 19–30, 1927.

240. Chemodanoff, S. N., *Istoriia muzyki v sviazi s istorie obschestvennogo razvitiiazopyt Marksistskogo postroeniia istorii muzyki*. 204 pp. Kiev, 1927. LC.

241. Claiborne, Robert W., *The Way Man Learned Music*. Vol. I, 103 pp. New York, 1927.

242. Della Corte, *Disegno storico dell'arte musicale, con esempi*. 202 pp. Paravia, Milan, 1927, 1929.

243. Jeanson, Tunnar, and Rabe, Julius, *Musiken Genom Tiderna en popular Framstallning av den Vasterlandska Tonkunstens Historia*. 280 pp. Stockholm, 1927.

244. Hull, A. Eaglefield, *Music; Classical, Romantic and Modern*. 473 pp. Dent, London, 1927.

245. Chevailler, Lucien, *La musique*. E. de Boccard, Paris, 1928.

246. Gray, Cecil, *The History of Music* (History of Civilization series). 284 pp. A. Knopf, New York, 1928. Revised edition, 1931.

247. Isaacson, Charles D., *The Simple Story of Music*. 336 pp. Macy-Masius, New York, 1928.

248. Lorenz, Alfred, *Abendländische Musikgeschichte im Rhythmus der Generationen*. 123 pp. Hesse, Berlin, 1928.

249. Mayer, Anton, *Geschichte der Musik*, Deutsche Buchgemeinschaft, Berlin, 1928. For the new Nazi version see [291].

250. Machabey, Armand, *Histoire et évolution des formules musicales du Ier au XVme siècle de l'ère chrétienne*. Payot, Paris, 1928.

251. Moukhtar, Ahmed, *Mousiqui tarihi* (History of Music). 2 vols., illus. Stamboul, 1928. LC.

252. Scholes, Percy Alfred, *A Miniature History of Music for the General Reader and the Student*. 69 pp. Oxford University Press, 1928.

253. Scott, Cyril, *The Influence of Music on History and Morals, A Vindication of Plato*. Part III. Theosophical Publishing House, London, 1928. Historical section, pp. 157–239.

254. Unger, Hermann, *Musikgeschichte in Selbstzeugnissen*. 474 pp. Piper, Munich, 1928.

255. Buck, Percy C., *A History of Music*. 79 pp. Benn's Sixpenny Library, London, 1929, 1932.

256. Hewitt, Thomas J., and Hill, Ralph, *An Outline of Music History*. 2 vols. Woolf, London, 1929.
    Vol. I. From the Earliest Times to Handel and Bach. 98 pp.
    Vol. II. From C. P. E. Bach to Modern Music. 146 pp.

257. Percy C. Buck, editor, *The Oxford History of Music, Introductory Volume*. 236 pp. Oxford University Press, 1929.

258. Magni-Dufflocq, Enrico, *Storia della musica*. 2 vols. Soc. editrice libraria, Milan, 1929–1930.
    Vol. I. *Dalle origini al secolo XVIII*. 503 pp. 1929.
    Vol. II. *Del secolo XVIII ai nostri giorni nostri*. 595 pp. 1930.

362   BIBLIOGRAPHY

259. Müller, Erich H., *Deutsches Musiker-Lexikon.* 1643 pp. Limpert, Dresden, 1929.
260. Bücken, Ernst, editor, *Handbuch der Musikwissenschaft* and *Die grossen Meister der Musik.* Akademische Verlagsgesellschaft Athenaion, Potsdam. The 13 volumes of the *Handbuch* contain the following, issued originally in *Lieferungen* (parts) of about 30 pp. each:

   Lachmann, Robert, *Die Musik der aussereuropäischen Natur- und Kulturvölker,* 1929, 34 pp.

   Sachs, Curt, *Musik der Antike,* 1928, 32 pp.

   Panov, Peter, *Altslavische Volks- und Kirchenmusik,* 1930, 32 pp.

   Besseler, H., *Die Musik des Mittelalters und der Renaissance,* 1931, 338 pp. (10 parts.)

   Haas, Robert, *Die Musik des Barocks,* 1928, 291 pp. (9 parts.)

   Bücken, E., *Die Musik des Rococos und Klassiks,* 1928, 248 pp. (8 parts.)

   Bücken, E., *Die Musik des 19ten Jahrhunderts,* 1928, 320 pp. (10 parts.)

   Mersmann, Hans, *Die moderne Musik, seit der Romantik,* 1928, 222 pp. (7 parts.)

   Heinitz, Wilhelm, *Instrumentenkunde,* 1931, 160 pp. (5 parts.)

   Haas, Robert, *Aufführungspraxis der Musik,* 1931, 299 pp. (9 parts.)

   Ursprung, Otto, *Die katholische Musik,* 1931, 312 pp. (9 parts.)

   Blume, Franz, *Die evangelische Musik,* 1931, 170 pp. (5 parts.)
261. Wolf, Johannes, *Geschichte der Musik in allgemeinverständlicher Form.* 3 vols. Quelle & Meyer, Leipzig, 1929-1930. 2nd edition, 1934.

   Vol. I. *Die Entwickelung der Musik bis etwa 1600,* 159 pp. Only the first 10 pp. are devoted to antiquity.

   Vol. II. *Die Musik des 17ten Jahrhunderts und Opera und Kirchenmusik im 18ten Jahrhundert,* 144 pp. Pp. 105-144 are devoted to examples.

   Vol. III. *Die Entwickelung der Musik vom 18ten Jahrhundert (Lied, Instrumentalmusik, opéra comique, Theorie) bis zur Jetztzeit,* 128 pp. Pp. 99-128 are devoted to examples. Only 4 pp. are given to the twentieth century.

   A Spanish edition, translated by Higini Angles, appeared in Barcelona in 1934.
262. Gabeaud, Alice, *Histoire de la musique.* 204 pp. Larousse, Paris, 1930. Adopted for the city schools of Paris.
263. Moser, H. J., *Die Epochen der Musikgeschichte im Ueberblick.* Cotta, Berlin, 1930.
264. Meyer, Dorothy Tremble, *Introduction to Music Appreciation and History.* Published for the Division of University Extension, Massachusetts Dept. of Education. 156 pp. Oliver Ditson Co., Boston, 1930. At the end is printed a chronological table, paralleling events in music and general history.

265. Neretti, L., *Compendio di storia della musica per uso commune e specialmente dei maestri elementari e degl'insegnanti e alunni degl'instituti magistrali e della altre scuole medie*. 241 pp. Bemporad, Florence, 1930.

266. Sachs, Curt, *Vergleichende Musikwissenschaft in ihren Grundzügen*. Quelle & Meyer, Leipzig, 1930.

267. Subira, José, *La música, sus evoluciones y estado actual*. 206 pp. Biblioteca de Ensayos, Madrid, 1930.

268. Torrefranca, Fausto, *Le origini italiane del romanticismo musicale: i primitivi della sonata moderna*. 775 pp. Bocca, Turin, 1930.

269. Wilm, Mrs. Grace (Gridley), *A History of Music*. 382 pp. Dodd, Mead and Co., New York, 1930.

270. Cesari, Gaetano, *Lezioni di storia della musica — nella Regia Universita di Milano*. 170 pp. Ricordi, 1931.

271. Coeuroy, André, and Jardillier, Robert, *Histoire de la musique avec l'aide du disque*. 238 pp. Delagrave, Paris, 1931.

272. Herrera y Ogazon, Alba, *Historia de la música*. 504 pp. National University of Mexico, 1931.

273. Levi, Lionello, *Profile di storia della musica*. 259 pp. Zanichelli, Bologna, 1931.

274. Szendrei, Aladár Alfred, *Rundfunk und Musikpflege*. 199 pp. Kistner and Siegel, Leipzig, 1931.

275. Ponten, Theodore, *Musica ars: Leiddraad voor Muziekgeschiedenis en algemeene Musikleer*. 173 pp. Groningen, 1931.

276. Höweler, Casper, *Muziek Geschiedenis in Beeld*. 120 pp. H. J. Paris, Amsterdam, 1931.

277. Corte, Andrea della, *Le teorie delle origini della musica e le musiche dei populi antiche o primitivi*. 26 pp. Paravia, Turin, 1932.

278. Bauer, Marion, and Peyser, Ethel, *Music through the Ages*. 572 pp. G. P. Putnam's Sons, New York, 1932.

279. Dauter, Hans, *Musikgeschichte in graphischer Darstellung*. 6 large chronological charts. Frommhold & Wendler, Leipzig, 1932.
   Chart I, 3000 B.C.–1430 A.D.; II, 1430–1630; III, 1630–1830; IV, 1760–1860; V, 1760–1860; VI, 1760–1860.

280. Dyson, George, *The Progress of Music*. 238 pp. Oxford University Press, 1932.

281. Eichenauer, Richard, *Musik und Rasse*. 286 pp. Lehmann, Munich, 1932.

282. Müller-Blattau, Josef Maria, *Einführung in die Musikgeschichte*. 95 pp. C. F. Vieweg, Berlin, 1932.

283. Turner, W. J., *Music, A Short History*. No. 8 in the "How and Why Series." 96 pp. Black, London, 1932.

284. Ascherfeld, Clara, *Outlines of the History of Music*. 4 vols. Peabody Conservatory of Music, Baltimore, 1932–1933.

285. Bauer, Marion, *Twentieth-Century Music, How It Developed; How to Listen to It*. 339 pp. G. P. Putnam's Sons, New York, 1933.

286. Ewen, David, editor, *From Bach to Stravinsky, The History of Music by Its Foremost Critics.* W. W. Norton, New York, 1933. A series of critical essays by various writers, with a reprint of [151].

287. Moser, H. J., *Musiklexicon.* Originally in 16 *Lieferungen,* 1005 pp. in all. Hesse, Berlin, 1932–1935.

288. Yasser, Joseph, *A Theory of Evolving Tonality.* American Library of Musicology, Vol. I, New York, 1932.

289. Forns y Quadra, J., *Historia de la música.* 2 vols. Emprenta Clásica Española, Madrid.
    Vol. I. To the XVIth Century, 1929.
    Vol. II. XVIth to XXth Century, 1933.

290. Hegar, Elisabeth, *Die Anfänge der neueren Musikgeschichteschreibung um 1740 bei Gerbert, Burney und Hawkins.* 86 pp. Heitz, Strassburg, 1933.

291. Mayer, Anton, *Geschichte der Musik, mit einem Vorwort von Georg Vollerthum.* 414 pp., illus. Deutsches Leben und Sieben-Stäbe, Hamburg, 1933.

292. Osthoff, Helmuth, "Die Anfänge der Musikgeschichteschreibung in Deutschland," *Acta musicologica,* 1933, July–Sept., Vol. V, Fasc. 3.

293. Prunières, Henri, *Nouvelle histoire de la musique.* 4 vols. Rieder, Paris.
    Vol. I. *La musique du moyen âge et de la Renaissance,* 1933, 312 pp.
    Vol. II. *La musique des XVIIme et XVIIIme siècles,* 1936, 321 pp.
    Vol. III. *La musique classique et romantique* (in preparation).
    Vol. IV. *La musique moderne* (in preparation).

294. Dumesnil, René, *Histoire de la musique.* 292 pp., illus. Plon, Paris, 1934.

295. Glyn, Margaret H., *Theory of Musical Evolution.* 315 pp. Dent, London, 1934.

296. Lambert, Constant, *Music Ho! A Study of Music in Decline.* 342 pp. Faber and Faber, London, 1934, 1936.

297. Mersmann, Hans, *Eine deutsche Musikgeschichte.* 523 pp. Sans-Souci, Potsdam-Berlin, 1934.

298. Naumann, Emil, *Illustrierte Musikgeschichte,* new edition by Eugen Schmitz. 560 pp. Union Deutsche Verlags., Stuttgart, 1934.

299. Pecchiai, Pietro, *Occorre rifare la storia della musica! Valutazioni e paralleli.* 87 pp. Pacini Mariotti, Pisa, 1933. XI. Reprint of articles from *L'idea Fascista,* 1932–1933.

300. Ferguson, Donald N., *A History of Musical Thought.* 563 pp. Crofts, New York, 1935.

301. Finney, Theodore M., *A History of Music.* 618 pp. Harcourt, Brace & Co., New York, 1935.

302. Luciani, S. A., *Mille anni de musica.* 161 pp. Hoepli, Milan, 1936.

303. Moereman, L., *Histoire de la musique en Europe.* 163 pp. Cnudde, Ghent, 1936.

304. Rougnon, Paul, *La musique et son histoire.* 297 pp. Garnier, Paris, 1936.
305. Kinkeldey, Otto, "Changing Relations in Musicology," in *Proceedings,* M.T.N.A. Oberlin Press, 1936.
306. Bücken, Ernst, *Die Musik der Nationen.* 494 pp. Kröner, Leipzig, 1937.
307. Chavez, Carlos, *Toward a New Music.* W. W. Norton, New York, 1937.
308. Barrenechea, M. A., *Historia estética de la música.* A. Garcia Santos, Buenos Aires, 1924.
309. Andrade, Mario de, *Compendio de historia da musica.* 211 pp. Sao Paolo, 1929, 1932.
310. Vaughan-Williams, R., *National Music.* Oxford Press, 1934.
311. Osborn, A. S., *Centuries of Progress in Music.* 378 pp. Ann Arbor, Mich., 1937.
312. Parkhurst, Winthrop, and de Bekker, L. J., *The Encyclopedia of Music and Musicians.* 662 pp. New York, 1937.
313. Leichtentritt, Hugo, *Music, History and Ideas.* Harvard University Press, 1938.
314. Láng, Paul H., *Music in the History of Western Civilization* (in preparation). W. W. Norton, New York.
315. Thompson, Oscar, ed., *International Cyclopedia of Music and Musicians,* 2287 pp. Dodd, Mead and Co., New York, 1938. The articles on "Histories of Music," and "History of Music" are by W. D. Allen and Marion Bauer, respectively.
316. Einstein, Alfred, *Beispielsammlung zur Musikgeschichte.* Teubner, Berlin, 1917. A music history with musical examples only. These examples are now included in the 1939 edition of Einstein's *Short History of Music* [204A].
317. Schering, Arnold, *Geschichte der Musik in Beispielen, 350 Tonsätze aus neun Jahrhunderten.* Breitkopf, Leipzig, 1931. A music history with musical examples only.

INDEX OF NAMES

(Bracketed numbers refer to the Bibliography)

A

Aber, Adolf, xxiii
Acosta, Paul d', [132], 265
Acta musicologica, [292], xxiii
Addison, Joseph, 27, 64, 75, 191 n., 200, 222 n.
Adler, Guido, [207], [224], xi, 135–136, 140, 206, 266–267
Alexandre, Père, 82 n.
Allen, Frederick H., 319 n.
Allen, Warren D., 3 n., 145 n.
Ambros, August Wilhelm, [67], viii, 47 n., 109, 120, 139, 141–142, 266
American Musicological Society, 20 n., 193 n., 317 n., 333 n.
Amphion, 24
Anaximander, 185
Anderson, W. R., 142 n.
Andrade, Mario de, [309], 174, 310 n.
Andries, Jean Jacques, [68]
Année Musicale, L', xxiii
Antcliffe, Herbert, 287 n., 293
Apthorp, William F., 69
Apollo, 8, 13, 31, 99
Apollodorus, 53
Ariosto, 78
Aristides Quintilianus, 48
Aristotle, 25, 32, 36 n., 58, 95, 182, 183, 186, 199, 231, 242–243, 248, 249, 256 n., 318
Aristoxenus, 9, 58, 217, 257
Ascherfeld, Clara, [284]
Aubry, Pierre, 38 n., 164 n.
Augustine, St., 88 n., 249

B

Bach, C. P. E., 156, 251
Bach, J. S., 6, 10, 24, 59, 64, 74, 79, 83, 84, 117, 118, 125, 133, 134, 141, 147, 156, 172, 189, 212, 220, 238, 242, 245, 252, 253, 257, 264, 265, 271, 279, 291, 301, 309, 314, 328, 329, 331, 333 n.
Bach, the family, 308, 309
Bacon, Roger, 191
Bagehot, Walter, 42–43
Baïf, Antoine de, 42
Bain, Alexander, 155
Baini, Giuseppe, 87
Baker, Theodore, [205], 24
Baldwin, J. M., 180, 312 n., 315

Baltazarini (Beaujoyeulx), 42
Baltzell, Winton J., [152], 130, 158
Baronio, Cardinal, 22
Barrenechea, M. A., [308], 174
Basevi, A., [76], 122
Bastianelli, G., 168 n.
Batka, Richard, [173]
Bauch, Wilhelm, [69]
Bauer, Marion, [231], [278], [285], [315], xi, 252–253
Bawr, Mme. Alexandra Sofia, [38], 98
Bayle, Pierre, 64
Bayreuth, 119
Beaumarchais, Pierre Augustin Caron de, 242
Becker, Carl F., xxiii
Becking, Gustav, 252 n.
Bedford, Arthur, 75
Beethoven, Ludwig van, 59, 90, 100, 102, 120, 139, 140, 141, 159, 172, 188, 189, 209 n., 220, 224, 239, 260 n., 264, 265 n., 278, 290, 291, 293, 299–300, 301, 303, 307, 326, 333
Behrend, William, 138, 174
Bekker, L. J. de, [312]
Bekker, Paul, [238], 132, 181, 224 n., 225, 302
Bell, Nancy R. E., [103], 125
Bellaigue, Camille, [174]
Bergmans, Paul, 138
Berkeley, Bishop George, 74
Bernfeld, Siegfried, 318
Berrien, William, 310 n.
Bertrand, Paul, [193], 137, 265
Besseler, Heinrich, [260], 275
Billings, William, 170, 330
Bird, Joseph, [59], 126
Bisson, A. C. A., [108]
Bjerregard, C. H. A., 273 n.
Blainville, C. H. de, [21], 54
Blom, Eric, xxiii
Blondeau, A. L., [58], 102
Blume, Otto, [260]
Bobstiber, H., [153]
Bodin, Jean, 33, 95–96
Boethius, 9, 31, 70
Boileau-Despréaux, Nicolas, 42
Boletin Latino-americano de Música, 310 n.
Bonald, Louis de, 54

INDEX

(Subject Matter)

A CATALOGUE OF SELECTED DOVER BOOKS
IN ALL FIELDS OF INTEREST

A CATALOGUE OF SELECTED DOVER BOOKS
IN ALL FIELDS OF INTEREST

WHAT IS SCIENCE?, *N. Campbell*
The role of experiment and measurement, the function of mathematics, the nature of scientific laws, the difference between laws and theories, the limitations of science, and many similarly provocative topics are treated clearly and without technicalities by an eminent scientist. "Still an excellent introduction to scientific philosophy," H. Margenau in *Physics Today*. "A first-rate primer . . . deserves a wide audience," *Scientific American*. 192pp. 5⅜ x 8.
60043-2 Paperbound $1.25

THE NATURE OF LIGHT AND COLOUR IN THE OPEN AIR, *M. Minnaert*
Why are shadows sometimes blue, sometimes green, or other colors depending on the light and surroundings? What causes mirages? Why do multiple suns and moons appear in the sky? Professor Minnaert explains these unusual phenomena and hundreds of others in simple, easy-to-understand terms based on optical laws and the properties of light and color. No mathematics is required but artists, scientists, students, and everyone fascinated by these "tricks" of nature will find thousands of useful and amazing pieces of information. Hundreds of observational experiments are suggested which require no special equipment. 200 illustrations; 42 photos. xvi + 362pp. 5⅜ x 8.
20196-1 Paperbound $2.75

THE STRANGE STORY OF THE QUANTUM, AN ACCOUNT FOR THE GENERAL READER OF THE GROWTH OF IDEAS UNDERLYING OUR PRESENT ATOMIC KNOWLEDGE, *B. Hoffmann*
Presents lucidly and expertly, with barest amount of mathematics, the problems and theories which led to modern quantum physics. Dr. Hoffmann begins with the closing years of the 19th century, when certain trifling discrepancies were noticed, and with illuminating analogies and examples takes you through the brilliant concepts of Planck, Einstein, Pauli, Broglie, Bohr, Schroedinger, Heisenberg, Dirac, Sommerfeld, Feynman, etc. This edition includes a new, long postscript carrying the story through 1958. "Of the books attempting an account of the history and contents of our modern atomic physics which have come to my attention, this is the best," H. Margenau, Yale University, in *American Journal of Physics*. 32 tables and line illustrations. Index. 275pp. 5⅜ x 8.
20518-5 Paperbound $2.00

GREAT IDEAS OF MODERN MATHEMATICS: THEIR NATURE AND USE, *Jagjit Singh*
Reader with only high school math will understand main mathematical ideas of modern physics, astronomy, genetics, psychology, evolution, etc. better than many who use them as tools, but comprehend little of their basic structure. Author uses his wide knowledge of non-mathematical fields in brilliant exposition of differential equations, matrices, group theory, logic, statistics, problems of mathematical foundations, imaginary numbers, vectors, etc. Original publication. 2 appendixes. 2 indexes. 65 ills. 322pp. 5⅜ x 8.
20587-8 Paperbound $2.50

THE MUSIC OF THE SPHERES: THE MATERIAL UNIVERSE — FROM ATOM TO QUASAR, SIMPLY EXPLAINED, *Guy Murchie*
Vast compendium of fact, modern concept and theory, observed and calculated data, historical background guides intelligent layman through the material universe. Brilliant exposition of earth's construction, explanations for moon's craters, atmospheric components of Venus and Mars (with data from recent fly-by's), sun spots, sequences of star birth and death, neighboring galaxies, contributions of Galileo, Tycho Brahe, Kepler, etc.; and (Vol. 2) construction of the atom (describing newly discovered sigma and xi subatomic particles), theories of sound, color and light, space and time, including relativity theory, quantum theory, wave theory, probability theory, work of Newton, Maxwell, Faraday, Einstein, de Broglie, etc. "Best presentation yet offered to the intelligent general reader," *Saturday Review*. Revised (1967). Index. 319 illustrations by the author. Total of xx + 644pp. 5⅜ x 8½.
21809-0, 21810-4 Two volume set, paperbound $5.00

FOUR LECTURES ON RELATIVITY AND SPACE, *Charles Proteus Steinmetz*
Lecture series, given by great mathematician and electrical engineer, generally considered one of the best popular-level expositions of special and general relativity theories and related questions. Steinmetz translates complex mathematical reasoning into language accessible to laymen through analogy, example and comparison. Among topics covered are relativity of motion, location, time; of mass; acceleration; 4-dimensional time-space; geometry of the gravitational field; curvature and bending of space; non-Euclidean geometry. Index. 40 illustrations. x + 142pp. 5⅜ x 8½. 61771-8 Paperbound $1.50

HOW TO KNOW THE WILD FLOWERS, *Mrs. William Starr Dana*
Classic nature book that has introduced thousands to wonders of American wild flowers. Color-season principle of organization is easy to use, even by those with no botanical training, and the genial, refreshing discussions of history, folklore, uses of over 1,000 native and escape flowers, foliage plants are informative as well as fun to read. Over 170 full-page plates, collected from several editions, may be colored in to make permanent records of finds. Revised to conform with 1950 edition of Gray's Manual of Botany. xlii + 438pp. 5⅜ x 8½. 20332-8 Paperbound $2.50

MANUAL OF THE TREES OF NORTH AMERICA, *Charles Sprague Sargent*
Still unsurpassed as most comprehensive, reliable study of North American tree characteristics, precise locations and distribution. By dean of American dendrologists. Every tree native to U.S., Canada, Alaska; 185 genera, 717 species, described in detail—leaves, flowers, fruit, winterbuds, bark, wood, growth habits, etc. plus discussion of varieties and local variants, immaturity variations. Over 100 keys, including unusual 11-page analytical key to genera, aid in identification. 783 clear illustrations of flowers, fruit, leaves. An unmatched permanent reference work for all nature lovers. Second enlarged (1926) edition. Synopsis of families. Analytical key to genera. Glossary of technical terms. Index. 783 illustrations, 1 map. Total of 982pp. 5⅜ x 8. 20277-1, 20278-X Two volume set, paperbound $6.00

IT'S FUN TO MAKE THINGS FROM SCRAP MATERIALS,
Evelyn Glantz Hershoff
What use are empty spools, tin cans, bottle tops? What can be made from rubber bands, clothes pins, paper clips, and buttons? This book provides simply worded instructions and large diagrams showing you how to make cookie cutters, toy trucks, paper turkeys, Halloween masks, telephone sets, aprons, linoleum block- and spatter prints — in all 399 projects! Many are easy enough for young children to figure out for themselves; some challenging enough to entertain adults; all are remarkably ingenious ways to make things from materials that cost pennies or less! Formerly "Scrap Fun for Everyone." Index. 214 illustrations. 373pp. 5⅜ x 8½.   21251-3 Paperbound $2.00

SYMBOLIC LOGIC and THE GAME OF LOGIC, *Lewis Carroll*
"Symbolic Logic" is not concerned with modern symbolic logic, but is instead a collection of over 380 problems posed with charm and imagination, using the syllogism and a fascinating diagrammatic method of drawing conclusions. In "The Game of Logic" Carroll's whimsical imagination devises a logical game played with 2 diagrams and counters (included) to manipulate hundreds of tricky syllogisms. The final section, "Hit or Miss" is a lagniappe of 101 additional puzzles in the delightful Carroll manner. Until this reprint edition, both of these books were rarities costing up to $15 each. Symbolic Logic: Index. xxxi + 199pp. The Game of Logic: 96pp. 2 vols. bound as one. 5⅜ x 8.
20492-8 Paperbound $2.50

MATHEMATICAL PUZZLES OF SAM LOYD, PART I
selected and edited by M. Gardner
Choice puzzles by the greatest American puzzle creator and innovator. Selected from his famous collection, "Cyclopedia of Puzzles," they retain the unique style and historical flavor of the originals. There are posers based on arithmetic, algebra, probability, game theory, route tracing, topology, counter and sliding block, operations research, geometrical dissection. Includes the famous "14-15" puzzle which was a national craze, and his "Horse of a Different Color" which sold millions of copies. 117 of his most ingenious puzzles in all. 120 line drawings and diagrams. Solutions. Selected references. xx + 167pp. 5⅜ x 8.
20498-7 Paperbound $1.35

STRING FIGURES AND HOW TO MAKE THEM, *Caroline Furness Jayne*
107 string figures plus variations selected from the best primitive and modern examples developed by Navajo, Apache, pygmies of Africa, Eskimo, in Europe, Australia, China, etc. The most readily understandable, easy-to-follow book in English on perennially popular recreation. Crystal-clear exposition; step-by-step diagrams. Everyone from kindergarten children to adults looking for unusual diversion will be endlessly amused. Index. Bibliography. Introduction by A. C. Haddon. 17 full-page plates, 960 illustrations. xxiii + 401pp. 5⅜ x 8½.
20152-X Paperbound $2.50

PAPER FOLDING FOR BEGINNERS, *W. D. Murray and F. J. Rigney*
A delightful introduction to the varied and entertaining Japanese art of origami (paper folding), with a full, crystal-clear text that anticipates every difficulty; over 275 clearly labeled diagrams of all important stages in creation. You get results at each stage, since complex figures are logically developed from simpler ones. 43 different pieces are explained: sailboats, frogs, roosters, etc. 6 photographic plates. 279 diagrams. 95pp. 5⅜ x 8⅜.
20713-7 Paperbound $1.00

PRINCIPLES OF ART HISTORY,
H. Wölfflin
Analyzing such terms as "baroque," "classic," "neoclassic," "primitive," "picturesque," and 164 different works by artists like Botticelli, van Cleve, Dürer, Hobbema, Holbein, Hals, Rembrandt, Titian, Brueghel, Vermeer, and many others, the author establishes the classifications of art history and style on a firm, concrete basis. This classic of art criticism shows what really occurred between the 14th-century primitives and the sophistication of the 18th century in terms of basic attitudes and philosophies. "A remarkable lesson in the art of seeing," *Sat. Rev. of Literature.* Translated from the 7th German edition. 150 illustrations. 254pp. 6⅛ x 9¼. 20276-3 Paperbound $2.50

PRIMITIVE ART,
Franz Boas
This authoritative and exhaustive work by a great American anthropologist covers the entire gamut of primitive art. Pottery, leatherwork, metal work, stone work, wood, basketry, are treated in detail. Theories of primitive art, historical depth in art history, technical virtuosity, unconscious levels of patterning, symbolism, styles, literature, music, dance, etc. A must book for the interested layman, the anthropologist, artist, handicrafter (hundreds of unusual motifs), and the historian. Over 900 illustrations (50 ceramic vessels, 12 totem poles, etc.). 376pp. 5⅜ x 8. 20025-6 Paperbound $2.50

THE GENTLEMAN AND CABINET MAKER'S DIRECTOR,
Thomas Chippendale
A reprint of the 1762 catalogue of furniture designs that went on to influence generations of English and Colonial and Early Republic American furniture makers. The 200 plates, most of them full-page sized, show Chippendale's designs for French (Louis XV), Gothic, and Chinese-manner chairs, sofas, canopy and dome beds, cornices, chamber organs, cabinets, shaving tables, commodes, picture frames, frets, candle stands, chimney pieces, decorations, etc. The drawings are all elegant and highly detailed; many include construction diagrams and elevations. A supplement of 24 photographs shows surviving pieces of original and Chippendale-style pieces of furniture. Brief biography of Chippendale by N. I. Bienenstock, editor of *Furniture World.* Reproduced from the 1762 edition. 200 plates, plus 19 photographic plates. vi + 249pp. 9⅛ x 12¼. 21601-2 Paperbound $4.00

AMERICAN ANTIQUE FURNITURE: A BOOK FOR AMATEURS,
Edgar G. Miller, Jr.
Standard introduction and practical guide to identification of valuable American antique furniture. 2115 illustrations, mostly photographs taken by the author in 148 private homes, are arranged in chronological order in extensive chapters on chairs, sofas, chests, desks, bedsteads, mirrors, tables, clocks, and other articles. Focus is on furniture accessible to the collector, including simpler pieces and a larger than usual coverage of Empire style. Introductory chapters identify structural elements, characteristics of various styles, how to avoid fakes, etc. "We are frequently asked to name some book on American furniture that will meet the requirements of the novice collector, the beginning dealer, and . . . the general public. . . . We believe Mr. Miller's two volumes more completely satisfy this specification than any other work," *Antiques.* Appendix. Index. Total of vi + 1106pp. 7⅞ x 10¾. 21599-7, 21600-4 Two volume set, paperbound $10.00

THE BAD CHILD'S BOOK OF BEASTS, MORE BEASTS FOR WORSE CHILDREN, and A MORAL ALPHABET, *H. Belloc*
Hardly and anthology of humorous verse has appeared in the last 50 years without at least a couple of these famous nonsense verses. But one must see the entire volumes — with all the delightful original illustrations by Sir Basil Blackwood — to appreciate fully Belloc's charming and witty verses that play so subacidly on the platitudes of life and morals that beset his day — and ours. A great humor classic. Three books in one. Total of 157pp. 5⅜ x 8.
20749-8 Paperbound $1.25

THE DEVIL'S DICTIONARY, *Ambrose Bierce*
Sardonic and irreverent barbs puncturing the pomposities and absurdities of American politics, business, religion, literature, and arts, by the country's greatest satirist in the classic tradition. Epigrammatic as Shaw, piercing as Swift, American as Mark Twain, Will Rogers, and Fred Allen, Bierce will always remain the favorite of a small coterie of enthusiasts, and of writers and speakers whom he supplies with "some of the most gorgeous witticisms of the English language" (H. L. Mencken). Over 1000 entries in alphabetical order. 144pp. 5⅜ x 8.
20487-1 Paperbound $1.25

THE COMPLETE NONSENSE OF EDWARD LEAR.
This is the only complete edition of this master of gentle madness available at a popular price. *A Book of Nonsense, Nonsense Songs, More Nonsense Songs and Stories* in their entirety with all the old favorites that have delighted children and adults for years. The Dong With A Luminous Nose, The Jumblies, The Owl and the Pussycat, and hundreds of other bits of wonderful nonsense. 214 limericks, 3 sets of Nonsense Botany, 5 Nonsense Alphabets, 546 drawings by Lear himself, and much more. 320pp. 5⅜ x 8. 20167-8 Paperbound $1.75

THE WIT AND HUMOR OF OSCAR WILDE, *ed. by Alvin Redman*
Wilde at his most brilliant, in 1000 epigrams exposing weaknesses and hypocrisies of "civilized" society. Divided into 49 categories—sin, wealth, women, America, etc.—to aid writers, speakers. Includes excerpts from his trials, books, plays, criticism. Formerly "The Epigrams of Oscar Wilde." Introduction by Vyvyan Holland, Wilde's only living son. Introductory essay by editor. 260pp. 5⅜ x 8.
20602-5 Paperbound $1.50

A CHILD'S PRIMER OF NATURAL HISTORY, *Oliver Herford*
Scarcely an anthology of whimsy and humor has appeared in the last 50 years without a contribution from Oliver Herford. Yet the works from which these examples are drawn have been almost impossible to obtain! Here at last are Herford's improbable definitions of a menagerie of familiar and weird animals, each verse illustrated by the author's own drawings. 24 drawings in 2 colors; 24 additional drawings. vii + 95pp. 6½ x 6. 21647-0 Paperbound $1.00

THE BROWNIES: THEIR BOOK, *Palmer Cox*
The book that made the Brownies a household word. Generations of readers have enjoyed the antics, predicaments and adventures of these jovial sprites, who emerge from the forest at night to play or to come to the aid of a deserving human. Delightful illustrations by the author decorate nearly every page. 24 short verse tales with 266 illustrations. 155pp. 6⅝ x 9¼.
21265-3 Paperbound $1.50

THE PRINCIPLES OF PSYCHOLOGY,
William James
The full long-course, unabridged, of one of the great classics of Western literature and science. Wonderfully lucid descriptions of human mental activity, the stream of thought, consciousness, time perception, memory, imagination, emotions, reason, abnormal phenomena, and similar topics. Original contributions are integrated with the work of such men as Berkeley, Binet, Mills, Darwin, Hume, Kant, Royce, Schopenhauer, Spinoza, Locke, Descartes, Galton, Wundt, Lotze, Herbart, Fechner, and scores of others. All contrasting interpretations of mental phenomena are examined in detail—introspective analysis, philosophical interpretation, and experimental research. "A classic," *Journal of Consulting Psychology.* "The main lines are as valid as ever," *Psychoanalytical Quarterly.* "Standard reading . . . a classic of interpretation," *Psychiatric Quarterly.* 94 illustrations. 1408pp. 5⅜ x 8.
20381-6, 20382-4 Two volume set, paperbound $6.00

VISUAL ILLUSIONS: THEIR CAUSES, CHARACTERISTICS AND APPLICATIONS,
M. Luckiesh
"Seeing is deceiving," asserts the author of this introduction to virtually every type of optical illusion known. The text both describes and explains the principles involved in color illusions, figure-ground, distance illusions, etc. 100 photographs, drawings and diagrams prove how easy it is to fool the sense: circles that aren't round, parallel lines that seem to bend, stationary figures that seem to move as you stare at them — illustration after illustration strains our credulity at what we see. Fascinating book from many points of view, from applications for artists, in camouflage, etc. to the psychology of vision. New introduction by William Ittleson, Dept. of Psychology, Queens College. Index. Bibliography. xxi + 252pp. 5⅜ x 8½. 21530-X Paperbound $1.75

FADS AND FALLACIES IN THE NAME OF SCIENCE,
Martin Gardner
This is the standard account of various cults, quack systems, and delusions which have masqueraded as science: hollow earth fanatics. Reich and orgone sex energy, dianetics, Atlantis, multiple moons, Forteanism, flying saucers, medical fallacies like iridiagnosis, zone therapy, etc. A new chapter has been added on Bridey Murphy, psionics, and other recent manifestations in this field. This is a fair, reasoned appraisal of eccentric theory which provides excellent inoculation against cleverly masked nonsense. "Should be read by everyone, scientist and non-scientist alike," R. T. Birge, Prof. Emeritus of Physics, Univ. of California; Former President, American Physical Society. Index. x + 365pp. 5⅜ x 8. 20394-8 Paperbound $2.00

ILLUSIONS AND DELUSIONS OF THE SUPERNATURAL AND THE OCCULT,
D. H. Rawcliffe
Holds up to rational examination hundreds of persistent delusions including crystal gazing, automatic writing, table turning, mediumistic trances, mental healing, stigmata, lycanthropy, live burial, the Indian Rope Trick, spiritualism, dowsing, telepathy, clairvoyance, ghosts, ESP, etc. The author explains and exposes the mental and physical deceptions involved, making this not only an exposé of supernatural phenomena, but a valuable exposition of characteristic types of abnormal psychology. Originally titled "The Psychology of the Occult." 14 illustrations. Index. 551pp. 5⅜ x 8. 20503-7 Paperbound $3.50

FAIRY TALE COLLECTIONS, *edited by Andrew Lang*
Andrew Lang's fairy tale collections make up the richest shelf-full of traditional children's stories anywhere available. Lang supervised the translation of stories from all over the world—familiar European tales collected by Grimm, animal stories from Negro Africa, myths of primitive Australia, stories from Russia, Hungary, Iceland, Japan, and many other countries. Lang's selection of translations are unusually high; many authorities consider that the most familiar tales find their best versions in these volumes. All collections are richly decorated and illustrated by H. J. Ford and other artists.

THE BLUE FAIRY BOOK. 37 stories. 138 illustrations. ix + 390pp. 5⅜ x 8½.
21437-0 Paperbound $1.95

THE GREEN FAIRY BOOK. 42 stories. 100 illustrations. xiii + 366pp. 5⅜ x 8½.
21439-7 Paperbound $2.00

THE BROWN FAIRY BOOK. 32 stories. 50 illustrations, 8 in color. xii + 350pp. 5⅜ x 8½.
21438-9 Paperbound $1.95

THE BEST TALES OF HOFFMANN, *edited by E. F. Bleiler*
10 stories by E. T. A. Hoffmann, one of the greatest of all writers of fantasy. The tales include "The Golden Flower Pot," "Automata," "A New Year's Eve Adventure," "Nutcracker and the King of Mice," "Sand-Man," and others. Vigorous characterizations of highly eccentric personalities, remarkably imaginative situations, and intensely fast pacing has made these tales popular all over the world for 150 years. Editor's introduction. 7 drawings by Hoffmann.
xxxiii + 419pp. 5⅜ x 8½.
21793-0 Paperbound $2.25

GHOST AND HORROR STORIES OF AMBROSE BIERCE,
edited by E. F. Bleiler
Morbid, eerie, horrifying tales of possessed poets, shabby aristocrats, revived corpses, and haunted malefactors. Widely acknowledged as the best of their kind between Poe and the moderns, reflecting their author's inner torment and bitter view of life. Includes "Damned Thing," "The Middle Toe of the Right Foot," "The Eyes of the Panther," "Visions of the Night," "Moxon's Master," and over a dozen others. Editor's introduction. xxii + 199pp. 5⅜ x 8½.
20767-6 Paperbound $1.50

THREE GOTHIC NOVELS, *edited by E. F. Bleiler*
Originators of the still popular Gothic novel form, influential in ushering in early 19th-century Romanticism. Horace Walpole's *Castle of Otranto*, William Beckford's *Vathek*, John Polidori's *The Vampyre*, and a *Fragment* by Lord Byron are enjoyable as exciting reading or as documents in the history of English literature. Editor's introduction. xi + 291pp. 5⅜ x 8½.
21232-7 Paperbound $2.00

BEST GHOST STORIES OF LEFANU, *edited by E. F. Bleiler*
Though admired by such critics as V. S. Pritchett, Charles Dickens and Henry James, ghost stories by the Irish novelist Joseph Sheridan LeFanu have never become as widely known as his detective fiction. About half of the 16 stories in this collection have never before been available in America. Collection includes "Carmilla" (perhaps the best vampire story ever written), "The Haunted Baronet," "The Fortunes of Sir Robert Ardagh," and the classic "Green Tea." Editor's introduction. 7 contemporary illustrations. Portrait of LeFanu. xii + 467pp. 5⅜ x 8.
20415-4 Paperbound $2.50

EASY-TO-DO ENTERTAINMENTS AND DIVERSIONS WITH COINS, CARDS,
STRING, PAPER AND MATCHES, *R. M. Abraham*
Over 300 tricks, games and puzzles will provide young readers with absorbing
fun. Sections on card games; paper-folding; tricks with coins, matches and
pieces of string; games for the agile; toy-making from common household
objects; mathematical recreations; and 50 miscellaneous pastimes. Anyone in
charge of groups of youngsters, including hard-pressed parents, and in need of
suggestions on how to keep children sensibly amused and quietly content
will find this book indispensable. Clear, simple text, copious number of delightful line drawings and illustrative diagrams. Originally titled "Winter Nights'
Entertainments." Introduction by Lord Baden Powell. 329 illustrations. v +
186pp. 5⅜ x 8½.   20921-0 Paperbound $1.25

AN INTRODUCTION TO CHESS MOVES AND TACTICS SIMPLY EXPLAINED,
Leonard Barden
Beginner's introduction to the royal game. Names, possible moves of the
pieces, definitions of essential terms, how games are won, etc. explained in
30-odd pages. With this background you'll be able to sit right down and play.
Balance of book teaches strategy — openings, middle game, typical endgame
play, and suggestions for improving your game. A sample game is fully
analyzed. True middle-level introduction, teaching you all the essentials without oversimplifying or losing you in a maze of detail. 58 figures. 102pp.
5⅜ x 8½.   21210-6 Paperbound $1.25

LASKER'S MANUAL OF CHESS, *Dr. Emanuel Lasker*
Probably the greatest chess player of modern times, Dr. Emanuel Lasker held
the world championship 28 years, independent of passing schools or fashions.
This unmatched study of the game, chiefly for intermediate to skilled players,
analyzes basic methods, combinations, position play, the aesthetics of chess,
dozens of different openings, etc., with constant reference to great modern
games. Contains a brilliant exposition of Steinitz's important theories. Introduction by Fred Reinfeld. Tables of Lasker's tournament record. 3 indices.
308 diagrams. 1 photograph. xxx + 349pp. 5⅜ x 8.20640-8Paperbound $2.50

COMBINATIONS: THE HEART OF CHESS, *Irving Chernev*
Step-by-step from simple combinations to complex, this book, by a well-
known chess writer, shows you the intricacies of pins, counter-pins, knight
forks, and smothered mates. Other chapters show alternate lines of play to
those taken in actual championship games; boomerang combinations; classic
examples of brilliant combination play by Nimzovich, Rubinstein, Tarrasch,
Botvinnik, Alekhine and Capablanca. Index. 356 diagrams. ix + 245pp.
5⅜ x 8½.   21744-2 Paperbound $2.00

HOW TO SOLVE CHESS PROBLEMS, *K. S. Howard*
Full of practical suggestions for the fan or the beginner — who knows only the
moves of the chessmen. Contains preliminary section and 58 two-move, 46
three-move, and 8 four-move problems composed by 27 outstanding American
problem creators in the last 30 years. Explanation of all terms and exhaustive
index. "Just what is wanted for the student," Brian Harley. 112 problems,
solutions. vi + 171pp. 5⅜ x 8.   20748-X Paperbound $1.50

SOCIAL THOUGHT FROM LORE TO SCIENCE,
H. E. Barnes and H. Becker
An immense survey of sociological thought and ways of viewing, studying, planning, and reforming society from earliest times to the present. Includes thought on society of preliterate peoples, ancient non-Western cultures, and every great movement in Europe, America, and modern Japan. Analyzes hundreds of great thinkers: Plato, Augustine, Bodin, Vico, Montesquieu, Herder, Comte, Marx, etc. Weighs the contributions of utopians, sophists, fascists and communists; economists, jurists, philosophers, ecclesiastics, and every 19th and 20th century school of scientific sociology, anthropology, and social psychology throughout the world. Combines topical, chronological, and regional approaches, treating the evolution of social thought as a process rather than as a series of mere topics. "Impressive accuracy, competence, and discrimination . . . easily the best single survey," Nation. Thoroughly revised, with new material up to 1960. 2 indexes. Over 2200 bibliographical notes. Three volume set. Total of 1586pp. 5⅜ x 8.
20901-6, 20902-4, 20903-2 Three volume set, paperbound $10.50

A HISTORY OF HISTORICAL WRITING, Harry Elmer Barnes
Virtually the only adequate survey of the whole course of historical writing in a single volume. Surveys developments from the beginnings of historiography in the ancient Near East and the Classical World, up through the Cold War. Covers major historians in detail, shows interrelationship with cultural background, makes clear individual contributions, evaluates and estimates importance; also enormously rich upon minor authors and thinkers who are usually passed over. Packed with scholarship and learning, clear, easily written. Indispensable to every student of history. Revised and enlarged up to 1961. Index and bibliography. xv + 442pp. 5⅜ x 8½.
20104-X Paperbound $3.00

JOHANN SEBASTIAN BACH, Philipp Spitta
The complete and unabridged text of the definitive study of Bach. Written some 70 years ago, it is still unsurpassed for its coverage of nearly all aspects of Bach's life and work. There could hardly be a finer non-technical introduction to Bach's music than the detailed, lucid analyses which Spitta provides for hundreds of individual pieces. 26 solid pages are devoted to the B minor mass, for example, and 30 pages to the glorious St. Matthew Passion. This monumental set also includes a major analysis of the music of the 18th century: Buxtehude, Pachelbel, etc. "Unchallenged as the last word on one of the supreme geniuses of music," John Barkham, Saturday Review Syndicate. Total of 1819pp. Heavy cloth binding. 5⅜ x 8.
22278-0, 22279-9 Two volume set, clothbound $15.00

BEETHOVEN AND HIS NINE SYMPHONIES, George Grove
In this modern middle-level classic of musicology Grove not only analyzes all nine of Beethoven's symphonies very thoroughly in terms of their musical structure, but also discusses the circumstances under which they were written, Beethoven's stylistic development, and much other background material. This is an extremely rich book, yet very easily followed; it is highly recommended to anyone seriously interested in music. Over 250 musical passages. Index. viii + 407pp. 5⅜ x 8.
20334-4 Paperbound $2.50

THE TIME STREAM
John Taine
Acknowledged by many as the best SF writer of the 1920's, Taine (under the
name Eric Temple Bell) was also a Professor of Mathematics of considerable
renown. Reprinted here are *The Time Stream*, generally considered Taine's
best, *The Greatest Game*, a biological-fiction novel, and *The Purple Sapphire*,
involving a supercivilization of the past. Taine's stories tie fantastic narratives
to frameworks of original and logical scientific concepts. Speculation is often
profound on such questions as the nature of time, concept of entropy, cyclical
universes, etc. 4 contemporary illustrations. v + 532pp. 5⅜ x 8⅜.
21180-0 Paperbound $3.00

SEVEN SCIENCE FICTION NOVELS,
H. G. Wells
Full unabridged texts of 7 science-fiction novels of the master. Ranging from
biology, physics, chemistry, astronomy, to sociology and other studies, Mr.
Wells extrapolates whole worlds of strange and intriguing character. "One
will have to go far to match this for entertainment, excitement, and sheer
pleasure . . ."*New York Times*. Contents: The Time Machine, The Island of
Dr. Moreau, The First Men in the Moon, The Invisible Man, The War of the
Worlds, The Food of the Gods, In The Days of the Comet. 1015pp. 5⅜ x 8.
20264-X Clothbound $5.00

28 SCIENCE FICTION STORIES OF H. G. WELLS.
Two full, unabridged novels, *Men Like Gods* and *Star Begotten*, plus 26 short
stories by the master science-fiction writer of all time! Stories of space, time,
invention, exploration, futuristic adventure. Partial contents: *The Country of
the Blind, In the Abyss, The Crystal Egg, The Man Who Could Work Miracles,
A Story of Days to Come, The Empire of the Ants, The Magic Shop, The
Valley of the Spiders, A Story of the Stone Age, Under the Knife, Sea Raiders*,
etc. An indispensable collection for the library of anyone interested in science
fiction adventure. 928pp. 5⅜ x 8. 20265-8 Clothbound $5.00

THREE MARTIAN NOVELS,
Edgar Rice Burroughs
Complete, unabridged reprinting, in one volume, of Thuvia, Maid of Mars;
Chessmen of Mars; The Master Mind of Mars. Hours of science-fiction adventure by a modern master storyteller. Reset in large clear type for easy reading.
16 illustrations by J. Allen St. John. vi + 490pp. 5⅜ x 8½.
20039-6.Paperbound $2.50

AN INTELLECTUAL AND CULTURAL HISTORY OF THE WESTERN WORLD,
Harry Elmer Barnes
Monumental 3-volume survey of intellectual development of Europe from
primitive cultures to the present day. Every significant product of human
intellect traced through history: art, literature, mathematics, physical sciences,
medicine, music, technology, social sciences, religions, jurisprudence, education,
etc. Presentation is lucid and specific, analyzing in detail specific discoveries,
theories, literary works, and so on. Revised (1965) by recognized scholars in
specialized fields under the direction of Prof. Barnes. Revised bibliography.
Indexes. 24 illustrations. Total of xxix + 1318pp.
21275-0, 21276-9, 21277-7 Three volume set, paperbound $7.75

HEAR ME TALKIN' TO YA, *edited by Nat Shapiro and Nat Hentoff*
In their own words, Louis Armstrong, King Oliver, Fletcher Henderson, Bunk Johnson, Bix Beiderbecke, Billy Holiday, Fats Waller, Jelly Roll Morton, Duke Ellington, and many others comment on the origins of jazz in New Orleans and its growth in Chicago's South Side, Kansas City's jam sessions, Depression Harlem, and the modernism of the West Coast schools. Taken from taped conversations, letters, magazine articles, other first-hand sources. Editors' introduction. xvi + 429pp. 5⅜ x 8½.   21726-4 Paperbound $2.50

THE JOURNAL OF HENRY D. THOREAU
A 25-year record by the great American observer and critic, as complete a record of a great man's inner life as is anywhere available. Thoreau's Journals served him as raw material for his formal pieces, as a place where he could develop his ideas, as an outlet for his interests in wild life and plants, in writing as an art, in classics of literature, Walt Whitman and other contemporaries, in politics, slavery, individual's relation to the State, etc. The Journals present a portrait of a remarkable man, and are an observant social history. Unabridged republication of 1906 edition, Bradford Torrey and Francis H. Allen, editors. Illustrations. Total of 1888pp. 8⅜ x 12¼.
        20312-3, 20313-1 Two volume set, clothbound $30.00

A SHAKESPEARIAN GRAMMAR, *E. A. Abbott*
Basic reference to Shakespeare and his contemporaries, explaining through thousands of quotations from Shakespeare, Jonson, Beaumont and Fletcher, North's *Plutarch* and other sources the grammatical usage differing from the modern. First published in 1870 and written by a scholar who spent much of his life isolating principles of Elizabethan language, the book is unlikely ever to be superseded. Indexes. xxiv + 511pp. 5⅜ x 8½. 21582-2 Paperbound $3.00

FOLK-LORE OF SHAKESPEARE, *T. F. Thistelton Dyer*
Classic study, drawing from Shakespeare a large body of references to supernatural beliefs, terminology of falcony and hunting, games and sports, good luck charms, marriage customs, folk medicines, superstitions about plants, animals, birds, argot of the underworld, sexual slang of London, proverbs, drinking customs, weather lore, and much else. From full compilation comes a mirror of the 17th-century popular mind. Index. ix + 526pp. 5⅜ x 8½.
        21614-4 Paperbound $3.25

THE NEW VARIORUM SHAKESPEARE, *edited by H. H. Furness*
By far the richest editions of the plays ever produced in any country or language. Each volume contains complete text (usually First Folio) of the play, all variants in Quarto and other Folio texts, editorial changes by every major editor to Furness's own time (1900), footnotes to obscure references or language, extensive quotes from literature of Shakespearian criticism, essays on plot sources (often reprinting sources in full), and much more.

HAMLET, *edited by H. H. Furness*
Total of xxvi + 905pp. 5⅜ x 8½.
        21004-9, 21005-7 Two volume set, paperbound $5.50

TWELFTH NIGHT, *edited by H. H. Furness*
Index. xxii + 434pp. 5⅜ x 8½.   21189-4 Paperbound $2.75

La Boheme by Giacomo Puccini,
translated and introduced by Ellen H. Bleiler
Complete handbook for the operagoer, with everything needed for full enjoyment except the musical score itself. Complete Italian libretto, with new,
modern English line-by-line translation—the only libretto printing all repeats;
biography of Puccini; the librettists; background to the opera, Murger's La
Boheme, etc.; circumstances of composition and performances; plot summary;
and pictorial section of 73 illustrations showing Puccini, famous singers and
performances, etc. Large clear type for easy reading. 124pp. 5⅜ x 8½.
20404-9 Paperbound $1.50

Antonio Stradivari: His Life and Work (1644-1737),
W. Henry Hill, Arthur F. Hill, and Alfred E. Hill
Still the only book that really delves into life and art of the incomparable
Italian craftsman, maker of the finest musical instruments in the world today.
The authors, expert violin-makers themselves, discuss Stradivari's ancestry, his
construction and finishing techniques, distinguished characteristics of many
of his instruments and their locations. Included, too, is story of introduction
of his instruments into France, England, first revelation of their supreme
merit, and information on his labels, number of instruments made, prices,
mystery of ingredients of his varnish, tone of pre-1684 Stradivari violin and
changes between 1684 and 1690. An extremely interesting, informative account
for all music lovers, from craftsman to concert-goer. Republication of original
(1902) edition. New introduction by Sydney Beck, Head of Rare Book and
Manuscript Collections, Music Division, New York Public Library. Analytical
index by Rembert Wurlitzer. Appendixes. 68 illustrations. 30 full-page plates.
4 in color. xxvi + 315pp. 5⅜ x 8½. 20425-1 Paperbound $3.00

Musical Autographs from Monteverdi to Hindemith,
Emanuel Winternitz
For beauty, for intrinsic interest, for perspective on the composer's personality,
for subtleties of phrasing, shading, emphasis indicated in the autograph but
suppressed in the printed score, the mss. of musical composition are fascinating
documents which repay close study in many different ways. This 2-volume
work reprints facsimiles of mss. by virtually every major composer, and many
minor figures—196 examples in all. A full text points out what can be learned
from mss., analyzes each sample. Index. Bibliography. 18 figures. 196 plates.
Total of 170pp. of text. 7⅞ x 10¾. 21312-9, 21313-7 Two volume set, paperbound $5.00

J. S. Bach,
Albert Schweitzer
One of the few great full-length studies of Bach's life and work, and the
study upon which Schweitzer's renown as a musicologist rests. On first appearance (1911), revolutionized Bach performance. The only writer on Bach to
be musicologist, performing musician, and student of history, theology and
philosophy, Schweitzer contributes particularly full sections on history of German Protestant church music, theories on motivic pictorial representations
in vocal music, and practical suggestions for performance. Translated by
Ernest Newman. Indexes. 5 illustrations. 650 musical examples. Total of xix
+ 928pp. 5⅜ x 8½. 21631-4, 21632-2 Two volume set, paperbound $5.00

THE METHODS OF ETHICS, *Henry Sidgwick*
Propounding no organized system of its own, study subjects every major methodological approach to ethics to rigorous, objective analysis. Study discusses and relates ethical thought of Plato, Aristotle, Bentham, Clarke, Butler, Hobbes, Hume, Mill, Spencer, Kant, and dozens of others. Sidgwick retains conclusions from each system which follow from ethical premises, rejecting the faulty. Considered by many in the field to be among the most important treatises on ethical philosophy. Appendix. Index. xlvii + 528pp. 5⅜ x 8½.
21608-X Paperbound $3.00

TEUTONIC MYTHOLOGY, *Jakob Grimm*
A milestone in Western culture; the work which established on a modern basis the study of history of religions and comparative religions. 4-volume work assembles and interprets everything available on religious and folkloristic beliefs of Germanic people (including Scandinavians, Anglo-Saxons, etc.). Assembling material from such sources as Tacitus, surviving Old Norse and Icelandic texts, archeological remains, folktales, surviving superstitions, comparative traditions, linguistic analysis, etc. Grimm explores pagan deities, heroes, folklore of nature, religious practices, and every other area of pagan German belief. To this day, the unrivaled, definitive, exhaustive study. Translated by J. S. Stallybrass from 4th (1883) German edition. Indexes. Total of lxxvii + 1887pp. 5⅜ x 8½.
21602-0, 21603-9, 21604-7, 21605-5 Four volume set, paperbound $12.00

THE I CHING, *translated by James Legge*
Called "The Book of Changes" in English, this is one of the Five Classics edited by Confucius, basic and central to Chinese thought. Explains perhaps the most complex system of divination known, founded on the theory that all things happening at any one time have characteristic features which can be isolated and related. Significant in Oriental studies, in history of religions and philosophy, and also to Jungian psychoanalysis and other areas of modern European thought. Index. Appendixes. 6 plates. xxi + 448pp. 5⅜ x 8½.
21062-6 Paperbound $2.75

HISTORY OF ANCIENT PHILOSOPHY, *W. Windelband*
One of the clearest, most accurate comprehensive surveys of Greek and Roman philosophy. Discusses ancient philosophy in general, intellectual life in Greece in the 7th and 6th centuries B.C., Thales, Anaximander, Anaximenes, Heraclitus, the Eleatics, Empedocles, Anaxagoras, Leucippus, the Pythagoreans, the Sophists, Socrates, Democritus (20 pages), Plato (50 pages), Aristotle (70 pages), the Peripatetics, Stoics, Epicureans, Sceptics, Neo-platonists, Christian Apologists, etc. 2nd German edition translated by H. E. Cushman. xv + 393pp. 5⅜ x 8.
20357-3 Paperbound $3.00

THE PALACE OF PLEASURE, *William Painter*
Elizabethan versions of Italian and French novels from *The Decameron*, Cinthio, Straparola, Queen Margaret of Navarre, and other continental sources — the very work that provided Shakespeare and dozens of his contemporaries with many of their plots and sub-plots and, therefore, justly considered one of the most influential books in all English literature. It is also a book that any reader will still enjoy. Total of cviii + 1,224pp.
21691-8, 21692-6, 21693-4 Three volume set, paperbound $8.25

THE WONDERFUL WIZARD OF OZ, *L. F. Baum*
All the original W. W. Denslow illustrations in full color—as much a part of "The Wizard" as Tenniel's drawings are of "Alice in Wonderland." "The Wizard" is still America's best-loved fairy tale, in which, as the author expresses it, "The wonderment and joy are retained and the heartaches and nightmares left out." Now today's young readers can enjoy every word and wonderful picture of the original book. New introduction by Martin Gardner. A Baum bibliography. 23 full-page color plates. viii + 268pp. 5⅜ x 8.
20691-2 Paperbound $1.95

THE MARVELOUS LAND OF OZ, *L. F. Baum*
This is the equally enchanting sequel to the "Wizard," continuing the adventures of the Scarecrow and the Tin Woodman. The hero this time is a little boy named Tip, and all the delightful Oz magic is still present. This is the Oz book with the Animated Saw-Horse, the Woggle-Bug, and Jack Pumpkinhead. All the original John R. Neill illustrations, 10 in full color. 287pp. 5⅜ x 8.
20692-0 Paperbound $1.75

ALICE'S ADVENTURES UNDER GROUND, *Lewis Carroll*
The original *Alice in Wonderland*, hand-lettered and illustrated by Carroll himself, and originally presented as a Christmas gift to a child-friend. Adults as well as children will enjoy this charming volume, reproduced faithfully in this Dover edition. While the story is essentially the same, there are slight changes, and Carroll's spritely drawings present an intriguing alternative to the famous Tenniel illustrations. One of the most popular books in Dover's catalogue. Introduction by Martin Gardner. 38 illustrations. 128pp. 5⅜ x 8½.
21482-6 Paperbound $1.00

THE NURSERY "ALICE," *Lewis Carroll*
While most of us consider *Alice in Wonderland* a story for children of all ages, Carroll himself felt it was beyond younger children. He therefore provided this simplified version, illustrated with the famous Tenniel drawings enlarged and colored in delicate tints, for children aged "from Nought to Five." Dover's edition of this now rare classic is a faithful copy of the 1889 printing, including 20 illustrations by Tenniel, and front and back covers reproduced in full color. Introduction by Martin Gardner. xxiii + 67pp. 6⅛ x 9¼.
21610-1 Paperbound $1.75

THE STORY OF KING ARTHUR AND HIS KNIGHTS, *Howard Pyle*
A fast-paced, exciting retelling of the best known Arthurian legends for young readers by one of America's best story tellers and illustrators. The sword Excalibur, wooing of Guinevere, Merlin and his downfall, adventures of Sir Pellias and Gawaine, and others. The pen and ink illustrations are vividly imagined and wonderfully drawn. 41 illustrations. xviii + 313pp. 6⅛ x 9¼.
21445-1 Paperbound $2.00

Prices subject to change without notice.

Available at your book dealer or write for free catalogue to Dept. Adsci, Dover Publications, Inc., 180 Varick St., N.Y., N.Y. 10014. Dover publishes more than 150 books each year on science, elementary and advanced mathematics, biology, music, art, literary history, social sciences and other areas.